The Political Uses
of Literature

The Political Uses of Literature

Global Perspectives and Theoretical Approaches, 1920–2020

Edited by
Benjamin Kohlmann and
Ivana Perica

BLOOMSBURY ACADEMIC
NEW YORK • LONDON • OXFORD • NEW DELHI • SYDNEY

BLOOMSBURY ACADEMIC

Bloomsbury Publishing Inc, 1385 Broadway, New York, NY 10018, USA
Bloomsbury Publishing Plc, 50 Bedford Square, London, WC1B 3DP, UK
Bloomsbury Publishing Ireland, 29 Earlsfort Terrace, Dublin 2, D02 AY28, Ireland

BLOOMSBURY, BLOOMSBURY ACADEMIC and the Diana logo are trademarks of
Bloomsbury Publishing Plc

First published in the United States of America 2024
This paperback edition published 2025

Copyright © Benjamin Kohlmann and Ivana Perica, 2024

Each chapter © of Contributors

Cover design: Eleanor Rose
Cover image: Literacy, the Path to Communism, 1920. Publisher: Gosudarstvennoe Izd, Moscow © Heritage Image Partnership Ltd / Alamy

All rights reserved. No part of this publication may be: i) reproduced or transmitted in any form, electronic or mechanical, including photocopying, recording or by means of any information storage or retrieval system without prior permission in writing from the publishers; or ii) used or reproduced in any way for the training, development or operation of artificial intelligence (AI) technologies, including generative AI technologies. The rights holders expressly reserve this publication from the text and data mining exception as per Article 4(3) of the Digital Single Market Directive (EU) 2019/790.

Bloomsbury Publishing Inc does not have any control over, or responsibility for, any third-party websites referred to or in this book. All internet addresses given in this book were correct at the time of going to press. The author and publisher regret any inconvenience caused if addresses have changed or sites have ceased to exist, but can accept no responsibility for any such changes.

Library of Congress Cataloging-in-Publication Data

Names: Kohlmann, Benjamin, 1981- editor. | Perica, Ivana, 1984- editor.
Title: The political uses of literature : global perspectives and theoretical approaches, 1920-2020 / edited by Benjamin Kohlmann and Ivana Perica.
Description: New York : Bloomsbury Academic, 2024. | Includes bibliographical references and index. | Summary: "Analyses the rich global histories of 20th- and 21st-century politicized writing in order to provoke new debate about the complex intersections between literature and political action"– Provided by publisher.
Identifiers: LCCN 2023025723 (print) | LCCN 2023025724 (ebook) | ISBN 9781501399336 (hardback) | ISBN 9781501399299 (paperback) | ISBN 9781501399329 (epub) | ISBN 9781501399312 (pdf) | ISBN 9781501399305 (ebook other)
Subjects: LCSH: Politics and literature.
Classification: LCC PN51 .P5565 2024 (print) | LCC PN51 (ebook) | DDC 809/.933581–dc23/eng/20230830
LC record available at https://lccn.loc.gov/2023025723
LC ebook record available at https://lccn.loc.gov/2023025724

ISBN: HB: 978-1-5013-9933-6
PB: 978-1-5013-9929-9
ePDF: 978-1-5013-9931-2
eBook: 978-1-5013-9932-9

Typeset by Deanta Global Publishing Services, Chennai, India

For product safety related questions contact productsafety@bloomsbury.com.

To find out more about our authors and books visit www.bloomsbury.com and sign up for our newsletters.

CONTENTS

List of Figures vii

Introduction *Benjamin Kohlmann and Ivana Perica* 1

PART I Revolution, Internationalism, and Literary Politics: Interwar Paradigms 21

1   Marxists Out of Work: Literature and the Useless in Interwar India *Ben Conisbee Baer* 23

2   Politics and Literature on the Peruvian Periphery: Realism and Experimentation in the Works of César Vallejo and José Carlos Mariátegui *Juan E. De Castro* 42

3   Reusing Artaud? On the Contemporaneity of *Messages révolutionnaires* (1936) *Sandra Fluhrer* 56

4   On the German Popular Front Novel in Historical and International Context *Hunter Bivens* 69

5   Narrative Struggle: 'Good' and 'Bad' Uses of Literature in the Committed Novel of the 1930s (Aragon, Dos Passos) *Aurore Peyroles* 87

6   Moscow, 1934–Yan'an, 1942: The Manifesto as Lived Experience *Steven S. Lee* 102

PART II Politicizing Theory and Literary Practice in the Global 1960s: Inflection Points 119

7   Militant Structures of Feeling: Raymond Williams, Claude Lefort, and Workers' Inquiry *Daniel Hartley* 121

8   Solidarity in Black and White *J. Daniel Elam* 137

9   Notes from the Underground, or: Why and How Was Non-Marxist Theory Resisted by Non-Marxists in a Totalitarian Society *Galin Tihanov* 150

10 Workshops of Abolition: Attica Print Culture and Small Press Poetry *Mark Nowak* 161

11 An Autofictional Intervention into Working-Class Literature: Karin Struck's *Klassenliebe* and the *Werkkreis Literatur der Arbeitswelt* *Christoph Schaub* 181

12 Feminism and Progressive Writing in Twentieth-Century India *Ulka Anjaria* 199

PART III Political Uses of Literature Today: Legacies and Departures 215

13 Cultural Politics after the Arab Spring: A New *Lotus* for a New World? *Maryam Fatima* 217

14 Segments of a Larger Narrative: Political Formalism and Working-Class Story Cycles *Dirk Wiemann* 232

15 Sedimented Reading Habits? The Future Utopia in Contemporary African Science and Speculative Fiction *Peter J. Maurits* 250

16 Literary Activism in Contemporary Africa: Praxis, Publics, and the Shifting Landscapes of the 'Literary' *Madhu Krishnan* 265

Notes on Contributors 279
Index 283

FIGURES

0.1 Brecht, "Eingreifendes Denken," Notebook, 1931–2, Akademie der Künste, Berlin; Bertolt Brecht Archiv, BBA 325/36. © Suhrkamp Verlag   8

10.1 Clockwise from top left: *Betcha Ain't: Poems from Attica* (Celes Tisdale, ed.); *The Last Stop: Writing from Comstock Prison* (Joseph Bruchac, ed.); *Convicted Voices* (Antu Satya); *Awakening of a Dragon* (Attica Brother Jomo); *Fighting Back: Attica Memorial Book, 1974*. Photo © Mark Nowak   165

14.1 Drawing, from Deepak Unnikrishnan, *Temporary People* (London: Restless Books, 2017), p. 252. © Restless Books   243

Introduction

Benjamin Kohlmann and Ivana Perica

"Only a new purpose can lead to a new art," the German playwright Bertolt Brecht declared in a short essay of 1929 entitled "On Form and Subject-Matter."[1] Presented as a rationale for the development of his *Lehrstücke* ("pedagogical plays") around 1930, Brecht's comment offers a useful route into the conversations about the political uses of literature that this volume traces from the interwar years to our own contemporary times. While Brecht's phrasing ("*Only* a new purpose . . .") is intended to give the sentence an air of unshakable artistic dogma, the comment in fact hovers ambivalently between two seemingly contrary positions that concern the question of committed art's primary obligations. On the one hand, Brecht's sentence appears to insist on the absolute priority of political commitment over aesthetic concerns by suggesting that literature's internal workings are by necessity subservient to some external (i.e., political or social) purpose; on the other hand, it contends that politics is of value to the artist only insofar as it enables a radical remaking of the patterns and forms of art itself. To put it another way: artistic innovation seems unthinkable without some prior commitment to (political, social) purposes that are imagined as existing outside of art; yet at the same time, as far as the work of the writer is concerned, the value of these 'prior' commitments must be measured in light of their ability to generate new aesthetic forms. Brecht presents the question of art's commitments as an unresolvable dialectic: in his formulation, art and political purpose are not external to one another; their relationship is characterized not by conflict and mutual exclusion but rather by the promise of generative friction and mutual enrichment.

This is not how literary scholars have traditionally thought about literature's relationship to the sphere of politics. Instead, those working within the discipline of literary studies have tended to see the attempt to make art do political work as a category mistake—as an alien imposition that does damage to art *and* politics. To provide a particularly well-known example: if we want to understand how the exclusion of political 'purpose' from the sphere of literature became part of the disciplinary DNA of literary studies, we can think back to the key works of the New Criticism of the 1950s. New Critics such as Cleanth Brooks, Allen Tate, and William K. Wimsatt explicitly presented their protocols of 'close reading' as a response to the intensely politicized writing of the interwar years: for these critics, praising the inner formal complexities of literary works became a way of denouncing politicized writing as a literary-historical aberrance.[2] "For the poet as a public performer," Wimsatt declared, "poetic language is a complex and treacherous medium."[3] Key to this endeavor was the attempt—itself not without historical precursors, of course—to translate the instrumental logic of (artistic) means and (political) ends into a complex internal dynamic of parts and the whole: "Inside the poem," Wimsatt concluded in his influential book *The Verbal Icon* (1954), "there are no ends and means, only whole and parts."[4] The influence such arguments had on the disciplinary configuration of literary studies within the Anglo-American academy (and beyond) is remarkable—indeed, they find surprising echoes even in scholarship that decisively breaks with many of formalism's key tenets. To offer only one particularly prominent example, the Marxist literary and cultural critic Fredric Jameson influentially proposed that the politics of literary works are located at the level of a textual 'unconscious.' Rejecting the attempt to think of politics in terms of a manifest or explicit purpose, Jameson argued that the politics of aesthetic objects are best described in terms of the relations that obtain between the text's various formal and generic structures: the political unconscious is found "not by abandoning the formal level for something extrinsic to it—such as some inertly social 'content' [or political 'purpose']—but rather immanently, by construing purely formal patterns as a symbolic enactment of the social within the formal and the aesthetic."[5] On this view, politics is intimately woven into the texture of the literary work itself: by sublimating politics into form, literature carries politics within itself as its immanent or intrinsic subtext. We do not wish to appear facetious in placing Wimsatt and Jameson side by side in this way, or to suggest that there is a straight line that runs from the conservative New Critics to more recent "suspicious readers."[6] However, it is worth reminding ourselves that Jameson's work forms part of a longer critical history—as well as a particular disciplinary formation—that privileges formal complexity at the expense of political purpose and that tends to discount activist writing.

In reclaiming buried literary-historical genealogies and offering up alternative routes for theoretical inquiry, the present volume takes its cue from recent attempts to think of the politicized writing of the interwar years not as a literary-historical anomaly but as a key moment in the configuration of the relationship between literature and politics—as an influential epicenter of interventionist art from which debates about literary politics and practices of committed writing were able to radiate out into new and globally expansive contexts.[7] The experimental periodization proposed in this book connects three periods of intensely politicized and activist art by proceeding in leaps from the interwar years to the 'long 1960s' and the present.⁸ This reperiodization is meant to make visible "alternative traditions" which, according to Raymond Williams, have too often been left abandoned "in the wide margin of the century."⁹ The book's three-part structure—its movement from the interwar years to the long 1960s and our contemporary moment—very deliberately resists advancing a single or univocal history of politicized art. However, the contributions to this book all join forces in restoring to view what the artist and art-theorist Gregory Sholette has recently called the "fragmented and boisterous reservoir of past interventions."¹⁰ Sholette emphasizes the unauthorized and non-formalized quality of this "reservoir of past interventions"—he also speaks of the non-canonized "phantom archive of activist art, overflowing with interventions, experiments, repetitions, compromises, minor victories and outright failures."¹¹ Sholette suggests that the reasons for the 'fragmentation' of this buried archive—and also for a good deal of its 'boisterousness'—derive from the highly particularized nature of activist art, that is, from the fact that it addresses itself so intently to the specific situations and historical moments in which it seeks to intervene.

There is another sense in which Brecht's comment affords insight into the broader problematic addressed by this volume. For, while Brecht's observation seems to dispense a general truth about the relationship between literature and politics, it is arguably best understood as an immediate response to the darkening political atmosphere of the later Weimar Republic—to the rise of fascism, to the Communist Party's (CP) 'class-against-class' policy, to the banning of the CP's paramilitary organization (the *Roter Frontkämpferbund*) by the governing Social Democrats, and to the subsequent denunciation of Social Democrats as 'social fascists' by the CP. In the eyes of Brecht and his collaborators, these developments necessitated a new type of interventionist, activist art capable of educating the masses—a pedagogico-artistic weapon suited to the new stage in the political struggle, which the *Lehrstücke* were meant to provide.

The case of Brecht shows that certain literary–political constellations cannot be understood without taking into account their immediate (historical, geographical, social, political, but also aesthetic) contexts. Taking their cue from this insight, several chapters in this book explore texts, performances, and artworks which are focused very intensely on specific local situations, whereas others investigate works that seek to intervene in broader historical conjunctures. Viewed in its entirety, however, the structure of the present volume echoes the logic of site specificity that characterizes art which aims to be politically 'useful' in the broadest sense. This means that while individual chapters rarely set out to propose a unified ontology of interventionist art, the volume as a whole can be seen to build toward a broader account of politically 'useful' art: taken together, our contributors indicate that such art is unintelligible without its constitutive orientation toward a particular site or historical situation in which it seeks to intervene. Sandra Fluhrer's chapter about the Mexican work of Antonin Artaud is relevant in this context as it discusses Artaud's concept of *culture orientée*. As Fluhrer notes, Artaud's concept *orientée*, while conveying "a semantic content similar to *engagé*," (62) usefully shifts the emphasis implicit in the latter concept: whereas the Sartrean term *littérature engagé* implies a decisionist emphasis—that is, humans' ability to commit themselves freely to this or that cause rather than another[12]—Artaud's *orientée* conveys the sense of an ineradicably anthropological orientation toward the world, a quasi-physical 'positioning' that is also foundational to all types of literary-political commitment. It is in this sense that the local explorations undertaken by the individual contributors to this volume build toward a larger sense of literature's interventionist potential, not as a historical dead end or aberrance, but as a foundational modality of artistic production as such.

New Commitments: Literary Studies and the Uses of Literature

Scholarship in literary studies has long been interested in the politics of writing, although comparatively less attention has been paid to works that explicitly seek to intervene in their historical contexts of production or reception—as though these works maintained too narrow a focus on a particular extraneous 'purpose' to matter artistically. Among the scholars who have defended literature's political usefulness, many have taken recourse to well-rehearsed twentieth-century arguments about the ways in which the political commitments of literary texts become encoded in their formal features; by contrast, others have defaulted to the assumption that literature's engagement with politics is best understood as a form of metapolitics, that is, that literary works are political insofar as they defamiliarize the hegemonic social protocols that create forms of political visibility or enforce political invisibility.[13] While it is true that some scholars have recently begun to think about the concrete uses that literature has served in a wide range of different contexts, this scholarship has generally subscribed to a pragmatist interpretation of the concept of 'use': literature is useful, critics such as Rita Felski inform us, to the extent that it meets some individual (affective or intellectual) need. This line of inquiry has produced much important critical work, but it has tended to sideline the question of literature's explicitly *political* uses: in rejecting the binary between "the Scylla of political functionalism and the Charybdis of art for art's sake,"[14] recent scholars have inadvertently neglected the diverse purposes that literary texts have served in the contexts of the countless social and political movements evolving 'out there.'[15]

Literary theorists have developed rich critical vocabularies to displace the question of direct agency or instrumental use from the academic study of literature. "It is crucial," observes Gabriel Rockhill in a notable recent study, "to rethink the operative logic of political efficacy outside of the instrumentalist framework": instead, we are told, we need to understand literature's attempts at agency in the context of a complex "conjuncture of determinants with multiple tiers, types, and sites of agency."[16] The present collection of chapters is very much in agreement with the second half of this statement: political agency is always complex and the sense of what it means for a text to intervene and become politically active will depend on the particular historical moment and situation in question.[17] However, taken together, the chapters in this book significantly complicate the first half of this statement: literary critics, we submit, have precisely *failed* to think hard enough about the attractiveness which the 'instrumentalist framework' has held for writers seeking to endow their works with a sense of 'political efficacy' and purpose. These, then, are some of the questions addressed in this book: How do literary works respond to the powerful and attractive fantasy of direct instrumental agency? How do certain works seek to align themselves with this fantasy while others endeavor to resist its allure?

While the contributions to this collection consider literary texts from a wide range of geographical contexts, they do not advance a single or unified vision of a world literary space centered around a transhistorically stable ontology of political writing. This book resists some of the guiding ideas that have characterized the study of world literature, while allying itself with certain new and emerging trends in the field. Among the more familiar critical assumptions that are interrogated in this volume is the displacement—in a good deal of scholarship about world literature—of the question of politics in favor of more specifically ethical considerations. As several of our contributors point out, the idea of *world literature*—from the concept's initial articulation by Johann Wolfgang von Goethe to its diverse afterlives, for example, in the important work of Pascale Casanova, Gayatri Chakravorty Spivak, or David Damrosch—has too often served to sideline or eclipse literature's complex local entanglement in the grassroots struggles that characterize practical politics. In a related vein, the category of *cosmopolitanism* is mostly conspicuous by its absence from this volume: while the study of cosmopolitanism has helped to bring much-needed attention to the production and reception of literary texts under conditions of globalization, some of this scholarship has prioritized the possibility of an "aesthetic education in the era of globalization"—that is, the expansion of (Western) readers' *ethical* imagination—at the expense of a more detailed consideration of the ways radical politics play out in a wide range of historical situations and geographical locales.[18]

Our contributors reopen the discussion of literature's political and activist potential by considering individual literary works as well as by reclaiming broader theoretical debates about literature's ability to intervene in social reality. Their chapters trace the mobilization of related conversations and artistic practices across two subsequent historical conjunctures—the committed literature of the long 1960s and our own present. In doing so, this project allies itself to a growing body of scholarly work that has homed in on the long cultural (after)lives and global entanglements of literary production in the transnational world of the 'Cominternians' as well as in the colonial peripheries, past and present.[19] For example, we are deeply sympathetic to recent efforts—for instance by the contributors to Amelia Glaser and Steven Lee's edited collection *Comintern Aesthetics*—to "unearth a lost genealogy for present-day activism, demonstrating ways of connecting the local and the global, the personal-as-political and world revolution."[20] Similarly, we take inspiration from the work of scholars of anticolonial literature, including J. Daniel Elam, who seeks to reclaim a spirit of "egalitarian readerly internationalism,"[21] and Sonali Perera, who remarks that "an aesthetics and politics" of politicized writing "cannot be gauged on the basis of a direct, unbroken line of institutions and traditions extending from the Communist Internationals to the World Social Forum."[22] Indeed, it might not be too much to say that what emerges from the present book is a kind of non-formalized International of engaged writers whose works contribute to a shared project of political construction and renewal. Literature, in the hands of these writers, does not appear primarily as a commodity that competes with other commodities for the limited attention of potential consumers—as it does in Casanova's model of the world literary system, for example—but as a medium of world-making that opens out toward larger political projects of collaborative world-making.

This collection is able to build on an important new body of scholarship that draws attention to the interventionist arts emerging from the interstices between Western literatures and the literatures of anticolonial resistance around the world. We recognize that literature in the Global South has often sought (and still seeks) direct alliances with political movements—and that such alliances must be central to any account of politicized writing in the context of twentieth- and twenty-first-century processes of globalization.[23] As we have already noted, this horizontal extension across different geographical spaces and locales is complemented by a highlighting of affinities that manifest diachronically, that is, across several distinctive historical moments. However, rather than suggesting that these local affinities solidified into uninterrupted historical continuities or unified teleologies, this volume presents them in the spirit of a constellation or montage: glancing back at the use which left-wing filmmakers such as Chris Marker (e.g., *Le Fond de l'air est rouge*, 1977) have made of montage in their attempts to convey the (dis)continuity of revolutionary traditions, the individual case studies in this volume are offered as local instantiations of activist art that are capable of speaking to each other across time.[24] The literary activist constellations which this procedure brings to light resist a hardening into fixed genealogies—they remain open and malleable, offering new footholds for future political uses.

Eingreifendes Denken: Literature and Politics beyond Left-Wing Melancholy

Taken together, the chapters in this volume contribute to conversations about politicized art along *three interrelated axes*:

First, the volume's attention to especially intense moments of radical literary production is intended to create openings for *new and future-oriented genealogies of activist literature*. These plural histories, as we envision them, resist the tendency to associate the reclaiming of revolutionary pasts with the nostalgically retrospective (and politically impotent) mode of "left-wing melancholy."[25] In taking the discussion of such radical instants up to the present, our contributors trace how the vital literary and theoretical interventions that were formulated in Russia and Europe during the interwar period were rearticulated in the light of new and emerging political demands (including feminist and anticolonial struggles) in the long 1960s as well as in our own historical moment. It is certainly true that literature's political efficacy continues to be an open question today—a fact that is partly to do (as Hunter Bivens notes in his chapter) with politicized literature's enduringly uncertain position between a "fully revolutionary horizon" and a marginalized or subterranean "counter-public sphere" (74). Our volume indicates that critical analysis of the now can be invigorated by placing contemporary interventions in dialogue with earlier historical moments in which literature and politics vitally informed each other. In this context, as the chapters by Galin Tihanov, Bivens, and other contributors show, theoretical production itself came to perform a radical role, playing the part of what Brecht once called "interventionist thought" (Brecht's German phrase, penciled in radiant red into a 1931–2 notebook, is "eingreifendes Denken").[26] (Figure 0.1)

Second, the contributions to this volume indicate that explorations of the political uses of literature must take into account *the global portability of these practices and debates* as they evolved across a wide range of geographical contexts and historical situations. Several of the chapters in this collection show that configurations of the relationship between literature and politics in interwar Europe remained attuned to the particular articulations of this relationship in other far-flung ('peripheral') geographical contexts, and vice versa. As the literary scholar Snehal Shingavi has observed (in a passage quoted in Ulka Anjaria's chapter), "aesthetic and political notions put forward through various organs of the Communist

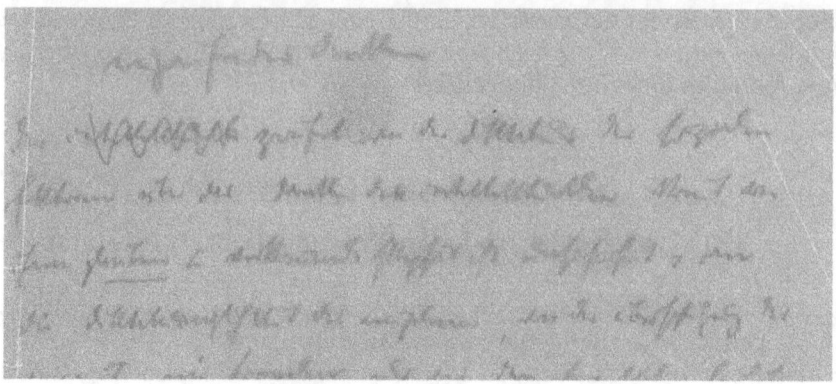

FIGURE 0.1 Brecht, "Eingreifendes Denken," Notebook, 1931–2, Akademie der Künste, Berlin; Bertolt Brecht Archiv, BBA 325/36. © Suhrkamp Verlag.

Party were translated, reinterpreted, reimagined, and refigured" in colonial contexts (199). As Anjaria explains, this critical attunement to processes of cultural translation and refiguration indicates that we are better served by attending to particular formations of the political rather than applying the term *political* as a blanket label. In this sense, the present volume adds up to more than the sum of its parts: the different episodes that are explored in the individual contributions appear in a new light when they are viewed from the perspective of an interconnected global literary history. In the words of Sholette, all activist art, "whether contemplating a prison break, or a revolution, or merely the reconceptualization of existing institutions," is "haunted by the elusive dream of historical agency and its unceasing hunger for total emancipation."[27]

Third, this volume builds toward *new conceptualizations of literature's 'uses' for literary history and literary theory*. While not all chapters contribute explicitly to this overarching theoretical project, the scholars represented in this book share the conviction that attending to the question of literature's overtly political uses is both a necessary task and an urgent one. Focusing on politics as conscious commitment and principled action, this volume pushes beyond the now-fashionable (and politically weak) assertion of form's literary "affordances" by exploring how literary works come to be deployed as moments of activist intervention.[28] This does not mean that our contributors take a naive view of literary agency as unmediated—on the contrary, they defend the recognition that even "the flat[test and most] ephemeral pamphlet" (to adapt W. H. Auden's famous phrase from 1937) is a highly mediated form of political engagement.[29] Responding to this insight, the chapters consider a diverse range of literary genres, textual forms, and artistic representations. And yet, our volume also ventures a crucial shift in emphasis: away from the belief that the question of 'use' depends primarily on the affordances of the object (literary forms, aesthetic structures, etc.), and toward the view that artists actively 'make use' of particular forms in order to achieve particular ends. The art theorist Stephen Wright has recently noted that 'making use' of artistic forms (rather than merely 'using' them) involves an activist 'retooling' and *'repurposing'* of these forms themselves.[30] This 'crafting' of new forms in response to new 'purposes' entails a distinctive set of difficulties: the attempt to turn literature into an instrument of social and political change does not mean that we should simply dispense with questions of (aesthetic) mediation altogether; rather, and as Brecht knew, this activist remaking of forms unsettles our understanding that the work of mediation is all we should be paying attention to, especially when it comes in the modernist guise of artistic 'complexity' or 'difficulty.'

As we have noted, calls for literature to be politically active have always been energized by situational and conjunctural pressures—that is, activist literature and art are always simultaneously *reactive* (i.e., they must be understood in terms of their openness to historical pressures) and *aspirational* (i.e., they seek to imagine and/or prefigure new spaces for historical agency). In their shared effort to shed light on this dialectic, the chapters in this volume will occasionally revisit and critique scholarly positions that bear the imprint of certain familiar twentieth-century debates about the nature of politicized art. For instance, the above-mentioned opposition of 'art for art's sake' and 'political functionalism' has been repeatedly identified with the stalemated confrontation between Formalism and Marxism—or between the avant-garde and realism—most commonly represented by theoretical greats such as Theodor W. Adorno and Georg Lukács. This volume illustrates just how problematic and historically contingent these binaries were to begin with. As Joe Cleary has noted, from the 1930s onward, modernism and realism were produced "at once as reified categories and as the obvious termini of modern 'world literature'": while the Soviet Union "took 'ownership' of realism, ... modernism was taken into custodianship by New York (with generous backing from Washington)."[31] Extending Cleary's world system perspective, we can now see that the view that pits a formally innovative but largely inward-looking modernism against an artistically retrograde but socially active realism is also implicitly affirmed in key left-wing contributions to the debate about literature and politics, such as *Aesthetics and Politics*, the landmark anthology of 1977 that brought together key contributions (by Ernst Bloch, Adorno, Lukács, and others) to the realism–modernism debate of the 1930s. *Aesthetics and Politics* has been the go-to book on the topic for several generations of literary scholars, but it has dramatically narrowed our understanding of the literary-historical map we seek to recover here. It is an unintended effect of the sedimentation and canonization of such theoretical constructs that they tend to dehistoricize certain oppositions, presenting them as natural or ontologically given rather than socially produced. As a result, the stark dichotomization of artistic debates that marked the Cold War years has led many critics to embrace misleading or reductive views of literature's political uses. While our volume does not engage in a systematic or sustained revision of the two key concepts ('realism' and 'modernism') around which these debates were structured, it moves toward an alternative configuration of the relationship between these concepts: on the one hand, literary realism does not appear as a "single form" but is rather defined "by what it is able to accomplish in the world";[32] on the other, formal experimentations of the kind often associated with modernism were themselves frequently deployed in the service of the 'realist' project of mapping and interrogating as social totality.

If it is true that "capitalist realism" (Mark Fisher's term for the contemporary closing down of revolutionary horizons) is today's hegemonic artistic, intellectual, and political "style," it becomes increasingly difficult to imagine any form of agency that will be capable of fundamentally challenging the status quo.[33] As the members of the communist Endnotes Collective have recently observed, our current historical situation produces "*revolutionaries without revolution*, as millions descend onto the streets and are transformed by their collective outpouring of rage and disgust, but without (yet) any coherent notion of transcending capitalism."[34] There are those who would argue that we should not bother looking to literature for solutions to these deeply political problems—and the present volume is far from engaging in any special pleading on behalf of the scholar-as-activist. And yet, it is a central contention of this book that the literary works under consideration here provide a reservoir of future-oriented modes of thinking, feeling, and being-in-the-world that we desperately need today.

Chapter Organization

This volume seeks to contribute to critical debates about literature and politics by mapping out a geographically expansive set of artistic and theoretical constellations. In doing so, our contributors hope to make questions pertaining to politicized art newly compelling to a broad and diverse readership. But they also reflect on the urgent need to think about literature's political uses today—at a time when it seems difficult to imagine any kind of political efficacy for art, even as the need to do so grows ever more acutely. Literature may not provide ready-made answers to our current political problems, yet as the chapters in this volume suggest, the committed literature of the twentieth century does hold out aesthetic resources for a fresh engagement with the dilemmas that face us now.

The first part turns to literary works of the interwar years as a way of anchoring the book's overarching questions. The chapters in this part provide a chronological starting point, but they also begin to illustrate the global and transnational perspective advanced by the volume as a whole.

Ben Conisbee Baer's chapter begins by asking what it means to imagine that literature has political uses and whether political commitment necessarily entails literature's subordination to the rationalities of political calculation. Baer turns to the case of colonial India, where literature was instrumentalized politically by the state through surveillance and proscription. Multiple political trials of communists in the 1920s and 1930s, culminating in the Meerut Conspiracy Case (1929–33), used sedition and conspiracy laws to disrupt the emergent workers' movement by incapacitating its leadership. As Baer shows, the defendants' legally useless strategy of wasting time in court enacts a paradoxically 'literary' gesture that unexpectedly communicates with India's progressive literary movement of the later 1930s. A short story by Manik Bandyopadhyay discloses this connection by questioning the radical reader's desire to see in the representation of subaltern or working-class figures necessarily insurgent or rebellious models for political use.

Developing the tension between literature's apparent 'usefulness' and an unassimilable literary 'surplus,' the chapters by Juan E. De Castro and Sandra Fluhrer turn to the Latin American context. De Castro's contribution examines the relationship between socialism and literary creation in the works of César Vallejo (1892–1938), generally considered one of the greatest Spanish-language poets of the twentieth century, and José Carlos Mariátegui (1894–1930), arguably the major Latin American Marxist thinker. In addition to analyzing Vallejo's *Human Poems* (1939) and Mariátegui's *Seven Interpretive Essays on Peruvian Reality* (1928), the chapter looks at less-known texts, such as the Peruvian poet's "Autopsy of Surrealism" (1930), his criticism of the European avant-garde, or the Marxist theorist's novella, *La novela y la vida: Siegfried y el profesor Canella* (1929). By looking at these and other texts, De Castro begins to trace the relationship among *indigenismo* (the representation of indigenous lives), the avant-garde, and Marxist ideas in the works of both Peruvian authors. De Castro shows that both authors found in social narrative and the avant-garde valuable resources for the creation of new and politically versatile modes of intervention. Sandra Fluhrer's chapter explores related questions by turning to the work of Antonin Artaud, the French surrealist whose politicized work was profoundly transformed by a sojourn in Mexico in 1936. Since at least 1968, Artaud's work has provoked questions concerning the political aspects of art, owing both to his radical proposals for a new theater and to his highly strung revolutionary sensibilities. Certain readers (including Susan Sontag) have regarded Artaud's engagement with revolution as decidedly *un*political. This chapter reassesses Artaud's relation to politics through a reading of *Messages révolutionnaires*, a central albeit rather neglected work of Artaud's. This collection of essays and talks, which Artaud wrote during his travels in Mexico, is his most trenchant engagement with the political debates of his time. The texts contain a strong critique of capitalist liberalism and a slightly weaker but still vital critique of Marxism.

This chapter argues that the revolution Artaud advocates is positioned against these two political systems: it is concerned with the fundamental problem of political anthropology, namely, finding a viable relationship between bodies and souls in space. Fluhrer's chapter crucially 'provincializes' the position of Europe in debates about the relationship between literature and politics: instead of presenting Europe (and the United States) as the single most important scene where this relationship was negotiated, Fluhrer indicates that the European case needs to be treated as part of a much more expansive global field.

Taking their cue from Fluhrer's chapter on Artaud, the next two contributions by Hunter Bivens and Aurore Peyroles turn to Europe (Germany, France) as well as to the United States. The Popular Front period of the mid-1930s is at the center of Bivens's explorations: this period is often thought of as a retreat from class in favor of nation and a retreat from the left avant-gardes of the 1920s in favor of more traditional and representational genres. German Popular Front literature did indeed witness a resurgence of the realist novel, precisely because the novel struck many authors as an ideal form for registering the subterranean and capillary processes that had contributed to the fascist state of exception over a long historical *durée*. Rhetorically, the Popular Front saw a shift from class to 'the people' or the nation. Both of these shifts can be read, Bivens argues, as an attempt to portray a kind of temporal alliance politics, linking the contemporaneous antifascist struggle to a *longue durée* of plebeian oppression and dispossession and their attendant nonsynchronisms. Focusing on debates around the Popular Front and the novel among authors in the milieu of the German Communist Party (KPD) in antifascist exile, this chapter draws on the notion of a popular avant-garde developed by Ernst Bloch and Hanns Eisler in their contributions to the Expressionism Debate to argue for a popular front novel that is post-novelistic, in that its protagonist is no longer the individual, but the historical horizon itself. Revisiting a closely related historical context, Peyroles's contribution aims to understand how the engaged novel of the 1930s—here represented by two large novel cycles (John Dos Passos's *USA* [1930–6] and Louis Aragon's *Le Monde réel* [1932–51])—participated in a 'struggle of stories.' As the chapter shows, both novels stage the pernicious power of hegemonic storytelling, which relies on occasionally crude but extremely effective narrative structures. It is precisely against these binary and simplifying narratives that the engaged novels of Dos Passos and Aragon define themselves. For novelists who conceive of their art as a way of intervening in the world, political commitment takes the form of a desire to upend and problematize dominant narratives, notably the way these narratives reflect the 'real world' and address the reader. The reader, for Dos Passos and Aragon, is an active collaborator rather than an impassive consumer. The final chapter in this part, by Steven S. Lee, shifts the focus to a new geographical context (China) while continuing the earlier chapters' interest in forms of literary internationalism. As Lee points out, revolution has long been regarded as generative for modernism, with several scholars noting the frequent, often troubled alignment of artistic and political vanguards. A key case in point is Martin Puchner's *Poetry of the Revolution* (2006), which presents the *Communist Manifesto* as a model for world literature—in particular, for avant-garde manifestos throughout the twentieth century. Lee expands Puchner's framework by applying it to the 1934 Soviet Writers Congress and Mao Tse-Tung's 1942 Yan'an Forum on Literature and Art, events which marked the subordination of artists and writers to the political vanguard. Reading the documents from these events as manifestos makes it possible to blur the boundary between modernism and (socialist) realism and, in the process, to expand the reach of global modernism to realms typically closed off from it—Stalin's Soviet Union and Mao's China.

The second part investigates how literary writers engaged with the new political demands that emerged during the long 1960s, a period marked by a wide range of counter-hegemonic struggles. While the first three chapters (by Daniel Hartley, J. Daniel Elam, and Galin Tihanov) study individual texts in order to raise broader conceptual questions, the last three chapters (by Mark Nowak, Christoph Schaub, and Ulka Anjaria) explore some of the radical recalibrations of aesthetic forms undertaken by committed writers of the period. Daniel Hartley's chapter begins by looking back at Karl Marx's publication in 1880 of a survey consisting of 101 questions about every aspect of working life, to be answered by workers themselves. This questionnaire inaugurated a tradition that became known as 'workers' inquiry' and that aimed to counteract the hegemony of official, 'objective' forms of knowledge by inviting workers to write about their daily experiences, producing militant knowledge as part of a project of autonomous worker organization. Considering the unauthorized forms of writing invited by these questionnaires, Hartley sets out the resemblances between Raymond Williams's theory of the 'structure of feeling' and the important philosophical justification for workers' inquiry written by the French militant and founding member of the heterodox Marxist group Socialisme ou Barbarie Claude Lefort in 1952: "L'expérience prolétarienne" (Proletarian Experience). The chapter concludes with a reading of Paul Romano and Ria Stone's *The American Worker* (1947), one of the best-known examples of twentieth-century workers' inquiry and a direct inspiration for Lefort's essay. J. Daniel Elam's contribution expands the geographical scope of this part—it traces the political uses of literature by way of Lorraine Hansberry's work in the 1960s, notably her posthumously produced play, *Les Blancs*. The essay provides an idiosyncratic but crucial prehistory of Hansberry's play, starting in sociology departments at Anglo-American universities in the early twentieth century and moving toward the 1960s, where Hansberry will wrestle with the implications of early sociology as it might hopefully be put to radical political use. Although Hansberry was not a sociologist, she was a key member of a transnational and radically minded network of sociologists and social theorists. Read in this light, the chapter demonstrates how *Les Blancs* unites, under the misleadingly simple name 'solidarity,' questions about the use of theater, aesthetic experimentation in social scientific writing, and political activism. Elam reads the provocation of the phrase 'the political uses of literature' to indicate not only the ways that literature has been used in politics and political activism, but also how literature is the place where politics can be thought through, debated, wrestled with, and tentatively expressed. For anticolonial and antiracist thinkers in the twentieth century, there was no literature without politics—but also, and perhaps more excitingly, no politics without literature. In other words, politics was a literary endeavor, an aesthetic project, and the grounds for imagining new political communities.

Turning more specifically to the field of literary *theory*, the title of Tihanov's chapter ("*Notes from the Underground*: Why and How Was Non-Marxist Theory Resisted by Non-Marxists in a Totalitarian Society") evokes Fyodor Mikhailovich Dostoevsky's *Notes from the Underground* because all of the action Tihanov refers to unfolds, just as in Dostoevsky's 1864 novella, in St. Petersburg, or Leningrad in the cases of Soviet resistance to theory. But the term *underground* also captures the location of this particular dissident protest: away from the mainstream, scattered in the pages of samizdat magazines, in articles some of which have never been (re)published and have therefore never left the dark room of subterranean critique. There is also a third reason for Tihanov's deployment of the term *underground*: when Friedrich Nietzsche, in 1886/7, encountered Dostoevsky's novella, in Nice, in a French translation titled *L'esprit souterrain*, he made a major discovery for himself that stimulated a rethinking of what a philosophical discourse is and how it functions. Marking out the instances of Russian resistance to theory, Tihanov argues, can also occasion some rethinking of the status of theory and its fortunes in the past century, and today.

The second set of chapters in this part on the long 1960s explores three specific literary case studies. Nowak's chapter turns to the early 1970s—a period when creative writing workshops proliferated in prisons across the United States in the wake of the murder of George Jackson and the Attica uprising. In seeking early precursors to what Mariame Kaba has recently called "the abolitionist imagination," Nowak's chapter investigates a prehistory of abolition studies in the writings of the incarcerated poets of the Attica generation. The chapter analyzes poems from a number of anthologies that published writings produced in 1970s prison workshops. By grounding the prehistory of carceral studies and prison abolition in the cultural production of prison poets, Nowak seeks to conjoin today's prison abolition theories and activism to the foundational literary work of incarcerated creative writers of the Attica generation. Shifting attention from the politics of abolition to emancipatory feminist politics, Schaub's chapter situates Karin Struck's autofictional novel *Klassenliebe* (1973) in the working-class literature of its time, in particular, the work of the group *Werkkreis Literatur der Arbeitswelt*. It analyzes how this German novel—through its form and discourse—lays bare blind spots and exclusionary politics in the project of constructing working-class literature. In sum, Schaub contends that the question of the political use of literature needs to be addressed on several interconnected analytical levels: central among these are the historically situated politics of literary representation (including its formal strategies) and the practices and institutions that enable and constrain political organizing around literature. In the closing chapter of this part, Anjaria turns to the Indian context to ask how women writers had to navigate India's complex political terrain, balancing class critique with questions of individual rights and sexual politics that were part of a burgeoning women's movement. Anjaria's chapter offers a new perspective on mid-twentieth-century Indian progressive writing through a focus on two major authors, Ismat Chughtai and Mahasweta Devi, both of whom reimagined the nature of progressive writing by writing female characters who challenge structures of power through resistance, refusal, joy, and desire rather than solely through collective revolutionary action. In doing so, their works displace the dominant perception that political possibility is primarily to be found in the public sphere, in revolutionary action, and in rational dissent.

The volume's closing part turns to the present moment. It explores the longevity of the debates mapped out in previous chapters, but it also homes in on new permutations in the relationship between literature and political commitment. Maryam Fatima's chapter investigates how mid-twentieth-century discussions of literature's political usefulness are mobilized by more contemporary cultural actors in order to respond to current crises of migration, globalization, and climate precarities. Fatima engages with two iterations of the literary magazine *Lotus*: the earlier version, *Lotus: Journal of Afro-Asian Writing*, which ran from 1968 to 1990, was issued by the Afro-Asian Writers' Association based in Cairo (and later Beirut and Tunis); relaunched after two and a half decades (now with a tricontinental focus on Africa, Asia, and Latin America), the new magazine builds on and deviates from the old *Lotus*'s conceptualization of political literature and cultural politics. In addition to conceptualizing a more capacious Global South geography, the new *Lotus* also broadens its scope of political intervention by unhitching itself from the ideological strictures of the previous magazine (which was funded and sustained by internationalist Soviet cultural bureaucracies) and claims to recenter the 'literary.' Fatima contextualizes the new magazine's lack of ideological coherence through current discussions on 'post-politics' and 'antipolitics,' which allows us to interrogate the stakes and limitations of depoliticizing aesthetics. How,

Fatima asks, might the new *Lotus* be imagined in the absence of a Third World project?

Dirk Wiemann's chapter takes a different approach by investigating the potentials and limitations of 'political formalism.' As Wiemann notes, political formalism signifies a set of literary-theoretical positions which aim to uphold the claim of literature's political efficacy in a largely anti-critical climate. From the standpoint of political formalism (here associated with the work of Jacques Rancière, Caroline Levine, Anna Kornbluh, and others), this efficacy is tied up with the situational transcendence that the literary text articulates through its formal deviance from hegemonic framings of the social world. Since these formalist distinctions of literature's political uses are by and large premised on an understanding of literature as autopragmatic, they have been fiercely interrogated by theorists who argue for an interventionist and antagonistic art practice that not only addresses but also tries to overcome its own implication in a hierarchically structured, exclusionary art field. The chapter brings this tension between formalist and activist literary theories to a reading of an exemplary dissident text, namely Deepak Unnikrishnan's story cycle *Temporary People* (2017). The next chapter, by Peter J. Maurits, combines literary-critical analysis and theoretical reflection. It identifies a peculiar friction between works of contemporary African science fiction and speculative fiction on the one hand and debates about this body of literature on the other. As Maurits shows, many critics assume that contemporary African speculative and science fiction (ASF) involves 'better future narratives'—in truth, however, this narrative form tends to be largely absent from works of ASF. ASF thus complicates our understanding that science fiction and its subgenre of the narrative utopia are the preeminent genres for imagining alternative or better futures. Maurits explores this deactivation of narrative strategies of speculation and extrapolation in a series of short stories by the Motswana writer Tlotlo Tsamaase.

Echoing the more site-specific insights of Maurits's chapter, Madhu Krishnan's contribution begins by noting that the concept of literary activism is as inchoate as it is (increasingly) ever present. Krishnan traces the contested genealogies of the term as well as the tensions which are linked to contemporary concerns about the nature of the literary and its uses. Against the argument that literature must be disinterested and singular in its forms, Krishnan argues that the work of literary activists on the African continent demonstrates how even the most carefully attuned work of aesthetics retains a political use and usage which cannot be separated from the question of activism. The chapter examines the case of the Cameroonian magazine *Bakwa*, setting its work within a longer continental history of literature and activism which has spanned at least seventy years. Focusing particularly on the ways in which the colonial invasion fractured the creative ecology and linguistic imaginary, Krishnan explores how contemporary efforts to revitalize Africa-centered literary networks around translation can be seen as a crucial node in the larger nexus of social production and political activism. Krishnan's chapter offers an apt conclusion to this part—it shows that the peripheral zones of today's globalized economic system provide especially fertile ground for activist modes of writing.

Notes

The editors would like to thank the participants of the "Political Uses of Literature" conference, held at LMU Munich in 2020. Funding by the German Research Foundation's Heisenberg Programme and LMU's research training group "Globalisation and Literature" is gratefully acknowledged. Special thanks are due to Myrjam Wallner and Kalina Janeva for assisting with the formatting of the manuscript.

1 Bertolt Brecht, "On Form and Subject-Matter," in *Brecht on Theatre: The Development of an Aesthetic*, ed. John Willett (London: Methuen, 1982), 29–30, here 30. Brecht's German reads: "Erst der neue Zweck macht die neue Kunst." See Bertolt Brecht, "Über Stoffe und Formen," in *Werke*, vol. 21: *Schriften I* (Frankfurt: Suhrkamp, 1992), 302–4, here 303–4.

2 On the "literary radicals" of the 1930s "whose influence the New Critics set out to combat," see, for example, Barbara Foley, *Radical Representations: Politics and Form in US Proletarian Fiction, 1929–1941* (Durham: Duke University Press, 1993), 5.

3 William K. Wimsatt, *The Verbal Icon: Studies in the Meaning of Poetry* (Lexington: University of Kentucky Press, 1954), 243.

4 Ibid.

5 Fredric Jameson, *The Political Unconscious: Narrative as a Socially Symbolic Act* (Ithaca: Cornell University Press, 1981), 63.

6 For a recent critique of the (Freudo-Marxian) "hermeneutics of suspicion," see Rita Felski, "Critique and the Hermeneutics of Suspicion," *M/C Journal* 15, no. 1 (2011), https://journal.media-culture.au.

7 For theorizations of a 'long 1930s' and its legacy of politicized art, see Leo Mellor and Glyn Salton-Cox, "Introduction: The Long 1930s," *Critical Quarterly* 57, no. 3 (2015): 1–9; and Benjamin Kohlmann and Matthew Taunton, "Introduction," in *A History of 1930s British Literature*, ed. Benjamin Kohlmann and Matthew Taunton (Cambridge: Cambridge University Press, 2019), 1–13.

8 Analogously to the concept of the long 1930s, Jameson has suggested that we treat the 1960s as an elongated decade, making it the focal point for new analyses of capitalism's crises and cultural transformations in the twentieth century. As such, *the 1960s* signifies not "an omnipresent and uniform shared style" or way of thinking and writing, but "the sharing of a common objective

situation to which a whole range of varied responses and creative innovations is then possible." See Fredric Jameson, "Periodizing the 60s," *Social Text*, 9–10 (1984): 178–209, here 178.

9 Raymond Williams, "When Was Modernism?" in *The Politics of Modernism: Against the New Conformists* (London: Verso, 2006), 131–5, here 135.

10 Gregory Sholette, *The Art of Activism and the Activism of Art* (London: Lund Humphries, 2022), 18.

11 Ibid.

12 See Jean-Paul Sartre, "What is Literature?" in *What Is Literature? And Other Essays* (Cambridge, MA: Harvard University Press, 1988), 21–245.

13 For an influential version of this account, see Jacques Rancière, *The Politics of Aesthetics: The Distribution of the Sensible* (London: Bloomsbury, 2011).

14 Rita Felski, *The Uses of Literature* (Oxford: Blackwell, 2008), 9.

15 As Dirk Wiemann notes in his contribution, for some proponents of "postcritique" "both literature and its analysis thus become an exercise in befriending the given and making peace with the status quo." (232)

16 Gabriel Rockhill, *Radical History and the Politics of Art* (New York: Columbia University Press, 2014), 53–4.

17 The Scottish playwright and theater theorist John McGrath, one of the great anglophone inheritors of the theatrical agitprop tradition of the later interwar years, cautioned that "perhaps the most important, and neglected, fact is that the relationship [between art and politics] is determined by many concrete historical phenomena, occurring on all kinds of level, so that the relationship *changes*. There is no point in elaborating a timeless, idealized structure somewhere outside history for this relationship." See McGrath, *Popular Theatre: Audience, Class, and Form* (London: Nick Hern, 1996), 82.

18 See Gayatri Chakravorty Spivak, *An Aesthetic Education in the Era of Globalization* (Cambridge, MA: Harvard University Press, 2013).

19 On the lost world of the Comintern, see, for example, Michael Denning, *Culture in the Age of Three Worlds* (London: Verso, 2004); Katerina Clark, *Moscow, the Fourth Rome: Stalinism, Cosmopolitanism, and the Evolution of Soviet Culture, 1931–1941* (Cambridge, MA: Harvard University Press, 2011); and *Comintern Aesthetics*, ed. Amelia M. Glaser and Steven Lee (Toronto: University of Toronto Press, 2020). On the complex positionality of anticolonial struggles within internationalist political projects, see, for example, Sonali Perera, *No Country: Working-Class Writing in the Age of Globalization* (New York: Columbia University Press, 2014); Rossen Djagalov, *From Internationalism to Postcolonialism: Literature and Cinema between the Second and the Third World* (Montreal: McGill-Queens University Press, 2020); and J. Daniel Elam, *World Literature for the Wretched of the Earth: Anticolonial Aesthetics, Postcolonial Politics* (New York: Fordham University Press, 2020).

20 Steven Lee, "Introduction: Comintern Aesthetics–Space, Form, History," in *Comintern Aesthetics*, ed. Amelia M. Glaser and Steven Lee (Toronto: University of Toronto Press, 2020), 3–29, here 14.

21 Elam, *World Literature*, xiii.
22 Perera, *No Country*, 9.
23 For usefully synthetic recent accounts, see, for example, on the Latin American context: Sophie Esch, *Modernity at Gunpoint: Firearms, Politics, and Culture in Mexico and Central America* (Pittsburgh: University of Pittsburgh Press, 2018); on artistic activism in the Middle East: Ryan Watson, *Radical Documentary and Global Crises Militant Evidence in the Digital Age* (Bloomington: Indiana University Press, 2021); and on the African context: *African Literatures as World Literature*, ed. Alexander Fyfe and Madhu Krishnan (London: Bloomsbury, 2022).
24 Marker's powerful *Le Fond de l'air est rouge* (1977) links up articulations of the revolutionary impulse across the twentieth century by connecting scenes from different radical moments, such as the 1917 Revolution and the anticolonial protests of the 1960s and 1970s.
25 For Walter Benjamin's influential discussion of this idea, see "Left-Wing Melancholy (On Erich Kästner's new book of poems)" (1931), *Screen* 15, no. 2 (1974): 28–32. For a related recent account, see Enzo Traverso, *Left-Wing Melancholia: Marxism, History, and Memory* (New York: Columbia University Press, 2016).
26 Bertolt Brecht, "Eingreifendes Denken," in *Werke*, vol. 21: *Schriften I* (Frankfurt: Suhrkamp, 1992), 524–5. By contrast, more recent accounts of the rise of literary theory and the institutionalization of ideology critique have emphasized that critique developed as an intellectual *ersatz* for 'real' revolutionary activity: on this reading, theory constituted a compensatory response to the failure of left-wing political revolutions in the West in the 1920s and 1930s. See, for example, Joseph North, *Literary Criticism: A Concise Political History* (Cambridge, MA: Harvard University Press, 2017).
27 Sholette, *The Art of Activism*, 151.
28 On the concept of affordances, which has roots in design theory, see Caroline Levine, *Forms: Whole, Rhythm, Hierarchy, Network* (Princeton: Princeton University Press, 2015).
29 For Auden's phrase "To-day the expending of powers / On the flat ephemeral pamphlet," see his civil war poem "Spain 1937," in *The English Auden: Poems, Essays and Dramatic Writing, 1927–1939*, ed. Edward Mendelson (London: Faber and Faber, 1986), 210–12, here 212.
30 The phrase *making use*, Wright observes, "suggests that using is not something given" but rather "that using itself needs to be crafted." See Stephen Wright, *Toward a Lexicon of Usership*, Arte Útil, www.arte-util.org.
31 Joe Cleary, "Realism after Modernism and the Literary World System," *Modern Language Quarterly* 73, no. 3 (2012): 255–68, here 262–3.
32 Lee, "Introduction," 17.
33 On capitalist realism, see Mark Fisher's eponymous *Capitalist Realism: Is There No Alternative?* (London: Zero Books, 2009).
34 Endnotes Collective, "Onward Barbarians," *Endnotes*, https://endnotes.org.uk/. Emphasis in original.

PART I

Revolution, Internationalism, and Literary Politics

Interwar Paradigms

1

Marxists Out of Work

Literature and the Useless in Interwar India

Ben Conisbee Baer

> *Every time the meaning of a discussion depends on the fundamental value of the word* useful—*in other words, every time the essential question touching on the life of human societies is raised . . . it is possible to affirm that the debate is necessarily distorted and that the fundamental question is eluded.*
> GEORGES BATAILLE, "THE NOTION OF EXPENDITURE" (1933)[1]

What is a political *use* of literature? The question posed by this volume *uses* the plural noun form of the word evoking, polysemically, several possibilities. First, and most obviously, that literature might be an instrument of politics, useful to or usable by some politics—a practice in principle distinguishable from literature. (One thinks, only half ironically, of national anthems. And despairingly of ethnonational epic poems that celebrate— and potentialize the structure of feeling for—genocide.) In 1920s India, journal editorials and poetry by Bengali writer and publisher Kazi Nazrul Islam (1889–1976), who translated the socialist *inter*national anthem into Bengali in that decade, were regularly proscribed, and their author briefly imprisoned, for political sedition.[2] His translation of the "Internationale" is cited incidentally in prosecution evidence during the Meerut Communist Conspiracy Trial (1929–33), an event I will return to below. It was sung at the opening of the first All-India Workers' and Peasants' Party Conference in Calcutta (December 1928), records of which are produced as proof that the Meerut accused conspired to violently overthrow British sovereignty. While Nazrul was by no means the only writer subject to proscription for political reasons, his example brings us to the subject of this chapter.

An extensive system of state surveillance of publication existed in colonial India. Its regulating law was designed to monitor and control "hatred," "contempt," or "disaffection" on the evidence of any kind of written, visible, or oral mark.[3] Sedition, then, was defined on a wide terrain of affect—the withdrawal of 'affection' toward the government—defined as the legally verifiable effect of some mark or trace. In the case of literary works, it could result in the banning and confiscation of texts, imprisonment, and fines. This represents one extreme of the political 'use' of literature: a calculated decision in advance regarding the sociopolitical effects of certain statements. What might have characterized the juridical reading machine that programmed such decisions? This is a difficult question, but an important clue appears in a librarian's 1924 note on Nazrul's poetry collection *Bisher Banshi* (Poison Flute) sent to the Director of Public Instruction recommending proscription: "the profusion of such words as blood, tyranny, death, fire, hell, demon and thunder."[4] The reading instrument thus operated as a predigital keyword search. Yet the extreme complexity of the question of modes of reading may be indicated by the fact that in the early 1920s Saumyendranath Tagore, who would become the first translator of the *Communist Manifesto* into an Indic language, received his initial schooling in socialism from the antisocialist tract *Socialistic Fallacies*. "I had no doubts," he writes, "about the accuracy of socialism, having read this book by socialism's *enemy*."[5] This raises questions about who is prepared to read in these ways and how, the incalculable effects of such modes of reading, and the epistemic terrains in which they are learned and practiced.

Politics is a domain necessarily oriented toward the calculable; toward predictability and probability; and toward the strategic practices of governance, legislation, and management of social space according to rational expectations. For there to be political use(s) of literature in this register, one would attempt to measure the extent to which literature is or could have utility according to these ultimately extraliterary criteria. Such a metric, for which one must immediately admit it is impossible to fix an irreducible standard, might also gauge the 'commitment' or engagement of writer or work, making comparative adjudication possible. One could calculate the degree to which a literature is the vehicle of a political communication (supplying unequivocal meaning, correct content, positive representations correlating to desired social effects, etc.). Or, conversely, condemn or proscribe in a determinate political interest certain works of literature as demonstrably subversive, decadent, or retrograde. One might have to decide, evoking the specter of Carl Schmitt, whether the literature in question (or literature as such) is a friend of politics or its enemy.[6]

Schmitt's contemporaneous (1927/32) definition founds 'the political' on a fundamental decision: identification of the enemy, from which all other political calculations would derive their rationality. Precisely because it does not consist in or sustain unequivocal, constative, verifiable statements lending themselves to clear-cut decision-making, literature can only supplement—or even menace—this political *logos* and reading protocol.[7] Saumyendranath's account of his reading already raises questions about the stability of the Schmittian definition, since the 'enemy' of socialism can be its friend if read in a certain way: *Socialistic Fallacies* is an antisocialist polemic. Likewise, the 'literariness' of a text depends on a mode of reading as much as a strict conformity with some set of objective characteristics. Thus, even if a literary work stages irreconcilable social antagonisms—within its very language forms for a V. N. Voloshinov, for example—it cannot simultaneously supply reliable criteria for a political decision regarding those antagonisms or the effects of reading them.[8]

This gives rise to a second possibility of reading our heading: 'uses' in the sense of customs or habits. To have political uses can mean, albeit slightly archaically, to have political habits. If there were political uses of literature in this sense, *literature* would have political habits, or even an addiction (becoming a 'user')—habitually, though not necessarily essentially or even intentionally, borrowing or repurposing signifiers belonging to a politics. With effects that may not be strictly political or that may question or alter the terms and laws by which such politics is articulated, understood, and practiced.

Neither of these readings of the rubric is exhaustive or ultimately cleanly separable from the other. Acknowledging this, my chapter attempts to torque the first interpretation of the phrase 'political uses of literature' toward the second.

From Paranoid Reading to Headless Organization

Let us return to the terrain of affect for a moment. For the paranoid apparatus of 1920s–30s colonial government, the greatest *imagined* political threat was communism. As Hari Vasudevan writes, "following the separate peace at Brest-Litovsk (1918), London and Delhi regarded Bolshevism as a security threat. The sentiment was compounded by Moscow's projection of militant opposition to colonialism."[9] This phantasmatic feeling of immediate existential threat to colonial power recalls—not coincidentally—the figure of a *Gespenst* that organizes the opening of the *Communist Manifesto*: a specter, terrifying to the "Powers of old Europe," envisioned by those powers in fictions, fables, or 'folktales' (*Märchen*), against which a counter-manifestation, in the form of a *manifesto*, should disclose and make public the communists' actual "views . . . aims . . . tendencies."[10] The *Manifesto* posits a frame for the preliminary reduction of paranoid affect, a repudiation of secretive conspiracy in the name of public enlightenment, turning the ghostly figure around to denounce the spectral powers of the state's spies and secret police.

In colonial India, paranoia was determined by the world-historical mutation represented by the 1917 Russian Revolution and the activities of the Comintern after 1919, the increasing consciousness of communist aims and strategies, the unstoppable flow of communist writings into and around the subcontinent, and the generalization of urban labor organization and the mass industrial strike, especially from the mid-1920s onward. It thrived in the residual atmosphere of prerevolutionary 'Great Game' international politics, given literary articulation in Rudyard Kipling's *Kim* (1901), in which Russia was already a figure of obsessive anxiety.[11] Colonial surveillance also recorded that small numbers of British communists traveled to India to work with organizations there. It matters little that paranoia was in large part phantasmatic and that organized communism occupied a limited sphere in interwar India: the 'specter of communism' nevertheless produced real effects in the legal-political system, resulting in a bizarre series of increasingly elaborate legal trials between 1922 and 1933.[12]

The last and largest of these trials, the Meerut Communist Conspiracy Case (1929–33), focalizes the juridico-political reading machine *in extremis*. This machine impossibly attempts to process the entire text of international communism to produce evidence of 'conspiracy' *beyond* the written, visible, or oral marks that exemplified sedition. In 1929, thirty-two men associated with the communist movement in India were arrested and placed on trial for "conspiracy to deprive His Majesty of the sovereignty of India . . . by means of a revolution" under section 121-A of the Indian Penal Code (Chapter VI: Of Offences Against the State).[13] In 1931, Meerut was accurately described as "the greatest State trial ever held in India," and in terms of its four-year duration and vast expense, it was perhaps the largest undertaken by any imperial power in the interwar epoch.[14] It is beyond my scope here to give a detailed account of the circumstances and unfolding of the Meerut trial, whose published documentation runs to thousands of pages. I will only examine the way its logic discloses unexpected configurations of the political and the literary, use and uselessness.

Those arrested represented the main organizational and intellectual leadership of the workers' movement, which—in a striking reflection of the regicidal charge against them—was effectively beheaded by their detention. Dipesh Chakrabarty, among others, has observed the "temporary lull"[15] in working-class militancy that coincided exactly with the years of trial and was determined by this decapitation. Chakrabarty's research sensitively accounts for the indigenous 'feudal' mode of leadership and organization that was powerfully effective for India's emerging socialist movement: a "*babu*–coolie"[16] relation that both regulated general industrial militancy and conditioned the terms in which socialist struggles for hegemony could be carried out. Contrasting with the hiatus of the industrial workers' movement in India after the arrests, there was a remarkable campaign of international publicity and support for the imprisoned leaders (involving renowned intellectuals such as Albert Einstein, H. G. Wells, Romain Rolland, and Harold Laski, as well as Indian and British politicians, clerics, and trade unions). The difference of social and epistemic levels should be noted and thought through: recent histories of Meerut have tended to celebrate this moment for its "international solidarity and anticolonial internationalism,"[17] its "cross-border alliances against imperialism,"[18] without sufficient attention to the class fix of such alliances. As Susan Pennybacker writes:

> [D]uring this time, there were as many as 23,000 political prisoners in India, many of whom had been picked up in raids and in house searches, beaten, and incarcerated without trial. Displays of military force accompanied arrests, and the courts often refused to grant bail. The leaders of India's social movements routinely faced imprisonment, but rank-and-file workers and militants did as well, and many under more onerous conditions, without the shield of celebrity.[19]

I will return to this question in reading a literary text at the end of the present chapter.

Wasting Time: Conspiracy, Intention, Program

Meerut is a trial for conspiracy: the worst sort of conspiracy thinkable by the law because it envisages the deposition of the sovereign, that unanswerable, sacred anchor point of the state's law itself. The maximum penalty for conspiracy—one step short of the capital crime of waging war against the sovereign—was 'transportation for life' or deportation to a penal colony.

Proposing that the Meerut accused were charged with 'thought crimes,' historians of the trial have identified an important paradox: the law's definition of conspiracy calls for verifying the unprovable.[20] When Macaulay drafted the first Indian Penal Code in 1837, English law included provisions for thought crime: "anyone who 'compasses' or 'imagines' the sovereign's death [comes] within the scope of treason."[21] Under 121-A (1870), the definition of the conspiratorial 'act' is so infinitely flexible that *no act need have been committed*. Does this already bring us to the realm of fiction if not necessarily literature? Conspiracy is not essentially defined by an 'act.' More precisely, 'to conspire' *is* the act itself, not necessarily entailing any other deed; but this requires supplementary definition drawn from elsewhere in the code stipulating the precondition of 'agreement,' since conspiracy is a crime of more-than-one perpetrator. From start to finish, the prosecution's argument is grounded on the concept of agreement and therefore (shared) conscious intention: "the essential ingredient in conspiracy ... is agreement," writes Judge Yorke in his final judgment, reprising the prosecution's opening statement four years previously that "the mere agreement to do these things is an offence."[22] This gives rise to an epistemological problem: how to know and how to prove agreement—and therefore criminal *intent*—to do a specific thing in the absence of demonstrable actions that attempt to realize it. At the very least a story must be told, since the accused's activities such as organizing labor, reading political texts, conducting secret correspondence, or receiving foreign funding were not technically illegal. Thus, it was necessary to reframe these acts in terms of a specific intention to deprive the king-emperor of his sovereignty by demonstrating, through textual exegesis, that 'conspiracy' is interior to the epistemology, structure, and system of communist organization as such—going all the way back to Marx. To be a communist *is to be* a conspirator. "Bolshevism ... is a rule of life,"[23] says the prosecution on day one of the trial. This ultimately sets the scene for the 1934 criminalization of the Communist Party as an 'unlawful association.'

This quasi-ontologization of the 'Bolshevik' communicates with a rich seam of literary, affective, and legal history in colonial India: the anxiety and paranoia of the early and mid-nineteenth-century British concerning 'thuggee.' The thug concept crystallizes to define a religious, hereditary, or communal criminal collectivity whose way of life is supposedly organized around plunder and murder on the highways. It is enshrined in a law of 1836 that supposes "criminal intention could be assessed not only from a specific criminal act but from the characteristics of a collectivity."[24] The thug was lastingly installed as an almost mythic figure of terror in colonial India through innumerable memoirs and fictional works written by Englishmen and Englishwomen. As well as raising the symbolic specter of 'mutiny,' then, Meerut transposes the thug question of guilt through group membership and 'way of life' onto the structure of international communism:

> Their object was, shortly put, to replace the Government of His Majesty, King George, in India, and in its place to put the Government of the Third Communist International. It might also fairly be stated that that was in effect to substitute for the Government of His Majesty the Government of Mr. Stalin as he is now called. In fact it is the case for the prosecution that these accused are Bolsheviks, that is to say that they aim at the Bolshevik ideal.[25]

It is at this point we see the convergence of two programs: the programmed outcome of the trial and the program of a reading protocol that quasi-automatically scours texts for evidence to produce legal proof. The juridical reading machine operates like the librarian who parsed Nazrul's poetry as a collection of subversive keywords. In this case, the crucial signifiers are 'violence,' 'dictatorship of the proletariat,' and 'revolution,' with Lenin's *State and Revolution* (1917) as exhibit A.[26] The crucial, criminalizing distinction from legal, that is, constitutional, struggle hinges on the question of force:

> A nationalist may desire complete independence of India, which in itself implies the cessation of the King's sovereignty, but this does not necessarily render him liable to prosecution under this section. The word deprive implies forcible dispossession. If a nationalist asks through the usual civil channels with a view perhaps to inducing the British Parliament on behalf of the King to give complete independence to India he cannot thereby be said to be planning to deprive the King of his Sovereignty.[27]

The question of this intended force or violence thereby places the accused in excess of constitutionality, and 'violence' becomes a crucial link in the prosecuting signifying chain.

The prosecution's giant hermeneutics links these keywords in a structural and causal chain. Program against program: the accused's guilt was defined in terms of an *intentional* agreement to "put in practice the creed of the Communist International and to carry out its programme"[28]—a program traced by the prosecution all the way back to the *Communist Manifesto*, through many other works by Marx and Engels, Lenin, Stalin, the *ABC of Communism*, and so on, to the manifestos, correspondence, and recorded speech produced by the accused themselves. The programmatic reading argues that communists are programmed by a signifying code (in words such as 'violence' and 'dictatorship') to *intend* and *agree* to enact a program of "forcible dispossession." An excess of text and quotation from communist writings fills the gap of proving agreement and intention to conspire (in its original pagination, the final judgment alone runs to over 1,700 pages). The prosecution's implicit logic is that intention is a calculable and causal movement along a signifying chain.

Second program: it is clear from documents now available (as it was, for different reasons, to the defendants at the time) that the Meerut trial was programmed in advance—from the highest levels of state—to convict. In other words, it was the fiction or simulacrum of a trial.[29] Everything about Meerut was set up to reproduce the formal structure of a legal trial: judge, defendants, lawyers, evidence, witnesses, questioning, testimony, and so on. The Meerut location also offered the symbolic satisfaction (and force) of being the site at which the 1857 'Mutiny' had begun, metonymically linking the trial to the colonial history of suppressing insurrection in the subcontinent. One crucial aspect permitted by the specificity of colonial legal structures, and deliberately exploited by the state, was the absence of a jury. This was made possible by the regionally differentiated legal institutions of colonial India in which trial in a Presidency town would be held in a High Court with a jury, whereas the district of Meerut (far from the large cities where the accused had mainly operated) worked on a Magistrate's and Sessions court system. 'Assessors,' whose recommendations carried no necessary influence in trials, substituted for jurors in district courts, and at Meerut the accused's petitions for moving to a trial by jury were refused.[30] In pretrial secret correspondence, Home Secretary Haig had already established the principle of prejudgment: "we could not, however, take the chance of submitting the case to a jury. . . . We cannot put the case into Court unless we are convinced it will result in conviction."[31] Replying to the Viceroy of India (Lord Irwin) in a telegram of February 1929, the secretary of state for India, Viscount Peel, wrote, "Of course it is essential that if the case is instituted there must be no doubt of its success."[32] If, in principle, legal trials are conducted so as to make possible a judgment, that is, a new decision, Meerut was demonstrably prejudged. It took no new decision even as it established novel precedents. That is, as a trial it was fictive, a simulacrum, precisely because it proceeded with a result guaranteed in advance.

The prisoners' dilemma was thus how to respond to an evident foregone conclusion structured as a theatrical excess. We must acknowledge that the accused were "not a homogenous group."[33] As Philip Spratt, one of three English communists arrested, observes in his memoir, "the 31 accused . . . split into two almost equal groups . . . the communists and the non-communists."[34] It was the self-identified communist eighteen who signed a *General Statement* of principle and analysis read aloud before the court in December 1931. Examination of the recorded individual statements of all defendants discloses significant doctrinal and experiential heterogeneity between and within both groups. Without being able to discuss these differences further here, I will focus on the communist responses. Their lengthy collective statement, which in book form exceeds 300 pages, was read in court by the accused R. S. Nimbkar.[35] It was largely assembled from parts of individual defendants' trial statements—many already significantly lengthier than the *General Statement* itself. A 'rational' response to the Meerut prisoners' dilemma might have been to plead guilty so as to decrease the trial period and even the actual sentences. In 1963, Muzaffar Ahmad, one of the accused and one of the first Indian communist leaders, wrote that they were advised by Congress Party leadership to immediately plead guilty as "the trial would end immediately and there would be very light sentences."[36] Scenting a self-serving strategy by their erstwhile allies, the prisoners did exactly the opposite, constructing interminable (word-)sentences and thereby indefinitely prolonging the trial by years.

A prevailing historical interpretation (apparently shared to some extent by the defendants) of the prisoners' recourse to these prodigious word-barrages is of a "propaganda coup" for the communists, a self-representation of "the voices of anticolonial resistance" on an international stage.[37] More modestly, Ahmad and others would make a retrospective claim for "the dissemination of our ideology."[38] It is true that in activist pamphlets, newspapers, and political speeches, short excerpts and digests of the defendants' statements received international publicity, though the *General Statement* was not widely published until 1967, and most of the other trial documents remain in state archives.[39] This confirms that the prisoners' strategy was—in rational–utilitarian terms—a risky wager at best, perhaps even a perverse decision. "The statements they made day after day in the Sessions Court, instead of establishing any grounds in their favor, foredoomed all chances of escape," writes Ahmad in retrospect. As Ahmad continues, the statements made were "not evidence" in legal terms; they were not *legal* testimony because they were not taken under oath.[40] They often repeat, again at great length, some of the most programmatic orthodoxies of Stalinist or Comintern doctrine. But the *use* of these statements remains incalculable, open-ended; their composition and utterance are at the same stroke a profoundly profitless squandering of signifiers, energy, time, and even health and life, prolonging the trial by years. (In addition to the shared privations of extended incarceration, defendant D. R. Thengdi died during the trial period and Kishorilal Ghosh died shortly afterward; Gopal Basak lost all his teeth through a botched dental procedure).[41]

An earlier tactic at Meerut had been hunger strike, that is, self-imposed refusal of food consumption.[42] Lester Hutchinson recalls the symbolic and political power of such a gesture of self-sacrifice in the subcontinent, used to great effect by Mahatma Gandhi and part of an indigenous lexicon of political leadership.[43] The prisoners soon change tack from this anorexic approach to a bulimic one. Gaining permission from the court to access a large archive of communist texts while in jail, including proscribed literature and prosecution evidence, they partially digest and protractedly regurgitate it over the months and years.[44]

If, to secure its programmed result, the prosecution utilizes fiction, simulacrum, and a reading pattern that is both extensive and reductive, the prisoners both repeat and displace this strategy: by wasting time, and by reframing the alleged determinism of a communist program in and as the open-endedness of wasted time. The communists know their statements are (legally) 'useless': the case has been decided in advance. A possible use remains in the restricted sphere of international publicity, but, as we have seen, claims for the effectiveness of international solidarity— indispensable though it is—are exaggerated because they remain constricted to high-level metropolis–colony circuits.[45] Social strata below this would have remained impermeable to thousands of pages of Marxist *professions de foi* recorded in English. While these statements by the accused are not conventionally recognizable as 'literature,' they hijack the political instrumentalization of a *fiction* (the trial as non-trial) by inflating and refiguring the prosecution strategy as a waste of everybody's time, in excess of any programmable outcome. They also subvert the program by imbuing their statements with their own heterogeneous personal and subjective narratives (fascinating in their own right) of how they arrived at socialist/communist positions. This latter dimension is necessarily but unfortunately lost in the more widely available and formally doctrinal *General Statement*.

One example will have to suffice here. The prosecution alleges that criminal conspiracy against the sovereign is an inevitable and intended agreement realized programmatically as a 'way of life' by its Bolshevik adherents. This reappears in the motif of determinism, affirmed by several defendants and the *General Statement* itself. In an ironic acceptance of the charges, the prisoners affirm that they are indeed personifications of an impersonal historical tendency. Raising the stakes, they contend that this logic in fact voids the charge of 'conspiracy' in the colloquial sense, because the historical antagonisms at play are far larger and more powerful than the intentional agency of this or that activist group. The king has, as it were, already been beheaded by the rise of bourgeois society; he is "already an alien . . . a puppet,"[46] instrumentalized by a system over which he has no real power. The future epoch of socialist difference from capitalism for which the defendants work is not within their power to bring about on such and such a day, though a calculation of the historical tendencies leads them to conclude its inevitability and to situate their agency therein precisely as a "subjective" event.[47] They are rather "faithful to the Leninist conception of politics as the art of intervening in the conjunctures that are themselves posited as specific modes of concentration of the 'main' contradiction (antagonism)."[48] As Sohan Singh Josh puts it in his own statement before the court, "Revolution is in the womb of the future. When it will take place do not know what I will do. Perhaps I will kill off the bourgeoisie perhaps I will not."[49] The prisoners declare a zone of non-knowledge for the agent in their own subjective actions, which they carry out with no final guarantees. Thus, even as they confess to "trying to set up an entirely new system of laws,"[50] the effects must ultimately be in excess of any existing program or plan (though a program and plan are needed). If the future epoch of socialist difference is therefore determined just as much by wasted time and effort, does this not echo Marx's own recourse to the literary imagination when he writes of insurrection that "the social revolution of the nineteenth century cannot draw its poetry from the past, but only from the future";[51] a situation in which 'content' will *exceed* (*hinausgehen über*) 'words'?

Waste as Proof

One of the difficulties indicated by Meerut and its aftermath was precisely that of developing hegemony in the long term as a supplement to the intellectual and political self-development of communist and socialist leaders. As we have seen, the movement could be beheaded, albeit temporarily, because of a persistent epistemic gap shaped by indigenous patterns of leadership. This epistemic–political conundrum determines an inventive response: the startling practice of unguaranteed 'wastage' in the trial that indicates the space of a socialist differential from both immediate calculations of usefulness and political rationality, and from the defendants' own often programmatic formalizations of Marxist theory. This, I contend, is one reason the struggle shifted in a cultural/literary direction during the later 1930s with the emergence of an organization such as the All-India Progressive Writers' Association (AIPWA) founded in London in 1934.[52] While the AIPWA was partly a response to shifting Comintern priorities such as the Popular Front, its attempts to close the epistemic gap (by negotiating with it) accommodated innovative practices in popular and public language and wider experimentation with regional and class-inflected idiom and modes of verse and narrative, while embracing forms of judgment at odds with political program alone. While I cannot elaborate this issue in detail here, I suggest an approach to it in closing my chapter with a literary work that stages a dilemma of the post-Meerut period and the question of political uses of literature.

In the late 1940s, just after Indian independence, AIPWA-affiliated Bengali author Manik Bandyopadhyay (1908–1956) published two collections of short stories that construct complex figurations from sedimented layers of historical experience. These include the rural and urban sociopolitical turbulence of the interwar period in India, the epoch of war itself (including the horrific Bengal Famine of 1943), and the effects of renewed rural struggles in postwar Bengal that straddled the moment of formal independence (especially the Tebhaga revolt of 1946–9, a landless sharecroppers' campaign against the concentration of power and property, focused on the proportion or share [*bhag*] of crops allotted to rural workers as their payment).

"Chhoto Bakulpurer Jatri" (Travelers to Chhoto Bakulpur, 1948) is the head story of an eponymous collection of eight tales.[53] I focus my concluding section on this story because, written by an avowedly communist and 'committed' author, it nonetheless cautions against attempts to render legalistic or decidable evidence for the political usability of literature. As a possible reflection on the incalculable consequences of the Meerut trial, it displaces the question of decidable use and proof of efficacy into questions of reading and readability, questioning the reader's desire for literature's immediate political effectivity or usefulness. In this sense, the story stages reading as both instrument and caesura in legal–political decision-making and action.

"Travelers to Chhoto Bakulpur" is set in Bengal at an indeterminate time of the recent past or near future (1940s). It tells the story of Dibakar Das, a Howrah factory worker who, with his wife Anna and their infant child, is attempting to visit Anna's parents' village home. Having learned that an ongoing factory strike near this village has resulted in violent conflict with the police and local gentry, the family travels to the area to check on Anna's relatives. Arriving at night by train on their way to the village of Chhoto Bakulpur, the group passes through an umbral, almost deserted landscape of thickly clustered shacks and an increasingly sinister series of human gatekeepers. There is first a "group of soldiers on the platform," silently overseeing the arriving travelers, a "sight that he [Dibakar] has become used to."[54] An atmosphere of exception and crisis is thus also normality in this quasi-subaltern universe. The soldiers, representatives of the official force of the state, do not expressly interact with the passengers. The next set of gatekeepers at the railway station, a seemingly self-appointed group of local men, "babumoto lok" (gentry-like persons),[55] do, however. Thus begins the first interrogation, instigated by a young, khadi-clad man who has been staring at Anna (the khadi possibly marking him as a Congress Party worker; hence another, explicitly political, level of the state). The family's tickets and destination are demanded, and the fact that they are headed to the very place a bloody conflict occurred arouses surprise. The whole interaction is staged in terms of the gentry's contemptuous superiority toward the subaltern group, and the latter's affectless disengagement. Having procured an oxcart to take them to Chhoto Bakulpur, the family passes through a further layer of sentries and interrogations. On the dark, abandoned road, flashlight beams shine out on them from "the porches of expropriated huts," followed by disembodied voices: "Who goes there? Where are you going?"[56] Passing a "huge encampment" at Kadamtala village, the family reaches the last set of gatekeepers and its final interrogation. "You could tell that the untimely arrival of Gagan's oxcart had aroused some happy excitement among those who had set up guard at the village entrance, cutting off the insurrectionary settlement from the outside world."[57] The final scene of questioning more closely resembles an arrest and trial than the preceding ones, focused as it is on identity, proof, witness, physical search, and conviction. By an ambiguous (free indirect) focalization of the leading sentry as "probably a non-government group leader [*besarkari dalpati*],"[58] the narrative suggests that Dibakar and his family have now entered an extrajudicial zone, a non-state space where normal legal protocol is suspended. This is underlined by Dibakar's question: "has one-forty-four been invoked?"[59]—a reference to Section 144 of the Indian Criminal Procedure Code that prohibits unlawful assembly. The answer is "No prohibition, why a prohibition?"[60] There is no formally legal ban on entering the area, and yet the family is extralegally detained. The ensuing scene of trial is therefore staged as a simulacrum of legality. Its scene depicts insistent questioning, multiple demands for 'proof' (*proman*) of identity, an aggressive search of the family's belongings, and a Meerut-like 'judgment.' Within the paranoid logic of the situation narrated, the very fact that the family's entire disposition presents as a "harmless, ordinary, bovine, farmworker couple" becomes "a reason for deep suspicion."[61] With an ordinary reflex cruelty toward subaltern persons, the sentinels confiscate and consume a package of *paan* chews that Dibakar had bought at the train station. This everyday cruelty communicates with the story's suggestion of the enjoyment experienced by the guardsmen on the arrival of a group to search, a pleasure in cruelty and authority that underlies and intensifies the affective tone of the story's scenography.

Here is my translation of the final passages of the story, in which 'proof' of Dibakar and Anna's guilt is ostensibly discovered. This follows on directly from the appropriation of Dibakar's *paan* packet:

> Three remaining *paan*s went into three men's mouths. Chewing on *paan*, casting an eye toward the printed-paper *paan* wrapper in the lanternlight, one of the men jumped as if he had received an electric shock. He stares with bulging eyes at the large letters printed on the paper he has carefully smoothed out. "To the Militant Heroes of Chhoto Bakalpur."
>
> Voice trembling with the excitement of this profound discovery, he yells, "Got it! Got a pamphlet!"
>
> Pamphlet? [*Istahar*?] Yes indeed. Dangerous pamphlet! Though folded and stained with lime and *paan* juice, it is completely legible with effort. Eye-opening reading.
>
> They breathe a sigh of relief, though. No more pointless effort, no more being plagued by imaginary doubts and suspicions, absolutely irrefutable proof is in their hands. Now the conspiracy [*sadajantra*] will come out.
>
> "Where'd you get this pamphlet?"
>
> The question is pronounced as if deliciously rolling off the tongue.
>
> "Pamphlet? I don't know about no pamphlet! Bought four paisa of *paan*, *paan*-seller wrapped it in that paper."
>
> "The *paan*-seller wrapped it, or you knowingly bought *paan* and wrapped it in the pamphlet?"
>
> "Why? Why'd I do that?"
>
> "No more messing. Tell us your real name now."
>
> Dibakar and Anna looked each other in the face.[62]

The story ends here. This final scene stages a terrible 'misreading' of text as evidence. Not only the phrase on the piece of paper (insurrectionary language), but the very designation of the paper as a pamphlet (*istahar*) suggests a field of communist significations. Evoking the Meerut period, *istahar* (also "manifesto") is the term under which the *Communist Manifesto* was translated into Bengali in 1927 by Saumyendranath Tagore, and *sadajantra* ("conspiracy") is the Bengali term applied to the communist trials of the 1920s and 1930s. Beyond these obvious signifiers, the absurdity and cruel irony of being convicted for possessing a militant text recycled as food wrapping highlights the protagonists' innocence while simultaneously dramatizing a politically (and existentially) consequential reading vector. Here, the interest of the story is that such a mode of reading may be shared by the thoughtless, self-appointed guardians of law and order and by the radical, 'committed' reader alike. The dramatized mistake intertwines two positions, effectively cross-contaminating the readers *in* the text and an implicit, extratextual, committed reader in search of politically usable meanings.

At a first level, metonymy from the printed slogan to the militant identity of its carrier is both 'relief' and wish fulfillment: a phantasmatic, "imaginary" (*mangara*, mind-made, even "fictive") political suspicion finds verification through a metonymic chain. The text dramatizes the limits of reading at the point where insurgent intention and identity are made to derive from the contingent possession of a particular object taken as a document. This hangs precisely on an instrumentalization of waste, excess, a recycled scrap of paper. It is political use insofar as it turns the innocent, the unmotivated, the 'useless' remainder into the pawn of political calculation, no matter how ultimately perverse or phantasmatic.

Second, while the printed text in the story clearly does not appear as a literary work, it articulates a point at which equivocal signifiers and traces (composing a figure) are interpreted and assigned determinate meaning. The scene is the focal point of text and reading *in* the text, also figuring the practice of reading (this) literature in terms of political use. The story thereby confronts us with a representation of political reading as the categorization and diagnosis of an iconic or representative character 'type': the peasant or worker (subaltern or working class) who *must* be rebellious, evidence for which is found in a useless piece of wastepaper, "folded and stained with lime and *paan* juice."[63] Such ordinary, worldly traces and marks, themselves in excess of the printed message, must be ignored for the extraction of the political signification 'militant.' The enigmatic figure of the Dibakar group is disfigured into unilateral meaning by the imposition of a signifier, making it useful for a political program of social control. Hence even the professed proper names of the protagonists must immediately be destroyed by being decrypted and known: "tell us your real name now."[64] If such a method is taken as a political allegory of reading for the literary text instrumentally usable as content, an example, or a diagnosis for politics, all openness to uncertainty, texture and trace, and a non-programmed futurity dissolves as it is coded into system. Reading ends when, as is perhaps inevitable, text is translated into the usefulness of a calculable action.

I am somewhat provocatively arguing, then, that "Travelers to Chhoto Bakulpur" discloses the desire of the radical, politicized reader in the figure of the gentrified hoodlum who wishes to find resistance or even revolution personified in the oppressed as such. In this way, "Travelers to Chhoto Bakulpur" also warns against the radical reader's desire to find insurgent consciousness—and thus an immediate criterion of evaluation and certitude—in depictions of the marginalized, rather than negotiate the more complex and equivocal terrain of a subalternity (or indeed a worldly ordinariness) that cannot be reduced (or inflated) to the sign of insurgency. As the AIPWA recognized, echoing its contemporary Antonio Gramsci who was writing in a Roman jail at the same moment, the making of socialist hegemony is surely a political task. Yet as the Meerut prisoners indicated by wasting time and words in their courtroom responses (and as the AIPWA also knew in practice), the political program and its assurances are persistently limited by a world it can neither definitively measure nor control. The 'pamphlet' is, after all, the sign of a larger political space beyond the narrowly delineated, claustrophobic landscape of the story, yet it also figures even that political space and sign as a limited envelope held in a worldly web of other traces and uses.

If we can call this supplementation 'ethical' rather than 'political,' and if it therefore represents a cesura in political epistemologies rather than an inscription of literature into their criteria without remainder, Manik Bandyopadhyay's story ends by prompting the reader to imagine such a disjuncture. Its externally focalized last sentence reads, "Dibakar and Anna looked each other in the face."[65] Diverging from the interrogation and exultation of the political operatives who have finally identified 'proof' they can use, the story ends with an image of gazes on faces. It withholds an interpretative gesture, such that this image of subjectivity may depict the mutually unknowable in the world of the story just as much as it signs off with an enigma for the reader. Such a gesture toward a place of vagueness and non-understanding is exactly what literature can 'do,' even if it is ultimately not of direct use for practical politics.

Notes

1 Georges Bataille, "The Notion of Expenditure," in *Visions of Excess: Selected Writings, 1927–1939*, ed. Allan Stoekel (Minneapolis: University of Minnesota Press, 1985), 116–129, here 116.

2 A list of Nazrul's banned books may be found in Hiranmay Bhattacharya, *Nirbasita Sahitya* vol. 2 (Kolkata: Sagar, 1987), appendix p. 18; discussion in vol. 1, p. 162–88. See also Priti Kumar Mitra, *The Dissent of Nazrul Islam* (New Delhi: Oxford University Press, 2007), 127–46. In the 1920s, more of Nazrul's works were proscribed than those of any other named author, though

proscription extended to significant numbers of anonymous pamphlets, and publishers and presses were also subject to liabilities.

3 John D. Mayne, *Commentaries on the Indian Penal Code* (Madras: Higginbotham and Co., 1872), 104.

4 Sisir Kar, *Bengali Books Proscribed under the Raj* (New Delhi: Samskriti, 2009), 355. Sisir Kar, *Nishiddha Nazrul* (Kolkata: Ananda, 1983) offers a fuller account of the various proscriptions of the poet's writing.

5 Saumyendranath Tagore, *Jatri* (Calcutta: General Printers and Publishers, 1975), 60. Emphasis added, trans. B. C. B. He read Yves Guyot's *Socialistic Fallacies* (1910), an English translation from the French.

6 See Carl Schmitt, *The Concept of the Political*, trans. George Schwab (Chicago: University of Chicago Press, 2007 [1932]).

7 "If no word which enters a literary work ever wholly frees itself from its meaning in ordinary speech, so no literary work . . . leaves these meanings unaltered." This literary excess goes for political discourse, too. See Th. W. Adorno, "Commitment," in *Aesthetics and Politics*, ed. Fredric Jameson, trans. Ronald Taylor (New York: Verso, 1980), 177–97, here 178.

8 See V. N. Voloshinov, *Marxism and the Philosophy of Language*, trans. L. Matejka and I. L. Matunik (Cambridge, MA: Harvard University Press, 1986 [1930]).

9 Hari Vasudevan, "India and the October Revolution," in *The Global Impacts of Russia's Great War and Revolution* Book 2, Part 2, ed. Choi Chatterjee, Steven G. Marks, Mary Neuburger, and Steven Sabol (Bloomington: Slavica, 2019), 199–324, here 299. See also Juned Shaikh, "Marxism, Language, and Social Hierarchy, 1920–1950," in *Outcaste Bombay: City Making and the Politics of the Poor* (Seattle: University of Washington Press, 2021), 46–84; and Ali Raza, "Red Scare," in *Revolutionary Pasts: Communist Internationalism in Colonial India* (Cambridge: Cambridge University Press, 2020), 177–208.

10 Karl Marx and Friedrich Engels, *Manifesto of the Communist Party*, in *Marx-Engels Collected Works*, vol. 6 (London: Lawrence and Wishart, 1976), 481.

11 See Peter Hopkirk, *The Great Game: The Struggle for Empire in Central Asia* (New York: Kodansha International, 1992).

12 The major communist conspiracy cases are Peshawar, Cawnpore (Kanpur), and Meerut. For a sober assessment of the reality of Communist Party organizing on the ground in 1920s–30s India, see Sobhanlal Datta Gupta, *Comintern and the Destiny of Communism in India: 1919–1943* (Kolkata: Seribaan, 2006).

13 Langford James, Prosecution Opening Address, *Meerut Conspiracy Papers* (Meerut: Saraswati Printing Press, 1932), A–1. Thirty-one of the men were captured in March, and Hutchinson in June.

14 *The Meerut Prisoners and the Charge Against Them* (London: Modern Books, 1931), 3.

15 Dipesh Chakrabarty, *Rethinking Working-Class History* (Princeton: Princeton University Press, 1989), 118. In 1935, British intelligence noted the "marked

improvement in the industrial situation" following the detentions. Cited in Pramita Ghosh, *Meerut Conspiracy Case and the Left-Wing in India* (Calcutta: Papyrus, 1978), 164.

16 Chakrabarty, *Rethinking*, 143–53 and *passim*.

17 Michele L. Louro and Carolien Stolte, "The Meerut Conspiracy Case in Comparative and International Perspective," *Comparative Studies of South Asia, Africa and the Middle East* 33, no. 3 (2013): 310–15, here 311.

18 Priyamvada Gopal, *Insurgent Empire: Anticolonial Resistance and British Dissent* (London: Verso, 2019), 249.

19 Susan D. Pennybacker, *From Scottsboro to Munich: Race and Political Culture in 1930s Britain* (Princeton: Princeton University Press, 2009), 166.

20 Franziska Roy and Benjamin Zachariah, "Meerut and a Hanging: 'Young India,' Popular Socialism, and the Dynamics of Imperialism," *Comparative Studies of South Asia, Africa and the Middle East* 33, no. 3 (2013): 360–77, here 361; Ali Raza, "Separating the Wheat from the Chaff: Meerut and the Creation of 'Official' Communism in India," *Comparative Studies of South Asia, Africa and the Middle East* 33, no. 3 (2013): 316–30, here 317; Gopal, *Insurgent Empire*, 261. A. G. Noorani indicates a glitch in the legal code that requires a proven 'act' to be committed for *criminal* conspiracy, but only 'agreement' in the case of an offense against the state. *Indian Political Trials* (New Delhi: Oxford University Press, 2005), 238–9.

21 Wing-Cheong Chan, "Abetment, Criminal Conspiracy, and Contempt," in *Codification, Macaulay and the Indian Penal Code: The Legacies and Modern Challenges of Criminal Law Reform*, ed. Wing-Cheong Chan, Barry Wright, and Stanley Yeo (Farnham: Ashgate, 2011), 129–54, here 130. The IPC was effected only in 1860. The wording on imagining the king's death goes back to the Treason Act of 1351.

22 *Meerut Conspiracy Papers*. Judgment Delivered by R. L. Yorke (Simla: Government of India Press, 1932), 8; James, Opening Address, A–3.

23 James, Opening Address, A–3. See also Raza, "Red Scare," 191–3.

24 Radhika Sinha, *A Despotism of Law: Crime and Justice in Early Colonial India* (Oxford and New York: Oxford University Press, 1998), 214–15.

25 James, Opening Address, A–2.

26 See V. I. Lenin, *The State and Revolution* (New York: International Publishers, 1943 [1917]).

27 *Meerut Conspiracy Papers*, Committal Order of 1929, 10.

28 James, Opening Address, A–3. The case papers contain voluminous evidence lists of exhibits, police surveillance reports on meetings, and so on.

29 This is why historians have described it in terms of "political theater" (Roy and Zachariah, "Meerut and a Hanging," 361) and "self-fulfilling prophecy . . . foregone conclusion" (Raza, "Separating the Wheat from the Chaff," 323).

30 This feature was an inheritance of early nineteenth-century colonial legal organization. The use of assessors was not unusual in the legal system but

was conspicuously manipulated in this instance. National Meerut Prisoners' Defence Committee, *The Meerut Trial: Facts of the Case* (London, 1929), 4–5.

31 *Communism in India: Unpublished Documents, 1925–1934*, ed. Subodh Roy (Calcutta: Ganasahitya Prakash, 1972), 80.

32 Ibid., 98.

33 Louro and Stolte, "The Meerut Conspiracy Case," 313. Manu Goswami describes the internal differences of even the communist group in some detail, see Manu Goswami, "Conspicuous Communism," in *Political Imaginaries in Twentieth Century India*, ed. Manu Goswami and Mrinalini Sinha (London and New York: Bloomsbury, 2022), 73–98, here 82–7.

34 Philip Spratt, *Blowing up India: Reminiscences and Reflections of a Former Comintern Emissary* (Calcutta: Prachi Prakashan, 1955), 52. Another of the accused, Sohan Singh Josh, also comments on the split, noting that while imprisoned the communist group embarked on intensive autodidactic legal and theoretical study so as to maintain some consistency of principle and theory, see Sohan Singh Josh, *The Great Attack: Meerut Conspiracy Case* (New Delhi: People's Publishing House, 1979), 94–5.

35 The *General Statement* is published as *Communists Challenge Imperialism from the Dock* (Calcutta: National Book Agency, 1967).

36 Muzaffar Ahmad, "Mirat Mamlar Jatkinchit [A Little About the Meerut Trial]," in *Samkalaner Katha* (Calcutta: National Book Agency, 1963), 52–67, here 60. Trans. B. C. B.

37 Raza, "Red Scare," 194; Gopal, *Insurgent Empire*, 250–1.

38 *Communists Challenge Imperialism*, ii.

39 See *The Meerut Trial: Facts of the Case*; *The Prisoners' Reply*; *Meerut Conspiracy Case* (Rolland); *Indian Quarterly Register*; *The Times*, and so on. Moreover, a short work of street theater condemning the trial was staged in England.

40 *Communists Challenge Imperialism*, i–ii.

41 These aspects of the case are detailed in Lester Hutchinson, *Conspiracy at Meerut* (London: George, Allen & Unwin, 1935). The prosecution counsel, Langford James, also died during the trial. Hutchinson writes, "In dust alone the prosecution and defence were equal," 166.

42 See Hutchinson, *Conspiracy*, 98–112; also reported in the London *Times*, September 19 and October 2, 1929.

43 See Hutchinson, *Conspiracy*, 102. Referring to Sibnath Banerjee, one of the Meerut prisoners, Dipesh Chakrabarty observes that the "display of 'sacrifice'" made during the trial was a crucial aspect of his subsequent authority as a workers' leader. *Rethinking*, 151–2.

44 See Josh, *Great Attack*, 91–2; Hutchinson, *Conspiracy*, 126.

45 This explains why, in all the scholarship on Meerut, there is almost nothing that examines its publicity and contemporary effects in languages other than English. A suggestive exception is Juned Shaikh's *Outcaste Bombay*.

46 *Communists Challenge Imperialism*, 290–2.
47 Ibid., 5.
48 Slavoj Žižek, "A Leninist Gesture Today: Against the Populist Temptation," in *Lenin Reloaded: Toward a Politics of Truth*, ed. Sebastian Budgen, Stathis Kouvelakis, and Slavoj Žižek (Durham: Duke University Press, 2007), 74–98, here 83.
49 *Meerut Conspiracy Papers*. Statement of Sohan Singh Josh, 351.
50 *Communists Challenge Imperialism*, 1.
51 Karl Marx, "The Eighteenth Brumaire of Louis Bonaparte," in *MECW* vol. 11 (London: Lawrence and Wishart, 1979), 106.
52 See Talat Ahmed, *Literature and Politics in the Age of Nationalism: The Progressive Episode in South Asia, 1932–56* (London: Routledge, 2009); Ulka Anjaria, *Realism in the Twentieth-Century Indian Novel: Colonial Difference and Literary Form* (Cambridge: Cambridge University Press, 2012); Ben Conisbee Baer, "Shit Writing: Mulk Raj Anand's *Untouchable*, the Image of Gandhi, and the Progressive Writers' Association," *modernism/modernity* 16, no. 3 (2009): 575–95.
53 Manik Bandyopadhyay, "Chhoto Bakulpurer Jatri," in *Manik Granthabali*, vol. 11 (Kolkata: Granthalay Private Limited, 1978), 565–79. This story appeared in a periodical in 1948 before its inclusion in the collection in 1949 (Kolkata: Indian Publishing House). The related collection I referred to is titled *Chhoto Boro* (literally, "Little Large"; more idiomatically, "Great and Small") and was published in 1948. A translation of "Travelers to Chhoto Bakulpur" is available in Manik Bandyopadhyay, *Selected Stories*, ed. Malini Bhattacharya (Kolkata: Thema, 2003), 235–44. All translations here are my own. Peter Scharer has an excellent and related reading of "Chhoto Bakulpur," connecting it to the "terrorist" Bengali nationalism of the early twentieth century and the Alipore Bomb Trial of 1908–9. See Peter Scharer, *Contested Regimes: Revolutionary Signification in Colonial Bengal* (Princeton University Department of Comparative Literature, Senior Thesis: April 2022), 66–84.
54 Ibid., 565–6.
55 Ibid., 566.
56 Ibid., 569.
57 Ibid., 569–70.
58 Ibid., 570.
59 Ibid., 571.
60 Ibid.
61 Ibid.
62 Ibid., 572–3.
63 Ibid., 572.
64 Ibid., 573.
65 Ibid.

2

Politics and Literature on the Peruvian Periphery

Realism and Experimentation in the Works of César Vallejo and José Carlos Mariátegui

Juan E. De Castro

In 1931, Peruvian César Vallejo (1892–1938), the author of the poetry collection *Trilce*, perhaps the most radical of all the radical modernist masterpieces that appeared in 1922, published his first and only full-length novel: *El tungsteno* (Tungsten). However, unlike the experimentalism of his poetry, or, for that matter, his earlier short fiction,[1] *Tungsten* is written in a realistic, even naturalistic, style. In addition to often being considered one of the founding texts of the region's *indigenista* narrative (which depicts indigenous life and culture), Vallejo's novel is also seen as one of the main examples of the social and arguably social realist novel in Latin America, even if it predates the establishment of socialist realism as the official dogma of socialist art and literature. It was published in Madrid by Editorial Cenit in the series "novela proletaria" (proletarian novel), which also included no less a social text than Fyodor Gladkov's founding social realist novel *Cement*. *Tungsten*, in addition to describing the activities of a transnational mining corporation, as well as the resistance and action of the mostly indigenous miners, also depicts the life of an indigenous agrarian community. Nevertheless, if Vallejo's evolution from radical modernist in the 1920s to social realist in 1931 would seem to exemplify the trajectory of many a left-wing writer of the time, a closer look at his texts, both creative and critical, complicates this rather simplistic description. Even though, as we will see, he was extremely critical of much of the French avant-garde of his time, especially surrealism, his poetry published posthumously, *España, aparta de mí este cáliz* (Spain, Take This Chalice from Me, 1939) and the *Poemas humanos* (Human Poems, 1939), can be seen as brilliantly imbricating political topics, radical sentiment, and avant-garde techniques.

The conjunction of social realism, avant-garde literature, and *indigenismo*, found in Vallejo's oeuvre, is also characteristic of fellow Peruvian José Carlos Mariátegui (1894–1930). Often considered the "first Marxist of Latin America" if not the Americas,[2] during the 1920s Mariátegui produced a critical review of the relationship, or lack thereof, between the avant-garde/ modernism and radical politics that saw in Vallejo's *Trilce* and the earlier *Los heraldos negros* (The Black Heralds, 1919), a prototype for a decolonial Peruvian and Latin American literature. Moreover, in addition to his role as a seminal Marxist thinker, Mariátegui was "one of Latin America's first practicing literary critics."[3] As such, he was not only a promoter of the social literature coming out of the Soviet Union (Maxim Gorky, Gladkov), but also a critical supporter of the avant-garde. Thus, *Amauta*, the seminal political and artistic journal he founded in 1926 and directed until his death, became a venue for the political avant-garde, that is, for the left-wing and progressive social groups that flourished in 1920s Peru. But *Amauta*, in addition to promoting politically denunciatory texts, published key works of the artistic and literary avant-garde of Peru, Latin America, and the world.

Vallejo published only four texts in *Amauta* during Mariátegui's lifetime: "Me estoy riendo" (I am Laughing, 1926), a short avant-garde poem; the brief essay "Poesía nueva" (New Poetry, 1926), which attempted to define what constituted novelty in poetry; "Prohibido hablar al piloto" (It Is Forbidden to Talk to the Driver, 1926), a brief miscellany of thoughts on such diverse topics as the organic nature of poetry, the difference between the arts and the sciences, and the politics of the term *Latin America*; and "Sabiduría" (Wisdom, 1927), a dream sequence from what would later become *Tungsten*. Mariátegui is therefore not only a promoter of *indigenista* and social literature, like Vallejo's then unpublished novel—a position that could seem compatible with his role as a Marxist intellectual and politician[4]— but also a vocal admirer of artists as diverse as the aforementioned Vallejo and Gladkov, the Mexican novelist Mariano Azuela, Luigi Pirandello, James Joyce, André Breton, and Charlie Chaplin, to mention just a few. Mariátegui would be among the first Latin Americans to write—occasionally—on these artists.

In addition to examining "Proceso a la literatura" (Literature on Trial), the chapter on literature in Mariátegui's masterwork *7 ensayos de interpretación de la realidad peruana* (Seven Interpretive Essays on Peruvian Reality, 1928), this chapter examines some other of his essays on literature—such as "Arte, revolución y decadencia" (Art, Revolution, and Decadence, 1926) and "Populismo literario y estabilización capitalista" (Literary Populism and Capitalist Stabilization, 1930). The chapter will also briefly look at his novella, *La novela y la vida: Siegfried y el profesor Canella* (The Novel and Life: Siegfried and Professor Canella), originally published serially in 1929 in the Peruvian journal *Mundial* and in book form posthumously in 1955. Furthermore, in addition to Vallejo's poetry, in particular "Un hombre pasa con un pan al hombro" (A Man Walks by with a Baguette on His Shoulder),[5] this chapter will also study some of his essays written during the 1920s and early 1930s.[6]

The Peruvian Context

As should be obvious, the writings of both Vallejo and Mariátegui were impacted by their Peruvian origins. Peru is, after all, a country located on the periphery of world capitalism. During the twentieth century, the country progressively moved from the British sphere of influence to becoming a semicolony of the United States. Like Ecuador and Bolivia, Peru has a population mostly of indigenous origins and moreover, during the 1920s, Amerindian languages (such as Quechua and Aymara) and cultures were still dominant in the countryside. This national background can be seen as explaining not only the stress on indigeneity but also the explicit anti-imperialism found in both Vallejo's *Tungsten* and Mariátegui's *Seven Interpretive Essays*.

In addition to their national origin, their lives share some basic commonalities: instead of being members of the Peruvian Lima elites, both were born in the provinces (Vallejo in Santiago de Chuco, in La Libertad; Mariátegui in Moquegua); both spent years in Europe (Mariátegui mostly in Italy between 1919 and 1923; Vallejo emigrated to Paris in 1923, where he would die in 1938); both were acquainted with the European art and literature of the 1920s; and both embraced Marxism during their stay in Europe.[7] Their approach to the new literature of the 1920s and 1930s was, however, rooted in their original peripheric, Peruvian locations and was free of the idealization of European culture so characteristic of previous Latin American travelers. To the degree that they embraced modernism and the avant-garde, they did so in a critical manner, free from idealization or fanaticism. Moreover, even though both saw Andean indigenous cultures as a political resource that could be tapped in the construction of socialism, they were free from the primitivist idealizations of indigenous[8] and, more generally, Latin American cultures that often characterized European surrealist and avant-garde visitors to the region.[9] It is important to note that Vallejo and Mariátegui expressed their ideas on literature primarily in journalistic articles and did not produce anything resembling a systematic treatment. Nevertheless, this chapter attempts to trace how the fruitful conjunction of revolution in art and revolution in politics, characteristic of the 1920s, was experienced by these two Peruvian authors, and, by extension, by many writers from Latin America.

As mentioned above, underlying Mariátegui's appreciation of Vallejo is the former's belief that the poet represented the first expression of a decolonial Peruvian literature. In *Seven Interpretive Essays*, Mariátegui claims that Vallejo

> announces the birth of a new sensitivity. It is a new, rebellious art that breaks with the courtly tradition of a literature of buffoons and lackeys. The great poet of *Los heraldos negros* [*Black Heralds*] and of *Trilce*— that great poet who has been ignored and disregarded in the streets of Lima, where carnival mountebanks have been welcomed and praised— appears in his art as a precursor of the new spirit, the new conscience.[10]

Here, Vallejo's novelty is linked to his role as the "precursor of the new spirit." As should be obvious, the term "new spirit" is unusually vague. As Fernanda Beigel has accurately noted: "In general, he characterized his period as one that resulted in a 'new spirit' that expressed a global transformation in all orders."[11] This 'new spirit' is clearly represented in his journal *Amauta*. Its contributors included avant-garde writers and artists regardless of their real political position, as well as essayists whose politics ranged from liberal reformism to communism. However, rather than mere capaciousness, the variety of political and aesthetic positions represented in *Amauta* shows that, for Mariátegui, what characterized the new spirit was its opposition to the colonial and colonialist mainstream of the Peruvian culture of his time. The political use of literature resided precisely in its capacity to transmit this new spirit.

Underlying this assertion of the progressive nature of the avant-garde is Mariátegui's belief that, despite some partial exceptions, what by analogy could be called the 'old sensitivity' of Peruvian literature, and of Peru tout court, was colonial or neocolonial—what in the passage above he mercilessly calls "a literature of buffoons and lackeys."[12] Mariátegui identifies in this colonialist literature a key role in maintaining Peru's colonial structures. As he notes in his *Seven Interpretive Essays* with respect to the politically and aesthetically conservative Peruvian futurists—José de la Riva Agüero, Ventura García Calderón, José Gálvez—who then constituted the country's cultural and literary elite: "Meanwhile, the 'futurist' generation makes use of his nostalgia and romanticism in the serenade under the balconies of the vice-royalty, which is intended politically to revive a legend indispensable to the supremacy of the heirs to the colony."[13] (The Peruvian 'futurists' shared only their name with the Italian avant-garde movement.) Mariátegui, therefore, identified in literature a political function, either progressive or regressive, depending on whether it supports or undermines what he calls the "legend" that justifies Peru's colonial political and social structures.[14] Social literature that describes the injustices of class society; *indigenismo* that defends, even celebrates, indigenous cultures exploited and described as barbaric by the "heirs of the colony";[15] modernism that rejects this "nostalgia and romanticism"[16]—all can be seen as undermining the ideological underpinnings of neocolonial Peru. Thus, even if Mariátegui died before Vallejo published *Tungsten*, one can easily imagine him finding no contradiction between its social realism and the Peruvian poet's earlier modernism. However, one must add that neither a modernist style nor a political or especially an indigenous topic is per se seen by Mariátegui as automatically progressive. The example of Italian futurism, which supported fascism, or the exoticist Indianism of Ventura García Calderón's narrative, which presented Peru's indigenous population as fascinating barbarians, serves as counterexamples to the new spirit identified by Mariátegui in modernism and *indigenismo*.

The Avant-garde and Decadence

The text in which Mariátegui most fully develops his ideas about the political value of the avant-garde is his 1926 essay "Art, Revolution, and Decadence." Here Mariátegui attempts to differentiate the 'decadent,' that is, reactionary, aspects of the avant-garde, from those he considers revolutionary:

> We cannot accept as new any art that merely brings us a new technique. This would mean amusing ourselves with one of the most fallacious modern illusions. No aesthetic can reduce artistic work to a question of technique. New technique should also correspond to a new spirit. If not, the only things that change are the parameters, the decorations. And an artistic revolution does not content itself with formal conquests.[17]

However, in marked contrast to the Soviet-led Communist mainstream that was rapidly becoming dominant, Mariátegui does not come to the conclusion that content determines a work's political use: As he notes,

> The revolutionary aspect of these contemporary schools or tendencies does not lie in their creation of a new technique. Nor is it the destruction of the old technique. It is the repudiation, the removal, the mockery of the bourgeois absolute.[18]

The revolutionary character of a work is, therefore, not directly deduced from the technique used or the style it is written in—realist, *modernista*, avant-garde—or, in principle, from its topic. Beyond authorial intention or an author's explicit politics, it is this rejection of the bourgeois absolute that determines, for the Peruvian Marxist, the political valence of a specific work.

The notion of the "bourgeois absolute" is never fully explained by Mariátegui, even when he clearly notes that it plays a role in the maintenance and reproduction of social and economic structure.[19] However, given its independence from technique or subject matter, one can see the reproduction of the "bourgeois absolute" as playing a key role in the maintenance and reproduction of social and economic structures.[20] I do not think it is farfetched to argue that Mariátegui identifies literature, as well as other arts, as prescribing or questioning the cultural limits of what is possible within a specific society. Although undertheorized, Mariátegui's identification of not only ideological value in literary works, but also their role in the emotional underpinnings, or rejection, of existing social structures, foreshadows Antonio Gramsci's notion of hegemony,[21] Raymond Williams's idea of 'structure of feeling,' or even Fredric Jameson's 'political unconscious.' After all, his criticism of the Peruvian literary establishment described above saw in the Peruvian literary elites' celebration of colonialism a bulwark against the possibility of imagining a different country.

Literature as a Map of Reality

A brief examination of Mariátegui's lone work of fiction written during the 1920s, *La novela y la vida: Siegfried y el profesor Canella* (The Novel and Life: Siegfried and Professor Canella, 1929), can serve to clarify his ideas on the relationship between politics and literature.[22] One reads in *The Novel and Life*, based on a real-life case of mistaken identity in Italy after the First World War: "If the judges at the court of Turin had read Jean Giraudoux's 'Siegfried et le limousine' the extraordinary case of the typographer Mario Bruneri, who was claimed by two legal wives, under a different name and with different feelings, would not have seemed so unexplainable or unprecedented."[23] Here Mariátegui seems to go beyond the ideas presented in "Art, Revolution, and Decadence." Not only does literature reflect or contradict the values of a society, what Mariátegui called its 'absolute,' but it also seems to have something like a practical use: it helps the reader imagine and therefore understand reality. Although this quotation comes from a fictional text, this is an idea that the Peruvian Marxist also expressed in his essays. Writing about, of all texts, André Breton's *Nadja*, Mariátegui had argued that: "Proposing to literature the path of imagination and dream, the surrealists offer an invitation to the discovery, the recreation of reality."[24]

Even if Mariátegui's aesthetic ideas are never fully developed or expressed in a consistent manner, it is clear that he sees literature as serving to buttress existing society and its structures. As we saw above, for him, the literature of the conservative Peruvian 'futurists,' whose literature exuded nostalgia for the colony, helped maintain colonial structures. Likewise, those writers who wrote within what he called the 'bourgeois absolute' played a role in supporting bourgeois society. But additionally, for Mariátegui, literature helps provide mental maps of society that help readers better understand the world in which they live. The avant-garde and modernism—by bringing subjective aspects of reality into representation, as well as by going beyond the limits of the bourgeois and of what could be called the neocolonial absolute—can be seen as fulfilling a progressive political function. This is why, in a gesture that contradicts before the fact the founding gesture of socialist realism,[25] in one of his last articles on literature, Mariátegui stated: "On the table of the revolutionary critic, beyond any hierarchical consideration, a book by Joyce will in all instances be a more valuable document than one by any neo-Zola."[26] Moreover, for the Peruvian Marxist, the political value of avant-garde literature, of which *The Novel and Life* is an idiosyncratic example, did not depend on subject matter nor even on the explicit ideology of the text. After all, his is a novel about the Italian petty bourgeoisie and there are no calls for revolution.

Vallejo and the Avant-garde

If Mariátegui found much of value in the new literature of his time, Vallejo would, at least at first glance, seem to be a fierce critic of his time. If read superficially, one could see reflected in his criticism the orthodox Soviet position that posited the breakup between the avant-garde and the political left—a development that had culminated in the establishment of Soviet-style socialist realism. For instance, in his article significantly titled "Autopsia del superrealismo" (Autopsy of Surrealism), published in 1930, one year before *Tungsten*, the great poet argues about the avant-gardes of his day:

> [S]ince the advent of surrealism, a new literary school bursts forth on a nearly monthly basis. Never before has social thought been sectioned off into so many and such fleeting formulas. Never before did it experience such a frenetic pleasure and such a need to be stereotyped into prescriptions and clichés, as though it were afraid of its freedom or unable to emerge in all its organic unity. Such anarchy and disintegration hadn't been seen except among the decadent philosophers and poets at the dawn of Greco-Latin civilization. Those of today, in turn, reveal a new decadence of the spirit: the dawn of capitalist civilization.[27]

Whereas for Mariátegui decadence and revolution were found in all literature, for Vallejo the avant-garde is only an example of the former. It would thus seem that one could consider Vallejo to have evolved unproblematically from the avant-garde poet of *Trilce* to the social-realist novelist of *Tungsten*. One can almost imagine the commissars of socialist realism borrowing phrases from Vallejo's essay. However, even a superficial perusal of Vallejo's posthumous poetry published after the establishment of socialist realism in 1934—*Spain, Take This Chalice from Me* and *Human Poems* (both 1939)— problematizes this putative evolution. After all, his posthumous poetry reconciles avant-garde technique with radical albeit, it must be noted, nondogmatic content. In fact, even in "Autopsy of Surrealism" one finds the seeds of a literature that goes beyond not only the avant-garde but also the then burgeoning socialist realism: "Such is the fate of all unrest that, instead of becoming an austere creative laboratory, merely amounts to a formula. Useless then are the booming complaints, the calls for the vulgate, the color advertisements, and in the end, the sleights of hand and professional tricks. Alongside the aborted tree, dead leaves asphyxiate."[28] Implicit in this passage is the possibility of a "creative laboratory" that would go beyond the limitations Vallejo finds in surrealism—the reduction of creativity into a formula—and, one assumes, social realism. In fact, one could easily argue that Vallejo's posthumous poetry represents a clear example of this 'austere creative laboratory.'

One can read "A Man Walks by with a Baguette on His Shoulder" as Vallejo's *ars poetica*, and, as such, as representing his counterproposal to the avant-garde. This poem juxtaposes images that can be interpreted as representing class inequality in 1930s France—a man carrying a baguette, another killing a louse, a homeless person sleeping on the street, and so on—with an artistic or intellectual tendency fashionable at the time— writing on the *doppelgänger*, psychoanalysis, Picasso's cubism, and so on. The poem therefore questions the usefulness of the avant-garde in a world characterized by injustice and inequality. However, while the poem would seem to be presenting ideas in line with the left-wing orthodoxy of the time, it obviously differs from a hypothetical socialist, realist text by not presenting communism or the Soviet Union as the solution to the poem's tension between art and thought and social injustice. Moreover, the style of the poem can be seen as both commenting on the French avant-garde of Vallejo's time and as going beyond surrealism. This poem, like all of Vallejo's posthumous poetry, exemplifies his notion of poetry, literature, and art as an "austere creative laboratory." Susan Sontag noted:

> The Surrealist tradition in all these arts is united by the idea of destroying conventional meanings, and creating new meanings or counter-meanings through radical juxtaposition (the "collage principle"). Beauty, in the words of Lautréamont, is "the fortuitous encounter of a sewing machine

and an umbrella on a dissecting table." Art so understood is obviously animated by aggression, aggression toward the presumed conventionality of its audience and, above all, aggression toward the medium itself. The Surrealist sensibility aims to shock, through its techniques of radical juxtaposition.[29]

Vallejo's use of juxtaposition clearly seeks to go beyond this "aim to shock." Michelle Clayton has noted that it is a "staggering" and "shattering" poem.[30] Moreover, Clayton argues that "[t]he central question of the poem is not what an artist does while ignorant of social reality but what an artist can do and cannot do once he becomes aware of the iniquities that surround him, even if the question of what he must do is left unsaid."[31] The latter point is of importance, since it is what differentiates Vallejo from socialist realism.

Vallejo was aware of Sergei Eisenstein's cinema as a filmic practice, though he probably also knew of Eisenstein's ideas. Eisenstein attempted to use juxtaposition "[t]o form equitable views by stirring up contradictions within the spectator's mind, and to forge accurate intellectual concepts from the dynamic clash of opposing passions."[32] In fact, Vallejo noted that in both *Battleship Potemkin* and *The General Line* Eisenstein was "taking the theory of historical materialism to the screen."[33] However, "A Man Walks by with a Baguette on His Shoulder" goes beyond what Vallejo saw as the "propagandistic character" of Eisenstein's films.[34] Much like the surrealists and Eisenstein, Vallejo's juxtapositions also appeal to the 'passions.' That said, rather than creating shock or, for that matter, proposing the "accurate intellectual concepts" of Marxism, the misencounters detailed by Vallejo primarily aim to create an emotional awareness of the need not only for a better art, but also, more importantly, for a better world.[35]

Bach, Beethoven, and Vallejo

In a series of brief notes he planned to include in his *Arte y la revolución*, Vallejo asks:

> Does a socialist art currently exist? It obviously does. Examples: Beethoven, many Renaissance paintings, the pyramids of Egypt, Assyrian statuary, a few of Chaplin's films, Bach himself (Bach is played in Russia), etc. Why do those works correspond to the concept and content of a socialist art? Because, in our opinion, they respond to a universal concept of the masses, and to feelings, ideas, and interests—to use an epithet derived from the noun communism—common to all human beings without exception.[36]

One might note that Vallejo is, at least from a historical perspective, wrong: Renaissance paintings were made to order by the rich Italian clergy, nobility, or bourgeoisie, Bach composed for his local German nobility, and so on. Furthermore, would the workmen who labored, one assumes under grueling conditions, to make the pyramids, have considered them to express their "feelings, ideas, and interests"? Be that as it may, it is worth noting that Vallejo does not deny the value of political art; for instance, he had the highest opinion of Eisenstein's films. However, in his "Ejecutoria del arte bolchevique" (Judgment on Bolshevik Art), he distinguishes between what he calls "Bolshevik art"—one of "propaganda and agitation,"[37] traits which, as we have seen, he identifies in Eisenstein's works and which could also easily be considered to be represented by his own *Tungsten*—and a "socialist art" capable of going beyond the class struggle to address all of humanity and all that is human. For him, this art is adumbrated in the greatest of classics. If *Tungsten* can be seen as "Bolshevik art," his poetry, including "A Man Walks by with Baguette on His Shoulder," can be seen as aiming for the universality he ascribes to "socialist art."

Despite being contemporaries and compatriots, Vallejo and Mariátegui related to the new literary and artistic tendencies of the 1920s in different ways. As we have seen, Vallejo, despite being frequently considered the major Latin American *vanguardia* poet, together with his Chilean contemporary Pablo Neruda, was critical of the actual avant-garde. For him, it seemed trapped in individualism and, perhaps more importantly, lacked the universality he saw in the great classics of Western culture. Mariátegui, on the other hand, was an enthusiastic promoter of modern literature and poetry. In fact, *Amauta* became the main venue through which surrealism, as well as other new cultural proposals coming from the turbulent Europe of the 1920s, was disseminated throughout the often staid Peruvian and Andean cultural milieus.

However, in different ways, Mariátegui and Vallejo question the opposition between literary experimentation, often seen as necessarily linked to bourgeois decadence, and committed socialist realist writing. In the case of Mariátegui, together with a celebration of the subversive possibilities of the avant-garde, one finds a defense of *indigenismo*. In this manner, he set the bases for Peruvian literature for the next twenty or thirty years. While often dismissed as 'neo-Zolas,' to use Mariátegui's phrase, the two major Peruvian *indigenista* writers who came of age in the 1930s and 1940s— Ciro Alegría (1909–1967) and José María Arguedas (1911–1969)—were in dialogue with modernism: Alegría uses interior monologues in both *Los perros hambrientos* (The Hungry Dogs, 1939) and *El mundo es ancho y ajeno* (Broad and Alien is the World, 1941), and José María Arguedas in *Los ríos profundos* (Deep Rivers, 1958) depicts with unusual intensity, not only the experiences but also the emotions and fantasies of a young mestizo boy in the Andes.[38] The case of Vallejo would, in principle, seem more complex.

After all, unlike Mariátegui, he was far from a promoter of most avant-garde writers, while his support for "Bolshevik art" was clearly qualified. However, his writing became a laboratory in which avant-garde, social realist, and other techniques were incorporated into an oeuvre with the aim of universality. In fact, both Alegría and Arguedas found in his prose and poetry a precedent for the creation of politically committed writing that was also the highest expression of literature.[39]

As we have seen, Mariátegui and Vallejo differed in their evaluations of the actual new literatures and arts that were being developed in the hectic 1920s. However, for both Peruvian Marxists, social narrative and the avant-garde were valuable resources for the creation of a new, more human, and therefore politically useful, literature.

Notes

1 Vallejo had previously published in Lima, Peru, a collection of short stories and vignettes, see *Escalas melografiadas* (Lima: Talleres Gráficos, 1923), and a novella, titled *Fabla salvaje* (Lima: La novela peruana, 1923).

2 Antonio Melis, "Mariátegui, primo marxista d'America," *Critica Marxista* 5, no. 2 (1967): 132–57, here 132.

3 Vicky Unruh, "Mariátegui's Aesthetic Thought: A Critical Reading of the Avant-Gardes," *Latin American Research Review* 24, no. 3 (1989): 45–69, here 45.

4 In 1928, Mariátegui founded the Socialist Party, which became the Communist Party after his death.

5 César Vallejo, "A Man Walks by with a Baguette on his Shoulder," in *The Complete Poetry: A Bilingual Edition/César Vallejo*, ed. and trans. Clayton Eshleman (Berkeley: University of California Press, 2007), 516–17.

Clayton Eshleman mistranslates the title of Vallejo's poem. A more accurate translation would be "A Man Walks by with a Loaf of Bread on His Shoulder." It should be noted that in Spanish *pan* can be loaf or bread.

6 Vallejo organized his articles in two collections titled *Contra el secreto professional* (Against the Professional Secret, Lima: Mosca Azul, 1973) and *Arte y revolución* (Art and Revolution, Lima: Mosca Azul, 1973). However, these were only published in book form in 1973.

7 Nevertheless, it seems Vallejo and Mariátegui had very limited personal contact, perhaps due to the fact that Vallejo lived in Lima during the time Mariátegui was mostly in Europe. After Vallejo left for France in 1923, he wrote Mariátegui twice: first, in 1926, thanking him for his positive evaluation of his poetry, and a second time in 1928, suggesting Mariátegui's editorial *Amauta* publish a book by an acquaintance. Mariátegui wrote him once in 1929. See José Carlos Mariátegui, *Correspondencia*, ed. Antonio Melis (Lima: Amauta, 1984), 203, 650.

8   Comparing Vallejo's "Telluric and Magnetic" with Pablo Neruda's *Heights of Macchu Picchu*, Efraín Kristal notes, "Vallejo is ... more guarded than Neruda in his attitude toward the indigenous world. He does not attempt to become the voice of the Sierra (as the Andean region is called in Peru). His yearnings are more challenging: to alter his own consciousness by engaging with the indigenous world on terms other than his own." Efraín Kristal, "Introduction," in *César Vallejo, The Complete Poetry: A Bilingual Edition*, trans. Clayton Eshleman (Berkeley: University of California Press, 2007), 1–20, here 5. Mariátegui, for his part, argued that "the *ayllu* (agrarian commune), the basic cell of the Inca state, survives to this day, despite the attacks of feudalism and gamonalism. It still shows enough vitality to gradually become the basic cell of a modern socialist state." José Carlos Mariátegui, "Principios de política agraria nacional," in *Peruanicemos al Perú* (Lima: Amauta, 1981), 108–12, here 109–10.

9   As Sandra Fluhrer notes in her contribution to this volume, regarding Antonin Artaud's views on Mexico and Mexican indigenous culture: "Artaud repeatedly proposes Mexico as the only place in the world, or one of the very few places, where an organic and oriented culture still exists, or where it may become reawakened at any moment by indigenous rites connected to revolutionary movements."

10 José Carlos Mariátegui, *Seven Interpretive Essays on Peruvian Reality*, trans. Marjorie Urquidi (Austin: University of Texas Press, 1971), 257.

11 Fernanda Beigel, *El itinerario y la brújula: el vanguardismo estético-político de José Carlos Mariátegui* (Buenos Aires: Biblios, 2003), 114.

12 Mariátegui, *Seven Interpretive Essays*, 257.

13 Ibid., 226–7.

14 Ibid., 227.

15 Ibid.

16 Ibid., 226.

17 José Carlos Mariátegui, "Art, Revolution, and Decadence," in *José Carlos Mariátegui: An Anthology*, ed. and trans. Harry E. Vanden and Marc Becker (New York: Monthly Review, 2011), 423–7, here 423.

18 Ibid., 424.

19 As the reader is surely aware, Mariátegui has borrowed the notion of the 'absolute' from Henri Bergson. Mariátegui admired Bergson and argued that "Bergsonism has influenced such different, even contradictory, events of varied importance as the literature of Bernard Shaw, the Dada insurrection, the novels of Marcel Proust, the dissemination of Christian Science's neo-Thomism, Theosophy, and the mental confusion of Latin American college students, the theory of revolutionary syndicalism, Fascist squadrismo." José Carlos Mariátegui, "Veinticinco años de sucesos extranjeros," in José Carlos Mariátegui, *Historia de la crisis mundial* (Lima: Amauta, 1980), 173–202, here 199.

20 "Distinguishing between these two contemporaneous categories of artists is not easy. Decadence and revolution, as they coexist in the same world, also

coexist in some individuals. The artist's consciousness is the agonistic circle of struggle between these two spirits. The understanding of this struggle almost always escapes the artists themselves. But in the end, one of the two spirits prevails. The other is left strangled in the arena." Mariátegui, "Art, Revolution, and Decadence," 423.

21 Although Mariátegui knew of Gramsci and may have actually met him, the fact is that the Italian Marxist's writings on hegemony would only be published posthumously. On the influence of Gramsci—real and imagined—on Mariátegui, see Juan E. De Castro, *Bread and Beauty: The Cultural Politics of José Carlos Mariátegui* (Leiden: Brill, 2020), 38–43.

22 *La novela y la vida* was first published serially in the Peruvian magazine *Mundial* between February 15 and April 26, 1929. It was only published in book form posthumously, in 1955.

23 José Carlos Mariátegui, *La novela y la vida: Siegfried y el profesor Canella* (Lima: Amauta, 1980), 19.

24 José Carlos Mariátegui, "*Nadja*, de Andrés Breton," in *El artista y la época* (Lima: Amauta, 1980), 178–82, here 178.

25 I am, of course, referring to the well-known statement by Karl Radek, one of the main leaders of the Communist International, who, during the First Congress of Soviet Writers in 1934, famously described *Ulysses* as "A heap of dung, crawling with worms, photographed by a cinema apparatus through a microscope." Karl Radek, "Contemporary World Literature and the Tasks of Proletarian Literature," in *Soviet Writers' Congress 1934*, ed. Maxim Gorki, Nikolai Bukharin, Karl Radek, Andrei Zdhanov, and A. I. Stetsky (London: Lawrence & Wishart, 1977), 73–182, here 153.

26 José Carlos Mariátegui, "Populismo literario y estabilización capitalista," in *El artista y la época* (Lima: Amauta, 1980), 32–6, here 34.

27 César Vallejo, "Autopsy of Surrealism," in *Selected Writings of César Vallejo*, ed. and trans. Joseph Mulligan (Middletown: Wesleyan University Press, 2015), 201–5, here 202.

28 Ibid., 205.

29 Susan Sontag, "Happenings: An Art of Radical Juxtaposition," in *Against Interpretation and other Essays* (New York: Dell, 1966), 263–74, here 269–70.

30 Michelle Clayton, *Poetry in Pieces: César Vallejo and Lyric Modernity* (Berkeley: University of California Press, 2011), 215.

31 Ibid., 216.

32 Sergei Eisenstein, "A Dialectical Approach to Film Form," in *Film Form: Essays in Film Theory*, ed. and trans. Jay Leyda (New York: Harcourt Brace Jovanovich, 1949), 45–63, here 46.

33 César Vallejo, "Russia Inaugurates a New Era on the Silver Screen," in *Selected Writings of César Vallejo*, ed. and trans. Joseph Mulligan (Middleton: Wesleyan University Press, 2015), 355–9, here 357.

34 Ibid., 355.

35 Ibid.
36 César Vallejo, "Existe el arte socialista," in *El arte y la revolución* (Lima: Mosca Azul, 1973), 37–42, here 37.
37 César Vallejo, "Ejecutoria del arte bolchevique," in *El arte y la revolución* (Lima: Mosca Azul, 1973), 26–7, here 26.
38 Both Alegría and Arguedas would express their debts to Mariátegui; see Ciro Alegría, *Mucha suerte con harto palo* (Buenos Aires: Losada, 1976), 87; José María Arguedas, "I Am not an Acculturated Man," in José María Arguedas, *The Fox from Up Above and the Fox from Down Below* (Pittsburgh: Pittsburgh University Press, 2000), 268–70, here 270.
39 See Alegría, *Mucha suerte con harto palo*, 396; José María Arguedas, "La novela y el problema de la expresión en el Perú," in *Qepa Wiñaq . . . Siempre literature y antropología*, ed. Dora Sales (Madrid: Iberoamericana, 2009), 153–60, here 157.

3

Reusing Artaud? On the Contemporaneity of *Messages révolutionnaires* (1936)

Sandra Fluhrer

In January 1936, the poet, theater utopist, actor, visual artist, and film maker Antonin Artaud (1896–1948) left Paris to take a ship to Mexico, where he was to spend nine months as one of the most peculiar cultural ambassadors in global history. Thanks to personal connections Artaud managed to travel under the auspices of the French Secretary of Education, with the task of investigating and recording the forms of expression of Mexican theater.[1] His aim was to find practices of regeneration for a Europe that was apparently in the process of succumbing to decadence and political despair. In his investigations, Artaud turned in particular to the Mexican revolutionary movements, which were then in a period of consolidation, albeit not exclusively in the direction of socialism.[2] Above all, however, Artaud was interested in Mexican indigenous cultures in which he hoped to discover sources of 'genuine' revolutionary forces. In Artaud's thinking, Mexico had already come to act as one of 'theater's doubles' he envisaged: only a few years before his journey, he had finished his manifestos on the "Theater of Cruelty." These contained a sketch for his first 'cruel' play, *La conquête du Mexique* (The Conquest of Mexico, 1932), the central theme of which is the clash between the European and the Aztec monarchies and which focuses on, among other things, "the spirit of the crowds" in Mexico.[3] Artaud's 1936 trip to Mexico thus served the purpose of artistic research. However, the journey was also of great personal importance to Artaud as it promised relief from financial and mental crises as well as an opportunity to leave behind his opium addiction. As far as we know, Artaud did undergo a transformation of sorts in Mexico. Yet after his return to Paris in late 1936, his medical condition deteriorated rapidly, punctuated by a number of hospitalizations and culminating in a series of horrific electroshock treatments at the asylum in Rodez.

The textual outcome of Artaud's Mexico trip amounts to three lectures, delivered at the University of Mexico City in late February 1936, and a number of short journalistic pieces published in Mexican newspapers in Spanish translation. These are the texts on which this chapter focuses. Another series of texts emerged from Artaud's visit to the indigenous community of Tarahumara or Rarámuri in the late summer of 1936. From 1936 until his death, Artaud continued writing on the Tarahumara and their rites involving the psychoactive cactus peyote. Whether his accounts were based on inner travels supported by ethnographic literature and drugs or on a concrete, venturous journey into the depths of the Sierra Madre remains debated.[4] The texts were published as a collection entitled *Les Tarahumaras* in 1974 (and as *The Peyote Dance* in English in 1975). In 2019, they received attention again when the Soundwalk Collective together with Patti Smith released the album *The Peyote Dance*, based on some of Artaud's texts on the Tarahumara.[5] Artaud intended to have his cultural/political and journalistic Mexico texts published in French as a collection of essays entitled *Messages révolutionnaires*—a plan only fulfilled in 1970, long after his death. By then, most of the original French manuscripts had been lost. While the French versions of the lectures are based on the original French typescripts, the journalistic texts are by and large back-translations from Spanish.[6] The Guatemalan poet Luis Cardoza y Aragón, one of Artaud's contacts in Mexico, had republished the Spanish texts under the title *México* in 1962, whereas only a small selection of the Mexico articles exist in English translation.[7]

The late republication and the difficult editing circumstances might account for the rather weak reception of *Messages révolutionnaires*.[8] I regard them as the most pertinent to the present of Artaud's texts, also in relation to the pandemic present with its new or sharpened polarities. Artaud's Mexico texts open new ways of thinking about Artaud's connection to the political beyond pathos, pathologizing, and pity. They are Artaud's most explicit and straightforward engagement with politics, and they suggest a concept of the political as an anthropological and a thoroughly aesthetic phenomenon— as a form of experience. From 1968 onward—that is, from Gilles Deleuze and Félix Guattari's *Anti-Œdipe* (1972) up to twenty-first-century political aesthetics—Artaud's writings have served as a prompt for fundamental questions of coercion and representation.[9] Susan Sontag, one of the most incisive commentators on Artaud, described Artaud's ideas as "deliberately not political," despite their revolutionary label and outlook: "Not only does Artaud share the widespread (and mistaken) belief in the possibility of a cultural revolution unconnected with political change," she writes, "but he implies that the *only* genuine cultural revolution is one having nothing to do with politics."[10] Yet, at least as far as the Mexican lectures and articles are concerned, this is not quite true. Not only do they specifically address politics (and politicians), but they also suggest that Artaud's concept of culture is political.

In the article "Ce que je suis venu faire au Mexique" (What I Came to Mexico to Do), published in *El Nacional* on July 5, 1936, Artaud writes: "I came to Mexico in search of politicians [*hommes politiques*], not artists."[11] Another 'revolutionary message' is his "Lettre ouverte aux Gouverneurs des États du Mexique" (Open Letter to the Governors of the States of Mexico), communicating his interest in Mexican indigenous cultures as forms of theatrical expression in everyday life.[12] The reason Artaud addresses politicians is the change he perceives in the social function of art and the social role of artists. From a holistic "'one-man band' or 'Protean man'" (*'l'homme orchestre' ou 'l'homme Protée'*) uniting "in his person all the faculties and all the sciences," the artist in Artaud's view has become a "slave[]" without influence on public affairs.[13] The division and specialization of cultural labor and the differentiation of the social make Artaud turn to politicians rather than to artists. "[S]ince politicians have replaced artists in the management of public affairs," he writes, it is now their "task" to "resist [the] superstition about progress" plaguing European societies.[14] This implies that politicians eventually need to become Protean artists.

Artaud's Mexico texts are often contradictory, provocative, and eclectic. They are fascinating in the sense that they provoke an ambivalence of attraction and repugnance. They possess an enormous energy for reform, but they also contain resentment, traces of (decidedly anticolonial) primitivism and exoticism celebrating ideas of renewal through the Tarahumara as "a Principle Race" (*une Race-Principe*).[15] They even include passages bordering on an apology for the political murder of artists who, in the French and Russian Revolutions, did not manage to create universal sentiments to solve the problems of their times.[16] The texts become readable and admissible as theatrical texts—as affective, performative, and self-conscious, as related to the co-presence of bodies (and words as bodies) within a concrete and collectively shared space. "On stage, everyone is right," claimed Heiner Müller, evoking a radical democracy of the stage that allows the experience of contradictions and radical positions.[17] Artaud's texts are a series of dramatic messenger's reports. They are hazardous, vocal even in their written form,[18] and they are mimetic: they show Artaud's transgressive journey as an attempt to reverse the European colonization of Mexico and to infect Europe with the remnants of Mexican nativism.

In their performativity, Artaud's Mexico texts express the Greta Thunbergian beauty of carrying out an 'official mission' no civic authority has ever commissioned—although Artaud did travel owing to diplomatic courtesy—a beauty traversing the border between cultural criticism and literature. Artaud's revolutionary writing shows a commitment that, for times running short of utopias, may still be of use. To a reading beyond pathos, pathology, and pity, Artaud's texts offer a pragmatic dimension containing impulses for both contemporary social and academic politics: a manual for a physiological revolution, and a praxeological plea for a dissolution of disciplines.

Political Critique in *Messages révolutionnaires*

Artaud's Mexico texts contain a detailed critique of both capitalist liberalism and Marxism. The former, according to Artaud, is based on "dead reason" and only produces a further loss of consciousness. Artaud's main point of attack is Europe's celebration of rationality and mechanization since Descartes, which in his view has led to a steep decline in our knowledge about nature and human culture. To observe rationally, according to Artaud's second university lecture "L'Homme contre le destin" (Man against Destiny), is to observe the dead: "That which the reason of the mind looks at can always be said to partake in death. Reason, a European faculty, exalted beyond measure by the European mentality, is always an image of death. History, which records facts, is an image of dead reason."[19] Modernity's capitalist liberalism deprives us of a comprehensive view of the world and its intricate web of connections, Artaud writes. We only get in touch with "these truths," he maintains, "when they turn into acts, when they manifest as earthquakes, epidemics, famine, wars, that is, as the rumbling of cannons"[20]—the form of the catastrophe is the only way left to us to grasp the workings of the world. The static and specialized character of rational science has severe consequences for the entire cultural world:

> When one speaks today of culture, governments think in terms of opening schools, grinding out books, spilling printer's ink, whereas, to let culture mature, one should close the schools, burn the museums, destroy the books, smash the printing presses.
>
> To be cultivated is to eat one's destiny, to assimilate it through knowledge.
> . . .
> Europe has dismembered nature with her separate sciences.
>
> Biology, natural history, chemistry, physics, psychiatry, neurology, physiology, all these monstrous germinations which are the pride of the Universities, just as geomancy, chirology, physiognomy, psychurgy, and theurgy are the pride of a few separate individuals, are to enlightened minds merely a *loss of consciousness*.

Antiquity had its labyrinths, but it did not know the labyrinth of divided science.[21]

Artaud argues in favor of the ancient Greek comprehensive understanding of arts and sciences, a profound and complex intellectualism shaped and practiced by a form of aesthetic experience he calls theater.[22]

Marx's thinking, Artaud asserts, did take the right direction, but Marx missed the point of human wholeness and with his mode of thinking history paved the way for a "false metaphysics".[23] When in 1926/7 members of the French Surrealist movement, among them André Breton, Louis Aragon, and Paul Éluard, joined the Communist Party, Artaud left the Surrealists (whose mystic and concrete aesthetics and rejection of all father figures he had shared) because they "had become a party, too," as he says in his first lecture in Mexico, "Surréalisme et révolution" (Surrealism and Revolution).[24] "The revolt for experience, which the surrealist revolution wished to be," he holds, "had nothing to do with a revolution that pretended to already know man and imprisoned him within the frame of his basest needs."[25] "All in all," he continues, "Surrealism descended into Marxism, while Marxism should have tried to elevate itself towards Surrealism."[26]

Artaud's critique of Marxism is not as sharp as his rejection of capitalist liberalism—or of German and Italian fascism, upon which he touches briefly but fiercely.[27] He observes that "of the ancient values of man Marx reorganized what the Bourgeoisie had left behind."[28] "French youth" (a construct on which he frequently relies in the texts, and with which he seems to identify), he states, regards Lenin's "materialist organization" in Russia as "transitory" and "punitive," conducted with "sheer cruelty."[29] He acknowledges Marx's attempt to think history beyond "an image of dead reason" and "sense the meaning of history in its particular dynamism" instead.[30] Yet Marx's thought also came down to facts: "the capitalist fact, the bourgeois fact, the congestion of the machine, the asphyxia of the economy of the age caused by a monstrous abuse of the use of the machine. Out of this true fact there came, *also in history*, a false ideology."[31]

According to Artaud, Marxist materialism above all ignores the interconnection between body and mind in the materiality and spirituality of both: "Spirit matter, matter spirit: They [French youth] affirm the interdependence of those two aspects of their being. For while they eat they feel, and while they think they eat. They accuse modern Europe of having invented an antagonism that in fact does not exist." Marxism thus fails to grasp "the whole human being" (*l'Homme entier*); it lacks a "metaphysics of nature"[32] while providing a "false metaphysics" in the way of the "materialist explanation of the world."[33] Moreover, Marxism still claims to be scientific and does not renounce the idea of individual consciousness.[34] Still, Artaud tries to connect to Marxist movements in Mexico, drawing on pertinent vocabulary to describe his own project: He considers a "social and economic revolution *indispensable*,"[35] he advertises his idea of the soul as a type of common good,[36] and approves of the Tarahumaras' "communism" as a "spontaneous feeling of solidarity."[37]

Toward an 'Organic and Oriented' Culture: Artaud's Political Theory

Artaud draws on Chinese and Paracelsian medicine and on homeopathy to describe his idea of wholeness.[38] In his third university lecture, "Le Théâtre et les dieux" (Theater and the Gods), he elaborates on his idea of "organic culture" as the precondition for wholeness:

> I call organic culture a culture based on the mind in relation to the organs, and the mind immersed in all the organs, and responding to one another simultaneously.
> There is an idea of space in this culture, and I say that real culture can only be understood spatially, and that this is an 'oriented culture' [*une culture orientée*] in the way theater is oriented.[39]

These thoughts pertain to the fundamental problem of political anthropology, which is to find a viable relation between bodies and souls in space. In the history of political ideas, this was a problem for Thomas Hobbes, who proposed an authoritarian contract to solve it. In Artaud's time this was also a problem for Carl Schmitt, who tried to solve it with a model of radical difference and conflict, as well as for Helmuth Plessner, who proposed a more moderate model of tact and social armor.

Moreover, Artaud's reference to organs evokes the history of political and theological organology. This is not the Artaud of the 'body without organs' yet. This is an attempt to restore political organology by taking it seriously and literally, rather than as a metaphor that tends to bury the concrete bodies within the figure of the political body. Metaphors of the political body have emerged from antiquity to the present when the unity or persistence of political and religious communities has been perceived to be in danger.[40] They operate with a topology of above and below (as in the head and the feet of the state in medieval concepts, sometimes still present in contemporary political speech) or of center and periphery (as in the fable of the belly and the members in Aesop and Livius). The images express a functional way of thinking politics. The organ of the community is also its instrument. Political body imagery is always also related to the political history of violence in and of *being made useful*.[41]

A decade later, Artaud's critique of this structure culminates in the idea of the 'body without organs,' a dancing body, liberated from authority, famously devised in his last work, the tormenting radio piece *Pour en finir avec le jugement de dieu* (To Have Done with the Judgment of God, 1947). In 1936, Artaud's texts still showed remnants of organological optimism. He demanded that the revolution aim not only for a new "constitution of society" but also for a new "inner constitution of man"[42] with organs in touch with one another, with the soul, and vice versa. Artaud's texts keep stressing the double meaning of *état* as a (political) state and a physical/emotional condition.[43]

For Artaud, physiological and sensory training is a pivotal task of revolutionary arts. In the article "The Social Anarchy of Art," he explains how artists should get involved with the bodies and souls of their time:

> Art has the social duty of giving an outlet to the anxieties of its age. The artist who has not auscultated the heart of his time, the artist who ignores that he is a scapegoat, that his duty is to magnetize, to attract, to bear on his shoulders the errant rage of his time in order to release it from its psychological malaise.[44]

A detailed description of this task can be found in Artaud's acting theory, outlined in his 1935 essay "An Affective Athleticism," published in *The Theater and Its Double*—a text whose Mexican publication he mentions in *Messages révolutionnaires*.[45] The actor, Artaud holds, possesses an "affective musculature which corresponds to the physical localizations of feelings" and intuitively conjures up collective "affective powers" which "have their material trajectory *by and in the organs*."[46] For Artaud, language, too, belongs to the collective affective powers bodies suffer and emit; it turns the body with which it interacts into a "'corps social.'"[47]

According to Artaud, the political emerges when bodies and souls come together in space, when they express, speak out, experience. This is what he calls 'oriented' and compares to theater. Theater is characterized by an orientation of bodies in space, a three-dimensional space that is always perceived in perspective and concretely, with respect to its material conditions. Artaud thus speaks of a located, positioned, materialized culture, a culture of gravity. "Theater," he says in the lecture "Theater and the Gods," "is an art of space, and by weighing on the four points of space, it risks touching upon life."[48] With a semantic content similar to *engagé*, perhaps less straightforward but more physical, *orientée* implies a political positioning. Moreover, being oriented means focusing on the sun, the East, the Orient; it refers to rising, stirring, getting up, appearing, to coming into being, into life.

Throughout his speeches and articles, Artaud repeatedly proposes Mexico as the only place in the world, or one of the very few places, where an organic and oriented culture still exists, or where it may become reawakened at any moment by indigenous rites connected to revolutionary movements.[49]

Artaud's talk of revolution in Mexico always implicitly criticizes the neglect of indigenous cultures in Mexico's various revolutionary movements (and tacitly comments on the exporting practices of the French Revolution). Artaud's revolutionary hope lies in indigenous life in Mexico.[50] His idea of a *culture orientée* reappears in a text on the Tarahumara community entitled "Une Race-Principe" (A Principal Race):

> Each Tarahumara village is preceded by a cross, surrounded by crosses in the mountains' four cardinal points. This is not the cross of Christ, the Catholic cross, but the cross of Man quartered in space, of Man with open arms, invisible, nailed to the four cardinal points. The Tarahumara thus express an active geometric worldview, to which the very shape of Man is connected.[51]

In short, Artaud's concept of revolution centers on the idea of grounded, gravitating, physically present, life-affirming, and mutually responding bodies and souls—on the idea of theatrical bodies. "[T]here is no better revolutionary instrument than theater," he claims in his article "The False Superiority of Elites."[52] Behind this claim lies the conviction that affect, suffering, and desire will prevail over means of sublimation; that as long as coercion and fear prevent organisms from running organically, no political movement will be effective; that because bodies and souls cannot be brought under control, politics can never be ultimately institutionalized. Unless institutions become truly theatrical, that is, metamorphic, the political cannot be a phenomenon of representation; rather, it needs to be a continuous and metamorphic practice involving minds and bodies in spatial orientation to one another.

Reusing Artaud to Theatricalize Life

We could regard Artaud's 'messages' to and from Mexico, including their primitivism, from a historical perspective, in context with other travelers to Mexico,[53] and, for instance, find similarities to Vladimir Mayakovski's transformational experience as described by Steven Lee in *The Ethnic Avant-Garde* (2015),[54] or to Aby Warburg's idea of relations and his critique of Western technological rationality, especially in his reports on his visits to the Pueblo Indians in New Mexico.[55] If we want to go beyond an exclusively historical perspective, the esoteric, mystical, contradictory, eclectic, and sometimes erratic character of Artaud's thinking makes it difficult to rely on him for present insights. At several points, his accounts are exoticist and tendentious. If we trust him at all, we do so because of his awareness of the "childish appearance" of his appeals,[56] because of the "baroque idea" of traveling to Mexico as a European "in search of living foundations of a culture the notion of which seems to be crumbling away here,"[57] and because of the peculiarity of his agenda and its implementation: ultimately, he is a cultural ambassador who aims at experience rather than at specific interests and intentions.[58]

"In a world without poets and madmen Artaud has become untimely," Jacob Rogozinski writes in his 2011 book on Artaud.[59] Over the past decade, however, the number of essays and studies on Artaud has been growing.[60] The pandemic has added further perspectives—Artaud's most notorious 'double' for theater is in fact the plague.[61] In *Messages révolutionnaires*, too, he mentions epidemics as opportunities to get in touch with the "truths" of the world again.[62] "Artaud's words seem both uncannily appropriate and utterly outmoded," Samuel Weber wrote in 2004 on a passage from Artaud's essay "No More Masterpieces" (1933) from *The Theater and Its Double*: "Utterly outmoded in the political and cultural importance he attaches to theater. Uncannily appropriate in his vision of 'war, plagues, famine, and massacres' that are the result, not of any special action, but of simply 'carrying on' as consumers of 'this or that admirable show.'"[63] Both findings have been confirmed during our pandemic times. We are, perhaps more than ever, distanced spectators of global catastrophes, and, less than ever, we take part in theaters of experience. Political decision-making processes during the pandemic have often been marked by a belief in the imperturbable truths of the 'hard sciences,' so strong that it has verged on irrationality and has contributed to triggering and strengthening esoteric reactions to the virus and pandemic-related policies.

Strikingly similar structures are present in Artaud's *Messages révolutionnaires*, including antiscientific affect and esoteric romanticism. They are therefore crucial texts for our time. Yet they are not so much to be read than to be *used* and experienced theatrically, *worked with* in the sense of Heiner Müller's assertion that "[t]his may be an archaic position, but it seems to me that we have not really worked with texts in theater yet, that texts still have not been used as material, as bodies there."[64] Perhaps these times, when theaters have reopened but audiences have failed to return, are inviting us to start this kind of work of addressing bodies and souls (of language, flesh, and blood) not *in politics* or as a political task but *as the political*, as political organs in the literal sense—of practicing new ways of political orientation.

Notes

1 Antonin Artaud, *Messages révolutionnaires* (Paris: Gallimard, 1971), 72. See also Florence de Mèredieu, "L'aventure mexicaine," in *C'était Antonin Artaud* (Paris: Fayard, 2006), 543–78.

2 See Hans Werner Tobler, *Die mexikanische Revolution: Gesellschaftlicher Wandel und politischer Umbruch 1876–1940* (Frankfurt am Main: Suhrkamp, 1992), 494–505, 598–9.

3 Antonin Artaud, "The Theater of Cruelty (Second Manifesto)," in *The Theater and Its Double*, trans. Mary Caroline Richards (New York: Grove Press, 1958), 122–32, here 127.

4 See Lars Krutak, "(Sur)real or Unreal? Antonin Artaud in the Sierra Tarahumara of Mexico," *Journal of Surrealism and the Americas* 8, no. 1 (2014): 28–55; Friedhelm Schmidt-Welle, *Mexiko als Metapher: Inszenierungen des Fremden in Literatur und Massenmedien* (Berlin: Ed. Tranvia, Frey, 2011), 106–9; J. M. G. Le Clézio, "Antonin Artaud, or the Mexican Dream," in *The Mexican Dream: Or, The Interrupted Thought of Amerindian Civilizations*, trans. Teresa Lavender Fagan (Chicago and London: University of Chicago Press, 2009), 161–72.

5 They also composed a bilingual radio play for the Deutschlandfunk in January 2020 with the German voice provided by filmmaker Werner Herzog.

6 Luis Cardoza y Aragón, "Pourquoi le Méxique?" trans. Juan Marey, *Europe: Revue littéraire mensuelle* 62, no. 667–8 (1984): 94–109, here 100.

7 For example, see Antonin Artaud, *Selected Writings*, ed. Susan Sontag (Berkeley: University of California Press, 1976), 357–94.

8 Florence de Mèredieu provides a detailed description of the context and conditions of Artaud's journey, see de Mèredieu, "L'aventure mexicaine." See also David A. Shafer, *Antonin Artaud* (London: Reaktion Books, 2016), 124–42. There are a few substantial discussions of the Mexico texts with an emphasis on Artaud's accounts and/or fictionalization of his visit to the Rarámuri, see Krutak, "(Sur)real or Unreal?"; Melanie Nicholson, "Surrealism's 'Found Object': The Enigmatic Mexico of Artaud and Breton," *Journal of European Studies* 43, no. 1 (2013): 27–43; Tsu-Chung Su, "Artaud's Journey to Mexico and His Portrayals of the Land," *Comparative Literature and Culture* 14, no. 5 (2013): n.p., docs.lib.purdue.edu/clcweb/vol14/iss5/17; Schmidt-Welle, *Mexiko als Metapher*, 100–10; Uri Hertz, "Artaud in Mexico," *Fragmentos*, no. 25 (2003): 11–17; Leslie Anne Boldt-Irons, "In Search of a Forgotten Culture: Artaud, Mexico and the Balance of Matter and Spirit," *The Romanic Review* 89, no. 1 (1998): 123–38; Jane Goodall, "Voyaging into Gnosis," in *Artaud and the Gnostic Drama* (Oxford: Clarendon Press, 1994), 134–64. Recently, Luciana Da Costa Dias has argued that the Mexico texts play a pivotal role for Artaud's late œuvre, because they condense Artaud's attempt to overcome structures of othering with the mind–body divide at their center, see Luciana Da Costa Dias, "Beyond the Peyote Dance: The Raramuri Tribe and 'Mexico' Representations in Antonin Artaud's Work," in *The Palgrave Handbook of Theatre and Race*, ed. Tiziana Morosetti and Osita Okagbue (Cham: Palgrave Macmillan/Springer, 2021), 407–23.

9 For recent political readings of Artaud, see Mehdi Belhaj Kacem, *Artaud et la théorie du complot* (Auch: Tristram, 2015); Jay Murphy, *New Media and the Artaud Effect* (Cham: Palgrave Macmillan/Springer, 2021); Soumyabrata Choudhury, "Eating Dissidence of Antonin Artaud: Towards a Poor

Aesthetics," in *Humanities, Provocateur: Towards a Contemporary Political Aesthetics*, ed. Brinda Bose (Delhi: Bloomsbury India, 2021), 282–300; Ronojoy Sircar, *Remember, Repeat, Inhabit: A Study of Antonin Artaud, Krzysztof Kieslowski, and Nikhil Chopra* (Delhi: Bloomsbury India, 2020). Martin Esslin harshly criticized the way the Paris student movement made political use of Artaud: "*He* had the right to utter those heart-rending screams of pain we can still hear in his last recording, because he suffered the pain from which they sprang. But that does not give others, who have not felt that pain, the justification to start uttering equally loud and strident cries. Without the suffering such screams are hollow, empty, superficial and fake. And what is true of the screams is equally true of violent talk and violent action. The middle-class student revolutionaries of the Paris riots of May 1968 who used Artaud's aggressiveness to power their own frustrations did not share these sufferings and, ultimately, merely exploited them for their own shallow ends and to provide cheap thrills for themselves." Martin Esslin, *Artaud* (London: John Calder, 1976), 113.

10 Susan Sontag, "Approaching Artaud," in *Under the Sign of Saturn* (New York: Vintage Books, 1981), 45–6. Emphasis in original.
11 Artaud, *Selected Writings*, 370; Artaud, *Messages révolutionnaires*, 97.
12 See Artaud, *Messages révolutionnaires*, 68.
13 Artaud, *Selected Writings*, 370; Artaud, *Messages révolutionnaires*, 97.
14 Ibid.; Artaud, *Messages révolutionnaires*, 98.
15 Antonin Artaud, *Les Tarahumaras* (Paris: Gallimard, 1971), 87. See also Nicholson, "Surrealism's 'Found Object'," 29–33; Schmidt-Welle, *Mexiko als Metapher*, 100–10. With a less critical take on Artaud's primitivism, Luciana Da Costa Dias stresses the importance of "racial issues" for the development of Artaud's work, see Da Costa Dias, "Beyond the Peyote Dance," 409. Artaud's sketch for *La conquête du Mexique* is also a harsh critique of colonialism, see Artaud, "The Theater of Cruelty (Second Manifesto)," 127.
16 See Artaud, *Messages révolutionnaires*, 136–7.
17 Alexander Kluge and Heiner Müller, *Ich bin ein Landvermesser: Gespräche, Neue Folge* (Hamburg: Rotbuch, 1996), 24. Trans. S. F.
18 On the presence of Artaud's speech/voice in his written texts, see Jacques Derrida and Evelyn Grossman, "Les voix d'Artaud (la force, la forme, la forge)," *Magazine littéraire*, no. 434 (September 2004): 34–6.
19 Artaud, *Selected Writings*, 358; Artaud, *Messages révolutionnaires*, 25–6.
20 Artaud, *Messages révolutionnaires*, 129.
21 Artaud, *Selected Writings*, 359; Artaud, *Messages révolutionnaires*, 27.
22 See Artaud, *Messages révolutionnaires*, 122.
23 Artaud, *Selected Writings*, 358; Artaud, *Messages révolutionnaires*, 25.
24 Artaud, *Messages révolutionnaires*, 18.
25 Ibid., 17.
26 Ibid., 19.

27 See ibid., 132.
28 Ibid., 19.
29 Ibid.
30 Artaud, *Selected Writings*, 358; Artaud, *Messages révolutionnaires*, 25.
31 Ibid. Emphasis in original.
32 Artaud, *Messages révolutionnaires*, 19.
33 Artaud, *Selected Writings*, 358; Artaud, *Messages révolutionnaires*, 25.
34 Artaud, *Messages révolutionnaires*, 85.
35 Ibid., 121. Emphasis in original.
36 Ibid., 86.
37 Artaud, *Les Tarahumaras*, 103. Trans. S. F. I was not able to obtain a copy of the English edition of *The Peyote Dance*.
38 See Artaud, *Messages révolutionnaires*, 21, 32, 34, 114.
39 Ibid., 42.
40 See Susanne Lüdemann, *Metaphern der Gesellschaft: Studien zum soziologischen und politischen Imaginären* (Munich: Fink, 2004).
41 See Iris Därmann, *Undienlichkeit: Gewaltgeschichte und politische Philosophie* (Berlin: Matthes & Seitz, 2020).
42 Artaud, *Messages révolutionnaires*, 122.
43 See also Artaud's text "Description of a Physical State" from *The Umbilicus of Limbo* (1925), in Artaud, *Selected Writings*, 64–5.
44 Artaud, *Messages révolutionnaires*, 127.
45 Ibid., 83.
46 Antonin Artaud, "An Affective Athleticism," in *The Theater and Its Double*, trans. Mary Caroline Richards (New York: Grove Press, 1958), 133–41, here 133–4. Emphasis in original.
47 Elena Kapralik, "Selbstmörder durch die Gesellschaft," in Antonin Artaud, *Van Gogh, der Selbstmörder durch die Gesellschaft und Texte über Baudelaire, Coleridge, Lautréamont und Gérard de Nerval*, ed. and trans. Franz Loechler (Munich: Matthes & Seitz, 1977), 127–49, here 142.
48 Artaud, *Messages révolutionnaires*, 42.
49 See ibid., 46–7, 72–3, 80–6, 104, 128, 130–1.
50 See ibid., 122, 128.
51 Artaud, *Les Tarahumaras*, 90. Artaud's account of the Tarahumara is less anthropocentric than it sounds here (in French and English). Artaud celebrates not only the Tarahumaras' presence in space (they were able to "preserve the natural force of gravity of the first humans," he writes. Ibid., 104.) but also their hermaphroditic symbolism and their metamorphic rites, see ibid., 105–6.
52 Artaud, *Messages révolutionnaires*, 122.
53 For example, Vladimir Mayakovski, Sergej Eisenstein, D. H. Lawrence, Aldous Huxley, André Breton, Leon Trotsky, or Anna Seghers. See Schmidt-Welle,

Mexiko als Metapher, 93–110 for a comparative reading of Breton's and Artaud's travels.

54 Steven S. Lee, *The Ethnic Avant-Garde: Minority Cultures and World Revolution* (New York: Columbia University Press, 2015), especially the chapter "Translating the Ethnic Avant-Garde," 47–82. Lee describes the transformative effect of Mayakovski's contact with Mexican art (esp. of Diego Rivera) on his poetry, leading to a pathic, 'Greek' performance in New York City with "words that could be *felt*" (ibid., 52, emphasis added). That Mayakovski seemed to "harness[] the exotic for revolution" (ibid., 58) and "seek new, revolutionary configurations of the modern and premodern" (ibid., 60) appears similar to Artaud's approach.

55 See Aby M. Warburg, *Images from the Region of the Pueblo Indians of North America*, trans. Michael P. Steinberg (Ithaca and London: Cornell University Press, 1995), www.degruyter.com/document/doi/10.7591/9781501707704/html. On connections between Warburg's, Artaud's and Eisenstein's America texts, see Murphy, *New Media and the Artaud Effect*, 23–31.

56 Artaud, *Selected Writings*, 372; Artaud, *Messages révolutionnaires*, 107.

57 Antonin Artaud, "Le Mexique et la civilisation," written before his departure, quoted in and translated by Eric Sellin, *The Dramatic Concepts of Antonin Artaud* (New Orleans: Quid Pro, 2017), 17. Artaud continues: "[B]ut I admit that the idea obsesses me; in Mexico there is to be found, linked to the earth, lost in the outflows of volcanic lava, vibrant in the Indian blood, the magic reality of a culture, and little would be required, no doubt, for its fire to be materially revived." Ibid.

58 On the openness of Artaud's journey, see Cardoza y Aragón, "Pourquoi le Méxique?"

59 Jacob Rogozinski, *Guérir la vie: La passion d'Antonin Artaud* (Paris: Cerf, 2011), 26. Transl. S. F.

60 The most recent examples include the 2021 study by Jay Murphy, *New Media and the Artaud Effect*, as well as Choudhury, "Eating Dissidence of Antonin Artaud"; Sircar, *Remember, Repeat, Inhabit*.

61 See Rustom Bharucha, "'The Theatre and the Plague': Revisiting Artaud in the Age of the Coronavirus," ep. 4 of *Theatre and the Coronavirus – A Speech-Act in Nine Episodes*, International Research Center "Interweaving Performance Cultures," Freie Universität Berlin, 2021, www.geisteswissenschaften.fu-berlin.de/en/v/interweaving-performance-cultures/online-projects/Theater-and-the-Coronavirus/Episode-4/index.html.

62 Artaud, *Messages révolutionnaires*, 129–30.

63 Samuel Weber, "'The Virtual Reality of Theater': Antonin Artaud," in *Theatricality as Medium* (New York: Fordham University Press, 2004), 277–94, here 277–8. Quotes within the quote are from Artaud's essay "No More Masterpieces."

64 Heiner Müller, "Gleichzeitigkeit und Repräsentation," in *Werke 11, Gespräche 2*, ed. Frank Hörnigk (Frankfurt am Main: Suhrkamp, 2008), 449–83, here 467. Trans. S. F.

4

On the German Popular Front Novel in Historical and International Context

Hunter Bivens

The popular front period is often thought of as a retreat from class in favor of nation and a retreat from the left avant-gardes of the 1920s in favor of more traditional and representational genres.[1] It is undeniable that German popular front literature witnessed a resurgence of the realist novel, precisely because the novel struck many authors as an ideal form for registering the subterranean and capillary processes that had contributed to the fascist state of exception over a long historical *durée*. In this chapter, I argue that this turn in the Popular Front, which lasted in the German context from roughly 1935 until 1939,[2] from class to "the people," and from a more experimental proletarian modernism to a more realist aesthetic among artists and writers aligned with the Communist Party of Germany (KPD) and the international communist movement,[3] can be read as an attempt to portray a kind of temporal alliance politics linking the contemporaneous antifascist struggle to a *longue durée* of plebeian oppression and dispossession and their attendant nonsynchronisms both nationally and internationally.[4] The major signposts here are the discussions leading up to adoption of socialist realism in the Soviet Union, the strategic shift to the strategy of the Popular Front at the Seventh World Congress of the Communist International in 1935, the Spanish Civil War, and the so-called Expressionism Debate of the late 1930s, carried out between 1937 and 1939 largely in the pages of the exile journal *Das Wort*, but also in the International Bureau of Revolutionary Literature's (IBRL) *International Literature* and other venues between figures such as

Georg Lukács, Anna Seghers, Bertolt Brecht, and Ernst Bloch. This debate, ostensibly one about the status of realism and modernist aesthetic techniques for a socialist literary practice, soon became, as Fredric Jameson has pointed out, one that "quickly extends beyond the local phenomenon of expressionism, and even beyond the ideal type of realism itself, to draw within its scope the problems of popular art, naturalism, socialist realism, avant-gardism, media, and finally modernism—political and non-political—in general."[5] This chapter draws on the notion of a popular avant-garde developed by Ernst Bloch and Hanns Eisler in their contributions to the Expressionism Debate to argue for a popular front novel that is post-novelistic, in that its protagonist is no longer the individual, but the historical horizon itself.

What the literature of the Popular Front shares with the proletarian-revolutionary literature of the Weimar Republic is a notion of culture as both a terrain and a weapon of political struggle, no longer in the streets of Germany itself, but now largely from the marginal spaces of exile and Hitler's camps. Precisely the collapse of the revolutionary proletarian counter-public sphere around the KPD after 1933, authors on the left were forced to reconceive a theory and practice of the political efficacy of literature. In this context the novels of the Popular Front increasingly turn to the form of the novel—ideal for isolated production—as well as to realism and social and historical analysis.[6] At the same time, given the institutional precariousness of the German popular front movement and the lack of a consensus among authors and critics, the literature of the German popular front moment is more productive as one that dwells on questions of the political uses of literature. This chapter will follow a particular strand of the publications among authors and thinkers on the left and either aligned with the KPD or uncomfortably within its orbit.

The Cultural Popular Front

It was only with the Popular Front policy that the KPD and the communist movement turned decisively to the question of national historical traditions in their analysis of fascism.[7] In his address to the Seventh World Congress of the Communist International in 1935, the Comintern's leader Georgi Dimitroff argued, "The fascists are rummaging through the entire history of every nation so as to be able to pose as the heirs and continuators of all that was exalted or heroic in its past."[8] Dimitroff implies that this fascist scramble for national traditions is enabled by a working-class politics that brackets out the national dimension:

> Communists who suppose that all this has nothing to do with the cause of the working class, who do nothing to enlighten the masses on the part of

their people in a historically correct fashion, in a genuinely Marxist-Leninist spirit, *who do nothing to link up the present struggle with the people's revolutionary traditions and past*—voluntarily hand over to the fascist falsifiers all that is valuable in the historical past of the nation, so that the fascists may fool the masses.[9]

The linkage of working-class struggles of the day with the revolutionary traditions of the past requires a popular understanding of history that would have to account for the social and spatial integration, or marginalization, of the working class from the discourse and practice of the nation. "The cultural arms of the Popular Front had begun invoking precisely authority and tradition," Katerina Clark argues. "Many intellectuals had begun to reject the avant-garde experimentalism as jejune and self-indulgent in the face of the world crisis. In their stead, writers were gravitating back toward the grand narrative."[10] Nevertheless, thinking about Popular Front culture purely in terms of nation and tradition fails to do justice to the cultural constellation of the 1930s. As Clark stresses, this was not a culture of insular nationalism, especially not in the Soviet Union or among the geographically dispersed German exiles. "Arguably," she writes, "in the 1930s the causes of nationalism, internationalism, and even cosmopolitanism were not distinct, but to a significant degree imbricated with each other in a mix peculiar to that decade."[11] Yet, if other Popular Fronts could appeal culturally and politically to a national popular progressive tradition, the German exiles could only appeal to the so-called better Germany through an analysis of the misery of German popular life, the poverty of the German progressive tradition, and their own exclusion from a thoroughly Nazified public sphere.

The discourses of antifascist exile were largely shaped by a significant shift in the cultural politics of the international communist movement in the 1930s: the official codification of socialist realism at the 1934 First All-Union Writers' Congress in Moscow, which set the scene for the adoption of the Popular Front policy the following year.[12] Sheila Fitzpatrick argues that socialist realism fits with "the firm establishment in Soviet ideology of the concept of a classless and apolitical 'classical heritage' in culture."[13] Removing the class status of the writer as a criterion of literary criticism, socialist realism marked a reconciliation with the bourgeois literary intelligence, both within the USSR and among potential allies abroad that included André Malraux, Heinrich Mann, and Lion Feuchtwanger.[14] Socialist realism should therefore be understood in the context of the Popular Front that it somewhat anticipates, emphasizing the classical realist novel, national cultural traditions, and the political significance of perspective rather than the class origin of the work.[15] In many ways, the relative openness of the debate at the 1934 Moscow Conference, with Willi Bredel's plea for the continued vitality of proletarian-revolutionary authorship and Wieland Herzfelde's emphasis on the usefulness of modernist techniques, set the tone for a broad antifascist literary alliance.[16] The result of this, organized largely by Johannes R. Becher, Mikhail Koltsov, and Sergei Tretyakov, was the first International Congress of Writers for the Defense of Culture, which took place in Paris in June 1935.[17]

The latter event conspicuously focused on a broad alliance politics, with many of the speeches concentrating on the preservation of Enlightenment values, the moral responsibilities of the writer in the face of the fascism, and the defense of reason and humanism.[18] For Clark, the reciprocal connections between a reinvestment of national traditions on the one hand, and a commitment to internationalism on the other, were key to the structure of feeling of the Popular Front, and the Paris Congress represented its high tide.[19] Some speakers, notably Anna Seghers and Bertolt Brecht, who critically introduced the idea of property relations, challenged this vague humanistic consensus, attempting to frame fascism as a symptom of the crisis of mid-twentieth-century capitalism.[20] Nevertheless, the congresses in Moscow and Paris articulated a certain implicitly conservative formal consensus. Largely eclipsed were the production aesthetics of figures like Brecht, Walter Benjamin, and Tretyakov. For many, the Paris Congress marked a decisive break between aesthetic and political avant-gardes.[21]

The years of exile were also the time of the Expressionism Debate.[22] The discussion, which Clark sees as an "approximate analogue" to the Soviet anti-'Formalist' campaign of the mid-1930s,[23] circled around the status of modernism and realism within Marxist aesthetics, but also around the relationship of art and culture to political struggle and social life, and history more generally.[24] A primary factor of the debate dealt with the question of popularity, or *Volkstümlichkeit*; how could a literary culture that was literally separated from the German people through exile, ideology, and contesting reconstructions of the German cultural tradition, or *Erbe*, nevertheless maintain a connection to that people? Perhaps more important than the local arguments about the status of Expressionism were the attempts by figures like Bloch, Eisler, Seghers, Brecht, and from the other side, Georg Lukács, to shift the debate to the problematic relationship between the political and the aesthetic avant-gardes in the context of Popular Front politics. As Bloch and Eisler put it in a 1937 article in *Die neue Weltbühne*, the aesthetic avant-garde needed the Popular Front in order to give focus to their work, to prevent them from producing into the void, whereas the Popular Front needed the avant-garde to give reality "its most contemporary, precise, and colorful expression."[25] Moving away from the question of whether or not the masses could 'understand' nonfigurative art, Bloch and Eisler maintain, as did Brecht, that art must keep pace with the most advanced forces of production. This implies not only the political refunctioning of mass media like newspapers, film, and radio but also the transformation of older forms like the drama and the novel to take these newer technologies into account.[26] Eisler and Bloch argue that aesthetic and political avant-gardes march separately and often do not strike together.[27] Acknowledging the critiques that pre- and postwar German avant-gardes often remained elitist, abstract, or culinary, Bloch and Eisler nevertheless insisted that precisely the Popular Front should and must open up a space for a new, popular avant-garde, arguing that "today the artist only remains avant-garde when he succeeds in making the new means of art useful for the struggle of the broad masses."[28] Against the argument that the difficulty of avant-garde art isolates it from the masses, Bloch and Eisler insist that it is precisely the question of aesthetic level that lends urgency to avant-garde art on the left, since only here, from a socially critical perspective, can new mass media technologies be refunctioned as instruments of political engagement.[29]

In a follow-up article "Die Kunst zu erben" (To Inherit the Arts), Bloch and Eisler address the problem of cultural heritage, noting that the tendency to dismiss modernism as decadence has the corresponding effect of fetishizing the classics, a left-wing version of the National Socialist canonization of a properly German tradition.[30] If the bourgeois heritage is to be engaged from the left, it must be a critical engagement that recognizes the aesthetic as historically dynamic and understands modernism as a mode of resistance to the commodification of culture and social life under industrial capitalism.[31] As Bloch and Eisler point it, the avant-garde exercises an emancipatory function, developing new ways of seeing and feeling the modern social world, a world which is not only that of the dissolution of the bourgeoisie, but also that of the rise of the proletariat. From the very artifacts of bourgeois decay, according to Bloch and Eisler, we catch glimpses of the socialist future. "Therefore," they write, "the achievements of Picasso and Einstein acquire something of the anticipatory; they are illuminated from the world that is not yet here."[32] Rather than judge the cultural production of the day by the aesthetic standards of the past, Bloch and Eisler end their piece with the slogan: "critical acceptance of the present, and through this the facilitation of productive access to the traditions of the past."[33] For Bloch and Eisler, the vocation of a popular front culture is to integrate modernist techniques into forms of figural and realist representation that will now address itself to popular labors and struggles. This "social modernism," with its collective stance and reliance on techniques of documentary and reportage,[34] emerges clearly in Anna Seghers's Popular Front novels, but also, for example, in the photomontages of John Heartfield and in Brecht's exile dramas. Thus, if the Popular Front era seems marked by a return to realism, it is now a realism that has already passed through the modernist avant-gardes.[35]

What Is a Popular Novel?

Lukács famously theorized the novel as the epic collision of the "problematic individual" with the reified edifice of social convention or "second nature."[36]

In the conjuncture of social revolution and the hypermodernity of the Weimar Republic, this opposition was seen by many theorists and writers to be rooted in a form of bourgeois market capitalism that had been swept away by the First World War and the October Revolution. As Siegfried Kracauer notes in 1930, "it is no accident that one speaks of the 'crisis' of the novel. This crisis resides in the fact that the reigning compositional model of the novel has been invalidated by the abolition of the contours of the individual and its antagonists."[37] Indeed, for Benjamin, "the novelist" has historically "secluded himself from people and their activities,"[38] and the proliferation of biographies, dime novels, and historical novels in this period was a symptom of the crisis of a genre rooted in a bourgeois individuality in dissolution. In the 1920s and 1930s, writers found themselves faced with the urgent problem of the masses, confronting their own transforming status as producers of content for what Brecht called the "great apparati" of literature, theater, and the press,[39] as well as trying to develop new ways of addressing mass audiences beyond the mechanism of the market. The proletarian-revolutionary novels of the Association of Proletarian-Revolutionary Writers (Bund proletarisch-revolutionärer Schriftsteller, or BPRS) represented one path of doing this within the context of Germany's Third Period Communist Party-affiliated counter-public spheres in the late 1920s and early 1930s.[40] The proletarian novel differed from its bourgeois counterpart, as F. C. Weiskopf points out in a 1930 radio interview with Kurt Hirschfeld, in its documentary style and through the "capturing of collective actions and collective feelings" instead of individual psychological portrayals.[41] Likewise, the plots of proletarian novels were driven more by social than individual processes.[42] The final important innovation that Weiskopf saw in the proletarian novel was the "widening of the realm of language" to include the language of the communist movement, trade union and factory culture, and working-class speech in general.[43] For Weiskopf, these novels were no longer novels in a strict sense, but hybrid post-novelistic epic forms: half novel half biography, half protocol half novel, half reportage half novel.[44]

Similarly, novels written within the ambit of Popular Front culture continued this formal hybridity, but often by adapting popular mass literary forms, from the thriller to the romance to the historical novel.[45] To borrow a phrase from Miriam Hansen, Popular Front culture might be thought of as a highly politicized variant of "vernacular modernism," a mapping of complicated cultural responses to modernization through the negotiation of the increasingly contested boundaries between mass culture and high culture.[46] At the same time, many Popular Front novels reach toward a deeper sense of the popular, pushing toward what Benjamin describes in his review of Seghers's 1937 novel *Die Rettung* (The Rescue) as the chronicle. Benjamin uses the term to grasp the complicated ways in which Seghers refracts the contingencies of everyday life through the very architecture of her narratives. Unlike the conventional novel, "in which episodic figures appear through the medium of the main character," in the chronicle that medium—"the character's 'fate'—is absent."[47] Seghers's epics are "not organized in terms of episodes and a principle plot line," instead containing "an abundance of short episodes often building to a climax."[48] The chronicle, as we know from his theses "On the Concept of History," has a special place in Benjamin's thought as the epic form of a redeemed history; one that "narrates events without distinguishing between major and minor ones" in accord with the principle that "nothing that ever happened should be regarded as lost to history."[49] Like Lukács's theorization of the historical novel, the chronicle "brings the past to life as the prehistory of the present" and opens onto the "portrayal of the past as history,"[50] but now freed of the Lukácsean category of the typical, and with it perhaps the fundamentally biographical form of the novel, while preserving the novel's epic quality of time and duration.[51]

Writing on Benjamin's twelfth thesis on the philosophy of history, Michael Löwy illuminates the fundamental attitude of Popular Front culture on the popular, a key term in the debates on the literary left in the 1930s, along with realism and partisanship. Lukács defined the popular in his major contribution to the Expressionism Debate, "Realism in the Balance," which appeared in 1938 in *Das Wort*, in terms of cultural heritage and "the progressive tendencies of the people," which would be expressed in popular literature through a realist aesthetic that would support "a genuine popular culture, a manifold relationship to every aspect of the life of one's own people as it has developed in its own individual way in the course of history."[52] Brecht defined the popular in a more operative fashion in his unpublished riposte, "Popularity and Realism," in terms of intelligibility, partisanship, and "relating to traditions and developing them."[53] In both cases, the popular is also a question of cultural heritage and popular history, or *Erbe*. Benjamin, however, highlights the dispersed and discontinuous character of popular tradition, which is silenced, broken, and driven underground by the history of the victors. Benjamin, Löwy argues, "contrasts the historical continuum, which is the creation of the oppressors, with tradition, which is that of the oppressed."[54] Activating this popular tradition of resistance requires an act of intervention into the present that would "weave into the 'warp' of the present the threads of a tradition that has been lost for centuries."[55] Indeed, this weaving of the promises and horrors of the past into the warp of the present is an attempt to redeem history as tragedy through the genre of the epic. Raymond Williams writes, "the successful revolution . . . becomes not tragedy but epic; it is the origin of a people or its valued way of life."[56] Epic—in the more prosaic usage of narrative prose but also in the sense of a redemptive recovery of the unity between popular history and everyday life as a source of plebeian resistance and a resource for antifascist struggle—haunts the literature of the German Popular Front. The epic in this doubled sense informs the renewed urgency of the novel in exile as a genre uniquely suited to the weaving of the past into the present, and the weaving of the present itself into the fractured and precarious traditions of the oppressed, a "plebeian tradition," to borrow the title of Hans Mayer's famous essay on Brecht.[57]

Similarly, the shift in focus from class to nation can be read, at least in some of the novels of the Popular Front, as an attempt to portray a kind of temporal alliance politics of the oppressed. To take an example, in the midst of Eduard Claudius's Spanish Civil War novel, *Grüne Oliven und nackte Berge* (Green Olives and Bare Mountains, 1944), the German Interbrigadist Jak Rhode has a vision of the eternal soldier after he is wounded in battle. In this vision, Jak is confronted with the dead of all past wars, and, lined faceless among corpses, he finds himself, not as Jak Rhode, but as a "strange dead peasant, who held an old musket on his arm, his body mutilated by a halberd."[58] Jak asks himself if it hurt, and the reply is the voice of that history without history that defines the trope of the eternally suffering peasant who now is also his partisan interlocutor:

> [W]hat are you asking, the peasant answered, dying doesn't hurt. Living, like we have lived, hurts; it was an eternal fear of the power of the lords. This life hurts, it wastes you away; you can never be what you might have been. Why are you asking? You are fighting, and I have fought; we have both fought since many centuries past.[59]

Jak is here briefly re-inscribed within the plebeian tradition as a static continuum of oppression, punctuated by the occasional disaster, of temporality as a circle of scarcity, toil, and death. Bent and distorted by fear, the life of the peasant is identical to its own foreclosure—"you can never be what you could have been"[60]—determined by the narrow confinement of an oppression so ancient as to become ontological. Jak's response—"I have a rifle, and I have hand grenades, and I have the courage not to tolerate this life any longer!"—marks the break between communist and plebeian violence,[61] between a violence in service to feudal and capitalist masters on the one hand and the violence of self-liberation on the other. Yet at the same time, this exchange marks not only the difference between the conscious partisan and the armored, yet creaturely peasant, the *Landsknecht* (peasant mercenary), but at the same time reveals that peasant heritage as the deep structure of partisan commitment, linking both the traditions of popular suffering and the present antifascist struggle across Europe, from Germany to Spain.

In other words, for Claudius, the communist struggle is popular precisely as the very break into a human history denied to the peasantry. In the prologue of the novel, Claudius writes,

[I]t is only worth fighting and dying for all of the smells you have yet to smell. For each taste that you have never tasted. For all of the melodies you have not heard. For all of the things that you have never done and that you have been denied from doing. For all of the thoughts that you have not thought and that you have been denied from thinking.... Only for the future that they wish to deny you is it worth living and dying.[62]

The future that Claudius evokes here is very much the future of a redeemed plebeian past, of the life in which one can never become what one could have become. In this sense, one is reminded again of Benjamin's theses, for here Claudius is evoking not a historicist model of progress, but rather the kind of thinking that Benjamin juxtaposes to it:

The Social Democrats preferred to cast the working class in the role of a redeemer of future generations, in this way cutting the sinews of its greatest strength. This indoctrination made the working class forget both its hatred and its spirit of sacrifice, for both are nourished by the image of enslaved ancestors rather than the ideal of liberated grandchildren.[63]

What Claudius contributes to this Benjaminian insight is that the future and the redeemed past cannot be thought separately, just as the peasantry and the proletariat are both articulations of a *longue durée* of oppression and subalternity.

Anna Seghers's 1942 novel *The Seventh Cross* provides another example of this historical front. The novel opens with a historical panorama of the Rhine-Main lowlands. These lowlands initially appear in a pastoral vision, neither rural nor urban, where the fields and fruit trees stand side by side with the railroad tracks and smoke of the nearby factory.[64] Yet this is but a moment of repose for a region that has been shaped by a long history of struggle. "This is the land," Seghers writes, "of which it is said that the last war's projectiles plow from the ground the projectiles of the war before the last."[65] In a sweeping historical panorama, Seghers emplaces the Rhine-Main lowlands at the border between empires, religions, and revolutions:

For a long time, though, this chain of hills meant the edge of the world; it was here that the Romans drew their *limes*. So many races had perished here since they burned the Celts' sun altars, so many battles had been fought, that the hills themselves might have thought that what was conquerable had finally been fenced and made arable.... Here camped the legions, and with them all of the Gods of the world: city gods and peasant gods, the gods of Jew and Gentile, Astarte and Isis, Mithras and Orpheus. Here ... stood the peoples' cauldron. North and south, east and west, were brewed together, and while the country as a whole remained unaffected by it all, yet it retained a vestige of everything. Like colored bubbles, empires rose up from that country, rose up and as soon burst again. They left behind no *limes*, no triumphal arches, no military highways; only a few fragments of their women's golden anklets. But they were as hardy and imperishable as dreams.[66]

Seghers provides an epochal history of the Rhineland, from the invasion of the Franks at the close of the fifth century to the 1936 arrival of Nazi regiments. The history of empires is briefly interrupted by moments of resistance, for example, the Mainz Republic founded by German Jacobins inspired by the French Revolution, reminding us of the fractured and discontinuous character of Germany's progressive tradition.[67] At the same time, it is connected in Seghers's narratives to the contemporaneous anti-imperialist struggle in China and antifascist struggle in Spain; she writes of the inmates of the concentration camp Westhofen, "a certain natural law, or a mysterious circuit, seemed to connect this group of chained up miserables with world centers."[68] Bernard Spies points out that Seghers's account dwells less on the singularity of the succession of historical powers that have crossed over and tarried in this landscape than on "a continuum of historical acts of violence."[69] Spies notes that here Seghers casts history itself as "the progress of violence"[70] in a rather Benjaminian vein. Only against the continuum of domination does the "eschatological point" of Seghers's historical understanding come into view, "which does not after all expect salvation at the end of historical upheavals, but rather beholds it in its immanence: what asserts itself in the continuum of violence in other words is in the long run not the violence itself, but rather humanity, which each power tramples underfoot without being able to destroy."[71] Regarded from this epochal vantage point, the pageantry of the Nazis already augurs their downfall, the ephemeral quality of their rule when measured against the mute solidity of the quotidian, and the persistence of nature itself: "in the morning," Seghers writes, "when the stream left the city behind beyond the railroad bridge, its quiet bluish-gray was in no way altered. How many field standards had it lapped against? How many flags?"[72] This fundament of the natural aligns itself in Seghers's novel with the stories and legends of revolt and resistance from the peasant uprisings, from Mainz Republic and the workers' movement, and, as Spies points out, with the great leitmotifs of human culture (understood now in the broad sense of the cultivation of nature), "culled from the natural wealth of the region, refined through the labor of centuries: apples and wine."[73]

This brings us to the key debates in the German literary emigration on the status of the historical novel, best memorialized in Lukács's book of the same name. In other words, the debate around the historical novel in the German antifascist emigration was a debate about the relative serviceability of the novel itself. The novel reemerges as a privileged genre in the 1930s for coordinating the uneven timescales and nonlinear histories of everyday life in Germany that underlie the National Socialist political and social synthesis.[74] While neither work mentioned above is a historical novel in the proper sense, they both attempt to fulfill the historical novel's vocation of historical orientation and localization. In different ways, they present popular genealogies of fascism and antifascist resistance as embedded in the present of the 1930s. For Fredric Jameson, these are the axes of contradiction of the historical novel: on the one hand, the opacity of the mediations between the level of experience and the givenness and institutionality of the world, and on the other hand, the discrepancy between power and events, since neither the center of power nor popular life can be represented.[75] One could say the same about the great cataclysms of history, in the sense that, as Lukács points out, it is a mistake to think of these catastrophes as being punctual. "In reality," Lukács writes, "'sudden' catastrophes are actually long in preparation." Thus, the "epic gives a broadly unfolded, entangled picture of the varied struggles—great and small, some successful, some ending in defeat—of its characters, and it is through the totality of these that the necessity of social development is expressed."[76] *The Historical Novel* closes with an invocation of a new epic tendency in Popular Front novels, reaching beyond the prose of capitalist society, where "the only result of the people's colossal heroic efforts was the replacement of one form of exploitation by another," to the "heroic upsurge" of the "revolutionary liberation of the people."[77]

Following Lukács, then, the historical novel is in fact not to be regarded as an independent practice of the novel proper. Echoing Alfred Döblin's formulation that "every good novel is a historical novel," Lukács insists that, on the one hand, the novel as a genre is itself centrally concerned with the relationship between the present and the past, and that, on the other hand, the historical novel both rises from and returns to the social novel.[78] As Agnes Heller notes, the historical character of the novel has less to do with any direct depiction of historical figures and events than it does with the sensitivity of the modern novel to "a very special kind of kairos: social character, personal fate, story, historical moments, all of them need to be interwoven in a unique pattern, since what can happen with a particular social character cannot happen with another."[79] It is this notion of the epic portrayal of the past as history, enabled by the durational and capillary form of the novel, that both grounds Lukács's critique of novels that use historical settings merely as backdrop and also unexpectedly draws his account of the novel within range of Benjamin's notion of the chronicle.

Tyrus Miller argues that for Lukács, "novels . . . can be understood as a sort of rhetorical laboratory for constituting and nominating 'the people,' exhibiting the conditions under which this succeeds or fails and with what social, political, and existential results."[80] Indeed, as J. M. Bernstein argued in *The Philosophy of the Novel*, "at the horizon of the history of the novel, just as it was at the horizon of the history of modern philosophy, there stands the question of the 'we,' the we who shall speak and make history."[81] Yet, this epic "we" is not, as it perhaps was for the young Lukács, some prelapsarian utopia; it is not something that has been lost. Nor is it something that in some way is already present beneath the reified divisions of social life. Rather, as Bernstein points out, the project of an epic narrative is itself the production of an emancipated future, the narrative production of both a subject and a world in which social action and social meaning might for the first time find themselves in equipoise. For Bernstein, this project of collective narration is precisely what links representation to political practice under the sign of the Marxist project.[82]

Jameson cast doubt on the viability of a contemporary popular front politics as early as 1977, given the lack of a progressive bourgeoisie or mass workers' parties in late capitalism,[83] and we are at least as far from an epic "we" as we were in the 1930s. Indeed, contemporary realism in literature, for example, Uwe Tellkamp's sprawling post-GDR Bildungsroman *Der Turm* (The Tower, 2008), feels increasingly like capitalist realism, the exploration of individual subjectivities in a moment of, to quote Mark Fisher, "the widespread sense that not only is capitalism the only viable political and economic system, but also that it is now impossible even to imagine a coherent alternative to it."[84] Instead, the realism of the German Popular Front novels discussed here portrays the present itself as an intense experience of defeated historical and political alternatives to that very present. In a review of Anna Seghers's later GDR novel *Die Entscheidung* (The Decision, 1959), East German writer Christa Wolf notes that there is something profoundly "non-novelistic" about Seghers's GDR novels.[85] Seghers's novels do not offer "the history of a subject or subjects removed from their limited context," but rather narrate the emergence of "new societies" and "new forms of human living together."[86] "These great processes," Wolf writes, "are only to be registered in their complex epic multiplicity."[87] This complex epic structure, I would argue, is in part a legacy of the proletarian modernism that persists through the Popular Front novel and beyond, not only in a novel like Peter Weiss's monumental portrayal of the literary and political struggles of the Popular Front itself, *Aesthetics of Resistance* (1971–81), a novel that, for Klaus Scherpe and James Gussen, "wishes to be an indication, a sign of this historical work of liberation that has not yet become history,"[88] as much as it does through the "historical novels" of the present that Lauren Berlant discusses in her *Cruel Optimism*, such as Colson Whitehead's *The Intuitionist* (1999) or William Gibson's *Pattern Recognition* (2003), which aspire to "induce certain affects into the reader whose value sutured that reader to history and genealogy, producing a capacity to sense historical experience in an aesthetic feedback loop,"[89] thereby preserving the vocation of the novel as a tool for social and historical feeling and recognition.

Notes

1. This chapter draws on material from my book, Hunter Bivens, *Epic and Exile: Novels of the German Popular Front 1933–1945* (Evanston: Northwestern University Press, 2015).

2. On the German Popular Front, which remained more of a project than a political formation in its own right, see Ursula Langkau-Alex, *Deutsche Volksfront: Zwischen Berlin, Paris, Prag, und Moskau*, 3 vols. (Berlin: Akademie-Verlag, 2004). Neither the opponents of National Socialism at home in Germany, nor in the centers of the German antifascist emigration charted in the subtitle to Langkau-Alex's work, were able to develop a unified position, but at the same time, the Popular Front as a cultural politics was decisive for German intellectuals in exile from Moscow to Los Angeles and provided them with a discourse to relate to the international struggles of the 1930s. See Jean-Michel Palmier, *Weimar in Exile: The Antifascist in Europe and America*, trans. David Fernbach (New York: Verso, 2017) and the series *Kunst und Literatur im antifaschistischen Exil 1933–1945: In sieben Bänden*, ed. Simone Barck and Klaus Jarmatz (Leipzig: Reclam, 1989). On the 1930s as a political conjuncture, see Marc Matera and Susan Kingsley Kent, *The Global 1930s: The International Decade* (New York: Routledge, 2017).

3. On this shift, see Bivens, *Epic and Exile*. For an account of the proletarian modernism of the Weimar Republic, see Sabine Hake, *The Proletarian Dream. Socialism, Culture, and Emotion in Germany, 1863–1933* (Berlin and Boston: Walter De Gruyter, 2017).

4. On the notion of nonsynchronism, see Ernst Bloch, *Heritage of Our Times*, trans. Neville and Stephan Plaice (Cambridge: Polity Press, 1991), 97–148.

5. Fredric Jameson, "Reflections in Conclusion," in *Aesthetics and Politics*, ed. Fredric Jameson (New York: Verso, 1977), 196–213, here 196–7.

6. See Sigrid Bock, "Roman im Exil: Entstehungsbedingungen, Wirkungsabsichten und Wirkungsmöglichkeiten," in *Erfahrung Exil: Antifaschistische Romane 1933–1945*, ed. Sigrid Bock and Manfred Hahn (Berlin: Aufbau-Verlag, 1979), 7–49, here 7, 33.

7. See Birgit Schmidt, *Wenn die Partei das Volk entdeckt: Anna Seghers, Bodo Uhse, Ludwig Renn, u.a.: Ein kritischer Beitrag zur Volksfrontideologie und ihrer Literatur* (Münster: Unrast, 2002).

8. Georgi Dimitroff, *Against Fascism and War* (New York: International Publishers, 1986), 76.

9. Ibid.

10. Katerina Clark, *Moscow, the Fourth Rome: Stalinism, Cosmopolitanism, and the Evolution of Soviet Culture 1931–1941* (Cambridge, MA: Harvard University Press, 2011), 171.

11. Ibid., 5.

12. The speeches at the First All-Union Writers Congress are reproduced in H. G. Scott, *Problems of Soviet Literature: Reports and Speeches at the First Soviet*

Writers' Congress (Westport: Hyperion Press, 1981). See also Hans-Jürgen Schmitt and Godehard Schramm, *Sozialistische Realismuskonzeptionen* (Frankfurt am Main: Suhrkamp, 1974).

13 Sheila Fitzpatrick, *The Cultural Front. Power and Culture in Revolutionary Russia* (Ithaca and London: Cornell University Press, 1992), 250.

14 See ibid., 243. On the cultural pull of in the mid-1930s and socialist realism as an appeal to bourgeois intellectuals, see Clark, *Moscow*, esp. 169–209.

15 For a discussion of the role of Lukács and the German *émigrés* in the USSR in the formation of a Popular Front discourse, see Clark, *Moscow*, 136–68.

16 See Simone Barck, "Die Mission des Dichters 1934," in *Wer schreibt, handelt: Strategien und Verfahren literarischer Arbeit vor und nach 1933*, ed. Silvia Schlenstedt (Berlin and Weimar: Aufbau-Verlag, 1983), 520–31, here 520.

17 On the Paris Congress, see *Paris 1935: Erster Internationaler Schriftstellerkongreß zur Verteidigung der Kultur*, ed. Alfred Klein (Berlin: Akademie-Verlag, 1982). See also Wolfgang Klein and Silvia Schlenstedt, "Wirkungsstrategien auf dem Pariser Schriftstellerkongreß 1935," in *Wer schreibt, handelt: Strategien und Verfahren literarischer Arbeit vor und nach 1933*, ed. Silvia Schlenstedt (Berlin and Weimar: Aufbau-Verlag, 1983), 532–58.

18 See Clark, *Moscow*, 178.

19 See ibid., 5.

20 See Klein and Schlenstedt, "Wirkungsstrategien," 548.

21 See Clark, *Moscow*, 198–9.

22 There is a copious literature on the so-called Brecht–Lukács debate, or the Expressionism Debate. One of the better accounts in English is the essay collection edited by Fredric Jameson, *Aesthetics and Politics*. See also Eugene Lunn, *Marxism and Modernism: An Historical Study of Lukács, Brecht, Benjamin and Adorno* (Berkeley: University of California Press, 1982). Important German work on this debate includes the collection edited by Hans-Jürgen Schmitt, *Die Expressionismus-Debatte: Materialien zu einer marxistischen Realismuskonzeption* (Stuttgart: Suhrkamp, 1973). See also, from a GDR perspective, *Dialog und Kontroverse mit Georg Lukács*, ed. Werner Mittenzwei (Leipzig: Reclam, 1973) and Dieter Schiller, *Der Traum von Hitlers Sturz: Studien zur deutschen Exilliteratur 1933–1945* (New York and Frankfurt am Main: Peter Lang, 2010).

23 See Clark, *Moscow*, 211.

24 Brecht's contributions to the debate appeared only with the posthumous publication of his "Volkstümlichkeit und Realismus" (Popularity and Realism, 1938) in the GDR journal *Sinn und Form* in 1958 and his *Schriften zur Literatur und Kunst* in 1966. See *Lexikon sozialistischer Literatur: Ihre Geschichte on Deutschland bis 1945*, ed. Simone Barck, Silvia Schlenstedt, Tanja Bürgel, Volker Giel, and Dieter Schiller (Stuttgart and Weimar: J. B. Meltzer, 1994), 143.

25 Ernst Bloch and Hanns Eisler, "Avantgarde-Kunst und Volksfront," in *Zur Tradition der deutschen sozialistischen Literatur: Eine Auswahl von Dokumenten 1935–1941*, ed. Alfred Klein (Berlin and Weimar: Aufbau-Verlag, 1979), 401–9, here 401.

26 See ibid., 406.

27 See ibid., 404.

28 Ibid., 406.

29 See ibid., 407.

30 See Ernst Bloch and Hanns Eisler, "Die Kunst zu erben," in *Zur Tradition der deutschen sozialistischen Literatur: Eine Auswahl von Dokumenten 1935–1941*, ed. Alfred Klein (Berlin and Weimar: Aufbau-Verlag, 1979), 409–15, here 411.

31 See ibid., 412.

32 Ibid., 414.

33 Ibid., 415.

34 Michael Denning, *The Cultural Front: The Laboring of American Culture in the Twentieth Century* (New York: Verso Press, 1997), 122.

35 On this point, see Devin Fore, *Realism After Modernism: The Rehumanization of Art and Literature* (Cambridge, MA: MIT Press, 2012).

36 Georg Lukács, *Theory of the Novel: A Historico-Philosophical Essay in the Forms of Great Epic Literature*, trans. Anna Bostock (Cambridge, MA: MIT Press, 1971), 78, 62.

37 Siegfried Kracauer, "The Biography as an Art Form of the New Bourgeoisie," in *The Mass Ornament: Weimar Essays*, ed. and trans. Thomas Y. Levin (Cambridge, MA: Harvard University Press, 1995), 101–6, here 102.

38 Walter Benjamin, "The Crisis of the Novel," in *Selected Writings. Volume 2, Part 1, 1927–1930*, ed. Howard Eiland, Michael W. Jennings, and Gary Smith (Cambridge and London: Belknap Press, 1999), 299–304, here 299.

39 Bertolt Brecht, "The Modern Theater is the Epic Theater," in *Brecht on Theatre: The Development of an Aesthetic*, ed. John Willett (New York: Hill & Wang, 1964), 33–42, here 35.

40 The BPRS was founded under the auspices of the Comintern's IBRL in October 1928 and was disbanded in 1935. Bringing together radical left-wing authors from the bourgeoisie like Seghers and Becher on the one hand and proletarian writers like Hans Marchwitza and Bredel on the other, the BPRS was a key organization for the development of Marxist aesthetic theory and literary practice in the interwar period. Its journal, *Linkskurve*, saw a lively debate between the developing positions of Georg Lukács and various leftist positions. For a comprehensive history of the organizational politics and literary debates within the BPRS, see Helga Gallas, *Marxistische Literaturtheorie: Kontroversen im Bund proletarisch-revolutionärer Schriftsteller* (Neuwied and Berlin: Luchterhand, 1971). The GDR perspective on the BPRS is sketched in Alfred Klein, "Zur Entwicklung der sozialistischen

Literatur in Deutschland 1918–1933," in *Literatur der Arbeiterklasse: Aufsätze über die Herausbildung der deutschen sozialistischen Literatur (1918–1933)*, ed. Irmfried Hiebel (Berlin and Weimar: Aufbau-Verlag 1976). James F. Murphy situates the BPRS debates in the context of developments in the USSR and the American left in the 1920s and 1930s in *The Proletarian Moment: The Controversy over Leftism in Literature* (Urbana and Chicago: University of Illinois Press, 1991).

41 F. C. Weiskopf and Kurt Hirschfeld, "Um den proletarischen Roman," in *Zur Tradition der deutschen sozialistischen Literatur: Eine Auswahl von Dokumenten 1935–1941*, ed. Alfred Klein (Berlin and Weimar: Aufbau-Verlag, 1979), 1926–1935, 210–18, here 215.

42 See ibid., 216.

43 Ibid.

44 See ibid., 215.

45 See Alexander Stephan, *Anna Seghers*: Das siebte Kreuz: *Welt und Wirkung eines Romans* (Berlin: Aufbau-Verlag, 1997), 79–93.

46 Miriam Bratu Hansen, "The Mass Production of the Senses: Classical Cinema as Vernacular Modernism," *Modernism/Modernity* 6, no. 2 (1999): 59–77, here 60.

47 Walter Benjamin, "A Chronicle of Germany's Unemployed," in *Selected Writings. Volume 4, 1938–1940*, ed. Howard Eiland and Michael W. Jennings (Cambridge and London: Belknap Press, 2003), 126–34, here 128. We know from Helen Fehervary's work the impact that Seghers had on Benjamin's conception of the chronicle. See Helen Fehervary, *Anna Seghers: The Mythic Dimension* (Ann Arbor: University of Michigan Press, 2001), 148–74.

48 Benjamin, "A Chronicle of Germany's Unemployed," 131.

49 Benjamin, "On the Concept of History," in *Selected Writings Volume 4, 1938–1940*, ed. Howard Eiland and Michael W. Jennings (Cambridge and London: Belknap Press, 2003), 389–400, here 390.

50 Georg Lukács, *The Historical Novel*, trans. Hannah and Stanley Mitchell (Lincoln and London: University of Nebraska Press 1983), 53, 83.

51 See Lukács, *Theory of the Novel*, 83, 121–3.

52 Georg Lukács, "Realism in the Balance," in *Aesthetics and Politics*, ed. Fredric Jameson (New York: Verso, 1977), 28–59, here 57.

53 Bertolt Brecht, "Popularity and Realism," in *Aesthetics and Politics*, ed. Fredric Jameson (New York: Verso, 1977), 79–85, here 81.

54 Michael Löwy, *Fire Alarm: Reading Walter Benjamin's "On the Concept of History,"* trans. Chris Turner (New York and London: Verso Press, 2005), 89.

55 Ibid.

56 Raymond Williams, *Modern Tragedy* (Peterborough: Broadview Press, 2001), 64.

57 Hans Mayer, "Die plebejische Tradition," in Hans Mayer, *Brecht* (Frankfurt: Suhrkamp, 1966), 309–22, here 310.

58 Eduard Claudius, *Grüne Oliven und nackte Berge* (Halle an der Saale: Mitteldeutscher-Verlag, 1976), 166.
59 Ibid.
60 Ibid., 167.
61 Ibid.
62 Ibid., 8.
63 Benjamin, "The Concept of History," 394.
64 Anna Seghers, *The Seventh Cross*, trans. James A. Galston (Boston: David R. Godine, 2004), 8–9. The standard edition of the novel is Anna Seghers, *Das siebte Kreuz: Roman aus Hitlerdeutschland*, Werkausgabe I/4 (Berlin: Aufbau-Verlag, 2000).
65 Ibid., 9.
66 Ibid.
67 See Seghers, *The Seventh Cross*, 9.
68 Ibid., 219.
69 Bernard Spies, "Kommentar," in Anna Seghers, *Das siebte Kreuz: Roman aus Hitlerdeutschland*, Werkausgabe I/4 (Berlin: Aufbau-Verlag, 2000), 445–96, here 474.
70 Ibid., 464.
71 Ibid.
72 Seghers, *The Seventh Cross*, 12.
73 Spies, "Kommentar," 465.
74 See Matthias Bertram, "Literarische Epochendiagnosen der Nachkriegszeit," in *Deutsche Erinnerung: Berliner Beiträge zur Prosa der Nachkriegsjahre (1945–1960)*, ed. Ursula Heukenkamp (Berlin: Erich Schmidt Verlag, 1999), 11–100, here 61.
75 See Fredric Jameson, "A Monument to Radical Instants," in Peter Weiss, *Aesthetics of Resistance*, vol. 1, trans. Joachim Neurgoschel (Durham: Duke University Press, 2005), vii–xlix, here xviii, xx.
76 Lukács, *Historical Novel*, 146.
77 Ibid., 346–7.
78 Ibid., 83. For Alfred Döblin's position, see "Der historische Roman und wir," in *Schriften zur Ästhetik, Politik und Literatur* (Frankfurt: Fischer Verlag, 2013), 292–316.
79 Agnes Heller, "History and the Historical Novel in Lukács," in *The Modern German Historical Novel: Paradigms, Problems, Perspectives*, ed. David Roberts and Philip Thomson (New York: Berg, 1991), 19–34, here 27.
80 Tyrus Miller, "Editor's Introduction: The Phantom of Liberty: György Lukács and the Culture of 'People's Democracy'," in György Lukács, *The Culture of People's Democracy. Hungarian Essays on Literature, Art, and Democratic Transition, 1945–1948*, ed. and trans. Tyrus Miller (Chicago: Haymarket Books, 2013), vii–xxxvi, here xxxv.

81 J. M. Bernstein, *The Philosophy of the Novel: Lukács, Marxism, and the Dialectics of Form* (Minneapolis: University of Minnesota Press, 1984), 257.

82 Ibid., 266.

83 Jameson, "Reflections," 203.

84 Mark Fisher, *Capitalist Realism: Is there No Alternative?* (Winchester: Zero Books, 2009), 2.

85 Christa Wolf, "Das Land, in dem wir Leben," *Neue Deutsche Literatur* 9, no. 5 (1961): 49–65, here 54. For a discussion of this aspect of Seghers's novels, see Hunter Bivens, "Aufbauzeit oder flaue Zeit? Anna Seghers's GDR Novels," in *Dimensions of Storytelling in German Literature and Beyond: 'For Once Telling It All from the Beginning,'* ed. Kristy R. Boney and Jennifer Marston William (Rochester: Camden House, 2018), 70–81. For an account of Uwe Tellkamp's novel as a postcommunist project of literary restoration, see Julia Hell, "Demolition Artists: Icono-Graphy, Tanks, and Scenarios of (Post-)Communist Subjectivity in Works by Neo Rauch, Heiner Müller, Durs Grünbein, and Uwe Tellkamp," *The Germanic Review* 89, no. 2 (2014): 131–70.

86 Ibid.

87 Wolf, "Das Land," 54.

88 Klaus Scherpe and James Gussen, "Reading *The Aesthetics of Resistance*: Ten Working Theses," *New German Critique* 30, no. 30 (1983): 97–105, here 104. As of the publication of this chapter, two volumes of Weiss's *Aesthetics of Resistance* have been published by Duke University Press in English translation by Joachim Neugroschel (2005) and Joel Scott (2020), respectively.

89 Lauren Berlant, *Cruel Optimism* (Durham: Duke University Press, 2011), 66. See also Fredric Jameson's speculations on "historical novels of the future" in Jameson, *The Antinomies of Realism* (New York: Verso Press, 2013).

5

Narrative Struggle

'Good' and 'Bad' Uses of Literature in the Committed Novel of the 1930s (Aragon, Dos Passos)

Aurore Peyroles

Few terms have been as vulnerable to misunderstanding as the idea of literary–political commitment. As Jacques Rancière explains, when it comes to commitment (*engagement*), it often happens that "one of the interlocutors both hears and does not hear what the other is saying."[1] The concept of commitment is notoriously unstable—so much so that its constitutive ambiguities sometimes seem to produce a total absence of meaning. These ambiguities are further intensified in the context of literary fiction: Is literature's primary commitment to literature itself or to some cause outside it? When it comes to politicized literature, commitment often tends to be associated with an oversimplification of literary writing, on the level of both style and plot, that is, with privileging intention over literary expression.

This chapter reflects on the elusive notion of literary commitment, not merely from a theoretical point of view but also by examining the views embodied in two politically committed novel series: Louis Aragon's *Le Monde réel*, written between 1932 and 1951 (though my focus here will be on the first three volumes, written before the Second World War), and

John Dos Passos's *USA*, a trilogy written between 1930 and 1936. These two voluminous series, adding up to several thousand pages, attempt to answer a question that was particularly acute in the 1930s: How did we get here? They anticipate Jean-Paul Sartre's theorization in *What Is Literature?* (1947) but deliver a political interpretation of their present situation, one that censures and places responsibility on the powerful. With these series, Aragon and Dos Passos left behind the surrealist and modernist experiments of their youth to answer the decade's unprecedented call for a gesture of commitment. More precisely, they rearticulated these literary experiments by investing them with a political function. Their commitment consists in tracing a chronology of the compromise of republican ideals by the various powers claiming to defend them. It is this effort to understand that makes them committed novels: in these books, commitment refers less to a political doctrine or an ideological conviction than to taking into account the present situation, which one must understand in order to act.[2]

This gesture of commitment has rarely been expressed as acutely as during the 1930s. Beginning with the Great Depression and ending with the specter of Nazism looming over Europe, this decade elicited intensely political reactions from many artists. Its tumultuousness, the crises that plagued it, and the exacerbation of social inequalities and political antagonisms seemed to render impossible any posture of indifference. Writers were no exception: literary writing was part of a context in which any commitment was encouraged, regardless of the side taken or form adopted. Many writers intervened as public intellectuals, but the movement of commitment that characterized this period both ran alongside the literary field and also involved literature itself.

The awareness of living in particularly volatile times prompted writers to reexamine their choice of instruments, themes, and communication strategies. If the historical context profoundly affected the ethical conduct of writers, pushing them to intervene in the political and intellectual fields, it also modified their literary practice. As Benoît Denis reminds us, it was during these years that the very notion of literary commitment appeared: "The interwar period corresponds to a period of intense conflict between the literary and the political and thus constitutes a laboratory of sorts in which various forms of literary commitment were experimented with."[3] These were the years of debate and experimentation as to the possible reconciliation between literature and politics, not those of the "dogmatic moment of commitment" associated with "Sartre's hegemony."[4] Lacking obvious artistic precursors, writers had to invent what it meant to commit oneself in literature. There is a real sense in which the 1930s were the years in which the idea of literary commitment—understood as political purpose inseparable from literary style—first emerged.

Rather than providing a general definition of what the committed novel is—as distinct from the *roman-à-thèse*, for example—I propose to examine the way in which the two novel series under consideration here stage the political power of literature and how they define themselves in contrast to dominant storytelling—or what their authors consider as such. By choosing to write novels, Aragon and Dos Passos aimed to exert political influence by narrating fictional stories. They thus shared their ambition with the (un)official narratives deployed by the political powers of the day, that is, the very persons and institutions these writers aimed to condemn: both Aragon and Dos Passos sought to persuade. Both authors felt the need to forge alternative stories, distinguished both in form and content from the dominant stories whose harmful effects on public opinion are illustrated by the committed novel. In the novels, this resulted in a highly political clash between the official narratives and their respective counter-narratives.

Denouncing Dominant Storytelling: Hegemonic 'Thrillers'

Seen through the lens of Dos Passos's and Aragon's novels, both American and French societies appear to be saturated with hegemonic fictions disguised as fact. These fictions falsify reality and manipulate the public; they shape national views and opinions, holding the public captive. These hegemonic narratives, disseminated through the mainstream press, seem absolute in that they imperceptibly substitute facts and rational arguments with often misleading fictions serving propagandistic ends. The main characteristic of the official (hegemonic) stories alluded to in *USA* and *Le Monde réel* is that they transfigure the real world, camouflaging it, as it were, to serve the ends of the established order and those in power. Formally and fundamentally simplistic, these omnipresent narratives are as hostile to counter-hegemonic narratives as they are convincing to large portions of the population.

What the hegemonic narratives denounced by Dos Passos and Aragon have in common is that they all articulate what Christian Salmon calls a "national security thriller."[5] The purpose of the thriller, of course, is to thrill; whether the enemies of authority are internal or external, they are always hyperbolically presented as threatening and formidable. The basic storyline tends to be simple and highly productive: socialists, or any individuals that challenge the established order, threaten the nation's cohesion, just as it is preparing to go to war in the late 1930s. This basic blueprint, relying on the figure of the scapegoat, is developed using caricatures and unfounded associations. The designation of a common and pernicious enemy inevitably bolsters the powers that be, which present themselves as the last bulwark against the onslaught of hostile forces. Thus, the socialist, be he French or American, is systematically portrayed as the adversary in national narratives, one whose existence justifies the repressive policies carried out against his fellow human beings.

The Red Scare that gripped the interwar United States and permeates Dos Passos's *USA* was based on such caricatures, which created a binary between socialists and 'good' Americans. This is evidenced by the snippets collected in the "Newsreel" sections of the trilogy, where headlines, article excerpts, images, light song lyrics, and sensationalist announcements are bundled together, reflecting "the common mind of the epoch."[6] For instance, the utter fabrication in the headline "IWW [Industrial Workers of the World] IN PLOT TO KILL WILSON"[7] defines the united 'Red Front' in terms of its alleged opposition to American democracy, embodied in the person of its president. These narratives, with varying success, devalue all political dissenters, who are invariably represented as traitors, manipulators driven by mediocre ambitions, and outsiders.

The political benefit of the false stories staged and denounced by *USA* and *Le Monde réel* is not limited to the dismissive caricature of the contesters of power or to the equivalent praise of its (nationalist) defenders. The frantic narrative production in which the opponents engage aims to mobilize its recipients and to turn them into unwavering supporters of an order that is both unjust and untenable. The modern exercise of a power that has become "symbolic"[8] and not (too) openly repressive or directly violent requires the active support of the dominated class. To maintain the subject-citizens in a minoritarian and inferior position, it is necessary to obtain from them "a kind of active complicity."[9] This complicity is doubly paradoxical: firstly, because it links the powerful and "those who benefit least from the exercise of power," who are thus "led to participate, to a certain extent, in their own subjugation";[10] secondly, because this 'active complicity' only serves to ensure effectively the passivity of the majority. In committed novels, this narrative production appears essential to this voluntary submission.

This is why the hegemonic production of stories by the state and its agents aims to terrify its readers: it presents an imminent danger that demands urgent response. Thus, the scenarios developed by the dominant class have as their "ultimate goal . . . not so much the annihilation of the enemy as its mythical construction," as Christian Salmon notes.[11] The purpose of these false narratives is to create a horizon of expectation, narrative as well as political. They warrant, and thereby make logical and desirable, the repressive policies pursued by the state's authorities. It is in their name that certain decisions are taken, no matter how contrary to tradition or the law: the arrests of trade union leaders, expelling or even assassinating activists in the United States, extending military service, suppressing any form of strike action or protest in France—all this is done in full view of the population. Moreover, if these violent and illegal actions do not offend public opinion, it is because the even more violent if not downright shocking stories with which the public are continually bombarded make them seem necessary and therefore entirely justified.

The hegemonizing influence of the thrillers created by the dominant class is inseparable from the media power they have at their disposal. The mass dissemination of such stories is in fact an indispensable condition that shapes the political expectations of the American and French publics. The mainstream press, as staged in the committed novel, has the power to impose a fixed and deceptive language that articulates dominant public thought because it is shaped by the ideology of the dominant class. It also molds its readers' perception of the world with deliberately misleading stories: be they true or false, the stories disseminated by mainstream media always reinforce the established order. For instance, the news headline "LENIN SHOT BY TROTSKY IN DRUNKEN BRAWL"[12] is probably one of the most blatant media lies featured in the novels under consideration.[13] The mainstream press distorts the facts and sometimes simply invents them.

In *Le Monde réel*, the newspaper *Le Petit Républicain* uses the same tactic, exonerating those responsible for wrongdoing and blaming the strikers. When fires break out in the taxi company's garages, the chief investigator raises the possibility that "the culprits are to be found among the drivers, hired every day since work has resumed"[14]—an interpretation that does not suit the company bosses. The fiction machine is immediately set in motion, and the printed version conforms with the bosses' interests in every respect: "The *Petit Républicain* decided between the options of the day before: It opted for the missing striker. Only he could be the perpetrator of the attacks; look for the person who benefits from the crime."[15] Fully fictional characters, protagonists of stories manufactured by official power-holders, appear and disappear to suit narrative and political needs. The mainstream press is presented as a disinformation factory.

Dominant narrative production, as seen through the lens of the committed novel, serves not to *explain* the real world, not even in a biased way, but rather to create what Christian Salmon calls a fully formed "counter-reality": it aims to build "a new virtual universe, an enchanted kingdom populated by heroes and anti-heroes into which the citizen-actor is invited to enter,"[16] full of imaginary dangers, troubling specters, and heroic saviors. All dominant narratives are based on dichotomies, which coincide with moral and axiological oppositions, such as barbaric Germans versus virtuous Americans, good workers versus bad strikers, true patriots versus deceitful traitors, or acceptable Social Democrats versus intolerable Marxists. Mainstream narratives are quick to transpose the confrontation between the two opposing camps onto this axiological terrain. The characterization of the antagonistic forces is no longer dependent on the situation but is fixed by reference to definitive values. Moreover, these dominant stories are not illustrations of an explicit (political) thesis *about* the world but rather present themselves as simple accounts of reality as such, that is, as accounts in which ideology or the attempt to cajole the reader plays no part. Novels never disguise their fictional status—official storytelling, on the other hand, as it is presented in Dos Passos's and Aragon's novels, seeks to impose a false view of reality while pretending to be a true factual narrative.

Combined with widespread media dissemination, its narrative mechanisms, extremely simple insofar as they favor immediate and unquestioning endorsement, thus ensure that dominant storytelling monopolizes the public spaces staged by Aragon and Dos Passos. The novelists portray the "cultural hegemony"[17] of the powerful, that is to say, the cultural and ideological domination of the ruling class, as theorized by Antonio Gramsci. Relying on such effective means of dissemination as schools, mass media, and popular culture, the 'enemies' have succeeded in imposing a uniform and univocal narrative hegemony, shaping the perceptions and opinions of French and American societies. The monopoly on legitimate violence held by the state is coupled with a narrative monopoly, the repressive power with a prescriptive power, the exercise of force with obtaining consent. It is this prerogative, typical of all narration, that Yves Citton calls "scénarisation":

> Telling a story to someone not only means articulating certain representations of actions according to certain types of sequences; rather it also leads to the conduct of the listener, according to these articulations and sequences. By staging the actions of the (fictional) characters in my story, I contribute—more or less effectively, more or less marginally—to scripting the behavior of the (real) people to whom I address my story.[18]

Yet the insistence of Dos Passos and Aragon on showcasing the formidable power of official storytelling does not just serve a denunciatory purpose. It also aims to convince the reader of the need to reappropriate the prescriptive power of narrative activity, as illustrated by their very plots. Staging the influence of hostile official stories also means staging the need to develop equally effective narratives that, rather than maintaining established order, would help undermine it.

Inventing New Stories

What is at stake here is the opposition between dominant narratives and narratives that are different in content and form—in other words, developing left-wing storytelling, which (Dos Passos and Aragon hoped) would have the same impact and opinion-shaping power as its conservative counterpart. In an era of proliferating narratives and the development of technologies that allow for their widespread dissemination, political struggle necessarily involves a narrative struggle too.

Insofar as they write novels—and not essays or journalistic articles—Aragon and Dos Passos also choose to tell stories, trusting in the powers of narration and fiction to exert political influence on their readers. By challenging the official storytelling monopoly, the committed novel undermines the foundations of the dominant narrative and makes another narrative heard, both in terms of its proposed interpretation of the world and in terms of the way in which it deploys said interpretation. The narrative enterprise is therefore not condemned as such, since "it is by no means wrong in itself to 'tell oneself stories': it all depends on what these stories tend towards."[19] Instead, the novels emphasize the need to distance themselves from the narratives disseminated by the various powers—political and economic—while at the same time exploiting the effectiveness of the very processes they censure.

The objective of committed fiction writing is thus analogous to the objectives of those it presents as its adversaries. Dos Passos's character Dick Savage, who becomes a protégé of the powerful and unscrupulous J. W. Moorehouse, notes, "Whether you like it or not, the molding of the public mind is one of the most important things that goes on in this country."[20] The author describes what he deems the mission of the "professional writer" in similar terms: "[He] discovers some aspect of the world and invents out of the speech of his time some particularly apt and original way of putting it down on paper. If the product is compelling, and important enough, *it molds and influences ways of thinking* to the point of changing and rebuilding the language, which is the mind of the group."[21] The propagandist and the novelist, therefore, have the same goal—namely, to influence and shape 'the mind of the group.' But whereas the former only aspires to ensure personal advantage by endorsing and helping maintain the status quo, the latter claims to strive for a more just political order. *USA* and *Le Monde réel* aim to substitute the dominant scripts of power with a counter-*scénarisation*.

Hence, along with the will to persuade there is the need to reconfigure the narrative enterprise: if the political ambition of these novels does not necessarily involve the wholesale renunciation of existing forms, it nevertheless implies a reflection on the practice of storytelling. Benoît Denis emphasizes the extent to which literary commitment leads to a reflexive return to literature itself: "If the question of commitment forms an integral part of aesthetic modernity, it is precisely because of the movement of generalized reflexivity that it induces. . . . The committed writer, however he may position himself, is always led to become the theorist of his practice."[22] Literary commitment is thus linked to literary experimentation: in its ambition to restore a perception of reality atrophied by discourse and habit and to question the order of things, commitment leads to a heightened interest in the radical potential of experimentation. Within the novel series considered in this chapter, dominant fictions provide numerous counter-models against which the committed fiction is conceived and developed.

What remains to be seen is how this is achieved and how a denunciation of a narrative model transforms into its productive reappropriation. How does committed fiction writing distinguish itself from what it designates as 'bad' stories, not only because they serve the 'wrong' side, but also because they rely on 'bad' narrative scripts?

Novels of the 'Real World'

The most obvious feature distinguishing 'good' stories from 'bad' is the former's commitment to fact as opposed to the latter's unacknowledged fictionality. Whereas official narratives create a world of myths and symbols, Aragon and Dos Passos write *as if* they refuse all simplification and schematization, in order to give us a brutal and stark rendering of reality. Of course, this 'real world' is a construct, whose composition and examination are framed by the novelists' own political convictions. The apparent erasure of mediation between the real world and the text is therefore a deliberate strategy, as Paul Ricœur suggests in *Temps et récit*: the illusion of "a story that seems to tell itself and let life speak" only testifies to "the subtlety of the rhetorical maneuvers"[23] behind which the author hides. The fact remains that Dos Passos and Aragon define their narratives by adherence to what they present as indisputable facts, pitting them against fictional invention. The committed novel is confrontational.

That is why it leaves little room for romance. Romance is largely absent from these texts, stifled by social conditions that appear to crush the spontaneity of erotic attraction. American romance thus carries little weight in the face of financial and social calculations and considerations. For the young upstart Moorehouse, the two heiresses Annabelle Strang and Gertrude Staple represent above all, if not exclusively, a means of climbing the social ladder: "Ward was very happy and decided he loved her very much,"[24] the text notes, once the family's objections have been overcome. Caught in the same social traps and deceptions, true love is nowhere to be found in *Le Monde réel* either: a surprising absence in the work of a novelist and poet who so often chose to write about it. One character, Catherine, correctly, if somewhat crudely, summarizes the situation in which upper-middle-class women are confined: "What do you want a woman to become, if not a worker? A kept woman [*une cocotte*], married or not."[25] There are neither romantic prospects nor opportunities for some form of escape. The task of literature, as performed by the committed novel, is not to entertain but rather to inform, not to evade but to confront the reality that only the dominant class has a vested interest in leaving obscured. This anticipates Sartre's assertion that "[t]he function of the writer is to make sure that no one can ignore the world and that no one can claim to be innocent of it."[26]

The refusal of committed novels to abstract themselves from reality is reinforced by a recurring tendency: the claim to reflect the complexity of reality leads these novels to multiply plots and fields of investigation, in order to explore various social milieus and various spaces. As mentioned earlier, dominant templates for political novels were often limited in scope, reduced as they were to the glorification of one side and the denigration of the other. Without completely abandoning this antagonistic structure, *Le Monde réel* and *USA* complicate it by introducing a multitude of stories, characters, and narrative detours. Meticulously exploring nations in upheaval, these series seem to strive to comprehend the whole of 'the real world,' as if no detail should escape them: "Everything must go in," Dos Passos insists.[27]

This ambition of the novel to capture a whole nation and an entire era is obviously overwhelming and disproportionate. Dos Passos's title reflects the trilogy's totalizing intention and the change of scale. "*Three Soldiers* and *Manhattan Transfer* had been single panels; now, somewhat as the Mexican painters felt compelled to paint their walls, I felt compelled to start on a narrative panorama to which I saw no end," he recalls.[28] Responding to the "effort to take in as much as possible of the broad field of the lives of these times,"[29] *USA* intends to measure itself against what Roland Barthes calls "the ubiquity of reality."[30] It aims to portray the collective life of the nation not through unifying symbols or through the fate of a representative character but in a more diverse, specific, and nuanced way. The plethora of characters strains the reader's attention. In addition to the dozen characters whose names punctuate the sequences of the American trilogy and the biographies of several great contemporary figures, many individuals gravitate around them—family, lifelong friends, and short-term acquaintances. "For Dos Passos, to tell a story is to add up,"[31] wrote Sartre of the man he considered "the greatest writer of [his] time."[32] But this addition concerns not only the traditional novelistic components such as characters and setting; it also applies to the narrative modes: the trilogy interweaves several plots but it also mixes different genres of prose-writing. Indeed, three nonfiction sections—"Newsreel," "Camera Eye," and the biographical sequences—are interspersed into the fictional plots. The simultaneity is not only rendered by the multiplication of plotlines: it applies to the generic setup of the novel itself. By the same token, Aragon's novel series multiplies the narrative threads, the cast of characters, and the narrative detours to dizzying effect. In *Les Beaux Quartiers*, plots proliferate as the story progresses, undermining the initial binary structure and the linear progression of the conflict between the two Barbentane brothers in which it originated. The novel is teeming with a growing network of additional characters: "Life is absurdly rich in people, in possibilities," observes a character.[33]

The profusion of plots, characters, and modes in *Le Monde réel* and *USA* helps to distinguish 'good' from 'bad' narratives: unlike the extreme simplification that reduces the world to a perfunctory set of values, the committed novel devotes sustained attention to the diversity of reality, to its abundance of possibilities and interpretations. The novel's depiction of reality does not seem to be filtered through any ideological lens. By continually exceeding what seems strictly necessary for narrative coherence and by multiplying the threads and characters, these novels unsettle the artistic logic of official propaganda narratives. Yet this proliferation, far from detracting from the argumentative logic of the novel's commitment, in fact enhances it. Not only does it distinguish committed narratives from their counters, but it also creates a type of fiction that reflects reality itself, without any apparent ideological slant.

In other words, the narratives of *USA* and *Le Monde réel* multiply the threads and narrative modes in apparent defiance of both narrative and political logic, thereby diffusing the linear progression into simultaneous abundance. They also multiply the obstacles between the political commitment they convey and its reception by the reader. Countering the formal oversimplification of official narratives, these novel series challenge the didactic monologism and narrative schematism that characterize 'bad' stories. The narrative choice to multiply and to complicate, as well as the nuances it inevitably produces, signals political and literary distrust in that which claims to be absolute and definitive, linear and unproblematic. What may be described as flaws from a purely artistic point of view is thus part of the political toolkit of committed novels. By multiplying characters and narrative forms, by incorporating all kinds of styles and discourses, Aragon and Dos Passos preclude the possibility of producing a single dogmatic discourse, thereby freeing their own narratives from any suspicion of authoritarianism. In this way, they undermine the narrative foundations of established order by opening up many narrative and political points of contention.

Democratic Novels?

The absence of a single didactic narrative authority overseeing this diffusion of viewpoints seems to imply the absence of an explicitly militant or accusatory discourse. The facts described are not filtered through a narrative voice that explains their meaning, causes, and consequences. The theoretical seems to have been eclipsed by the particular; similarly, the ideological has been eclipsed by the multitude of viewpoints and opinions, not all of which are equally justified or legitimate. The reader is confronted not with certainties to be accepted or contested but with disconcerting uncertainty. It is no longer possible to subscribe to the fiction of the novels, to suspend one's judgment completely through faith and voluntary submission: the novels force the reader to distance herself or himself from them.

The intricate narrative patterning of *USA* and *Le Monde réel* multiplies the blanks and gaps that unsettle the novel's coherence and linearity. Both series resemble complex jigsaw puzzles whose pieces have been deliberately scattered over several thousand pages. This very uncertainty created by the novels compels the reader to make a special interpretive effort by actively engaging in the social investigation performed by the novel series. Of course, everything is done to steer the investigation in a certain direction, and it is unlikely that these works could be interpreted as saying the opposite of what their authors intended—but the fact remains that the reader's collaboration is absolutely required for the development of the argument. It is therefore by creating distance between reader and text that the novels seek to enable his/her self-conscious commitment. By multiplying narrative levels and repeatedly breaking the realistic illusion, Dos Passos and Aragon make interpretative labor the precondition for literary commitment. In other words, the literary and political agenda of *USA* and *Le Monde réel* is to disrupt narrative order in order to create more opportunities for readerly involvement.

By enlisting the reader's participation, the committed novel is not content to offer a mere reflection of the social world. Rather, it involves the reader in the critical deciphering of the social reality it purports only to portray. To put it another way: the narrative complications mentioned above compel the reader to become actively involved in piecing the narrative together. Confronted with a multitude of scattered and isolated elements, some of which constitute essential pieces of the puzzle, the reader must collect them, connect them, and interpret them while reading. However, this principle of reading-as-interpretation calls into question the very notion of novelistic illusion. Readers of committed novels must learn to doubt before entering into a new type of (radical) political belief—they must learn to question 'the obvious' before recognizing the very appearance of 'obviousness' as a rhetorical construction. Reading thus becomes an experiment in the process of interpretation itself—based on both the disruption of linear reading and the realistic illusion. *USA* and *Le Monde réel* shape narratives that are immediately and structurally engaging: what seemed to be an obstacle to reading turns out to be an invitation to engage.

The decision to constitute the position of the reader as that of an active interpreter—along with the foregrounding of procedural argument rather than blunt assertion, of exchange rather than imposition—contributes to the sense that committed novels aim to call into being a world shared between the figures of the author and the reader in which the power of reasoning trumps mere coercion. Thus, we could say that Dos Passos's and Aragon's novel series are political novels not so much in an overtly militant sense as in a structural sense. In contrast to the societies staged in the texts and the absence of overt politics in them, the fictional space is the privileged site where politics can be deployed. The committed novel, instead of striving to impart knowledge, shatters illusions. The experiments that marked the early works of Dos Passos and Aragon and that paved the way to narrative dispersion—to the play of perspectives and the technique of montage—are invested with a political function: novel-writing, by enabling political engagement through critical distance and the renewed exercise of a radically democratic deliberative discourse.

In the very deployment of authoritarian narrative strategies, dominant storytelling substitutes the dialogic space of the political with the monological space of the ideological. "There are three specifically totalitarian elements that are proper to any ideology: the claim to explain everything, the emancipation from reality, the coherence that exists nowhere in the realm of reality," maintains Hannah Arendt in her seminal analysis of totalitarian systems.[34] Dominant storytelling pursues these three ambitions.[35] As part of a covert ideological propaganda, it experiments with a power relationship that has nothing democratic about it. *USA* and *Le Monde réel* are written, narratively and politically, against this dominant model, elaborating within them a political relationship that is radically different from that imposed by dominant storytelling. The enterprise of conviction renounces authoritarian intimidation and creates the conditions for critical interpretation; at the same time, it opens up the space—and the uncertainty—necessary for the deployment of politics. The tacit goal of the dominant fiction to achieve what Salmon calls "a less deliberative democracy"[36] is countered by the restoration of the democratic contract.

It is precisely in this requirement for readers' active collaboration that *USA* and *Le Monde réel*, and committed novels in general, become structurally political. Hannah Arendt defines politics as an "in-between space" (*Zwischenraum*) of "relating" (*Verknüpfung*)[37] in which both the "faculty of judging" (*Urteilskraft*) and "free speech" (*freie Rede*)[38] are fully exercised. It is this faculty of judging that the committed novel solicits through the very blanks it multiplies, and it is this speech freed from conventional and manipulative discourse that it produces. Its modes of operation and expression therefore make it an inherently political space. Renouncing a conventional authoritarian omniscient narrator, and thereby rejecting what Arendt calls "speech in the form of command and listening in the form of obedience,"[39] the politically engaged novel of the 1930s is based on collaborative engagement. Through the fragmentation of narrative threads, through montage, through the destruction of the realistic illusion, and the rejection of didactic certainties, it invites its reader to question it actively rather than passively trust it. In Arendt's terms, the "despotic power" of an omnipotent author over a submissive reader is replaced by "political power," which entails a collaborative relationship between reasoning equals.[40]

In the cases of Dos Passos and Aragon, the committed novel is animated by the narrative desire to offer a counter-model to hegemonic fictions—and indeed, in my understanding of the genre, the exposure of dominant fictions is foundational to the committed novel as such. In other words, the language and fictions deployed in the name of authority provide so many models against which committed fiction is developed. While they only rarely stage overt class struggle, which tends to end in defeat for the oppressed, *USA* and *Le Monde réel* fully engage in a *struggle of narratives*, which must replace the scripts produced by power with equally effective counter-scripts. They aim to reappropriate the narrative instruments powerfully misused by their political adversaries and turn them against those adversaries. What is at stake in the committed novel is not the attempt to uphold aesthetic singularity as a principled opposition to the opportunism of majority storytelling: winning the struggle of narratives, in the committed novel, sometimes appears even more pressing than the class struggle itself. In elaborating the idea of the *committed novel* through two major examples, this chapter has sought to help dispel the skepticism that often meets explicitly political literature by reintroducing the problematic of commitment into literary analysis itself: this type of inquiry encourages us to shift attention away from a 'political history of literature'—that is, from the study of writers' biographical involvement in the social and political arena of their time—to an analysis of authorial choices and modes of reading that are implied by the gesture of commitment within literature. This shift makes it possible to define literary commitment more precisely, both in terms of the portrayal of politics in a given literary work and in terms of transforming the literary work into a form of political argumentation sui generis. The political ambitions of literary writing can only be understood through the relationship between these two impulses.

Notes

1 Jacques Rancière, *La Mésentente: politique et philosophie* (Paris: Galilée, 1995), 12.

2 See Aurore Peyroles, *Roman et engagement: le laboratoire des années 1930* (Paris: Classiques Garnier, 2015).

3 Benoît Denis, *Littérature et engagement: de Pascal à Sartre* (Paris: Éditions du Seuil, 2000), 228. The quotations from Francophone texts were all translated by the author of this chapter.

4 Ibid., 25.

5 Christian Salmon, *Storytelling: la machine à fabriquer des histoires et à formater les esprits* (Paris: La Découverte, 2008), 166.

6 John Dos Passos, "Introductory Note to *The 42nd Parallel*," in *John Dos Passos: The Major Non Fictional Prose*, ed. Donald Pizer (Detroit: Wayne State University Press, 1988 [1932]), 177–85, here 179.

7   John Dos Passos, *USA* (London: Penguin Classics, 2001 [1930–6]), 613.
8   See Pierre Bourdieu, *Pouvoir et langage symbolique* (Paris: Éditions du Seuil, 2001).
9   John B. Thompson, "Préface," in Pierre Bourdieu, *Langage et pouvoir symbolique* (Paris: Éditions du Seuil, 2001), 7–82, here 40.
10 Ibid.
11 Salmon, *Storytelling*, 166.
12 Dos Passos, *USA*, 618.
13 According to the International Socialist Voice website, "LENIN SHOT BY TROTSKY IN DRUNKEN BRAWL" was a headline in the *Chicago Tribune* in the summer of 1919, see http://www.socialistparty.net/pub/pages/international/intrvoice07-10-09/5.html, August 1, 2022.
14 Louis Aragon, *Les Cloches de Bâle* (Paris: Gallimard, 1997 [1934]), 953.
15 Ibid.
16 Salmon, *Storytelling*, 134.
17 Antonio Gramsci, *Quaderni del carcere* (Torino: Einaudi, 1975 [1948]), 866.
18 Yves Citton, *Mythocratie: Storytelling et imaginaire de gauche* (Paris: Éditions Amsterdam, 2010), 12.
19 Ibid., 77.
20 Dos Passos, *USA*, 1145.
21 John Dos Passos, "The Writer as Technician," in *John Dos Passos: The Major Non Fictional Prose*, ed. Donald Pizer (Detroit: Wayne State University Press, 1988 [1935]), 80–1, here 81. Emphasis in original.
22 Denis, *Littérature et engagement*, 108.
23 Paul Ricœur, *Temps et récit* (Paris: Éditions du Seuil, 1991 [1983]), 291.
24 Dos Passos, *USA*, 220.
25 Aragon, *Les Cloches de Bâle*, 785.
26 Jean-Paul Sartre, *Qu'est-ce que la littérature?* (Paris: Gallimard, 2008 [1947]), 30.
27 Dos Passos, "What Makes a Novelist," in *John Dos Passos: The Major Nonfictional Prose*, ed. Donald Pizer (Detroit: Wayne State University Press, 1988 [1935]), 272.
28 John Dos Passos, *The Best Times: An Informal Memoir* (New York: New American Library, 1966), 172.
29 Dos Passos, "Introductory Note," 179.
30 Roland Barthes, *Le Degré zéro de l'écriture* (Paris: Éditions du Seuil, 1972), 66.
31 Jean-Paul Sartre, *Critiques littéraires* (Paris: Gallimard, 2000 [1938]), 17.
32 Ibid., 24.
33 Louis Aragon, *Les Beaux Quartiers* (Paris: Gallimard, 2000 [1936]), 304.

34 Hannah Arendt, *The Origins of Totalitarianism* (New York: Harcourt, 1973 [1951]), 219.
35 See Susan Rubin Suleiman, *Authoritarian Fictions: The Ideological Novel as a Literary Genre* (Princeton: Princeton University Press, 2006).
36 Salmon, *Storytelling*, 129.
37 Hannah Arendt, "Einführung in die Politik," in *Was ist Politik?: Fragmente aus dem Nachlaß*, ed. Ursula Ludz (Munich: Piper Verlag, 1993), 28–135, here 42.
38 Ibid., 52.
39 Ibid., 78.
40 Ibid., 75.

6

Moscow, 1934–Yan'an, 1942

The Manifesto as Lived Experience

Steven S. Lee

Western modernism of the early twentieth century offers a well-trodden reference point for the convergence of politics and literature, revolution and aesthetics. For Perry Anderson, the "imaginative proximity of social revolution" was one of three decisive coordinates (along with new technologies and an academism against which artists and writers could define themselves) overdetermining the modernist conjuncture.[1] However, this conjuncture did not last: as Anderson notes, after the Second World War, "the image or hope of revolution faded away in the West. The onset of the Cold War, and the Sovietization of Eastern Europe, cancelled any realistic prospect of a socialist overthrow of advanced capitalism, for a whole historical period."[2] Western attempts to assert otherwise—most notably in the 1960s, with figures like Jean-Luc Godard drawing inspiration from Mao Zedong's Cultural Revolution—instead signified "no more than the arrival of a long-overdue permissive consumerism."[3] The various exhibits, conferences, and other such events commemorating the 1917 centenary largely underscored revolution's even sorrier fate today: now ever more distant from us, revolution and its (sometimes thrilling, often oppressive) aftermath have been stripped of ideological content, while the aesthetic forms emerging from revolution have become objects to fetishize and commodify.

And so what is left to be gained from the intersection of revolution and aesthetics? The usual coordinates used to debate this subject—art versus propaganda, modernism versus (socialist) realism, Bertolt Brecht versus Georg Lukács—fail to register just how impotent the revolutions of the twentieth century seem from the vantage of our post-post-Cold War present. Yet given how precarious and crisis ridden this present is, it would be rash simply to eulogize the various revolutionary aesthetic projects of the twentieth century, which might yet point to political alternatives. Instead, recent work has been done to revive our grasp of these projects by foregrounding the affective charge generated by a wide range of leftist art and writing. For instance, Christina Kiaer finds in Aleksandr Deineka's 1930s paintings a "lyrical strand of Socialist Realism" that crossed "private emotion and publicly oriented feeling to create a shared visual language of socialism."[4] Kiaer moves beyond modernism versus realism via an overriding socialist feeling that hints at lost alternatives to contemporary commodity culture.

With a similar aim in mind, my chapter also blurs the boundaries between modernism and socialist realism—not through a focus on affect, but rather by thinking about some of the founding documents of socialist realism as manifestos. The manifesto, I argue, provides an enduring example of the political uses of literature; it points to a genealogy of revolutionary literature not so beholden to the interwar West. Here I will be building on Martin Puchner's use of the manifesto genre to connect art and revolution, specifically his connection of Karl Marx and Friedrich Engels's *Communist Manifesto* (1848) to a variety of avant-gardist manifestos. Puchner's *Poetry of the Revolution* has been so seminal in part because of the spatial and historical dispersion of the manifesto genre, spanning Italian and Russian futurism in the early 1900s, Latin American creationism in the 1920s, and *TDR*'s manifesto issues in the 1970s and 1980s. Throughout, Puchner's emphasis is less on literary form than on how these texts act upon the world. However, and for good reason, he pulls back from tracking this genre across what I see as the natural inheritors of the Marxist/avant-gardist manifesto, namely, the Soviet Union under Stalin and China under Mao. This is a glaring omission given the contemporary world system's tilt toward China,[5] and what I hope to show is how, in the most prominent vestige of international socialism and increasingly dominant center of global capitalism, the manifesto genre points to an enduring revolutionary aesthetic that carries both official weight and radical potential. Perhaps most concretely, it offers a model of representation that levels the hierarchies separating author and subject, artist and audience, 'modern' West and 'exotic' East—in short, an inclusive cultural practice best understood as neither modernist nor socialist realist, but as part of the still-unfolding manifesto genre.

Again, Puchner has good reason not to engage much with the Soviet Union or China, given his emphasis on theatricality: the fact that, upon writing, the 1848 *Communist Manifesto* and twentieth-century avant-gardist manifestos lacked authority. Instead, the manifesto is self-authorizing: the *Communist Manifesto* is a history of revolution that also tries to create history—"history *as* revolution."[6] It does not simply address, but actively seeks to forge "the proletariat" by telling them to unite.[7] That is, the manifesto's claim to authority rests on a revolution that has not yet happened, a history that has not yet been enacted. More specifically, central to Puchner's definition of the manifesto is a tension between unauthorized theatrical acts (as one might find on a theatrical stage) and performative speech acts, as defined by John Austin—speech able to project authority and act on the world by following accepted conventions. As Puchner writes:

> Speech acts must battle and conquer the threat of theatricality in order to become speech acts. Such a battle between theatricality and performativity is nowhere as visible as in the manifesto. Saying that the manifesto is theatrical means that its speech act occurs in an unauthorized and unauthorizing context; the theater, for Austin, is the paradigm for such an unauthorized context. However, the manifesto does not rest comfortably in this unauthorized space; indeed, it tries to exorcise its own theatricality by borrowing from an authority it will have obtained in the future. All manifestos are intertwined with the theatrical, driven by it and troubled by it, and they all seek to turn the theater into a source of authority.[8]

Implicit here is the possibility that once a manifesto ceases to be theatrical and gains authority—once the anticipated political and/or aesthetic revolution occurs and the performative purges the theatrical—the manifesto loses relevance or perhaps even ceases to be a manifesto. For Puchner the genre requires (or at least is most compelling when it features) an unresolved, recurring tension between the theatrical and performative, between texts that are ends in themselves and those that are means to ends.[9] This seems to be why the operations of specific communist parties and regimes fall beyond his purview. Instead, his coverage of the Soviet Union stops with Russian futurists—correctly depicted as embattled vis-à-vis the "manifestos and propaganda controlled by the emerging [Soviet] state"[10]—while his coverage of China stops with the Chinese liberal Hu Shi rather than Hu's Peking University colleagues Chen Duxiu and Li Dazhao, cofounders of the CCP.[11]

However, state socialism never ceased to be theatrical, as seen, for instance, in Alexei Yurchak's study of late Soviet culture. Interestingly, Yurchak, also drawing from Austin, notes how, even in official settings, performative utterances can advance the non-authorized, flexible meanings that Puchner associates with the theatrical. Specifically, Yurchak shows how Soviet society's performative dimension (e.g., the act of voting in a fixed election coupled with the context and conventions leading one to perform this ritual) overshadowed literal, "constative" meanings (e.g., the person for whom one was voting, guaranteed to win), rendering the latter "open-ended, indeterminate, or simply irrelevant."[12] This does not mean that the performative dimension was simply antistate or antisocialist; instead, it allowed the "last Soviet generation" to "preserve the possibilities, promises, positive ideals, and ethical values of the system while avoiding the negative and oppressive constraints within which these [were] articulated."[13] Yurchak thus uses the performative to move beyond the binaries typically applied to state socialism—for instance, the idea that Soviet subjects were either dissidents or conformists, pro-Soviet or pro-Western, authentic-selves or masked-selves. To this series we can add Puchner's opposition of the performative and theatrical, and suggest that in the realms of really existing socialism, the manifesto genre not only flourished but became lived experience.[14]

Moscow, 1934

This becomes evident by turning to the 1930s establishment of socialist realism, typically associated with Stalin's imperative that writers become 'engineers of the human soul.' At its official launch during the 1934 Soviet Writers' Congress, Bolshevik official Andrei Zhdanov elaborated in his keynote speech that such engineering entailed "knowing life so as to be able to depict it truthfully in works of art, not to depict it in a dead, scholastic way, not simply as 'objective reality,' but to depict reality in its revolutionary development."[15] Here Zhdanov, who would become an instrumental figure for both Stalinist terror and campaigns against cultural 'formalism,' lends credence to the common understanding of socialist realism as depicting life not as it is, but as it should be, that is, outright lies serving an authoritarian state. However, coming at the heels of a state-sanctioned Cultural Revolution (1928–32), which had elevated doctrinaire "proletarian" artists and writers over their avant-gardist counterparts, the Soviet-wide Writers' Union inaugurated by the Congress purportedly transcended sectarianism and signaled a more ecumenical approach to literature.[16] Accordingly, the lens provided by Puchner makes it possible to see Zhdanov's speech as future oriented rather than fixed in stone. Just as Marx and Engels's *Communist Manifesto* both "theoretically constructs" and "identifies with" a unified proletariat that does not yet exist—a class *in* itself that does not yet speak *for* itself[17]—Zhdanov's "reality in its revolutionary development" pushes writers to depict a revolution that has not yet been completed. They are to help enact this revolution through their writing, just as the *Communist Manifesto* tries to write its own history—namely "the history of the future"[18] in which everything described in the manifesto will have come to pass.[19]

The Writers' Congress specifically provided a glimpse of how, in this future to come, literature would be stripped of social and national hierarchies—as became evident in the Congress's reimagining of world literature and world literary history. Elaborating on Marx and Engels's famous claim that "from the numerous national and local literatures, there arises a world literature,"[20] Puchner describes the *Manifesto* as a new, future-oriented literary model, de-emphasizing itself as an original text and emphasizing instead "total translatability."[21] The Writers' Congress, in contrast, sought to reconceptualize *past* literary forms from the perspective of the liberated future. After declaring the proletariat the "sole heir of all that is best in the treasury of world literature,"[22] Zhdanov defined socialist realism as entailing an emphasis on "real life."[23] This in turn denoted

> a rupture with romanticism of the old type, which depicted a non-existent life and non-existent heroes, leading the reader away from the antagonisms and oppression of real life into a world of the impossible, into a world of utopian dreams. Our literature, which stands with both feet firmly planted on a materialist basis, cannot be hostile to romanticism, but it must be a romanticism of a new type, revolutionary romanticism.[24]

As Katerina Clark has elaborated, revolutionary romanticism meant an emphasis on the monumental and heroic; socialist realism thus combined "what hitherto seemed uncombinable: verisimilitude and mythicization."[25] However, this combination was not arbitrary, but drew from an unorthodox understanding of world literary history, combining realism, romanticism, folklore, and myth in a way that troubled the boundaries of literature itself. Maxim Gorky made this clear in his own keynote speech at the Congress, immediately following Zhdanov's:

> Myth is invention. To invent means to extract from the sum of a given reality its cardinal idea and embody it in imagery—that is how we got realism. But if to the idea extracted from the given reality we add—completing the idea, by the logic of hypothesis—the desired, the possible, and thus supplement the image, we obtain that romanticism which is at the basis of myth and is highly beneficial in that it tends to provoke a revolutionary attitude to reality, an attitude that changes the world in a practical way.[26]

Thus, myth yielded realism; combining this with the desired and possible yielded revolutionary, transformative romanticism hearkening back to myth. Unseating familiar notions of literary progression—romanticism giving way to realism giving way to modernism—here Gorky presents myth as cutting across modernity and pre-modernity. For him, myth, folklore, and "the people's oral tradition [*ustnoe tvorchestvo naroda*]" had always had a material basis since they were reflections "of the phenomena of nature, of the struggle with nature and of social life."²⁷ As examples, he cites ancient Greek and Russian medieval epics as well as Russian folktales, all harmoniously blending "reason and intuition, thought and feeling" in ways only possible when a "creator directly participates in the work of creating realities, in the struggle for the renovation of life."²⁸ Accordingly, if socialist realism centered positive heroes, for Gorky "the most profound and vivid, artistically perfect types of heroes were created by folklore, the oral tradition of the toiling people."²⁹

Socialist realism thus pointed to a world literature modeled not on the translatability and circulation of the *Communist Manifesto*, but on precapitalist forms that from the standpoint of a liberated, proletarian society were retrospectively granted revolutionary significance.³⁰ This helps to explain one of the most striking features of the Congress, as noted by Kathryn Schild: the fact that it served not just to inaugurate socialist realism but also to showcase Soviet minority literatures. Gorky asserted in his speech that Russian writers "obviously have no right to ignore the literary creation of the national minorities simply because there are more of us than of them," and despite his implicit Russo-centrism here, the majority of the almost 600 delegates belonged to minority groups. Gorky then quoted at length a letter from a Tatar writer who decried being treated like an "ethnographical exhibit" that drew interest only from "lovers of the exotic and the rare in the big cities."³¹ The Congress thus took a stand against modernist exoticism, which Soviet writers and artists had long come to associate with Western imperialism—in response, as I have shown elsewhere, experimenting with both anti-imperialist exoticisms and explicitly anti-exotic depictions of non-Western cultures.³² Clearly, however, more progress was needed: the speech by Emi Siao (Xiao San), one of two delegates from China, critiqued Soviet films and stories that still depicted the Chinese as opium smokers, the men with queues, and the women with small feet, calling this "exotica of the worst type." He also chided delegates for gawking, during a break between sessions, at the feet of the other Chinese delegate, Hu Lanqi.³³ Another decentering presence was the formerly impoverished Dagestani poet Suleiman Stal'skii, dressed in national costume and performing an *ashug* song and chant that concluded:

V bol'shoi prostor nagornykh stran
Prevetnyi znak ashugu dan.
I vot ia, Stal'skii Suleiman,
Na slavnyi s"ezd pevtsov prishel.

[Going to] the great expanse of mountainous lands
A sign of greeting is given to the *ashug* [poet-singer]
And so I, Stal'skii Suleiman,
Have come to this glorious congress of singers.³⁴

This staid Russian translation, which was read immediately after Stal'skii's chant, captures the conventions of the *ashug* form: three rhyming lines followed by a fourth line which is repeated in each stanza, slightly changing with every appearance.[35] In this closing stanza the Dagestani periphery blurs together with the Muscovite center—Stal'skii's destination rather than departure point recast as a mountainous expanse. The Congress of Writers becomes instead a congress of *ashug* singers like him. In short, Stal'skii's chant advanced Gorky's expansive understanding of socialist realism as incorporating minority cultures and oral traditions. Stal'skii—later declared a "Homer of the 20th Century" by Gorky[36]—showed how the alignment of socialist realism and myth could valorize minority cultures in the present rather than relegate them to the past.

While almost everything at the Congress was authorized in advance (Siao's critique of his fellow delegates providing one exception), Stal'skii also affirmed the event's theatrical quality: specifically, it was a theatrical performance that purported to solve once and for all the problem of getting a class *in* itself to speak *for* itself. I draw here from Petre Petrov, who describes the Congress as a carefully managed show in which the authors became the audience and their subjects took the stage:

> At intervals throughout the writers' debates, organized groups of common folk from various walks of life proceeded down the aisle of the magnificent Hall of Columns and ascended the podium. These were the "delegates without membership cards," as Boris Pasternak referred to them: industrial workers, representatives of kolkhoz collectives, Young Pioneers, soldiers, scientists. . . . All of them made, essentially, the same demand: "Show us." In different voices, the people's representatives were demanding that they be represented (*darstellt*). In the voice of comrade Bratanovskii, speaking on behalf of proletarian authors of technical literature: "Our collective order to you, comrade writers, is: get closer to the industry worker, depicting him not only at the machine, but also showing his fight for acquiring high technical qualification, for absorbing all achievements of world culture."[37]

In Petrov's account, life appeared to enter the Congress. These ostensibly unofficial participants became part of the text of the Congress, demanding to be represented by authors in the sense of *darstellen*, artistic representation. Petrov adds, however, that these participants also represented themselves—in the sense of *vertreten*, political representation—via "pure self-exhibition"[38] which succeeded in possessing and affecting the audience of authors, many of whom were moved to tears. In effect, this unseated the author's supposedly privileged position vis-à-vis those represented (*dargestellt*). The revolutionary class *in* itself—including workers, peasant, women, minorities[39]—was already speaking *for* itself. The author's task was simply to show the immanent truth emerging from the people themselves. According to Petrov, this required not empirical investigation, but an emotional openness to the new coming-to-be called socialism—"to be organically one with the Soviet style of life"[40]—which would yield a new way of seeing and, thus, representing. In this way, socialist realism resolved the *darstellen/vertreten* distinction found in Marx's *Eighteenth Brumaire of Louis Bonaparte* and famously highlighted by Gayatri Spivak. The key here was not naive faith in a speaking subaltern but a state of being in which the liberation of subalterns was assured by socialism. In response, the writer was, in Petrov's words, "to cease 'representing' (in the sense of *darstellen*) and begin the movement of showing."[41] Thus situated on the new ontological ground of Soviet socialism, the role of the author was greatly diminished, foreshadowing the fact that with the subsequent onset of Stalinist terror, many (including several who attended the Congress) would simply cease to be present.

In sum, the two-week Congress was a living manifesto that upended literary hierarchies and shattered the boundaries separating art and life. This does not change the fact that socialist realism was a Stalinist institution that oppressed countless writers and artists. After Nikita Khrushchev's 1956 secret speech, it increasingly became a historical curiosity even in the USSR.[42] Nonetheless, at its inception we find a remarkably inclusive instance of words becoming action via an anticapitalist ontology that is now all but lost to us. Present-day efforts to reproduce merely the form of revolutionary total art (e.g., Ilya Khrzhanovsky's *Dau* project or Soviet avant-garde exhibits) absent from this ontological content can only affirm what we already know: our ever-growing distance from social revolution.

Yan'an, 1942

This distance is less clear in countries that are still nominally socialist, most notably China, where revolutionary aesthetics maintain their historical imprimatur. To be sure, the continued appearance of revolutionary slogans and symbols seems cynically at odds with the country's capitalist hyperdevelopment. However, this gap reopens the specter of theatricality as discussed by Puchner: that is, though authorized by the state, revolutionary aesthetics in China today have the potential to break free from state aims and gesture to a still-unrealized socialist revolution. Here I am building on Xiaomei Chen's argument that in contemporary China, propaganda performances as well as the *Communist Manifesto* itself serve to monumentalize the CCP but also have the potential to highlight the country's "problematic and disappointing reality."[43] Chen explicitly expands Puchner's purview by describing the *Communist Manifesto*'s peculiar flexibility in China, where "after Mao's death, cultural officials and performing artists collaborated on and transformed, without seemingly obvious tensions, the Maoist socialist reading of the *Manifesto* into a postsocialist revisionist imagining."⁴⁴ In short, the manifesto genre seems to be alive and well in China: the rest of this chapter will show how the really existing manifesto continued its run from the Soviet Union of the Stalinist 1930s to China of the 1940s, specifically Mao Zedong's 1942 Yan'an Conference on Literature and Art, and from there I will leap to the present day via Xi Jinping's 2014 Beijing Forum on Literature and Art.

Puchner's manifesto framework makes it possible to connect Moscow 1934 and Yan'an 1942, which, surprisingly, tend not to be discussed in tandem. Though Soviet culture had long inspired several among the Chinese left, Mao's *Talks at the Yan'an Conference on Literature and Art* emphasized the need to draw from local cultures and center the masses. As one might expect given Moscow's vexed record with the CCP (most famously, the directive to ally with the Guomindang, which then nearly annihilated the CCP in 1927), he urged caution about foreign models and took aim at devotees of the May Fourth movement to modernize Chinese culture—especially those among them embracing 'enlightened,' European styles. Accordingly, his brief mention of "proletarian realism" instead of socialist realism has been taken as evidence that he was unfamiliar with recent Soviet literary developments.⁴⁵ He did mention one influential Soviet novel, but this is because its emphasis on a "small guerrilla band" offered a model for "serving the masses in the base areas," with little concern for "old world readers."⁴⁶ In short, one of the premises of the Talks was a critique of Eurocentrism and its imperialist underpinnings.⁴⁷

Though lacking the vivid theatrical performances of the Soviet Writers' Congress, the Yan'an Talks better fit Puchner's notion of the manifesto given the CCP's tenuous position at the time: forced to this remote city in the Northwest, living in loess caves, battling both the Guomindang and the Japanese. Unlike Zhdanov and Gorky, Mao needed to project an authority that was yet to come:⁴⁸ like the *Communist Manifesto*, the Talks endeavored not just to describe but to create—specifically, a new culture marked by a "unity of politics and art, a unity of content and form, a unity of revolutionary political content and the highest artistic form possible."⁴⁹ Mao went on to hint that this envisioned unity would exceed the manifesto genre itself:

> For someone to perform a task solely on the basis of his motives and not bother about its effect is equivalent to a doctor only being concerned with making out prescriptions and not caring whether his patients die as a result, or like a political party only being concerned with issuing manifestos and not bothering to see whether they are carried out or not; how is a position like this still correct?⁵⁰

If Puchner casts the manifesto as wavering between the performative and theatrical, here Mao seems to banish the latter in favor of verifiable action.

The Talks sought to inaugurate a "living Marxism-Leninism" not confined to the written page but "fully applicable in the life and struggles of the masses."[51] Intellectuals were to recognize that their "processed forms" were secondary and inferior to the "natural forms" of "popular life"[52]—namely, the "language of the masses,"[53] with their "budding literature and art (wall newspapers, murals, folk songs, folk tales, popular speech, and so on)."[54] Thus, writers and artists needed to learn the masses' "natural forms" so as to broaden their audiences; before they could educate the masses, they first needed to be educated by them.

Here Mao was grappling with the same problem of representation encountered both in the *Communist Manifesto* and the Soviet Writers' Congress: how get a class *in* itself to speak *for* itself. Just as at the Writers' Congress, this entailed the relegation of artists and writers vis-à-vis their audiences and the valorization of folk cultures as revolutionary. Again, Mao was critiquing urban transplants who had embraced European culture and, in many cases, had dismissed traditional Chinese culture as feudal remnants and the masses as irrational. As Shu-mei Shih notes, typically in such circles "it was only when Western modernists 'validated' Chinese aesthetics by appropriating it that Chinese culture was seen as having the capacity to be modern."[55] In contrast, Mao proposed that this culture itself could serve revolutionary, modernizing functions, without Western mediation—a valorization of folk cultures that curiously echoed the Soviet Writers' Congress. Indeed, despite Mao's seeming parochialism, debates about Stalin's call for culture to be 'national in form, socialist in content' had taken place in China from the 1920s on. However, Mao's Talks departed from the Congress by emphasizing empirical knowledge of the masses rather than an anticapitalist ontology—a simpler solution to the *darstellen/vertreten* tension, and therefore perhaps more portable and durable (able, for instance, to survive socialism's collapse). Intellectuals just needed to listen to the speaking subaltern, and one concrete effect of the Talks was that more artists and writers began incorporating folk cultures into their works.[56]

At the same time, Mao recognized the subaltern's limits, leaving room for representational and creative flexibility. He described the intellectuals' "processed forms" as superior to the masses' "natural forms," since the former were more effective at organizing and concentrating instances of everyday oppression. This made it possible to

> awaken and arouse the popular masses, urging them on to unity and struggle and to take part in transforming their environment. If there were no processed literature and art, but only literature and art in their natural form, it would be impossible to accomplish this task or at least to do it as powerfully and speedily.[57]

Thus, as Kang Liu notes, intellectuals were tasked not with "a simple, transparent representation of real life as a mimesis of unmediated reality," but rather a complicated process of "transcoding" crude, popular forms into "another ideological, textual form, which is also aesthetically more refined and polished."[58] A case in point can be found at the Lu Xun Art Academy, housed in a former Spanish mission on the outskirts of Yan'an and which had a Western orientation before 1942. David Holm describes how, after the Yan'an Conference and subsequent changes to the curriculum, the Academy combined elements of *yangge* (a "motley collection of songs, dances, and folk plays," often bearing sexual and religious undertones) with European-style "spoken drama" (*huaju*, which emerged in Shanghai during the May Fourth Movement and drew from Konstantin Stanislavsky).[59] The result was an eclectic repertoire of agitational performances performed by multiple, often touring troupes with up to 2,000 total participants—by Holm's count one in six of the region's public personnel.[60]

Mao's Talks thus yielded a new mass theater, or as Puchner puts it (describing futurist manifestos performed on stage), "the theatricality at work in all manifestos here returns to the actual stage and is allowed to develop its full force."[61] Indeed, Mao's Talks arguably provided a necessary precedent for Puchner. Upending notions of base determining superstructure (as he likewise did in his 1937 essay "On Contradiction"), Mao urged all writers and artists to produce works that could themselves claim historical agency, stating:

> Literature and art are subordinate to politics, and yet in turn exert enormous influence on it. Revolutionary literature and art are a part of the whole work of revolution.... If literature and art did not exist in even the broadest and most general sense, the revolution could not advance or win victory; it would be incorrect not to acknowledge this.[62]

The importance that Mao here grants to literature prefigures Puchner's account of a genre generating its own authority. In turn, Puchner draws from Louis Althusser's description of the manifesto as "not a text like others: it is a text which belongs to the world of ideological and political literature, which takes sides and a stand in that world. Better, a text that is an impassioned appeal for the political solution it heralds."[63] Althusser's debt to Maoism has been well established, but it would be speculative to suggest that Mao's engagement with the manifesto genre—again, his demand not just to issue but to carry out manifestos—also influenced Althusser.[64] What is clear, though, is that efforts to resolve the *Communist Manifesto*'s push-and-pull between the performative and theatrical, as well as the perennial task of representing (in both senses) the revolutionary class, persisted in China and the USSR alike.

The point here is not to retread the travels of radical tourists who, disillusioned with Western capitalism, sought revolution in a fetishized, red

East. Such journeys tended to turn a blind eye to the oppression that issued from such events as the Writers' Congress and the Yan'an Conference.⁶⁵ Accordingly, as alluded to near the start of this chapter, Anderson dismisses past efforts (for instance, in 1960s Paris) to revive modernism via "revolutionary tempests from the East."⁶⁶ With a generation having passed since the end of the Cold War's end—long enough for the emergence of a new Cold War, farcically devoid of ideological substance—these tempests from the past now seem purely theatrical, lacking any present authority or consequence. This makes it both remarkable and troubling that, in Beijing in 2014, Chinese president Xi Jinping convened his own Forum on Literature and Art, where he pressed "literature and art workers" to center and serve "the people" and to "carry forward the banner of the Socialist core value system"⁶⁷—the primary value being patriotism. Artists and writers were to reflect this system via a vivid, vigorous "lifelike manner" and were to employ "true-to-life images to tell people what they should affirm and praise, and what they must oppose and deny."⁶⁸ The result would be the attainment of quality, virtue, righteousness, and beauty. In short, Xi's speech was a straightforward endorsement of patriotism and realism, as well as a clear attempt to solidify his leadership by performing Mao's same role from Yan'an 1942. Curiously, Xi also echoed Stalin by calling artists and writers "engineers of the souls," a description not found in the Yan'an Talks, and yet there was obviously no sense in the 2014 speech of any Soviet-inspired anticapitalist ontology.⁶⁹ Instead, the point seemed to be to invoke the very heaviest hitters of state socialism, restoring to the manifesto genre a performative, authoritative dimension that seems utterly incongruous with the post-socialist present, but that in retrospect augured the heightened censorship and repression that we now see in Xi's China. However, situating his speech vis-à-vis past manifestos—1848, 1934, 1942— underscores the unwitting theatricality of the 2014 event. Pointing more to a revolutionary past rather than a revolutionary future, this theatricality opens the possibility that, as long as the CCP continues to stage this past, an international socialist horizon will remain latent in the new epicenter of global capital.⁷⁰

Notes

1 Perry Anderson, "Modernity and Revolution," *New Left Review* 144 (1984): 96–113, here 104.

2 Ibid., 107.

3 Ibid., 109.

4 Christina Kiaer, "Lyrical Socialist Realism," *October* 147 (Winter 2014): 56–77, here 60. Such work regears earlier connections made between the

Soviet avant-garde and socialist realism, most notably Boris Groys's influential argument that both shared a totalizing impulse.

5   However, Puchner's *The Written World* (New York: Random House, 2017) briefly notes how the *Communist Manifesto* was picked up by Mao, Ho Chi Minh, and Fidel Castro, see 268–70.

6   Martin Puchner, *Poetry of the Revolution: Marx, Manifestos, and the Avant-Gardes* (Princeton: Princeton University Press, 2005), 21. Emphasis in original.

7   Ibid., 31.

8   Ibid., 25.

9   See ibid., 262.

10 Ibid., 104.

11 Xiaomei Chen, *Staging Chinese Revolution* (New York: Columbia University Press, 2017), 8.

12 Alexei Yurchak, *Everything Was Forever, Until It Was No More* (Princeton: Princeton University Press, 2006), 26.

13 Ibid., 28.

14 Puchner acknowledges the "theatrical echoes" in Austin's speech act theory, but then asserts: "More important than these echoes, however, is the tension between Austinian performative speech acts and theatrical acts that informs Austin's theory throughout." As quoted above, this tension is then cast as hostile opposition: "Speech acts must battle and conquer the threat of theatricality in order to become speech acts. Such a battle between theatricality and performativity is nowhere as visible as in the manifesto" (*Poetry of the Revolution*, 24–5). Yurchak arrives at a more flexible view by drawing from Jacques Derrida's and Pierre Bourdieu's readings of Austin: Derrida's emphasis on the "semiotic power of discourse" and Bourdieu's emphasis on "the delegated power of external social contexts and institutions" point, for Yurchak, to the performative's "unpredictable meanings and effects in new contexts" (*Everything Was Forever*, 20–1).

15 A. A. Zhdanov, "Soviet Literature—The Richest in Ideas, the Most Advanced Literature," in *Problems of Soviet Literature*, ed. H. G. Scott (London: Martin Lawrence, 1934), 15–24, here 21.

16 Sheila Fitzpatrick, *The Cultural Front: Power and Culture in Revolutionary Russia* (Ithaca: Cornell University Press, 1992), 144. This ecumenicalism was belied by the speech by former Comintern official Karl Radek, which critiqued Marcel Proust, James Joyce, and their Soviet admirers for foregrounding the microscopic and turning a blind eye to "that storm reality, full of the most profound contradictions, which has been created by monopoly capitalism." Karl Radek, "Contemporary World Literature and the Tasks of Proletarian Art," in *Problems of Soviet Literature*, ed. H. G. Scott (London: Martin Lawrence, 1934), 73–162, here 155.

17 Puchner, *Poetry of the Revolution*, 30–1.

18 Ibid., 35.

19 Evgeny Dobrenko has lent credence to this socialist realism/*Communist Manifesto* connection—both converting language to action—by arguing that in the Soviet Union, socialist realism was an all-pervasive mechanism that itself produced Soviet socialism. See his *Political Economy of Socialist Realism* (New Haven: Yale University Press, 2007).

20 Karl Marx and Frederick Engels, *Manifesto of the Communist Party*, trans. Samuel Moore, Marxists Internet Archive, 2010, https://www.marxists.org/archive/marx/works/download/pdf/Manifesto.pdf, 16.

21 Puchner, *Poetry of the Revolution*, 52.

22 Zhdanov, "Soviet Literature," 21.

23 Ibid.

24 Ibid.

25 Katerina Clark, *The Soviet Novel* (Bloomington: Indiana University Press, 2000), 35.

26 Maxim Gorky, "Soviet Literature," in *Problems of Soviet Literature*, ed. H. G. Scott (London: Martin Lawrence, 1934), 27–69, here 44.

27 Ibid., 28. I have modified the 1934 translation slightly on the basis of the original. See Maxim Gorky, *Pervyi vsesoiuznyi s"ezd sovetskikh pisatelei, 1934* (Moscow: Sovetskii pisatel', 1990), 5–6.

28 Ibid., 36.

29 Gorky, *Pervyi vsesoiuznyi s"ezd sovetskikh pisatelei*, 8.

30 As Katerina Clark shows, Georg Lukács affirmed this notion in a 1935 article connecting socialist realism to both the European realist novel and ancient Greek epic, thus "according socialist realism a transnational, European context." Katerina Clark, *Moscow, the Fourth Rome* (Cambridge, MA: Harvard University Press, 2011), 164–5. Accordingly, Clark notes elsewhere an affinity between socialist realism and Walter Benjamin's storyteller, who bases "historical tales on a divine plan of salvation" and shows how events are "embedded in the great inscrutable course of the world" (see Clark, *Soviet Novel*, 159). Clark adds that the Stalinist novelist's "historical tales" were "based on something analogous to the 'divine plan of salvation' followed by the medieval chronicler, namely on the Marxist-Leninist account of history" (ibid., 159). Interestingly, Benjamin's 1936 "Storyteller" essay cites Gorky in its discussion of the Russian storyteller Nikolai Leskov, and Benjamin seems in accord with Gorky when he describes the storyteller as a "craftsman" who has not yet been alienated from labor: stories bear the imprint of experience and identity; they are "the raw material of experience" fashioned in a "solid, useful, and unique way." However, even while noting the alienating effects of what succeeds the story (namely, the novel), Benjamin, unlike Gorky, does not call for the modern revival or regearing of storytelling: "To present someone like Leskov as a storyteller does not mean bringing him closer to us but, rather, increasing our distance from him." Walter Benjamin, "The Storyteller: Reflections on the Works of Nikolai Leskov," in *Illuminations*, trans. Harry Zohn (New York: Schocken, 1969), 83–109, here 83, 96, 108.

31 Gorky, "Soviet Literature," 59–60. On the Congress's demographic and linguistic composition, see Kathryn Schild, "Between Moscow and Baku" (PhD diss., University of California Berkeley, Berkeley, 2010), 95, 121. Schild discusses how, in keeping with Stalin's 1925 call for culture to be "national in form, socialist [originally 'proletarian'] in content," the Congress featured multiple reports on the teleological advancement of individual minority literatures, the aim being to develop these to the level of Russian literature. This work builds on that of Yuri Slezkine, who situates these reports, specifically their emphases on national literary genealogies, vis-à-vis Soviet nationalities policy, which by the mid-1930s had reified national boundaries, traditions, and elites. As the decade proceeded, the policy would take an increasingly repressive, Russo-centric turn, culminating with several mass deportations; however, the reification of nationalities continued until—and arguably contributed to—the USSR's demise. Yuri Slezkine, "The USSR as a Communal Apartment, or How a Socialist State Promoted Ethnic Particularism," *Slavic Review* 53, no. 2 (Summer 1994): 414–52, esp. 446–8.

32 See Steven Lee, *The Ethnic Avant-Garde: Minority Cultures and World Revolution* (New York: Columbia University Press, 2015).

33 Gorky, *Pervyi vsesoiuznyi s"ezd sovetskikh pisatelei*, 365. Siao singled out the 1927 ballet *The Red Poppy*, which would later prove a sticking point in Sino-Soviet relations. See Edward Tyerman, "Resignifying *The Red Poppy*: Internationalism and Symbolic Power in the Sino-Soviet Encounter," *SEEJ* 61, no. 3 (2017): 445–66.

34 Ibid., 223–4. Trans. S. S. L.

35 Stal'skii is discussed in Schild, "Between Moscow and Baku," 121–2.

36 Gorky, *Pervyi vsesoiuznyi s"ezd sovetskikh pisatelei*, 676.

37 Petre Petrov, *Automatic for the Masses: The Death of the Author and the Birth of Socialist Realism* (Toronto: University of Toronto Press, 2015), 200–1.

38 Ibid., 202.

39 For a detailed list of Congress speakers, see Schild, "Between Moscow and Baku," 163–79.

40 Petrov, *Automatic for the Masses*, 210.

41 Ibid., 218. Given Spivak's use of Marx's *Darstellung/Vertretung* to emphasize a "divided and dislocated" subaltern subject unable to speak for herself, she would likely dismiss this solution as essentialist and utopian. "Can the Subaltern Speak?" in *Colonial Discourse and Post-Colonial Theory: A Reader*, ed. Patrick Williams and Laura Chrisman (New York: Columbia University Press, 1994), 66–111, here 71. However, in Petrov's account (linking Martin Heidegger and Stalinism), socialist realism foregrounds not an essentialized revolutionary subject, but rather "an immanent state of being that externalizes its essence and, in so doing, calls to life new phenomena, new realities of life." See Petre Petrov, "The Industry of Truing: Socialist Realism, Reality, Realization," *Slavic Review* 70, no. 4 (Winter 2011): 873–92, here 880.

42 See Evgeny Dobrenko, "When Comintern and Cominform Aesthetics Meet: Socialist Realism in Eastern Europe, 1956 and Beyond," in *Comintern*

Aesthetics, ed. Amelia Glaser and Steven Lee (Toronto: University of Toronto Press, 2020), 420–48.

43 Chen, *Staging Chinese Revolution*, 51.
44 Ibid., 12.
45 Bonnie McDougall, "Introduction: The Yan'an 'Talks' as Literary Theory," in *Mao Zedong's "Talks at the Yan'an Conference on Literature and Art*," ed. Bonnie McDougall (Ann Arbor: University of Michigan Center for Chinese Studies, 1980), 3–42, here 19.
46 Mao Zedong, "Talks at the Yan'an Conference on Literature and Art," in *Mao Zedong's "Talks at the Yan'an Conference on Literature and Art*," ed. Bonnie McDougall (Ann Arbor: University of Michigan Center for Chinese Studies, 1980), 55–86, here 85.
47 Though as Shu-mei Shih has shown, Republican China was no ordinary colony, given the many different European powers present, the ability of Chinese intellectuals to differentiate between European imperialism and European culture, and Japan's mediating role between Europe and Asia. Shu-mei Shih, *The Lure of the Modern: Writing Modernism in Semicolonial China, 1917–1937* (Berkeley: University of California Press, 2001), 1–45. According to Shih, post-1949 state denunciations of imperialism neglected this complexity, leading to the decades-long exclusion of modernism from Chinese literary studies, which instead emphasized realism and socialist realism—themselves foreign imports (ibid., 41).
48 As David Holm explains, the Talks were part of Mao's broader Rectification Movement (1940–2), which sought to overcome CCP sectarianism and boost morale amid an onslaught of political, military, and economic crises. David Holm, *Art and Ideology in Revolutionary China* (New York: Oxford University Press, 1991), 87–91.
49 Zedong, "Talks at the Yan'an Conference on Literature and Art," 78.
50 Ibid., 82.
51 Ibid., 67.
52 Ibid., 69.
53 Ibid., 61.
54 Ibid., 66.
55 Shih, *The Lure of the Modern*, 11.
56 For the long-running Chinese discussions of "national form," see Holm, *Art and Ideology*, 51–81. For the changes prompted by the Yan'an Conference, see ibid., 98–106.
57 Zedong, "Talks at the Yan'an Conference on Literature and Art," 70.
58 Kang Liu, *Aesthetics and Marxism: Chinese Aesthetic Marxists and their Western Contemporaries* (Durham: Duke University Press, 2000), 91. Liu notes that subsequent editions of Mao's Yan'an talks deemphasized this process through elisions that pointed instead to crude reflection (ibid., 92). See also McDougall, "Introduction," 18.

59 Holm, *Art and Ideology*, 115, 233–4.
60 Ibid., 253.
61 Puchner, *Poetry of the Revolution*, 89.
62 Zedong, "Talks at the Yan'an Conference on Literature and Art," 75.
63 Louis Althusser, *Machiavelli and Us*, trans. Gregory Elliott (London: Verso, 1999), 23. Quoted in Puchner, *Poetry of the Revolution*, 28.
64 Central to Puchner's notion of the manifesto is Althusser's and Antonio Gramsci's discussion of Niccolò Machiavelli's *The Prince*—specifically how this text creates its own political agent, the "New Prince." Accordingly, Liu writes that Mao's vision of Yan'an as a new worker-led dynasty "sounds much like a Gramscian vision come true—a new Jacobinian era of a 'Modern Prince' where 'national-popular collectives' hold sway." Liu then adds that Gramsci would have been horrified by the coercion of urban intellectuals under Mao's hegemony; Althusser, in contrast, seemed to endorse the Cultural Revolution. Liu, *Aesthetics and Marxism*, 86–7.
65 Warning Western scholars about applying seemingly progressive theories to the non-West, Xiaomei Chen notes: "In fact, to many Chinese readers and critics, the question of 'Can the subaltern speak?' is painfully reminiscent of the familiar question of 'For whom do we speak?' which was the central issue raised by Mao Zedong in his Yan'an Talk," leading to the imperative to extol rather than expose revolutionary reality, the Cultural Revolution, the suppression of intellectuals. Xiaomei Chen, *Occidentalism: A Theory of Counter-Discourse in Post-Mao China* (New York: Oxford University Press, 1995), 23–4. Chen thus affirms the Talks' relevance to postcolonial theory while also pointing to a long tradition of Western theorists (e.g., Althusser, Barthes, Kristeva) who romanticized Maoist China.
66 Anderson, "Modernity and Revolution," 108.
67 "Xi Jinping's Talks at the Beijing Forum on Literature and Art," *China Copyright and Media*, October 16, 2014, https://chinacopyrightandmedia.wordpress.com/2014/10/16/xi-jinpings-talks-at-the-beijing-forum-on-literature-and-art/ (accessed August 2, 2022).
68 Ibid.
69 Ibid.
70 Again, I am drawing here from Xiaomei Chen's argument in *Staging Chinese Revolution*. On socialism as a "necessary reserve" in contemporary China, see Perry Anderson, "Two Revolutions," *New Left Review* 61 (2010): 59–96, here 95.

PART II

Politicizing Theory and Literary Practice in the Global 1960s

Inflection Points

7

Militant Structures of Feeling

Raymond Williams, Claude Lefort, and Workers' Inquiry

Daniel Hartley

In 1880, Karl Marx published a questionnaire in *La Revue socialiste* consisting of 101 questions about every aspect of working life, to be answered by workers themselves. Despite not receiving a single response, it inaugurated an intermittent tradition that became known in French as *l'enquête militante* (literally, militant inquiry) and in English as "workers' inquiry." It has assumed various forms: from Lenin's own (unsuccessful) questionnaire and factory worker interviews to Mao Zedong's "investigations," the post-Trotskyist Johnson–Forrest Tendency (which expanded beyond the questionnaire to include worker reports or "narratives") and the postwar French group Socialisme ou Barbarie, to Italian workerist 'co-research' and beyond.[1] Workers' inquiry can thus be seen as a subterranean current of proletarian literary internationalism. Despite variations in form, the guiding principles of workers' inquiry remain constant: that the working class knows more about capitalist exploitation than anyone else (the epistemological principle); that by extension seemingly 'objective' bourgeois social scientific discourses embody reified conceptions of society and the workplace because they are not rooted in proletarian experience (the critical principle); and that by inviting workers to write about their experiences of work and daily life they would come to recognize their common lot, raising class consciousness and generating—via collection, publication, and dissemination—a nascent form of political organization (the political principle). As Davide Gallo Lassere and Frédéric Monferrand observe, "the objectification of the proletarian condition in the textual space of the inquiry *anticipates* the formation of a political subject that it aims to bring into being."[2] The political use of workers' inquiry as a literary mode is to root critical knowledge of capitalist society in proletarian experience with a view to organizing that experience into class-conscious subjectivity.

This anticipatory horizon, and the ambiguities involved in the textual 'objectification' of experience, connects workers' inquiry to Raymond Williams's concept of the 'structure of feeling,' and, more directly, to the early work of Claude Lefort. In what follows, I shall argue that although there was no known connection between the two thinkers, in his important 1952 essay on workers' inquiry, "L'expérience prolétarienne" (Proletarian Experience), Lefort effectively developed a militant, worker-based version of what Williams would come to call the 'structure of feeling.' The chapter will then conclude with a reading of Paul Romano and Ria Stone's *The American Worker* (1947), one of the best-known examples of twentieth-century workers' inquiry and a direct inspiration for Lefort's essay. In the course of the chapter, it emerges that workers' inquiry sits uneasily, but productively, between realism and modernism, especially as these modes were conceived in the interwar period.[3] Like Karin Struck's working-class autofiction, *Klassenliebe* (1973; Class Love), discussed by Christoph Schaub in the present volume, it is a heterodox type of writing that defies traditional classifications. Put in broad terms, to the extent that workers' inquiry seeks to capture linguistically the subjective experience of modern alienation—and of resistance to it—it extends the modernist tradition. However, unlike those modernists whom Georg Lukács criticized for failing to connect such immediate subjective experiences to the underlying objective unity of the capitalist social totality, workers' inquiry articulates the immediacy of proletarian experience with a critical analysis of the social relations and forces of production. As such, it can be read as an extension of realism. Its ultimate political horizon is a mode of social—and socialist—organization that would emerge from, and be adequate to, the proletarian 'structure of feeling.'

'Structure of Feeling'

To grasp the precise connection between the lines of argument in Williams and Lefort, it is necessary to reconstruct what was at stake for Williams in the conceptual innovation of the 'structure of feeling.' The concept emerged gradually in the immediate postwar period, most notably in his work on drama.[4] It was part of a two-pronged critique: of the dominant strand of English Marxist literary criticism of the 1930s (Christopher Caudwell,

Ralph Fox, Alick West), which Williams had absorbed enthusiastically as an undergraduate but whose simplistic applications of the base–superstructure argument he quickly came to find intellectually unsatisfactory, and of the literary-critical journal *Scrutiny* (1932–53), the influential Cambridge formation led by F. R. Leavis. From the latter, Williams inherited an attachment to 'experience.'[5] Whereas for Leavis the term was normative, denoting "the integrity of the subjective processes stimulated by literature that was especially attuned to its time, among those capable of its proper appreciation,"[6] for Williams 'experience' meant our inescapable, lived immanence to historically and socially determinate situations—our modes of dwelling, feeling, and acting within a specific present.[7] (Indeed, it is unfortunate that Williams's attachment to 'experience' is usually read as a residual humanism, when in fact it is more akin to a ruthless theoretical guarantor that critical thought steer clear of abstractions by 'dwelling within' historical actuality.) Precisely because experience, for Williams, is *determinate*, it is possible to speak of 'patterns' or 'structures' that (literally) inform it.[8] Williams's early work on drama constructed an expressivist artistic ideal on exactly this basis. Adapting T. S. Eliot's theory of the objective correlative, in which "a set of objects, a situation, a chain of events" serve to express (objectively) a "*particular* emotion,"[9] Williams's literary ideal can be defined as a unique pattern of experience achieving full expression in the objective facts of the work. In a slightly later iteration, this will become the expressivist logic of adequation between 'structure of feeling' and form. Literary creation is the combined result of a heightened sensitivity to the patterned minutiae of lived experience and a technical capacity to develop or identify forms adequate to their expression.

Lest this sound too functionalist, however, it is important to note that even in this early work Williams does not fully endorse Eliot's position.[10] He allows for a second scenario in which story, character, and idea

> may serve as a precipitant to the artist, in that through their comprehension the artist is able to find a provisional pattern of experience ... finding the objective correlative may often be for the artist the final act of evaluation of the particular experience, which will not have been completely understood until its mode of expression has been found.[11]

In Eliot, comprehended experience preceded expression in an adequate objective correlative, but Williams allows for a scenario in which the process of comprehending experience is *simultaneous* with the search for an adequate means of expressing it. In other words, writing or artistic creation is an act of cognitive discovery that (paradoxically) retroactively posits or 'reveals' the 'structure of feeling' it seeks to 'express.' This is crucial because it allows for the scenario—only fully developed in Williams's later work—in which, in seeking to express one's experience, one is initially forced to do so via preexisting hegemonic forms or styles that tend actively to *de-form* or *re-form* the unique experience from the inside (if they do not impede it fully), thereby incorporating it into the dominant dispensation of accepted values. Existing forms embody *effective* social relations: "When I hear people talk about literature," wrote Williams in 1980, "about describing what so-and-so did with that form—how did he handle the short novel?—I often think we should reverse the question and ask, how did the short novel handle him."[12] He gives an example that is acutely pertinent to the issue of workers' inquiry: the nineteenth-century working-class writers who wanted to write about their working lives, and who chose autobiography, passed down from the religious tradition of the witness confessing the story of her life, rather than the novel, which "was virtually impenetrable" to working-class writers because of its bourgeois presuppositions. "[T]he forms of working-class consciousness," writes Williams, "are bound to be different from the literary forms of another class, and it is a long struggle to find new and adequate forms."[13] Where the development of those new forms is prevented, working-class experience, if it is articulated at all, goes by way of the forms of its class antagonist and thus risks incorporation into the hegemonic order. The alternative, arguably the fate of most ordinary people, is to live forever with the discrepancy between "the articulated and the lived," to endure the "disturbance, tension, blockage, emotional trouble" of a life within modes of articulation that are inadequate to one's experience, itself thus incompletely understood, condemned to history's "vast areas of silence."[14]

By the time of *Marxism and Literature* (1977), Williams's theory of the 'structure of feeling' had reached its definitive form. It is to be distinguished from "formally held and systematic beliefs," referring to "specifically affective elements of consciousness and relationships ... practical consciousness of a present kind, in a living and interrelating continuity," but one which is at the same time structured: "a set, with specific internal relations, at once interlocking and in tension."[15] It denotes "social experiences *in solution*, as distinct from other social semantic formations which have been *precipitated* and are more evidently and more immediately available."[16] It is concerned with the living present of the sociocultural process *in general* within a given historical period. Against dogmatic forms of Marxism, it stresses the importance for revolutionary politics of grasping the experiential depths at which people are (ambiguously) determined *beneath* the level of formally articulated conviction.[17] Methodologically, it denotes a cultural hypothesis based on 'semantic figures,' usually in art and literature, which are interpreted as formalizations (or *failed* formalizations) of transindividual experiences, which may have been lived as isolated and unrelated at the time, but which emerge in analysis as common to a generation in a given time and place. The connection of 'structure of feeling' to the category of 'generation' came under attack by the *New Left Review* interviewers of *Politics and*

Letters (1979), who rightly pointed out that in any given period there can be three active generations or more, and that 'generation' tells us little about the relation of a 'structure of feeling' to a specific class.[18] This is arguably the weakest point of Williams's theory: in his desire to escape the conceptually redundant generalizations of the 1930s Marxist criticism of his youth (e.g., Caudwell's 'capitalist poetry'), he was reluctant to identify structures of feeling too closely with any given class or stage of historical development.[19] While his work on 'formations' certainly served to counteract this,[20] the relation of 'structure of feeling' as part of the *general* sociocultural process to the 'structure of feeling' of a *specific class* in a particular time and place remained undertheorized in his work. It is here that Lefort's essay offers a suggestive extension.

Claude Lefort's 'Proletarian Experience' (1952)

Following a break with the Trotskyist Fourth International over disagreements concerning the interpretation of Stalinism, Lefort and Cornelius Castoriadis formed the group Socialisme ou Barbarie, which published a journal of the same name from 1949 to 1967.[21] They argued that the Soviet system was a type of bureaucratic capitalism, an instance of the bureaucracy that had developed as a "new social form" in the postwar period, encompassing not only the USSR but also Western Fordist capitalist firms.[22] In their analysis, the chief characteristic of bureaucracy was the separation of *dirigeants* from *exécutants*, of those who command from those who carry out the commands.[23] This had repercussions for their conception of political organization—and of the party form in particular—since their critique "linked the separation of a cadre of professional revolutionaries from the masses to the development of the Stalinist state-bureaucracy."[24] Lefort's view was that *any* party organization contained within it the seeds of the bureaucratic state and was thus opposed to Sartre's (then influential) argument that the party was a necessary agent for synthesizing the atomized alienation of proletarian experience, offering a vision of a new life to which the worker could willingly convert.[25] Lefort's critique of Sartre followed the line of his former mentor, Maurice Merleau-Ponty, who in *Phenomenology of Perception* (1945) had opposed Sartre's decisionist conception *avant la lettre* by stressing precisely those elements of experience that Williams associated with the 'structure of feeling':[26]

> They reduce intentionality in general to the particular case of objectifying acts, they turn the proletarian condition into an object of thought.... Idealism is unaware of the interrogative, the subjunctive, the wish, the expectation, and the positive indetermination of these modes

of consciousness. . . . [C]lass is—prior to being conceived—lived as an obsessive presence, as a possibility, as an enigma, and as a myth.[27]

Where Williams was concerned with an expressivist ideal of adequation between 'structure of feeling' and form, Merleau-Ponty sought an expressivist ideal of adequation between proletarian experience and political organization.[28] Lefort, in effect, fused these ideas in his understanding of workers' inquiry.

"L'expérience prolétarienne" (Proletarian Experience) appeared in issue 11 of *Socialisme ou Barbarie* in 1952.[29] Lefort begins by targeting those economistic "pseudo-Marxists" who perceive historical change as the effect of objective economic laws, and in doing so elide proletarian experience and the agency of class struggle.[30] "While it would be absurd to interpret the history of the workers' movement without continuous reference to the economic structure of society as a whole at the time," writes Lefort, "to reduce workers to that structure is to condemn oneself to ignoring three-quarters of its concrete class conduct [*la conduite concrète de la classe*]."[31] Historically, the proletariat has not simply reacted to economic changes, but has engaged in revolution on the basis of its "total cumulative experience."[32] It thus demands a specific approach alert to its *subjective* development:

> The proletariat is subjective in the sense that its conduct [*sa conduite*] is not the simple result of the conditions of its existence, or, rather, its conditions of existence require of it a continuous struggle of transformation, thus a continuous release from its immediate fate. The progress of this struggle and the development of the ideological content enabled by this release form an experience through which the class constitutes itself.[33]

For Marxist analysis to capture this subjectivity, however, it must be able to answer such questions as: "how do people, placed in the conditions of industrial work, come to appropriate that work, build relations among themselves, perceive and fashion relations with the rest of society . . . how do they compose the shared experience which makes of them a historical force?"[34] The problem for Lefort is that existing Marxist analyses cannot answer these questions because they are only interested in the "results" and "fixed forms" of social life, rather than the human experience that corresponds to them.[35] It was for the same reason that Williams had insisted upon the structure of feeling: to move beyond that "*known* history, a known *structure*, known *products*" which assumed fully achieved articulation and ignored the realm of positive indetermination where so much, politically, was at stake.[36]

So what would a concrete analysis of the proletariat actually look like? Lefort enumerates four possible approaches. The first is objective and would describe the economic and social situation of the proletariat as well as detailing its specific work conditions. The second is 'subjective' in a limited sense and studies all official expressions of proletarian consciousness: primitive Marxism, anarchism, reformism, Bolshevism, Stalinism, and so on. The problem is that this approach remains focused on *explicit* experience, that which has been expressed and formalized in written programs or articles. Consequently, it misses what Lefort calls, in a phrase that repeats Williams's concerns almost verbatim, the "gap between what is lived and what is [explicitly] elaborated, transformed into an argument [*en thèse*]."[37] As soon as these thoughts become a system, Lefort argues, they break with proletarian experience.[38] The third approach is historical, seeking a continuity across major class manifestations (from revolutions to strikes) that have occurred in the course of industrial working-class existence. The final, and in Lefort's view most concrete, approach would seek to reconstruct the proletariat's attitudes toward work and society *from the inside*:

> Prior to any explicit reflection, to any interpretation of their lot or their role, workers have a spontaneous comportment with respect to industrial work, exploitation, the organization of production, and social life both inside and outside the factory. By any account, it is in this comportment that their personality most completely manifests. At this level, the distinctions between subjective and objective lose their meaning: this comportment includes ideologies which, to a certain degree, constitute its rationalization, just as it presupposes the economic conditions whose ongoing integration and elaboration it performs.[39]

Merleau-Ponty's "intentional arc" is now on the factory floor.[40] Just as Lefort's former mentor had criticized models of human experience premised upon an abstract consciousness confronted with a thetically posited 'objective' world, so Lefort argues that the necessary basis of revolutionary theory is proletarian phenomenology. Unlike the other approaches, which view the proletariat from the outside, the fourth approach is "recognized by workers as a moment of their own experience, a way to formulate, condense and confront a knowledge that is usually implicit, *more 'felt' than thought*, and fragmentary."[41] This is a militant version of Williams's 'structure of feeling'; workers' inquiry substitutes for the party as a form of expression adequate to proletarian experience.[42]

It is "worker testimonies," defined as "life narratives or narratives of individual experience," that are seen as the appropriate written form for such a proletarian phenomenology.[43] The aim, for militants, is to learn about every aspect of the worker's life: from work hierarchies, routines, and preferences to relations with fellow workers and management, to home life and his or her views on the world. The goal is then to accumulate such testimonies and tease out from the multiplicity of singular experiences a universal substructure with revolutionary potential, in a radicalized version of the eidetic reduction.[44] For the workers themselves, it is hoped that such an exercise enables them to recognize shared grievances and desires in common with other workers; the circulation of the testimonies serves to accelerate the process of autonomous, self-conscious class formation. Lefort does, however, recognize possible drawbacks to worker testimonies. The first is that by withdrawing into self-reflective isolation to write her narrative, the worker breaks with the very spontaneous, collective experience of work the inquiry had aimed to capture.[45] The second is that the proletariat remains under the cultural domination of the bourgeoisie, lacking belief in its own capacities.[46] Lefort seeks to overcome the latter by persuading his working-class readers that their culture, unlike the bourgeoisie's, which is disconnected from social life under the form of the production of ideas, "exists as a certain power of organization of things and of adaptation to progress, as a certain attitude regarding human relationships, a disposition to social community."[47] Yet, at the same time, he tends to underestimate the dangers of specifically *literary and linguistic* domination by the bourgeoisie, and of how this might internally limit working-class writing in general. In other words, Lefort overlooks the extent to which the *literary formalization of proletarian experience* is itself subject to the bourgeois—and also *bureaucratic*—hegemony of literary forms and of literacy as such.[48] Indeed, this problem of the politically inhibitive uses of literature was encountered by *Socialisme ou Barbarie*'s sister publication, the workers' newspaper *Tribune Ouvrière*, in the hegemony of a revolutionary rhetoric over the left political field, which made workers feel that to be taken seriously they had to express themselves in recognized rhetorical forms.[49] In effect, this reproduced the bureaucratic abstractions of the *dirigeants* precisely *within* the written forms designed to overcome them: "In the hands of the PCF–CGT, Marxism-Leninism became the language of command control."[50] It is in this sense that Lefort and Williams complement one another: Lefort makes possible the combination of 'structure of feeling' with site-specific class analysis, while Williams offers theoretical insights into the complex social mediations of literary forms.

Paul Romano and Ria Stone's *The American Worker* (1947)

Many of these tensions are at work in one of the best-known examples of workers' inquiry, Romano and Stone's *The American Worker* (1947), a direct inspiration for Lefort's essay. Grace Lee Boggs, code name Ria Stone, was part of the so-called Johnson–Forest Tendency, named after the code names of C. L. R. James (J. R. Johnson) and Raya Dunayevskaya (Freddie Forest), respectively. The Tendency emerged from a split within the US

Trotskyist Workers' Party in the early 1940s; contra Trotsky, they held that the USSR should be understood as a form of state capitalism. As James put it: "Ford's regime before unionization is the prototype of production relations in fascist Germany and Stalinist Russia."[51] It was out of the Tendency—and Correspondence, the organization and eponymous publication it subsequently became—that *The American Worker* arose. James suggested to young auto worker Phil Singer (Paul Romano) that he should keep a diary of his experiences at the General Motors plant where he worked. The diary became *The American Worker*, which is split into two halves: the first consists of Singer's reworked diary entries, the second of Grace Lee Boggs's Marxist analysis of Romano's account. The irony of this structure, of course, is that it seems to incarnate the very split between intellectual and manual labor that Correspondence wished to abolish, as no few commentators have noted.[52] What the latter tend to overlook, however, is that Romano's half contains a number of significant theorizations of its own, which the now commonplace practice of labeling his report a 'narrative' arguably causes to be missed.[53] The word 'narrative' appears nowhere in *The American Worker*, where reference is made instead to Romano's 'report,' a term that suggests slightly more potential for autonomous theoretical production. The label 'narrative' also potentially misleads readers into ignoring just how productively strange the form of Romano's report actually is—an odd hybrid of modernist and realist tendencies.

Romano begins by foregrounding the somewhat unexpected topic of *feelings*: "Their [the workers'] feelings, anxieties, exhilaration, boredom, exhaustion, anger, have all been mine to one extent or another. By 'their feelings' I mean those which are the direct reactions to modern high-speed production."[54] Given the Spinozist exactitude of the affective analyses that follow, the second sentence here must be accentuated: this is a *materialist analysis* of feelings rooted in modern high-speed industry. The aim is thus the articulation of the structure of feeling specific to this techno-productive configuration: "to express those innermost thoughts which the worker rarely talks about even to his fellow workers."[55] The genre of the pamphlet is ambiguous—"a diary, so to speak, of the day-to-day reactions of factory life."[56] What is then striking is that what follows is precisely *not* a diary, nor a conventional narrative of any kind. Instead, what presumably began as a chronological series of diary entries has been cut up and reordered into thematic units: the large-scale topics of the chapter titles (e.g., "The Effects of Production," "A Life-Time Transformed into Working Time") and subchapter titles which clearly began as colloquial formulations used by the workers: "You've Got to Live," "If I Had the Money Spent on This . . . ." The result is a slightly disconcerting deconstruction of narrative temporality. Certain chapters seem clearly rooted in specific historical situations, such as immediate postwar life or the increasing pushback against Jim Crow laws, while others seem at once specific and *sub specie aeternitatis*. Temporal markers hover between indexicality ('recently,' 'now,' 'at this time'), the simple or continuous present, and the classical narrative preterit with corresponding adverbs ('one day,' 'once'). There emerges, then, a tension between the *temporality of lived experience* that it was part of the aim of the report to capture, and the *rationalization of the presentation* into component parts which was intrinsic to Romano's own theoretical production.[57]

A further tension emerges between what one might call the realist and modernist aspirations of the text. It is realist in the precise sense described by Williams in *The Long Revolution*: "In the highest realism, society is seen in fundamentally personal terms, and persons, through relationships, in fundamentally social terms."[58] Such a realism pervades the text: from Romano's reading of older workers' assured physical movements as betraying their lived sense of a vested interest in the factory, to the complex motivations of the company stooge. One of the most powerful sections of the report is on Black workers, and the following passage merits quoting at length:

> There are many Negroes in the plant who have pride in their work. They are serious in their desires to give their best and to help their fellow workers. But the same pressures which drive workers as a whole apart, react doubly so on them. They deeply resent the humiliation which they suffer in production, and the failure on the part of society to give them an even break produces a negation of the qualities which workers as a whole admire. It confuses, distorts, and upsets them. They yearn for integration into the social process. They desire to be one with their fellow men. I have seen Negro workers deliberately turn their backs on a white worker. At another moment they have given of their best. The Negro's slacking on the job is directly traceable to his resentment at the restricted role he plays in production. Between these two tendencies the Negro is torn apart.[59]

Such passages have the ring of Benedict de Spinoza's *Ethics* about them.[60] Romano takes a racist cliché—the Black worker "slacking on the job"—which, in Spinozist terms, is the product of imaginary (inadequate) "knowledge from random experience" in which singular things "have been represented to us through the senses in a way which is mutilated, confused and without order for the intellect" (since we have failed to understand their true causes).[61] He then reconstructs the image according to reason, which clearly and distinctly grasps its object causally and conceptually.[62] In this case, he connects the Black worker's anguished withdrawal of effort to the racist pressures he experiences in society, which are redoubled *structurally* in the workplace where he is assigned the least desirable positions in the production process with little prospect of advancement. The worker is "torn apart" because the pride he takes in his work is inverted in practice by the structural racism of the production process, such that to resist the latter he must negate his own ideals.

These realist tendencies intersect with Romano's powerful art of modernist compression. An early example, though less elegant than those that follow, explicates his method:

> Monday morning on a dreary, cold, winter day: Workers are dressing and changing clothes. A worker comes in and in one word expresses the philosophical outlook and feelings of each worker present. In a frustrated, definitive, angry tone, he says, "Horse S" Everyone understands and says to himself, "You can say that again for me, brother."[63]

Romano repeatedly elucidates the hidden complexity of the transindividual "philosophical outlook[s] and feelings" that underlie punctual worker expressions. In this passage he overtly draws attention to the inverse relation between the concentrated economy of the outburst and the shared nexus of thoughts, frustrations, and resistances in which it is rooted. Ezra Pound defined the 'Image' as "that which presents an intellectual and emotional complex in an instant of time."[64] Romano punctuates his report, not with Images, but with equally 'compressed' expressions overheard in the factory. They have a similar effect on the reader to that which Fredric Jameson long ago observed of thoughts in the fiction of Sartre: they have the force of acts.[65] Unlike Pound, however, Romano is in a sense seeking to *reconstruct* the "intellectual and emotional complex" that gave rise to them:

> The life of a worker is transformed into working-time. He does not know how to play. After working hours, in the company of other workers, the conversation invariably returns to the shop. It is like a drug that will not release his mind. . . . When Sunday night arrives, he thinks dejectedly of returning to work on Monday morning. The incessant process continually repeats itself. He looks longingly for week-ends and they disappear before he has a real chance to absorb them. He says, "I work all week for Friday night."[66]

The last line would not be out of place in a pop song, which is unsurprising given the proletarian roots of popular music, though Romano here is less a crooner and more a psychoanalyst with his ear attuned to the political unconscious of the workplace.

He concludes his report where he started it. "Socialism," he writes, "is not merely an ideal to be wished for. It must grow out of the daily lives and strivings of the workers, and it must bring a new life to them in that which is closest to them and to society—their work."[67] This is the key political point of Williams's 'structure of feeling' and of workers' inquiry more generally: socialism is not a matter of dogmatic theories or abstract sloganeering, but must connect with and build upon the actual experience of workers in their daily lives. This experience is occluded by 'objective' theories of history and society which operate, for all their valuable insights, as extensions of capitalist reification. Workers' inquiry is designed to counteract the hegemony of these forms by producing militant knowledge as part of a project of autonomous worker organization. Its actual written results have been uneven, but Romano's report in particular illustrates the original and generative possibilities of the form. The promise of adequation between proletarian structure of feeling and social organization remains our contemporary horizon.

Notes

1. For a concise history of workers' inquiry, see Asad Haider and Salar Mohandesi, "Workers' Inquiry: A Genealogy," *Viewpoint Magazine* (2013), https://viewpointmag.com/2013/09/27/workers-inquiry-a-genealogy/, and in book-length form, see Marcelo Hoffman, *Militant Acts: The Role of Investigations in Radical Political Struggles* (New York: SUNY Press, 2019). Davide Gallo Lassere and Frédéric Monferrand suggest that the roots of workers' inquiry lie earlier in Friedrich Engels's *The Condition of the Working Class in England* (1845); see their "Les aventures de l'enquête militante," *Rue Descartes* 2, no. 96 (2019): 93–107, here 94–5.

2. Lassere and Monferrand, "Les aventures de l'enquête militante," 95. Emphasis in original.

3. The canonical anthology of the so-called realism-modernism debate remains, see *Aesthetics and Politics*, ed. Fredric Jameson (London and New York: Verso, 2007 [1977]), but see also Eugene Lunn, *Marxism and Modernism: A Historical Study of Lukács, Brecht, Benjamin and Adorno* (Berkeley: University of California Press, 1982).

4. John Higgins has rightly argued that Williams's early writing on drama was "the crucible in which he forged some of his central theoretical ideas." John Higgins, *Raymond Williams: Literature, Marxism and Cultural Materialism* (London and New York: Routledge, 1999), 21. For an alternative genealogy of Williams's concept of the structure of feeling, relating it to his lifelong reflections on style, see my *The Politics of Style: Towards a Marxist Poetics* (Leiden: Brill, 2017).

5. For an exploration of the conceptual trajectory of 'experience' from I. A. Richards, through Q. D. Leavis, Williams, and Stuart Hall, to E. P. Thompson, see Stuart Middleton, "The Concept of 'Experience' and the Making of the English Working Class, 1924–63," *Modern Intellectual History* 13, no. 1 (2016): 179–208.

6. Ibid., 184.

7. Note that my conception of Williams's understanding of 'experience' differs from Middleton's.

8   "The moral activity of the artist can also be an individual perception of pattern, or structure, in experience." Raymond Williams, *Drama from Ibsen to Eliot* (London: Chatto, 1954), 27.

9   T. S. Eliot, "Hamlet," in *Selected Essays* (London: Faber and Faber, 1932), 141–5, here 145. Emphasis in original.

10 I agree with Higgins on this point; see *Raymond Williams: Literature, Marxism and Cultural Materialism*, 30.

11 Williams, *Drama from Ibsen to Eliot*, 17.

12 Raymond Williams, "The Writer: Commitment and Alignment," in *Resources of Hope: Culture, Democracy, Socialism*, ed. Robin Gable (London and New York: Verso, 1989), 77–87, here 86.

13 Ibid.

14 Raymond Williams, *Politics and Letters: Interviews with* New Left Review (London: Verso, 1979), 168, 165. In *Marxism and Literature* (1977), Williams provides a gradation of correspondences between experience and sociocultural forms: "the experiences to which the fixed forms do not speak at all," "mixed experiences, where the available meaning would convert part to all, or all to part," and even within apparent adequacy "there can be qualifications, reservations, indications elsewhere." Raymond Williams, *Marxism and Literature* (Oxford and New York: Oxford University Press, 1977), 130.

15 Williams, *Marxism and Literature*, 132.

16 Ibid., 133–4. Emphasis in original.

17 I have expanded upon this idea in Daniel Hartley, "On Raymond Williams: Complexity, Immanence, and the Long Revolution," *Mediations* 30, no. 1 (Fall 2016): 39–60.

18 See Williams, *Politics and Letters*, 156–62.

19 See the tentative remarks in this respect in Williams, *Marxism and Literature*, 134–5.

20 See, for example, his superb essay on the Bloomsbury group: Raymond Williams, *Culture and Materialism* (London and New York: Verso, 2005 [1980]), 148–69.

21 The definitive study of Socialisme ou Barbarie is Stephen Hastings-King, *Looking for the Proletariat: Socialisme ou Barbarie and the Problem of Worker Writing* (Chicago: Haymarket Books, 2015 [2014]).

22 Hastings-King, *Looking for the Proletariat*, 40.

23 See ibid., 41.

24 Ibid., 33.

25 Sartre develops these arguments in the articles "Les Communistes et la paix" (1952–4) and "Réponse à Claude Lefort" (1953), reprinted in Jean-Paul Sartre, *Situations VI: Problèmes du marxisme, vol. 1* (Paris: Gallimard, 1964). For a succinct philosophical account of the dispute between Merleau-Ponty, Sartre, and Lefort, see Frédéric Monferrand, "Politiser l'expérience: Merleau-Ponty, Socialisme ou Barbarie et 'l'Expérience prolétarienne,'" *Chiasmi International*

19 (2017): 87–100. See also Jean-Philippe Deranty and Stéphane Haber, "Philosophie de l'histoire et théorie du parti chez Sartre et Merleau-Ponty," *Actuel Marx* 46, no. 2 (2009): 52–66.

26 Merleau-Ponty would go on to oppose Sartre at length and in detail in *Adventures of the Dialectic* (1955), though by then his position was distinct from his earlier conception.

27 Maurice Merleau-Ponty, *Phenomenology of Perception*, trans. Donald A. Landes (Abingdon: Routledge, 2012 [1945]), 472.

28 Monferrand suggests the qualification 'expressivist' for Merleau-Ponty's approach, in Monferrand, "Politiser l'expérience," 89.

29 Claude Lefort, "L'expérience prolétarienne," *Socialisme ou Barbarie*, no. 11 (November–December 1952): 1–19. A scanned PDF of the original issue can be accessed here: http://soubscan.org/books/pdf/soub_n11.pdf An English translation by Stephen Hastings-King was published online in *Viewpoint Magazine* in 2013, https://viewpointmag.com/2013/09/26/proletarian-experience/. Unless otherwise stated, the English translations come from this publication, but the page numbers refer to the original passages in the French publication.

30 Lefort, "L'expérience prolétarienne," 1.

31 Ibid., 2. Translation modified.

32 Ibid.

33 Ibid., 6. Translation modified.

34 Ibid. Translation modified.

35 Ibid., 7.

36 Williams, *Marxism and Literature*, 106–7. Emphasis in original.

37 Lefort, "L'expérience prolétarienne," 9. See also Williams, *Politics and Letters*, 168: "the peculiar location of a structure of feeling is the endless comparison that must occur in the process of consciousness between the articulated and the lived."

38 The philosophical repercussions of this argument are substantial but exceed the scope of this chapter.

39 Lefort, "L'expérience prolétarienne," 10. Translation modified.

40 Merleau-Ponty, *Phenomenology of Perception*, 137: "the life of consciousness—epistemic life, the life of desire, or perceptual life—is underpinned by an 'intentional arc' that projects around us our past, our future, our human milieu, our physical situation, our ideological situation, and our moral situation, or rather, that ensures that we are situated within all of these relationships. This intentional arc creates the unity of the senses, the unity of the senses with intelligence, and the unity of sensitivity and motricity." See also Conall Cash, "Politique symbolique et expression: 'L'expérience prolétarienne' entre Merleau-Ponty et le post-marxisme," *Rue Descartes* 2, no. 96 (2019): 117–26.

41 Lefort, "L'expérience prolétarienne," 11. Translation modified. Emphasis added.

42 See Monferrand, "Politiser l'expérience," 94.
43 Lefort, "L'expérience prolétarienne," 12. Translation modified.
44 See Hastings-King, *Looking for the Proletariat*, 110.
45 See Lefort, "L'expérience prolétarienne," 14.
46 See ibid., 17.
47 Ibid. Translation modified. This bears an uncanny resemblance to Williams's own famous definition of working-class culture: "the basic collective idea, and the institutions, manners, habits of thought and intentions which proceed from this." Raymond Williams, *Culture and Society: 1780–1950* (Harmondsworth: Penguin, 1963 [1958]), 313.
48 This is why I at once support Monferrand's Hegelian insistence (contra Lefort) on the positivity of linguistic inscription of proletarian experience (see Monferrand, "Politiser l'expérience," 95–6) while feeling that his claim that "it is in language that workers appropriate the political content of their experience" underestimates the potential infiltration of that linguistic appropriation by bourgeois or bureaucratic forms.
49 On this and related points, see the remarkable article by Daniel Mothé (Jacques Gautrat), a worker-member of Socialisme ou Barbarie: "Lecture en usine: pratique et subversion du tract politique," *Esprit*, Nouvelle série 1, no. 453 (January 1976): 117–33.
50 Hastings-King, *Looking for the Proletariat*, 221.
51 Cited in Hoffman, *Militant Acts*, 55.
52 For instance, Hoffman, *Militant Acts*, 57.
53 See, for instance, Haider and Mohandesi, "Workers' Inquiry: A Genealogy": "This was perhaps the most distinctive feature of all the inquiries sponsored by the Johnson–Forest Tendency—and perhaps one of the main reasons why they were never formally called 'workers' inquiries.' Workers' inquiry, in this variation, was specifically a *subjective narrative account*, not a response to a questionnaire." Emphasis added.
54 Paul Romano and Ria Stone, *The American Worker* (Detroit: Bewick Editions, 1972 [1947]), 21. At the time of writing, the text is out of print, but can be freely accessed and downloaded on the Internet Archive, https://archive.org/details/RomanoStoneTheAmericanWorker.
55 Ibid.
56 Ibid.
57 This might be said to reproduce the classical question of *Darstellungsweise* (mode of presentation) in Marx's *Capital*.
58 Raymond Williams, *The Long Revolution* (Harmondsworth: Penguin, 1965 [1961]), 314.
59 Romano and Stone, *The American Worker*, 115–16.
60 I am not, of course, suggesting that Spinoza was a philosophical touchstone for the Johnson–Forest Tendency (he was not), but I am arguing that a Spinozist logic informs Romano's report.

61 Benedict de Spinoza, *Ethics*, trans. Edwin Curley (London: Penguin, 1996), 57.
62 See Ibid.
63 Romano and Stone, *The American Worker*, 31.
64 Ezra Pound, "'A Retrospect' (1918) and 'A Few Don'ts' (1913)," reprinted on the *Poetry Foundation*, website: https://www.poetryfoundation.org/articles/69409/a-retrospect-and-a-few-donts.
65 See Fredric Jameson, *Sartre: The Origins of a Style* (New Haven and London: Yale University Press, 1961), 58.
66 Romano and Stone, *The American Worker*, 36.
67 Ibid., 165–6.

8

Solidarity in Black and White

J. Daniel Elam

This chapter attempts to trace the political use of literature by examining Lorraine Hansberry's work in the 1960s, especially in her posthumously produced play *Les Blancs*. I provide an idiosyncratic but crucial 'prehistory' of Hansberry's play, which begins at sociology departments at Anglo-American universities in the early twentieth century and stumbles toward the 1960s, where Hansberry would wrestle with the implications of early sociology as it might be put to radical political use. Although Hansberry was not a sociologist, she was a key member of a transnational network of sociologists and social theorists. Reading her work in this light, I demonstrate how *Les Blancs* unites, under the misleadingly simple term 'solidarity,' questions about the use of theater, aesthetic experimentation in social scientific writing, and political activism. I read the provocation of the phrase 'the political use of literature' to indicate not only the ways that literature has been used in politics and political activism, but also how literature is the place where politics can be thought through, debated, wrestled with, and tentatively expressed. For anticolonial and antiracist thinkers in the twentieth century, there was no literature without politics—but also, and perhaps more excitingly, no politics without literature. In other words, politics was a literary endeavor, an aesthetic project, and the grounds for imagining new political communities.

The path that ran between literature and politics in the twentieth century often tracked a circuitous route, winding its way first through sociology and social theory. A significant number of mid-twentieth-century anticolonial and antiracist thinkers—activists and writers alike—received university degrees in the social sciences in the early twentieth century, when these fields of inquiry had yet to find their disciplinary coherence and autonomy. Instead, these fields reveled in the porousness of their boundaries, the indefinability of their objects of study, and their commitment to fin de siècle philosophical projects like vitalism and pragmatism.

Students from the British and French Empires were drawn to the United States for their training in these nascent fields. Some of the most exciting students of early twentieth-century social theory left academia for political activism, especially as the so-called decolonial wave swept across the Third World in the 1950s and 1960s. Following the Second World War, and in response to the expansion of university education, the American social sciences turned rigidly empirical. In their writing, anticolonial and antiracist thinkers and activists retained the productive messiness of the early twentieth-century sociological imagination.[1] Thinkers across the Global South would take the implicit egalitarian promises of the early social sciences and render them explicit as a way of imagining new forms of political community.

Sociology's Hesitations

The nascent social sciences reveled in the fact of their porousness even as they sought to define the various fields' methodologies and units of study. In 1905, the sociologist W. E. B. Du Bois wrote that sociology was 'hesitant,' and hoped that this hesitancy might make it more conducive to antiracist and egalitarian politics. The social sciences' desire to align themselves with the natural sciences rather than the human sciences often meant that social theorists often overlooked the provocation at the center of their study: the creative unit of 'society': On the one hand, empiricism devoted to the rigorous analysis of this purely fictive unit could not afford to mimic the empiricism of biology and physics; thinkers like William James and Henri Bergson reworked empiricism to these ends. On the other hand, the advantage of an imagined object of study is precisely that it can be strategically imagined and reimagined; thinkers like Du Bois and Zora Neale Hurston took up this challenge with regard to race and Blackness.

Sociology's distinction from anthropology was its assertion of a concurrent, coeval, interrelated—and therefore potentially equivalent—world. This was especially appealing for students from Europe's imperial holdings, where anthropology's interest in isolated cultures, temporal difference, and belated human development made it an accomplice for colonial rule. Kwame Nkrumah was drawn to sociology for its ability to imagine human interconnectedness at various scales. B. R. Ambedkar pushed sociological thought to its limits in order to show how the caste system had rendered Hindus incapable of forming a coherent or cohesive society. Other students, like Jomo Kenyatta, turned to anthropology to assert cultural autonomy, therefore creating a defense against foreign occupation and misrecognition. Zora Neale Hurston, studying under Franz Boas, found the methodologies of anthropology and folklore conducive for an account of Black life in the US South.

'Society' was therefore loosely defined in various ways: as a 'collective conscious,' as 'organic filaments' tentatively held together, and as 'modes of communication.'[2] 'Society' was both greater and less than the sum of the individual humans that formed it. Early sociology often relied on metaphors borrowed from other sciences for these definitions rather than proffering their own.[3] What these metaphorical definitions share, however, is the idea that 'society,' an indivisible unit when it occurs, exists only as the collective product of humans who, in some way, commit to being a part of it. Dalit leader and anti-caste activist B. R. Ambedkar, who trained under John Dewey at Columbia University, showed how caste had rendered Hindus unable to make this commitment. For Ambedkar, caste had killed the possibility of a 'society' in India; any Indian anticolonial nationalism that pretended otherwise was to replicate the disastrous world that it ostensibly endeavored to escape.[4]

In contrast to the predominant practices of anthropology, sociology's haphazard methodologies relied on coevalness, contemporaneity, interconnectedness, and equivalence. With a few significant exceptions, anthropologists tended to freeze the people they studied in perpetual states of immaturity, belatedness, pastness, and incommensurable alterity; these methodological assumptions made anthropology particularly well suited to being the accomplice, alibi, and benefactor of exploitative colonial interests. Jomo Kenyatta, who studied anthropology under Bronisław Malinowski, reworked precisely these disciplinary pitfalls to produce an anthropological study that refuted empire in its own terms. His book, *Facing Mount Kenya*, was simultaneously a manifesto for an anticolonial cultural politics and a manifesto for an anticolonial anthropological method. Similarly, Franz Boas and his students at Columbia University reimagined anthropology to refute the field's own universalist tendencies and consequently produced rigorous theories of cultural relativism and commensurability.[5]

After the Second World War, the social sciences in the North Atlantic world turned decisively toward data-driven empiricism to meet the needs of the rapidly expanding university. The thinkers who had left academia to become activists, lawyers, and politicians across the Global South escaped this disciplinary turn and therefore retained the vibrant imagination of early sociological thought. In other words, the students of sociology who best redeemed the political vision of their nascent field were those from the colonized world. That is, sociology's students from the colonized world, who would become anticolonial and antiracist thinkers in the 1950s and 1960s, are the under-acknowledged benefactors of the 'sociological imagination.'

Lorraine Hansberry's Sociological Imagination

Lorraine Hansberry studied art at the University of Wisconsin–Madison, but she grew up in a family of social theorists and scholars. Her uncle, William Leo Hansberry, was an anthropologist and historian. His scholarship on Ethiopia was central to the inauguration of African Studies in the United States. Kwame Nkrumah, the first prime minister of Ghana, and Nnamdi Azikiwe, the first president of Nigeria, studied under his mentorship. The Hansberry family hosted leading Black intellectuals in their Chicago home, including Paul Robeson, Du Bois, and Duke Ellington. During her time in Madison, Hansberry joined the Communist Party. For her, the various political concerns that surrounded her were not merely inseparable; they were synonymous.[6]

Nevertheless, we should avoid thinking that there is a self-evident relationship here which would underestimate the imagination necessary for envisioning transnational solidarity and global/internationalist Blackness. Rigorously connecting the liberation and decolonization in Africa and Black civil rights in the United States required, first, inventing the grounds on which a shared collective consciousness could sustainably stand. As many anticolonial and antiracist activists who drew on their sociological training explained, there were many alluring but insufficient ways of forming political communities against, below, and beyond the nation-state. Neither shared identity nor shared history alone were sufficient for a sustainable and egalitarian community—and, in any case, no relationship between American Black people and Africans could be easily predicated on either. *Les Blancs* represents Hansberry's dedicated effort to ascertain the requirements of a political community forged through solidarity.

From *The Blacks* to *Les Blancs*

Les Blancs is undeniably a response to Jean Genet's *Les Nègres* (*The Blacks*), which Hansberry had seen during its run in New York. *The Blacks* is a play within a play, in which Black actors reenact the show trial and consequent murder of a white woman. The actors in the cast are all Black, but five of them wear 'whiteface' to represent establishment figures. Genet imagined the play to be a surrealist exposure of racial prejudice, racist stereotypes, and a critique of the French Empire in Africa. As a 'clown show,' the play presents Black characters as imagined by white audiences.[7] In his prefatory note to the play, Genet is clear that the intended audience is white; the play's force is the shock that white audiences are to feel when their racist imagination is portrayed back at them.

Genet's play is indebted to Henri Bergson, whose essay on laughter includes an attempt to answer the question, 'Why does one laugh at a negro?' One of Bergson's answers (albeit it quarantined in scare quotes) is that "a negro is a white man in disguise."[8] The mission of *The Blacks* is to stage a response to this question and therefore reveal the audience's complicity in this answer. The shock the white audience is to experience would theoretically lead them to reconsider the racism that undergirds their worldview. Many critics, especially of the American iteration, noted that white audiences tended to laugh at the clowning and did not demonstrate the shock they were supposed to receive.[9] In any case, *The Blacks* was one of the longest-running shows on Broadway in the 1960s, opening in May 1961 and running for over 1,400 performances. James Earl Jones and Maya Angelou were in the original cast. (James Earl Jones starred in the Broadway production of *Les Blancs*.)

In June 1961, Hansberry published an essay in *The Village Voice* which focused on Genet's play as well as Norman Mailer's response to it (published a month earlier in the same newspaper). Mailer's review of the play is largely positive while maintaining a hostile stance against Genet himself. Hansberry treats the two men together as exemplars of 'the new paternalism': a form of white liberal antiracism that nevertheless holds and deploys the same racism it is attempting to critique.

> The new paternalists really think, it seems, that their utterances of the oldest racial cliches are, somehow, a demonstration of their liberation from the hanky-panky of liberalism and God knows what else.[10]

Alternatively or additionally, this 'new paternalism' enables white antiracism to ensure a constant focus on white people through its concern with Black people. In this sense, Genet's prefatory note that the play is intended for white audiences is at least somewhat insightful and honest: the play is a conversation between a white playwright and his white audience. But this well-intentioned racial self-critique is done with Black actors and Black characters, effectively without acknowledging their presence.

The critique is, if obliquely, the centerpiece of Mailer's criticism of the play:

> The play entertains the forbidden nightmare of the liberal: what, dear Lord, if the reactionary is correct, and people are horrible. Yet, with the same breath, it is revolutionary. Genet's unconcealed glee at the turn of power from the White to the Negro would so charge the paranoia of the reactionary that he might suffer a heart attack.[11]

Mailer decides that the play is simultaneously revolutionary and impotent: a mirror held up between white people whose narcissism of minor differences has committed them to the political identities of 'liberal' and 'reactionary.' But what might be revolutionary about this project is ultimately rendered meaningless, according to Mailer, by Genet's commitment to theatrical flourish and his own homosexuality.

In her essay, Hansberry sees no difference between these two types of white antiracism. Between Mailer's hipster pity for Black people and Genet's defense of them, the primary concern of the new paternalism is the protection and cultivation of *white people's feelings* about Black people rather than about Black people themselves. The essay is only about Mailer and Genet insofar as it allows Hansberry to comprehend both the possibilities and the pitfalls of liberal white guilt and arrogance. Guilt and arrogance, for Hansberry, are not intrinsically bad places to start. But Mailer and Genet fail to chart a path from that starting point, and their projects stall even before they begin. Provocatively, Hansberry is attracted to arrogance as a political tool for white antiracist work. Arrogant white antiracists are "not the 'enemies' of Negros," and throughout her essay she is "disappointed and saddened" by her own "patches of anger and frequent flippancies."[12] Nevertheless:

> The wish is only that the arrogance become not shapeless; that it does not lose confidence in those of us who await the words which carry it with such hunger and need, on this barren landscape, knowing all the while the source and its truly monumental possibilities.[13]

Pity and arrogance do not necessarily prohibit solidarity with *les damnés de la terre*, but a belief that one can identify and move between the privileged and the damned is toothless piousness. In other words, the work of the antiracist white writer is not to loom in judgment over all other white people, but to realize that antiracism does not lift 'good' white people from their own whiteness. Hansberry gives an especially moving plea (focused specifically on Mailer but oriented toward Genet too):

> One hopes only that, recognizing his public turbulence as merely an echo of all thoughtful people these days, he will not let those forces with which he battles force him into such a rage that he cannot loom larger than their expectations and definitions of him. One powerfully hopes that.[14]

Solidarity in Black and White

Hansberry's essay in *The Village Voice* clarified a project that would continue for the rest of her tragically short life, but it would be shortsighted to describe *Les Blancs* as merely a response to Genet. Despite her allegedly 'visceral' reaction to seeing the play in New York, her 1961 review essay has a significantly wider purview of critique than the play alone.[15] The concerns of *Les Blancs* are an expansion and extension of her analysis in *The Village Voice*, but Hansberry's initial sketches for the play began in 1960.

Les Blancs is in English, but Hansberry's choice of a French title most clearly marks her response to Genet. Although 'The Whites' would be an accurate translation of the play's title, it would lose not only the reference to Genet, but it would also overlook a more significant implication that Hansberry makes by intertwining *blancs* with *nègres*. Genet's French title has more racist connotations than its English translation, and so Hansberry's choice of *blancs*, instead of 'whites,' is a provocation that word could also carry derogatory implications. In other words, Hansberry's *Les Blancs* responds to the not-so-subtle aggression of Genet's *Les Nègres* in a way that relative neutrality of 'whites' (in English) makes less possible. Similarly, the version of Genet's play that Hansberry saw on Broadway was in English and titled *The Blacks*; her response in French is a way to recenter the aggressive racist implications that might seem less obvious in English.

Les Blancs opens with two men arriving in a fictional village in Africa (implicitly under British rule): Tshembe, a Black African, who has returned for his father's funeral, and Charlie Morris, a white American journalist who has come to the village in order to understand the growing African anticolonial movement. Tshembe finds himself caught between his family's demands to join the anticolonial fight and his brother Abioseh, whose commitment (and recent conversion) to Catholicism stands in opposition to violence. Charlie stays at a local clinic overseen by missionary doctors, who have variously reconciled themselves to their position within the village. Charlie, in search of straightforward answers, debates race and colonialism with Tshembe, who cannot find—and refuses to offer—those straightforward answers.

In the Association of Artists for Freedom's Town Hall forum in 1945, Hansberry speaks to these questions:

> It's because that since 1619, Negroes have tried every method of communication, of transformation of their situation from petition to the vote, everything. We've tried it all. There isn't anything that hasn't been exhausted ... and now the charge of impatience is simply unbearable. I would like to submit that, yes, there is a problem about white liberals.... We have to find some way with these dialogues to show and to encourage the white liberal to stop being a liberal and become an American radical.... The basic fabric of our society, after all, is the thing which must be changed to really solve the problem.[16]

'Society' is not a flippant word choice here. The two questions that haunt and dominate the play are opposed and tragically intertwined: one, a debate about the use of violence in an anticolonial struggle; and two, the question of the use of well-intentioned humanitarianism as an alibi for colonial injustice. Tshembe and Charlie are not so much fully fledged characters as they are means by which these two questions confront each other in their starkest form.

Questions of anticolonial (and colonial) violence and humanitarian reason were not unique to Hansberry, who had watched the so-called Mau Mau revolution (and subsequent massacre) in Kenya in the 1950s, studied the horrors of the Belgian Congo under W. E. B. Du Bois, and had most likely read Frantz Fanon when his work reached the United States in 1963. Hansberry's interest in Africa, in the national independence of African countries, and in Pan-Africanism were not merely theoretical, but inherently tied to Black antiracist struggles in the United States. Blackness named the possibility of an alternative political community—not merely one of solidarity but one whose organic lineaments were a shared fate and destiny.

Before the lights are fully up, the first sound of *Les Blancs* is laughter—that of hyenas in the distance. Unlike *Les Nègres*, *Les Blancs* does not purport to stage a conversation between a playwright and an audience with a shared identity. Hansberry does not replicate (at least in any straightforward way) Genet's confrontational mode of theater, indebted to surrealism and Bertolt Brecht. But a certain audience-oriented didacticism does propel *Les Blancs* (and most reviews, as Robert Nemiroff discusses, focused almost exclusively on the tensions the Broadway production provoked in audiences).

Les Blancs occasionally responds to *The Blacks*. It does so with the aim of demonstrating that white guilt and paternalism more often reinforce colonial and racist hierarchies than dismantle them. Moreover, because it is possible to use guilt and paternalistic arrogance for antiracist and anticolonial justice, the fact that they often reinforce colonial and racist hierarchies is proof of a purposeful, rather than accidental, decision by white people to use antiracist and anticolonial activism to maintain supremacy. In other words, *blanc*-ness names a condition of refusing solidarity by proclaiming it, and in two senses: first, it is a rejection of solidarity with Black people; second, it is a refusal to admit the fact of one's inherent racial belonging. In the name of concern, pity, and magnanimity, *les blancs* reject solidarity with *les nègres*. In the name of antiracist outrage, *un blanc* believes himself to have transcended the racism of his fellow *blancs*. Put otherwise, *blanc*-ness reinforces white individuality (and autonomy) while insisting on Black homogeneity (a monolithic 'wretched').

Charlie's and Tshembe's ongoing conversation throughout the play stages this clearly. When Charlie asks Tshembe if he hates all white people, Tshembe responds:

> TSHEMBE (*A burst of laughter. Casting his eyes up.*) Oh, dear God, *why?* (*He crosses down and away.*) Why do you all *need* it so?! This absolutely *lo-o-onging* for my hatred! (*A sad smile plays across his lips.*) I shall be honest with you, Mr. Morris. I do not "hate" all white

men—but desperately wish that I did. It would make everything infinitely easier! But I am afraid that, among other things, I have *seen* the slums of Liverpool and Dublin and the caves above Naples. I have *seen* Dachau and Anne Frank's attic in Amsterdam. I have seen too many raw-knuckled Frenchman coming out of the Metro at dawn and too many hungry Italian children to believe those that raided Africa for three centuries ever "loved" the white race either. I would like to be simple-minded for you, but—(*Turning these eyes that have been "seen" up to the other with a smile.*)—I cannot. I have—(*He touches his brow*)—seen.[17]

And the two men argue about if the reverse is true:

CHARLIE (*Shaking his head.*) You really can't get rid of it, can you? The bitterness. No matter how you try, we've done it to you: *you do hate white men!*

TSHEMBE (*Gazing at him with open disgust.*) Mr. Morris, have it your way! No matter what delusions of individuality infect *my* mind, to *you* I am not an individual but a tide, a flood, a monolith: "The Bla-a-acks!"

CHARLIE Nonsense! To me you are no more "the Blacks" than I am "the Whites"—(*In his excitement* CHARLIE *steps on a swatch and* TSHEMBE *flicking his wrists, motions him back.*) That is, I can't speak for you—but *I* am myself.

TSHEMBE And *that* of course is nonsense! *You* are a tide, a flood—a tide, yes, I like that, a receding tide.[18]

And later, after Charlie accuses Tshembe of saying race is both real and 'a device':

TSHEMBE I am not playing games. (*He sighs and now, drawn out of himself at last, proceeds with the maximum precision and clarity he can muster.*) I am simply saying that a device *is* a device, but that it also has consequences: once invented it takes on life, a reality of its own. So, in one century, men invoke the device of religion to cloak their conquests. In another, race. Now, in both cases you and I may recognize the fraudulence of the device, but the fact remains that a man who has a sword run through him because he refuses to become a Moslem or a Christian—or who is shot in Zatembe or Mississippi because he is black—is suffering the utter *reality* of the device. And it is pointless to pretend that it doesn't *exist*—merely because it is a *lie!*[19]

If Tshembe's monologues to Charlie are didactic, it is because they are tied to Tshembe's own ambivalent commitment to anticolonial violence—an ambivalence that his comrades and family read as hypocrisy. Blackness does not necessarily guarantee political community, but it creates the conditions of possibility for it to occur.

The name 'Tshembe' would certainly remind contemporary audiences of Moïse Kapenda Tshombe, the president of Katanga State from 1960 to 1963 and the prime minister of the Democratic Republic of the Congo from 1964 to 1965. Tshombe was a celebrated figure among American conservatives who considered him the most (or perhaps only) acceptable African decolonial leader because of his support of anticommunist policies and his refusal to fundamentally alter the racial, ethnic, and economic structures of the Belgian Congo. Most Black Americans considered Tshombe to be a traitor to Black and African people because of his docility to Western Europe and the United States throughout the 1960s. The fictional Tshembe at the center of *Les Blancs* finds himself torn between his European education and violent anticolonial revolution; in this sense he resembles Hamlet, and his inner conflict is largely sympathetic. In a lecture in 1964, Hansberry declares that she would rather have a white comrade than fight alongside "a Moïse Tshombe."[20]

The point here is not to chide white people for bad antiracist solidarity, but rather to examine how whiteness itself is the rejection of solidarity altogether (marked, perhaps, by the desire to laugh). In the Association of Artists for Freedom's Town Hall forum in 1945, Hansberry speaks to these questions:

> Radicalism is not alien to this country, neither Black nor white, and we have a very great tradition of white radicalism in the United States, and I've never heard Negroes boo the name of John Brown. I don't think that we can decide ultimately on the basis of color that kind of thing.... The thing that is trying to be said is we want total identification. It's not a question of reading anybody.[21]

There are hardly any women in *Les Blancs*. Imani Perry notes that although Hansberry speaks through three African sons in the play (as opposed to three white Jewish daughters in *The Sign in Sidney Brustein's Window*), "the play is Lorraine's voice."[22] Perry's quick but incisive analysis of the play reconfigures its central questions as about inheritance. This combination of a biological and social imagination helps us think about the entanglement of Blackness and Africanness—or, alternatively, about how whiteness's refusal to participate in a collective consciousness is neither biological nor social.

Society as a Way of Life

One of the white doctors at the clinic describes her complicity in sustaining 'a way of life' that prohibits solidarity, or a shared 'society':

DEKOVEN Oh I have saved hundreds of lives; all of us here have. I have arrested gangrene, removed tumors, pulled forth babies—and, in doing so, if you will please try to understand, I have helped provide the rationale for genocide.
CHARLIE Genocide!? Come on now, DeKoven, you can't really—
DEKOVEN Mr. Morris, colonial subjects die mainly from a way of life. The incidentals—gangrene, tumors, stillborn babies—are only that: incidentals. Our work—(*He interlocks his fingers.*)—reinforces the way of life.[23]

What does it take to radically alter a way of life toward a decolonial and antiracist world? Hansberry's reply in a 1961 interview might finally give us a glimpse of the scope of this project:

Silberman: . . . It seems to me the question that I'm left with by this discussion is whether Mr. Jones and a good many people in the audience really want the merger which I think Miss Hansberry spoke about or whether they want to bring down the whole structure.
Hansberry: The latter may be necessary to make the first possible.[24]

To speak only of 'racial mergers' (meager solidarity), or to speak of them only in the service of radical structural change is to commit a fundamental misunderstanding. It is the error of *blanc*-ness, an error rooted in pious paternalism, and shortsighted political commitment. To approach the question the other way around, as Hansberry's response suggests, is to reimagine the lineaments of interpersonal connection. To imagine a 'society' in a politically potent way is to demand fungible contours of consciousness whereby the 'we' in whose name one speaks is infinitely inclusive. Put otherwise: the well-meaning 'we' of Genet, Mailer, and Charlie is limited in the first instance to white people, and in the second instance to white people who are not *those* ('bad') white people. This is built from good intentions but retains the same hierarchies and exclusions of racist and imperial projects. The alternative society of 'we' that Hansberry imagines in *Les Blancs*—that of 'Blackness'—relies on a politically catalyzed definition of 'society' that requires, by definition, the egalitarianism of a consciously shared consciousness.

A demand to change the 'whole structure' in the service of a proper 'merger'—rather than the other way around—is a vision for politics that required a literary imagination. I think we can understand this in a few different ways. On the one hand, the space of literature was the drafting board for revolutionary political visions. Novels and plays were the genres where internationalist, anticolonial, and antiracist utopias could be sketched out, given contours, and finessed. On the other hand, political thinkers in the Cold War world realized that literature was the realm where revolutionary politics could be enacted despite the unlikeliness of their realization in the real world. Forms of solidarity could be imagined, drafted, and staged as ways of offering glimpses of a world that could be otherwise—especially when this otherwise-world seemed impossible. In the first instance, literature was the first draft of imagined communities; in the second instance, literature *was* the imagined community, even if those communities were merely imagined.

In both cases, limiting our attention to the narrow category of 'literature' (or the recognizably 'literary') ignores how political and aesthetic thinkers in the twentieth century relied on the wildly experimental world of social theory, as it grasped for definitions of human collectivity that, by definition, relied on egalitarian politics as the basis for shared consciousness. Unlike other human collectivities (like the nation, for example), the curious unit of 'society' could be inclusionary, and infinitely so. The productively and provocatively undefinable unit of 'society' gave writers, thinkers, and activists fertile ground for cultivating political communities that had been written and staged into existence.

In their introduction to this volume, Benjamin Kohlmann and Ivana Perica argue for the necessity of taking literature serious as politics beyond the dismal rubrics of instrumentability. *Les Blancs* did not bring about the antiracist and anticolonial world that it staged—and in any case, it would be difficult to say that it staged an antiracist and anticolonial world. Rather, Hansberry combined the politically charged sociological imagination with a dramatic vision so that the stage became the ephemeral site for imagining that world (and its impossibility). Literature has political uses beyond 'the art of the possible'—and this is the realm where the use of literature is to imagine and commit to solidarities and political communities in their most revolutionary forms.

Notes

1 For a robust discussion of this, see Frederick Cooper, *Colonialism in Question: Theory, Knowledge, History* (Berkeley: University of California Press, 2005).

2 See Émile Durkheim, *Les formes élémentaires de la vie religieuse: La système totémique en Australie* (Paris: Alcan, 1912); Thomas Carlyle, *On Heroes, Hero-Worship, and The Heroic in History* (London: Chapman & Hall, 1841); John Dewey, *Experience and Education* (New York: Simon & Schuster, 1938).

3 See Gustave Le Bon, *Psychologie des Foules* (Paris: Alcan, 1895).

4 See B. R. Ambedkar, *The Collected Works of B. R. Ambedkar*, ed. Vasant Moon (New Delhi: Government of India, Ministry of Social Justice and Empowerment, 1990–ongoing); J. Daniel Elam, *World Literature for the Wretched of the Earth: Anticolonial Aesthetics, Postcolonial Politics* (New York: Fordham University Press, 2021); J. Daniel Elam, "Conscience and Conscious in the Global South: R. B. Ambedkar, Kwame Nkrumah, and

Anticolonial Sociology," *Comparative Literary Studies (Urbana)* 58, no. 3 (2021): 604–22.

5   See Jomo Kenyatta, *Facing Mount Kenya: The Tribal Life of the Gikuyu* (London: Secker & Warburg, 1938); Charles King, *Gods of the Upper Air: How a Circle of Renegade Anthropologists Reinvented Race, Sex, and Gender in the Twentieth Century*, 1st ed. (New York: Doubleway, 2019); Zora Neale Hurston, *Barracoon: The Story of the Last "Black Cargo,"* ed. Deborah G. Plant, 1st ed. (New York: Amistad, 2018).

6   See Fanon Che Wilkins, "Beyond Bandung: The Critical Nationalism of Lorraine Hansberry, 1950–1965," *Radical History Review* 95 (2006): 191–210.

7   Throughout this chapter, I follow current practices of writing Black with an upper-case 'B' to foreground its importance as a racial–political category (the formation of which this chapter partially traces).

8   Henri Bergson, *Laughter: An Essay on the Meaning of the Comic* (New York: Macmillan, 1914), 41.

9   For example, see even the most generous interpretation of the play in Edmund White, *Genet: A Biography* (New York: Knopf, 1993), 426–39.

10 Lorraine Hansberry, "Genet, Mailer, & the New Paternalism," *Village Voice*, June 1, 1961.

11 Norman Mailer on Jean Genet's 'The Blacks', *Village Voice*, May 11, 1961.

12 Hansberry, "Genet, Mailer, & the New Paternalism".

13 Ibid.

14 Ibid.

15 See Robert Nemiroff's notes on this in Lorraine Hansberry, *Les Blancs* (New York: Grove Press, 2010), 32.

16 Lorraine Hansberry, *Conversations with Lorraine Hansberry*, ed. Mollie Godfrey (Jackson: University Press of Mississippi, 1992), 5–9.

17 Hansberry, *Les Blancs*, 78.

18 Ibid., 90–1.

19 Ibid., 92.

20 Hansberry, *Conversations with Lorraine Hansberry*, 7.

21 Ibid., 7.

22 Imani Perry, *Looking for Lorraine: The Radiant and Radical Life of Lorraine Hansberry* (Boston: Beacon Press, 2018), 200.

23 Hansberry, *Les Blancs*, 114–15.

24 Hansberry, *Conversations with Lorraine Hansberry*, 9.SOLIDARITY IN BLACK AND WHITE

9

Notes from the Underground, or: Why and How Was Non-Marxist Theory Resisted by Non-Marxists in a Totalitarian Society

Galin Tihanov

The reason I evoke *Notes from the Underground* in the title of this chapter is seemingly a simple one: all of the action that my chapter refers to unfolds, just as in Fyodor Mikhailovich Dostoevsky's piece, in St. Petersburg, or Leningrad in the cases of Soviet resistance to theory. Of course, there is also another reason: "underground" captures the location of this particular protest—away from the mainstream, scattered in the pages of samizdat type-written magazines, in articles some of which have never been republished, that is, they have never left the darkroom of subterranean critique to break into the light of day. And for a third reason perhaps. When Friedrich Nietzsche, in the winter of 1886/7, encountered Dostoevsky's novella, in Nice, in a French translation titled *L'esprit souterrain*, he felt propelled by Dostoevsky's text into further reflection on the premises of his own philosophy (as he was, to an extent, through his encounter with Stendhal's writing). Marking out the instances of Soviet resistance to theory might also, let us hope, occasion some rethinking of the status of theory and its fortunes in the past century, and today. Ultimately, the three brief case studies I undertake here are meant to deliver a lesson about the rather different rationale and dynamics of the resistance to theory in a totalitarian society. The real question is why and how is non-Marxist theory resisted by non-Marxists in a society in which non-Marxist thought ought to be considered an ally of those opposing mainstream discourse and official dogma.

Let me begin with what I believe might be a much-needed differentiation between two fundamentally different meanings the word 'theory' has acquired over the last half a century or so. The first one (one can visualize the word 'theory' being written with an initial capital '*t*' here) is reserved for theory conceived of as an important but somewhat loosely defined body of thought that gravitates toward a substantial (if not full) overlap with continental philosophy. There are two versions of this understanding of theory (with a capital '*t*') that are worth pointing to, each represented by a seminal recent work. One is the equation of Theory with French post-Structuralism; in this version, Theory unfolded in France in the second half of the 1960s and migrated to the United States in the 1970s. François Cusset, who has studied the process of this migration, has written persuasively about "French Theory" (to quote the title of his book published in France in 2003, in which the words "French Theory," in English in the French original, drive home his point about the transformative—and global—power of Theory). Cusset produces an excellent argument about the possible reasons for this equation, or substitution. On reaching the shores of America, dominated as it was (and still is) by the traditions of analytic philosophy, French post-Structuralist philosophy (foremost Deconstruction) was appropriated not as philosophy per se but as a powerful method of analyzing (and putting in question) narratives: literary, religious, and legal. Theory, in Cusset's words, became "mysteriously intransitive": no longer a theory of something, but "above all a discourse on itself."[1] The second version is the equation of Theory with the dialectical method, honed by G. W. F. Hegel but detectable before him, right down to medieval philosophy and letters (in Andrew Cole's broad—perhaps a touch too broad—reconstruction). Theory, in this second version, allows one to perform a move within philosophy away from philosophy, as Andrew Cole would have it when he associates the birth of Theory with Hegel.[2] Again, the ensuing claim is all-encompassing: "theory historicizes thought, studying its materialization across disparate forms of human expression—music, literature, art, architecture, religion, philosophy—either in a diachronic or synchronic analysis—or, aspirationally, both at once."[3]

There is also, however, another understanding of theory (we could visualize the word being written with a small '*t*' here); it focuses on a particular time-limited episteme and on a much more well-defined area, that of literature or the other arts: music, architecture, theater, film, and so on. The episteme I am referring to must be time-limited, for it is itself the product of a time-limited regime of relevance that bestows on literature (or these other arts) a sense of autonomy and self-sufficiency without which the semblance of timelessness constituted in the act of theoretical reflection—with its uncovering of seemingly universal principles (or even immutable rules)—would not be possible.

The meaning I invest in the term 'regime of relevance' harks back to Foucault, but here it has a more specific semantic compass: it refers to a historically available constellation of social and cultural parameters that shape the predominant understanding and *use* of literature for the duration of that particular constellation. I submit that literary theory is the product of one specific phase in the evolution of one particular regime of relevance. Methodical reflection on literature, known to have existed in the Western tradition at least since Plato, should not be confused with literary theory. Literary theory is only a particular shade of that phenomenon; disciplined, rational thinking about literature does not come to an end with the demise of literary theory as a unique and time-limited episode within that disciplined, rational reflection. What makes this episode both characteristic and important is that it unfolds within the bedrock of a distinct, equally unique and time-limited, regime of relevance that posits and circumscribes literature's significance. To put it briefly, this specific regime of relevance sees literature as an autonomous discourse that tends to differ—in various ways and to a varying degree—from other discourses: journalistic, philosophical, quotidian, and so forth. This regime of relevance commences with the wider discursive formation we still refer to as Romanticism. But literary theory, I contend, was born later. Romanticism channels the notion of the autonomous worth of literature almost exclusively through the figure of the writer. With his doctrine of the literary field, Bourdieu has memorably rearticulated a long Romantic tradition of positioning literature as beneficially marginal, the product of writers who are both extraordinarily talented and unmistakably relegated to the periphery of society: prophets, madmen, and outcasts. Literary theory, however, emerges at a later stage in the life span of this particular regime of relevance that defines literature and its significance with reference to its autonomy. What is so distinct about literary theory is that it contemplates this autonomy (and the resulting uniqueness of literature as a discourse) not through the figure of the writer per se but through language. This, in a sense, is the great breakthrough of the Russian Formalists around the First World War: literature presents a specific and autonomous discourse, not because of the exceptionality of the writer who writes it, but because of the specific way in which language functions in it. Of course, after Jacques Derrida, we know that this is a claim that is not always possible to uphold: not because language in literature is not metaphoric or figurative, but because it is so not only in literature. Yet what the Formalists did amounted nonetheless to a veritable revolution: the writer was taken out of the equation; for the first time what really mattered was the text and its language.

This regime of relevance, in which literature is valued for its autonomy and uniqueness as a discourse that is unlike other discourses, breaks with previous regimes of relevance in which literature's significance is linked to its capacity to convey ideas, emotions, or knowledge of the world, or to instigate socially and politically oriented actions. Those previous regimes of relevance foreground forms of writing that still preserve the links of literature to an earlier state of symbiosis with philosophical, historiographical, pedagogical, and political discourses. This new regime of relevance, with its insistence on grounding literature's significance in the autonomy it derives from the special way in which language is used in it, sustained literary theory's dominant position among other modes of reflecting on literature into the early 1980s, when it gradually became untenable because the very way in which one conceives of literature's relevance was itself changing by then. The patrimony of literary theory is currently active within a regime of relevance that thinks literature through its market and entertainment value, with only residual recall of its previously highly treasured autonomy. The enduring legacy of literary theory is present in a spectral way: instead of assuming a reliably material form, it is available solely relationally; it disintegrates every time one forgets that it is the volatile product of a past regime of relevance still at work within a new regime vis-à-vis which it is no longer dominant.[4]

These two meanings—and manifestations—of theory (both with a capital and with a small 't') have over the last fifty years or so functioned not in isolation from one another, but in constant imbrication and overlap. Let me adduce an illustration of this complexity drawn from the scene of theory in Germany of the 1960s. In mid-1960s Germany, these two meanings—and projects—of theory intersect in a way that is indicative of, and marked by, earlier developments in the German humanities. The version of theory that tends to extend to a full overlap with dialectics is very much alive in the legacy of what we still refer to as 'critical theory,' an intellectual project that commenced in the 1920s and was already influential by the late 1950s. In the 1960s, this project revives Walter Benjamin's work which the '68-ers rediscover; it also formulates what Theodor Adorno would call 'negative dialectics': reversing Hegel's postulate that 'the whole is the true' but remaining dialectical nonetheless, albeit 'negatively' so. This extended understanding of Theory as coextensive with dialectics (almost exclusively of German provenance) is not the only one on offer in Germany during the 1960s. A competing version of Theory seeks inspiration in hermeneutics, and thus also largely in the domestic intellectual tradition. To some extent, of course, in the version practiced by Hans-Georg Gadamer, hermeneutics meets the dialectical method; Hegel is undoubtedly important (including on the level of vocabulary) for the subtle moves of mediation that are on display in *Truth and Method*, Gadamer's opus magnum published in 1960.[5]

On the other hand, literary theory as such (the second project of theory, 'theory' with a small 't') is barely present in Germany until the mid-1960s. If anything, a great deal of what constitutes literary theory arrives initially as an export from France, in the guise of Structuralist semiotics. Roland Barthes's *Mythologies*, in a severely abridged translation,[6] becomes the first harbinger of this particular project of theory in Germany. As Horst Brühmann notes,

Barthes's *Mythologies* appeared in Germany (as *Mythen des Alltags*) at a time when not a single book was available in German by Michel Foucault, Louis Althusser, Jacques Derrida, Jacques Lacan, or even the members of the Tel Quel Group; Claude Lévi-Strauss's *Tristes Tropiques* had been translated into German in 1960, but without the theoretical passages.[7] Thus, at least initially, French literary theory arrives in Germany without the supporting frame of French Theory. In both France and Germany, what anchors and advances Structuralist literary theory is the parallel revival, for the first time in Europe since the 1930s, of Russian Formalism; in retrospect this could be seen as a self-reflexive gesture, by some of the Structuralists, of establishing intellectual provenance for their own work. This process begins precisely in the mid-1960s. In 1964, a German translation of Victor Erlich's 1955 monograph on Russian Formalism is published in Munich; the next year, the first books of works by Russian Formalists appear in France and Germany: in France, the famous anthology edited in Paris by Tzvetan Todorov, with a preface by Roman Jakobson, and in Germany, a selection of Boris Eikhenbaum's writings brought out by Suhrkamp. To complicate matters, some of the essays included in Todorov's anthology of Russian Formalist literary theory (by Viktor Shklovsky and Eikhenbaum) are carefully read and referred to a few years later by Herbert Marcuse, the indisputable intellectual guru of the 1968 protests, thus staging a consequential meeting between theory and Theory.[8]

But while in the West the explosive mixture of theory (both with a capital and with a small '*t*') was celebrating its triumph throughout the late 1960s and the 1970s, in Soviet Russia the 1970s were already seeing theory fatigue, or even, as I will try to demonstrate briefly in what follows, an active resistance to theory. The political context should not be overlooked here. Literary theory, not just as a field, but as a university discipline based on textbooks and requiring the rituals of examinations, was first institutionalized precisely in Soviet Russia, beginning in the decade between the mid-1930s and the mid-1940s. But this institutionalization took place along strict Marxist lines, impoverishing Karl Marx's intellectual legacy and largely destroying the foundations of literary theory laid by the Russian Formalists (as in Boris Tomashevskii's early, non-Marxist but equally textbook-like summation, *Teoriia literatury: Poetika*, 1925). This is particularly true of the version of literary theory devised by Gennady Pospelov (1940), and less so of that cultivated by the more talented but only slightly less orthodox Leonid Timofeev (1934; then 1935 as an introduction to literary theory for fledgling writers with the title "Verse and Prose"; then 1945, as a university textbook).[9] The result of all this was that Russian Formalism, chastised so much and berated for so long, gradually acquired an aura of dissident aversion to dogma. The representative one-volume edition of Iurii Tynianov's writings on literary theory and poetics published in Moscow in 1977[10] was the work of scholars who were not prepared to talk, or walk, with the regime. Russian Formalism had become a byword for opposition to narrowly conceived Marxist theory.

It is against this background of canonizing Russian Formalism by, and among, those seeking to eschew the imposed ideological mainstream (*inakomysliashchie*, in Russian) that I wish to discuss now a stark example of resistance not to Marxist literary theory, but precisely to Russian Formalism, the guiding star—along with semiotics, on which a few words later—of those dissenting from official dogma. Not surprisingly, this voice against Russian Formalism comes from, as it were, a *practicing* dissident, the poet and journalist Viktor Krivulin (1944–2001). In the Leningrad samizdat magazine *37* (1976–81; twenty-one issues in total, which he edited with Tatiana Goricheva, his wife until her emigration in 1980), Krivulin published a long review article on the above-mentioned 1977 representative collection of Tynianov's works. The title of Krivulin's contribution, which translates as "Notes on the Margins of an Untimely Book," takes the reader back to Nietzsche and Maxim Gorky.[11] Krivulin attacks, to begin with, the principles of selection; he seems to be suggesting that after the republication of Tynianov's articles on verse theory in 1965,[12] the 1977 edition is an unnecessary monument to artificially arranged unity and cohesion. Yet the crux of his criticism is his profound disagreement with the technically pragmatic, ultimately 'cynical,' as he calls it, approach to literature introduced by the Formalists. This cynicism, Krivulin charged, was epitomized by Shklovsky's cold analysis of literature as the application of particular 'devices'; deprived of attention to content and ideas, this approach allowed Shklovsky to evade political commitment after the 1920s, turning his coat on occasion and adopting the position of a trickster interested in his own survival above all else. The same technical adroitness and pragmaticism marked Tynianov's approach to literature, according to Krivulin. In the end, the deeper problem here is that Tynianov, along with his fellow Formalists, was practicing an approach to literature that Krivulin found too secular, and in that sense too narrow. In a powerful passage in the last part of his long text, Krivulin concludes that Tynianov was eager to understand how literature behaves at "the lower limit of language," that which places language in contact with the everyday (*byt*). Alas, Tynianov had no sense at all for the importance of understanding how literature positions itself at what Krivulin calls "the upper limit of language," the contact zone in which literature faces metaphysics and religion.[13] For Tynianov, the "junior sister" of literature, in Krivulin's remarkable paraphrasing of Tynianov's term "junior genres," is the anecdote, the rumor, and other forms of everyday discourse—but literature's "senior sisters" are the Bible, the Koran, and the Vedas, which Tynianov does not know and does not want to know.[14]

My second example is Boris Groys's early piece "Istoki i smysl russkogo strukturalizma" (The Origins and Meaning of Russian Structuralism) published under the pseudonym 'Igor Suitsidov,'[15] just before Groys's emigration to West Germany in 1981; in the same issue, under his real name, Groys published an article on Kazimir Malevich and Martin Heidegger. The title, of course, is meant to reconnect the Russian reader with Nikolai Berdiaev and his book *The Origins and Meaning of Russian Communism* (English ed. 1937; first Russian ed. Paris 1955). Groys contends that in Soviet Russia, Structuralism had become just another ideology, rivaling in intelligentsia circles the official ideology of Marxism. In the absence of a philosophical tradition, in the absence, ultimately, of metaphysics (recall also Krivulin's critique of Tynianov), Soviet Structuralism put on that mantle. In Groys's account, it became nothing more than a "'conservative' version of the left materialist wing of the humanities": Soviet Structuralism succeeded Marxism in this role during the 1960s and 1970s.[16] Furthermore, Groys charges Soviet Structuralism with harboring the ambition of becoming an instrument of power and a tool of governance: "Structuralism insisted on becoming the ideology of the intelligentsia that was supposedly ready to begin to govern a society, in which all actions have only a systemic sense and which has lost intuition of its own historicity."[17] Yet Groys is under no illusion when it comes to the real potency of Structuralism to rival Marxism: "the [type of] rationality Structuralism [offered] turned out to be weaker than that of Marxism."[18] Those longing to take the fight into the open, beyond the conference halls or beyond their kitchens, were bound to end up frustrated; in the cold light of day, Groys recognized that "removed from participation in the institutions of power, the intelligentsia was able to deploy Structuralism in its capacity as metaphysics solely for the purpose of self-consolation."[19] Soviet Structuralism was no doubt often attacked by Soviet orthodoxy, but this only underlined the former's own growing monopoly on the humanities. It had thus become the new orthodoxy—even as some of its most talented practitioners, such as Juri Lotman and Sergey Averintsev, delivered truly inspiring examples of literary analysis (both Lotman and Averintsev are mentioned by Groys, the latter somewhat more ambivalently); in contradistinction, Viacheslav Ivanov's theory of the two hemispheres of the brain is ruthlessly ridiculed by Groys, as is Vladimir Toporov's attempt at a Structuralist-semantic reconstruction of 'wisdom' (Sophia).[20]

A third and final example. Attracting a relatively small group of academics brought together by admiration for Nikolai Marr's 'new theory of language' and his methodology of cultural analysis, 'semantic paleontology' (*semanticheskaia paleontologiia*) was a current in cultural and literary theory that had a considerable impact on some of its contemporaries (notably Bakhtin) and wider resonance beyond the 1930s. A major exponent of semantic paleontology, Olga Freidenberg (still best known in the West as Boris Pasternak's cousin), was at pains to negotiate the boundaries between her own para-Marxist cultural theory and orthodox sociologism. She was to face, much later, criticism from some of her own pupils, more often than not for methodological reasons. In an article surveying the history of the 'genetic method,' written decades after semantic paleontology had left the stage of Soviet literary theory, Sofia Poliakova charged Marr's followers with reducing cultural history to a "gigantic tautology" (*gigantskuiu tavtologiiu*). While in hot pursuit of primeval clusters of meaning, Poliakova maintained, Freidenberg produced a semantic universe in which everything resembled and echoed everything else: "We are thus in the kingdom of sameness clad in difference."[21] In 1979–80, Freidenberg once again became the target of criticism, this time by a group of young classicists at Leningrad University who believed her work to be lacking in methodological rigor and philological exactitude. Freidenberg was aligned with Lotman, Toporov, Averintsev, and Alexei Losev, who were all thought by these budding scholars to be representatives of a new—Structuralist—orthodoxy in philology, which, because it was perceived by many as a form of opposition to the regime, was felt to be beyond criticism (the proximity of this argument to Groys's critique of Soviet Structuralism is unmistakable). Seeking to rectify this undemocratic situation, the students organized small workshops in which they questioned the methodological untouchability of Structuralism and semiotics (of which Freidenberg was considered a predecessor sui generis, by Toporov and to some extent by Lotman, whose notion of "explosion" [*vzryv*] as a mechanism of cultural and historical change undoubtedly drew on her idea of the fitful birth of qualitatively new cultural formations[22]). The discussions (except for the one on Averintsev, which had not been recorded) were later published in the samizdat journal *Metrodor*.[23] Many of these discussions, I should add, were jocular and playful in style, thus deliberately challenging the position of authority Soviet Structuralism and semiotics had assumed.

In conclusion, I should like to make three brief points. First, there was no hiding place for theory in the Soviet Union. Often itself beginning as a form of resistance to Marxism, theory's own symbiosis with power and authority would be readily detectable and assailable. Second, and this is a really novel and important point, critique of Russian Formalism and Soviet Structuralism came not just from within Soviet Marxism, as is still generally assumed today, but also from the opposite end of the ideological spectrum, with arguments that were no less forceful, and certainly often more valid. Third, my reflections here capture, ultimately, some of the inherent strains between theory and ideology, or, if you will, between theory with a small and a capital '*t*.' Here are the two faces of this intrinsic tension: Krivulin, who found Tynianov's take on literature wanting, because he pined for theory with a capital '*t*' that would grow into an engagement with metaphysics and religion—and, on the opposite side, Leonid Zhmud (the Ukrainian-born Soviet and Russian scholar of Ancient Greek philosophy and science who, while still a PhD student in Leningrad, would organize critical public discussions of Freidenberg's and the Soviet Structuralists' work), and even more so Groys, who were uncomfortable with Soviet Structuralism having turned into an ideology in its own right and sought to scale it back to a stricter and more specific method, a theory with a small 't.' The lesson that emerges, I suppose, is that the "resistance to theory," to borrow the title of Paul de Man's 1982 eponymous essay, was not confined to the West and to the intrinsic exhaustion of the trust in language to secure access to truth; this resistance had its own rationale and subtle dynamic in the Soviet Union, a society in which theoretical innovation could and did at times display unexpected complicities with the ideological mainstream. These complicities were diagnosed, in the case of both Russian Formalism and Soviet Structuralism, once the two previously undogmatic currents of thought had gradually assumed a position of authority in intellectual circles. The most compelling resistance to them would come from outside of Marxism, in fact often from thinkers steeped in conservative and/or religious thought (e.g., in Heidegger) rather than in radical intellectual traditions, and this non-Marxist critique would be much more difficult to address and ward off than the staple accusations leveled by the Soviet regime. All this means that the Soviet resistance to theory holds lessons for our somewhat self-obsessed Western debates on theory: we have to recognize that theory, even when it emits its own impulses of critique vis-à-vis the status quo, is not immune to complicity in the re-articulation of authoritarian claims to truth.

Notes

1 François Cusset, *French Theory: How Foucault, Derrida, Deleuze and Co. Transformed the Intellectual Life of the United States*, trans. Jeff Fort, Josephine Berganza, and Marlon Jones (Minneapolis: University of Minnesota Press, 2008), 99.

2 See the argument in Andrew Cole, *The Birth of Theory* (Chicago and London: University of Chicago Press, 2014); for a more recent location of the origins of (literary) theory in Hegel, see M. A. R. Habib, *Hegel and the Foundations of Literary Theory* (Cambridge: Cambridge University Press, 2019).

3 Andrew Cole, "The Function of Theory at the Present Time," *PMLA* 130, no. 3 (2015): 809–18, here 810.

4 Here I elaborate on arguments advanced in my recent book *The Birth and Death of Literary Theory: Regimes of Relevance in Russia and Beyond* (Stanford: Stanford University Press, 2019), see especially the Prologue.

5 This part of my essay expands and refines arguments made in Galin Tihanov, "Romanticism's Longue Durée: 1968 and the Projects of Theory," *Interventions* 23, no. 3 (2021): 463–80.

6 See Horst Brühmann, "'Als Diskussionsgrundlage für Großstadtbüchereien empfohlen.' Zu Übersetzung und Rezeption der *Mythen des Alltags* in Deutschland," in *Mythen des Alltags—Mythologies. Roland Barthes' Klassiker*

der Kulturwissenschaften, ed. Mona Körte and Anne-Kathrin Reulecke (Berlin: Kulturverlag Kadmos, 2014), 25–40, here 30 (nineteen of Barthes's fifty-three *mythologies* were translated in the 1964 Suhrkamp edition).

7   Ibid., 32.

8   See Galin Tihanov, "The Politics of Estrangement: The Case of the Early Shklovsky," *Poetics Today* 26, no. 4 (2005): 665–96, esp. 689–90.

9   Timofeev, it has to be noted, was one of Mikhail Bakhtin's guarding angels in the very early 1940s, thanks to whom Bakhtin got to present his paper "Epic and Novel" at the Gorky Institute of World Literature.

10 See Iurii Tynianov, *Poetika, istoriia literatury, kino* (Moscow: Nauka, 1977).

11 The Russian title of Krivulin's article is "Zametki na poliakh odnoi nesvoevremennoi knigi," *37*, no. 10 (1977): 227–48 (typescript, not republished since its appearance in the samizdat magazine). All quotations are from the online text provided by the samizdat collections of the University of Toronto Libraries: https://samizdatcollections.library.utoronto.ca/islandora/object/samizdat%3A37_10/datastream/PDF/view (accessed August 2022); all translations are mine. The table of contents for all issues of *37* can be found in Josephine von Zitzewitz, *Poetry and the Leningrad Religious-Philosophical Seminar, 1974–1980: Music for a Deaf Age* (Cambridge and Leeds: Legenda, 2015), 193–208.

12 See Iurii Tynianov, *Problema stikhotvornogo iazyka: stat'i* (Moscow: Sovetskii pisatel', 1965).

13 Krivulin, "Zametki na poliakh odnoi nesvoevremennoi knigi," 245.

14 Ibid., 246. For an analysis of a much earlier instance of a non-Marxist critique of Russian Formalism, highlighting as early as 1930 the fact that the literary texts discussed by the Formalists were almost all Western (which did not deter them from claiming universal validity for their literary theory), see Galin Tihanov, "On the Significance of Historical Poetics," *Poetics Today* 38, no. 3 (2017): 417–28.

15 Published in *37*, 1980–1981, no. 21 (the last issue before the magazine ceased publication). In 1976, very soon after *37* had been founded, Krivulin and Groys were engaged in its pages in a polemic on the limits of comprehension with reference to contemporary art and literature, see A. A. Zhitenev, *Poeziia neomodernizma* (St. Petersburg: INA-PRESS, 2012), 301–2.

16 Boris Groys, *Rannie teksty, 1976–1990* (Moscow: Ad Marginem Press, 2017), 257 (my translation). Trans. G. T. A brief summary of Groys's text, from a different perspective, is provided in Zhitenev, *Poeziia neomodernizma*, 119–20. It is important to note that Groys's critique of Soviet Structuralism as complicit with the totalitarian nature of intellectual life in the Soviet Union parallels his earlier, and well-known, misgivings regarding the Soviet avant-garde as implicitly totalitarian, see Boris Groys, *The Total Art of Stalinism*, trans. Charles Rougle (London: Verso, 2011).

17 Groys, *Rannie teksty*, 257.

18 Ibid., 258.

19 Ibid.

20 Ibid., 245–50. Groys is also rather caustic in relation to Alexander Pyatigorsky, see ibid., 240.

21 S. V. Poliakova, *'Oleinikov i ob Oleinikove' i drugie raboty po russkoi literature* (Moscow: INAPRESS, 1997), 370 ("Takim obrazom, my v tsarstve tozhdestv, oblechennykh v otlichiiakh"); the quotation is from Poliakova's article "Iz istorii geneticheskogo metoda: marrovskaia shkola," first published in *Literaturnoe obozrenie* 7–8 (1994): 13–20. Poliakova contrasts in her article Freidenberg and Izrail Frank-Kamenetskii; the latter is declared a true scholar and thinker, whereas Freidenberg is apportioned the dubious honor of a helpless and methodologically perplexed follower of Marr and Frank-Kamenetskii. This assessment is historically inaccurate and unfounded. Suffice it to point to Frank-Kamenetskii's unequivocal praise of Freidenberg's pioneering role in the mythological interpretation of the Greek novel, which overturned Erwin Rohde's false assumption of the importance of invention and foreshadowed "by three years" Karl Kerényi's 1927 study *Die griechisch-orientalische Romanliteratur in religionsgeschichtlicher Beleuchtung* (which, according to Frank-Kamenetskii, was, compared to Freidenberg's, rather narrow in scope, limiting itself to an examination of the Egyptian myth of Osiris and its impact on the Greek novel); see Frank-Kamenetskii, "K genezisu legendy o Romeo i Iulii," *Russkii tekst* 3 (1995): 167–203, here 187.

22 See Juri Lotman, *Culture and Explosion*, trans. Wilma Clark (Berlin: Mouton De Gruyter, 2009), 140 (first published in Russian as *Kul'tura i vzryv*, 1992); see also Lotman's 1976 article "O. M. Freidenberg as a Student of Culture," *Soviet Studies in Literature* 12, no. 2 (1976): 3–11 (first published in Russian in 1973 as 'O. M. Freidenberg kak issledovatel' kul'tury'). At the same time, one has to keep in mind that Lotman's understanding of 'explosion' was sometimes marked by a very non-Freidenbergian Romantic belief in the genius of individual writers and artists as the agents of change, see Susi K. Frank, Cornelia Ruhe, and Alexander Schmitz, "Explosion und Ereignis: Kontexte des Lotmanschen Geschichtskonzepts," in J. M. Lotman, *Kultur und Explosion*, trans. D. Trottenberg (Frankfurt am Main: Suhrkamp, 2010), 227–59, esp. 254, 259.

23 The ten issues of *Metrodor* were published between 1978 and 1982. Some of the materials, including articles critical of Freidenberg, by S. A. Takhtadzhian and A. K. Gavrilov, are republished in *Novoe literaturnoe obozrenie*, no. 15 (1995). For a fascinating retrospective by one of the participants, see Leonid Zhmud', "Studenty-istoriki mezhdu ofitsiozom i 'liberal'noi' naukoi," *Zvezda*, no. 8 (1998): 204–9; see also the retort by one of Lotman's defenders: Georgii Levinton, "Zametki o kritike i polemike, ili Opyt otrazheniia nekotorykh neliteraturnykh obvinenii (Iu. M. Lotman i ego kritiki)," *Novaia russkaia kniga*, no. 1 (2002): 14–17.

10

Workshops of Abolition

Attica Print Culture and Small Press Poetry

Mark Nowak

Abolition is grounded in futurity. It speculates on an as yet impossible space and organizes forces to begin to procure the properties of its utopic actualization. Mariame Kaba, in *We Do This 'Til We Free Us: Abolitionist Organizing and Transforming Justice*, describes such a practice as "an abolition imagination."[1] Such imaginations, Kaba and others argue, lead to new possibilities beyond (neo)liberal theories and practices that are directly accountable for the vast expansion of American prisons in the twentieth and twenty-first centuries. Similarly, Angela Davis and her coauthors in *Abolition. Feminism. Now.* call for "the radicalness of the imaginary as a space for what is yet unthinkable, at the edge of the possible."[2] In the chapter that follows, I examine the prison poetry workshops and small press print cultures of Attica, New York, as cultural incubators for and literary precursors of "an abolition imagination" and "the radicalness of the imaginary" in the decade following the Attica uprising of September 1971. I also explore how print cultures and small presses, particularly those founded and directed by writers and publishers of color, temporarily opened radical new spaces for imprisoned poets to write as progenitors of today's prison abolitionists.

The Foundations of Small Press Poetry and Print Culture at Attica

Dudley Randall's Broadside Press, founded in Detroit in 1965, became the central publishing house not only for Black Arts Movement poets like Sonia Sanchez and Haki Madhubuti, but for imprisoned poets too.[3] One of the early print technologies employed by Randall was the broadside for which he named his press. After printing two of his own poems as broadsides in 1965, Randall printed more than seventy-five broadside poems by established poets like Robert Hayden, Gwendolyn Brooks, and Langston Hughes as well as then-emerging poets like June Jordan, Alice Walker, and Lucille Clifton from the late 1960s through the mid-1970s. Writings from and about prisons regularly appeared in the series too. Randall released several broadsides by Etheridge Knight, a military veteran imprisoned at Indiana State Prison in Michigan City, Indiana, including "2 Poems for Black Relocation Centers" (1968), "For Black Poets Who Think of Suicide" (1970), and "Poem for Brother/Man (after his Recovery from an O.D.)" (1972).[4] The press also published broadsides like Jim Witherspoon's "County Jail" (1970), Kuweka Amiri Mwandishe's "The Nigger Cycle: For Angela Davis Kidnapped by the F.B.I. on Oct. 13, 1970" (1971), and Susan Cottrell's "To My Man in Jail" (1973).

Mwandishe's poem, for example, appears on the back of his broadside, a large, folded card (the forty-fifth in the series). The front of the card features a portrait of Angela Davis with lines radiating from her afro. Beneath the galvanizing image appears, in small text, an appeal: "50 cents / All receipts from sale of this Broadside / will be donated to the Free Angela Davis Defense Fund." As James Sullivan writes, the production, sales, and purchase of Mwandishe's broadside can be viewed as "elements of material political practice, acts of solidarity with a specific cause."[5] As he astutely shows, even though the sales of the 1,000 copies of the publication would result in 500 dollars (at best) for Davis's defense fund, the broadside forms "a site for concretizing political commitment."[6] Davis herself asserts, "In learning about my case they learned about the Soledad brothers, about the subhuman conditions of the jails . . . about racism and how it pervaded every corner of the prison system." As Davis concludes, "Many who began, reluctantly, demanding bail, ended up as strong and effective leaders of the campaign."[7] Broadside Press, through its design and production decisions in publishing Mwandishe's poem, became part of this abolitionist movement.

The revolt at Attica in September 1971 is still the deadliest prison uprising in US history; thirty-three prisoners and ten prison employees were killed. Thirty-nine of those men were shot and killed by state law enforcement officers after the latter were ordered by New York State governor Nelson Rockefeller to retake the occupied prison. Eight months after the Attica rebellion, Celes Tisdale, a poet, professor, and founding member of Buffalo's Nia Writers Workshop (*Nia* from the Swahili word for *intention* or *purpose*), began teaching a Black Arts Movement-grounded poetry workshop at Attica. He brought in poems and recordings from Nikki Giovanni, Amiri Baraka, The Last Poets, and others as well as copies of *The Black Poets*, an anthology edited by Dudley Randall and published by Bantam in 1971, to read and discuss with imprisoned writers. After teaching dozens of workshops in 1972 and 1973 and recognizing the quality of the poems being written in his weekly workshops (and at the urging of his writing students), Tisdale gathered poems and bios from the imprisoned poets, as well as his own journals written after his visits to teach at Attica, into a manuscript. After "striking out with the white publishers," Tisdale's anthology, *Betcha Ain't: Poems from Attica*, would be published by Broadside Press in 1974.[8] The minimalist cover of *Betcha Ain't*, printed on textured goldenrod-colored paper, contains the title at the top, the name of the press and the book price ($2.50) at the bottom, and a drawing of a barred prison window. The outdoor sun casts shadows through the window as it is seen from within a prison cell. The front inside cover contains a list of more than sixty titles from "Broadside Poets," most priced between one and two dollars. This act of placing the growing list of poets here sets the Attica writers in a continuum with the most important Black writers of the time in an act of radical solidarity.

The poems in *Betcha Ain't* cross a range of poetic styles. Traditional forms like haiku, sonnets, and cinquains are published alongside poems with rhyming four-line stanzas and longer free verse poems. Themes range from "A Humble Muslim" to "The Red-Neck Coke Machine." But the theme most often addressed is the assault on the occupied D-Yard by state troopers, local sheriffs, and armed prison guards on September 13, 1971. Scholar and prison abolitionist Joy James has termed writings such as these "(neo)slave narratives," that is, writings that "reflect the languages of master, slave, and abolitionist."[9] For James, imprisoned writers like the poets in Tisdale's anthology function "as progressive abolitionists and register as 'people's historians.'"[10] Those who have survived the Attica uprising are thus in the unique subject position to tell their personal histories and the history of mass incarceration under a regime of racial capitalism. And it is precisely this type of poem by people's historians from D-Yard on September 13, 1971, that makes up the largest percentage of poems in *Betcha Ain't*. From Isaiah Hawkins's "13th of Genocide" and Mshaka's (Willie Monroe) "Formula for Attica Repeats" to Hersey Boyer's "Attica Reflections," Sam Washington's "Was It Necessary," and John Lee Norris's "Just Another Page," the writers in Tisdale's anthology tell the history of the Attica uprising and its brutal ending from their point of view. At the end of his poem "At Last," Christopher Sutherland clearly delineates the telos of the abolitionary imagination in the workshops following the uprising: "I 'vacuated the building / and burnt the motherfucker down!"[11]

Imprisoned people at other New York State prisons felt the aftermath of the Attica uprising, and other small press publishers played important roles in the poetry and print culture that was produced and distributed at the time. Joseph Bruchac, a writer and publisher with Abenaki and Irish/Slovak heritage, founded Greenfield Review Press and regularly published imprisoned writers. Here is how Bruchac describes the origins of the press in 1971:

> A friend of mine, William Witherup, was teaching a poetry writing workshop at Soledad Prison. He sent me a hand-printed and illustrated anthology of work by his guys (smuggled out of the prison by Bill, since they were not allowing inmates to send their writing out at that time) that was sub-titled "A Kite From Soledad." "Kite" of course referring to a message sent out without the permission of the prison. I published that book in a 68-page edition of 500 copies as WORDS FROM THE HOUSE OF THE DEAD, AN ANTHOLOGY OF PRISON WRITINGS FROM SOLEDAD. It was Greenfield Review Press Chapbook # 1.[12]

Shortly afterward, America the Beautiful Fund contacted Bruchac to ask if he would like to teach a writing workshop at Great Meadow Correctional Facility, also called Comstock Prison, a maximum-security facility in the Adirondack region of northern New York. Bruchac began his workshop on January 6, 1972. Two years later, after a year of funded workshops and more writing workshops which he continued to lead as a volunteer, Bruchac published an anthology of writings from his workshop on Greenfield Review Press, *The Last Stop: Writings from Comstock Prison*.

The cover of *The Last Stop* is even starker than *Betcha Ain't*. In place of the drawing and goldenrod cover of Tisdale's anthology, the cover of Bruchac's anthology has an austere black-and-white photograph of the exterior of Comstock Prison. When I asked Bruchac about the relationship of his workshop to the recent uprising at Attica, he replied, "Half of the men in my workshop were survivors of the massacre that took place at Attica and a number of them were still recovering from gunshot wounds."[13] In Bruchac's February 4, 1972, journal entry that he included in the anthology, he tells readers about one of these transfers: "A new man in the class. A-Jabar. A transfer from Attica. The Attica men have been at Comstock for weeks now but haven't been processed until now so had to remain in cells."[14] (Figure 10.1)

Bruchac chooses to open *The Last Stop* with a poem from his newest student, Attica transfer A-Jabar's "This iS A recording."[15] A-Jabar's five-page, typographically experimental poem is written loosely in the form of an intercept message—a recording that would be played when the number a caller was trying to reach was unavailable or disconnected (i.e., a "dead" number):

FIGURE 10.1 *Clockwise from top left*: Betcha Ain't: Poems from Attica *(Celes Tisdale, ed.)*; The Last Stop: Writing from Comstock Prison *(Joseph Bruchac, ed.)*; Convicted Voices *(Antu Satya)*; Awakening of a Dragon *(Attica Brother Jomo)*; Fighting Back: Attica Memorial Book, 1974. *Photo © Mark Nowak.*

```
        This is a recording
    when u hear/Read/Read in 2
                    the following
                            lines
    u will u will u will uoooooooooh will
    will not b: hearing/ reading anything
                    at all
```

> that is
> out of the ordinary[16]

But in A-Jabar's case, what is "the ordinary"? The incarceration of Black men in numbers astronomically higher than their white counterparts? Police brutality? Racial hatred by both "the ordinary" white society and the exclusively white prison guards who now oversee his life? The massacre at Attica? A-Jabar sets himself against this omnipresent and seemingly omnipotent "ordinary," describing himself as a "hellbent young Blk / Man" who has been "molded ... by an existing world order / of negros [/] whities [/] & dog / eat dog."[17] He ends this opening section of his poem by concluding,

> thus
> the bulk of my life/existence
> which might-could
> better b. termed/considered
>   death[18]

This death, what Orlando Patterson referred to as "social death," is what has been "the ordinary" in America for A-Jabar.[19]

As he maneuvers through the narrow pathways open to his life ("childhood" to "Male hood" to "pseudo real Man hood" to, finally, "Them called [/] call me / A Hood," a life tracked in just five short lines), A-Jabar attacks white supremacy that desires to create only one space for Black people: the space of death ("caught a lite death stroke / uh the white plague").[20] Although he is temporarily able to stave off death, the visceral unfurling of failing technologies in a failing society explodes in the feverish final section of his poem about life among the "neo- / Genocidal" white race and the racist prison system that houses "Un-People" like himself:

> as a result
> Their little data machine r. computer
> keeps going beeeeeeeep does not compute
> beeep beeeep frm Slave Nigr 2 Blk Man
> beeeeeeeep does not compute
> beeeep beeeep frm. fool Nigr 2 Man Blk
> beeeeeeeeeeee-eeep rev-o-lu beeeep
> ca - an not com - pute
> beeeeeep frm. Blk Man 2oooo-OOoooh
> beee-eeep frizzit slurp spurt
> ******** curse words-Blooooom
> This is a recording
> whenuhear/read/read n2
> the next lines

u will realize that
this poem this poem this poem this poem
this poem is'
                 Over . . .[21]

Under white settler American capitalism, represented by its communication technologies in this poem, the transition from "Slave Nigr 2 Blk Man . . . does not compute"; in white settler American capitalism, Black radicalism and Black revolution "ca – an not com – pute." It's important to note that the word *revolution* cannot even be uttered here, and when A-Jabar tries to speak the word, it's cut off by the American-made machines: "beeeeeeeeeeeeeeep rev-o-lu beeeep." In fact, A-Jabar sees the potential for Black men to self-determine their lives in America as an impossibility: "beeeeeep frm. Blk Man 2oooo-OOoooh / beee-eeep frizzit slurp spurt."

Poetry by Black imprisoned writers in these small press anthologies from the early 1970s forms a previously forgotten tradition within the radical Black and abolitionist imaginations. Publishers like Dudley Randall and Joseph Bruchac made the important decision to publish these works beside established authors on small presses they founded and directed. Although *The Last Stop* would receive little to no media coverage or reviews, according to Bruchac, Greenfield Review Press would nevertheless go on to publish many individual books and anthologies by imprisoned writers including James Lewisohn's *Golgotha: Letters from Prison* (1976), Carolyn Baxter's *Prison Solitary and Other Free Government Services* (1979), and *Light from Another Country: Poetry from American Prisons* (a comprehensive anthology edited by Bruchac in 1984).

The Expansion of Poetry and Print Culture at Attica

In addition to these poems in broadsides and anthologies from the workshops of Tisdale and Bruchac, poetry and print culture in and around Attica in the mid-1970s flourished. *Attica News* (a newspaper produced inside the prison between 1974 and 1979) and groups like the Attica Brothers Legal Defense and Prisoners Solidarity Committee (both located in nearby Buffalo, New York) published poetry in an array of chapbooks, memorial books, broadsides, handbills, and other printed objects to publicize the conditions imprisoned men struggled against at Attica in the months and years after the massacre. Prison newspapers have a long history of publishing poetry by imprisoned writers. Russell N. Baird, writing in *The Penal Press* at the beginning of the modern prison movement in 1967, called prison newspapers and magazines "instruments of freedom."[22] *Forlorn Hope*, first published on March 24, 1800, at a prison in New York, was America's first penal newspaper and, perhaps unsurprisingly, its first issue included "a long poem bemoaning the imprisonment of war veterans for debt stemming from war service."[23]

Attica News often included poems by imprisoned writers in its pages too. The edition published on July 31, 1974, for example, includes a poem, "Death spoke," by Brother Thomas Hagen.[24] Hagen's poem ends by documenting the carnage at Attica:

> Death spoke—At Attica
> And 43 humans went forth to join
>   Death's ranks and oppression came forth
> To Take a bow and To Receive
>   Death's praise.[25]

Death, always in the indented line, is literally (and poetically) one step ahead. The dialectical play of Hagen's poem is writ large: death versus life, imprisoned people versus prison guards, freedom versus captivity. Along with exposés like Brother Ali's "A View from Erie County Jail" (the issue's cover story), a notice about the organizing drive of the Attica Prisoners Union, a story about Cesar Chavez and the United Farmworkers Union organizing in the fields, and ads for buttons (a choice of two, "Attica is All of Us," 1 ½ inches, 35 cents, and "Attica Is/Free the Brothers Now," 2 ¼ inches, 60 cents) to benefit Attica Brothers Legal Defense, the editors of *Attica News* believed that Brother Thomas Hagen's poem also played an important part in these political struggles.

In addition to the publication of workshop poems in small press anthologies and *Attica News*, poems regularly appeared in a number of staple-bound booklets produced by various support organizations and prison defense funds. The consistency of the appearance of poetry in so much of the print culture around Attica speaks to poetry's centrality within this freedom struggle. James Sullivan argues for the inclusion of these small press and ephemeral materials in our critical studies: "A materialist criticism that reads the whole artifact, rather than reading past it to the text alone, will come closer to a study of the real social and political function of literature."[26] Attica Brother Jomo's *Awakening of a Dragon*, for example, published in 1974 by the Attica Bond to Free Jomo, is a twenty-page stapled 8.5 inches by 11 inches booklet that includes numerous photographs of Attica Brother Jomo Omowale (Eric Thompson aka Cleveland Davis) as well as photos of his mother, sisters, children, and others; a six-page "Inner View" (interview); and a dozen letters to his Davis family, his lawyer, "Comrades," Indicted Attica Brothers in Special Housing Unit, and others.

Both the front and back covers contain poems. On the inside front cover above the booklet's dedication—"In Loving Memory of Our Teachers"

(Malcolm X, The Fallen Attica Brothers, George and Jonathan Jackson, musicians John Coltrane, Janis Joplin, and Jimi Hendrix, and others)—Jomo includes a poem, "Free the Young Dragons," by Bro. Bernard Shipman, an "Attica Indictee." The poem, written by Shipman at Erie County Jail in 1974, inverts the symbolism of the dragon from its historical usage in global northern literature.[27] From the author of *Beowulf* through Henry Wadsworth Longfellow, Alfred Lord Tennyson, and numerous other poets, dragons have been creatures to be colonized, defeated, slain. Imprisoned Attica poets like Shipman and Jomo, however, use the dragon as a fierce protector of the people. In Shipman's poem, the young dragons (i.e., those imprisoned at Attica, all imprisoned people, all colonized people) are "fearsome and fearless / for the poor peoples cause."[28] Shipman even depicts the dragons' eyes "as two / redhot burning coals / reflecting the poor peoples blood." Shipman critiques the state's bond to the elite instead of the people, and, as Shipman's poem concludes, "Now you see why the system won't free the young / dragons."[29]

On the back cover, a large photograph of the Attica guard towers rising above high prison walls is paired with Ho Chi Minh's short prison poem "Free the Dragons":

> People who come out of prison
>   can build up the country.
> Misfortune is a test of
>   people's fidelity.
> Those who protest at injustice
>   are people of true merit.
> When the prison doors are opened,
>   the real dragons will fly out.[30]

As in Shipman's poem (which was most likely influenced by this poem), the *people* are central; the first three stanzas all include the word.[31] Unlike the caged young dragons in Shipman's poem, however, the focus here is on the freedom of dragons and how dragons will help the people when "the prison doors are opened." For Ho Chi Minh, as for Jomo, the dragon symbolizes wisdom, power, and regeneration. Ho Chi Minh's dragon poem circulated in prison print culture of the era. One poster from the Free Bobby Seale campaign of the early 1970s shows Seale, wrists in large metal handcuffs but the chain between them broken, with Ho Chi Minh's poem beneath the image. Here, instead of being presented in two-line stanzas as in Jomo's book, the poem is presented in all capital letters and lineated as it was typically translated in one four-line stanza.[32] Two things are curious here. First, in the final line of Seale's poster, plural *dragons* become singular *dragon*, suggesting that only Seale himself can free the people. Second, Jomo's printing of the poem added more poetic features like breaking the single stanza into four separate stanzas, indenting the second line of each stanza, adding enjambment, all of which gives Jomo's version a look closer to a poem like Gwendolyn Brooks's "We Real Cool." Reprinting poetry, in this case, also opens a space for rethinking, restructuring, and reimagining political language and poetic form.

The center pages of *Awakening of a Dragon* contain the most extensive poem in the booklet, Jomo's "Don't I Know You?," written in Erie County Jail in July 1974. Unlike the terse lines and tight stanzaic structure of poems by Bro. Bernard Shipman and Ho Chi Minh, this poem fills two 8.5 inch by 11 inch pages with lineation similar to the tradition of Whitman and Ginsberg. The poem opens with the narrator responding to being told to be a strong, proud Black man:

> ... Black on a ghetto corner?
> ... Proud of a welfare hand-out?
> ... Be strong on cold bologna & t.v. dinners?[33]

As the poem continues to unfurl, the narrator asks if "our forefathers" really wanted 40 acres and two mules, or if, after slavery, perhaps they had grown "to hate the very land that soaked up their blood."[34] Jomo expands the definition of "proud" to include a growing awareness "beyond the state of individualism."[35] His analysis of racial capitalism critiques "Slavemaster's welfare, Unemployment & No-Housing System."[36] If abolition is grounded in futurity, if it reorganizes space for the speculative, this section of Jomo's poem serves as a salient precursor to the contemporary abolition movement.

The final third of Jomo's poem references fifteenth-century Portuguese trade with Angola and the Congo, the Haitian Revolution, Mau Mau fighters, Vietnamese resistance, Wounded Knee, George Jackson, the Symbionese Liberation Army, and more. The narrator also serves as a people's historian of the Attica brothers and their uprising: "You was at the side of the true Attica Brothers of September / 13th, 1971, when they asked to be treated as men / humans [/] and received pain & death, but they resisted."[37] Poetry writing, here, becomes "the fugitive art of social life," as Stefano Harney and Fred Moten have termed practices like those used by Jomo and other imprisoned poets.[38]

One of the most comprehensive of these types of stapled booklets, *Fighting Back: Attica Memorial Book 1974*, was produced and distributed by a "collective effort by many Brothers and Sisters of the Attica Brothers Legal Defense."[39] Even if one might misguidedly argue that the publication of the poetry anthologies was motivated more by their poet-teachers and the appearance of poetry in other stapled publications and prison newspapers was nominal, the central role of poetry in *Fighting Back* signals the centrality of poetry to imprisoned writers at Attica. Quantitatively, nearly a quarter of the book's 100 pages contain poems. Ho Chi Minh's dragon poem, used on the back of Attica Brother Jomo's book, appears again, this time beneath a photograph of two white New York State troopers exiting a building. It is presented here in yet a different format; the first line is broken at "Build up," resulting in a brief second line ("The country") and a five-line stanza overall. Jomo's long poem, "Don't I Know You?," is reprinted in the booklet as well.

The other poems in *Fighting Back* range from love poems to political poems and apologies to polemics. Two poems directly critique President Nixon, who was in communication with Governor Rockefeller about the plan to send New York State troopers to crush the uprising at Attica. In one of these poems, "Psalm of Nixon," Ellis Robinson rewrites Ps. 23:1–6 ("The Lord is my Shepherd") by replacing God with Nixon, who "leadeth me beside stilled factories" and "guideth me to the path of unemployment for the / Party's sake."[40] Several other poems similarly delve into critiques of racial capitalism. Dalau Asahi has four poems in the booklet. In "Hunger," Asahi takes readers through his young narrator's life in four seasons leading up to his imprisonment, repeating both the opening line, "i was a ghetto's kid...," and the closing line, "i was hungry," in each stanza.[41] In spring, the narrator, who has "no / clothes on easter," was "hitting / bodegas, getting caught / and cut loose."[42] While playing in the streets in the summer, he "got / hit by a car twice, / but it was nothing."[43] The autumn and winter stanzas develop similarly: lack of a public assistance check, a landlord who "cut off the light," throwing snowballs at cars, taxis, and busses. "I got kicked, / stabbed and shot," Asahi writes, "cause / i was hungry."[44] As he concludes, he must still be "a ghetto's kid" because, even here at Attica, "i am still hungry."[45] These and other poems, including Asahi's poem "He Vivido," the only poem in Spanish in the booklet, offer a clear vision of the political and economic conditions in America in the early 1970s and a space for those imprisoned at Attica to personally and collectively critique the broken system.

Yet it is the poems of people's historians, written in the aftermath of the Attica rebellion, that make up the largest percentage of poems in *Fighting Back*. W. L. Wilson, writing under the pseudonyms Xmielex and Xmilex Tourah Diva Tah, contributed two September 13 poems. In the first poem, "Suddenly," Wilson uses four-line stanzas, typically with six or seven beats per line, to recount the day when state troopers with "A vacant stare— through vacant holes" rained bullets down upon the men in D-Yard.[46] Wilson's poem details the day's degradation ("Stand up boy == take off your clothes"), desecration ("Bleeding bodies—torn and ripped"), and reestablishment of police and guard control of the prison.[47] He saves one entire stanza for the gauntlet, which Heather Ann Thompson described in horrific detail in *Blood in the Water*. The imprisoned men had been stripped (including eyeglasses, false teeth). Naked and their feet punctured and bleeding from glass fragments, they were forced to run for "50 yards...[and]

both sides were lined with officers with ax handles, 2 x 4s, baseball bats and rifle butts."[48] Wilson describes the gauntlet in one stanza:

> Long gray tunnels—dingy halls
> Side by side—guard the walls
> Sticks and clubs—taste thy flesh
> Hands on head—run a gauntlet.[49]

Wilson's retelling uses rhyme (halls/walls), personification (sticks and clubs that *taste* flesh), word play ("guard" functions as both noun and verb here), alliteration (side by side, hand on head), and so on. Near the end of the poem, he gives a name to the horrors of Attica: "Darkness comes—in black disguise / To mourn the deeds—of genocide."[50] In another poem, Wilson describes September 13, 1971, as a "Subterfuge—that sought revenge."[51] W. L. Wilson is no longer only someone interviewed by journalists or scholars for their articles or essays; instead, he becomes, via his poems, a people's historian and a published poet.

Similarly, poems by Iron Mike (aka, Bro. Bernard Shipman, whose poem opened Attica Brother Jomo's booklet) and Jaja S (N. Michael Phillips) recollect September 13, 1971, in vivid and horrid detail. Shipman's "Death" concludes by summarizing that "it was death / returning to correct its blunder / but (40) died at my side so this / history will be my guide."[52] History plays a similar role in the first of Phillips's two poems about the day, a two-page poem titled "Surrender in Attica." The poet repeats a command from the police, "Please Surrender. / Put your hands on your head and go to / the north wall / you will not be harmed," to reflect on the perfidious language of law enforcement.[53] As a people's historian of and participant in the Attica uprising, Phillips knows firsthand the emptiness of the police officer's words. In response to the narrator pleading "Please don't shoot me," the poem's law enforcement antagonist responds,

> I tell you what nigger
> I want to shoot you
> but I will shoot at you
> and if you can out run this white power bullet
> then you are safe.[54]

The lived realities illustrated in this stanza—racism, white power, state-sanctioned violence—are nothing short of a death sentence.

In the poem that ends the booklet, "Death of a Comrade," Phillips focuses on the guns of the state troopers on the roof of C-block on the day of the massacre, the same type of guns used at My Lai and Kent State. The author comments next on "the fat man" at the negotiation table (Russell Oswald, commissioner of New York Corrections), whom he refers to as "the head man of all these concentration camps."⁵⁵ Because history, as the poem makes clear, repeats, he expects no negotiation. Phillips's narrator knows intuitively that "the only reason he has come in here, is to see how he / will kill us from the outside." Phillips then pulls back to the lyric mode:

> you ever notice that when somebodys
>   about to die
>   it always rains
>   I wonder why?⁵⁶

But the lyric mode is short, and history's repetition is inevitable. In the very next line, the narrator tells Jaja, "Hey man wake up" as state troopers are about to enter with their guns ("bang-bang-bang"). The poem, like the history of September 13, 1971, ends on an excruciating note. The narrator asks, "hey Jaja, why are you crying like that"; Jaja responds that his comrade, "my maine man got killed in that / god-damn-yard."⁵⁷

"Poetry as a Liberating Force": Small Press Poetry and Print Culture after Attica

By 1975, one year after the publication of *Fighting Back*, the denouement of interest in Attica by popular culture and print subculture begins. Film and jazz recordings brought a few final references to Attica to movie theaters and record stores. In the fall of 1975, Charles Mingus released *Changes One*, an album that opened with "Remember Rockefeller at Attica." Perhaps the most widely known popular reference to the uprising at Attica occurred when Sidney Lumet's *Dog Day Afternoon* opened in September 1975 in theaters across the United States. Set in Brooklyn in August 1972, the film begins with three men robbing a bank. The armed robbers take bank staff and patrons as hostages, and soon a substantial number of police officers arrive. Protagonist Sonny Wortzik, played by Al Pacino, is lured outside by a police sergeant. During the tense dialogue with the sergeant, Sonny shouts, "He wants to kill me so bad he can taste it," then repeatedly screams the word "Attica!" With the story of the uprising now reduced to a single word, its importance in popular culture and print culture wanes. By the tenth anniversary of the uprising in September 1981, President Reagan would recommend that the federal government spend $2 billion to build new prisons to "protect" US citizens from "the human predator," "career criminals," and "a jungle which threatens this clearing we call civilization."⁵⁸

Yet poetry workshops continued at Attica. After Celes Tisdale's workshop stopped meeting in 1975, David Kelly, a creative writing professor at nearby SUNY Geneseo, led the workshop in 1975 and early 1976. But Kelly, looking for a way for the workshops to continue without him, coaxed Gerald McCarthy, a white Vietnam veteran and recent graduate from the Iowa Writers Workshop, to "cover the workshop" for the summer of 1976.[59] McCarthy would teach creative writing at Attica, first once a week and then twice a week, until August 1979. McCarthy started a poetry magazine, *La Huerta*, and after several issues began a chapbook series under the same name to publish imprisoned writers. In addition to the chapbooks, La Huerta released a small anthology of writers from McCarthy's workshop, *Inside: Writings by Attica Inmates, 1977–78*. One chapbook, *Convicted Voices*, by a poet in McCarthy's workshops, Antu Satya (aka Lawrence I. Dillard), illustrates the changes in small press poetry publishing and Attica print culture at the end of the 1970s.

Without outside grants or funding, McCarthy got La Huerta's chapbooks printed any way he could. Dillard's chapbook, for example, was typeset, designed, and printed by high school vocational-technical students at a regional Board of Cooperative Education Services center where McCarthy also taught. Dillard's poems depict a post-uprising American rust belt of closing factories and endless winters. Dillard's poem "Today I See" opens in a late winter geography: "Traces of snow along the building / base." Looking up, the poet sees "branches on the withered peach tree" that are "entangled & bound / by a discarded black typewriter ribbon"—perhaps an indication of writer's block or a statement on the surveillance and censorship of imprisoned writers' words.[60] Yet the scene remains bucolic: "Winter hangs on" while garden tools, "untouched by winter's bitter cold," rest on a hallway door.[61] In the second and final stanza, Dillard metaphorically represents late 1970s American society via "broken shingles" that remind him "of poverty [/] / broken lives." He notices "evergreens across the grey wall" and remarks, "Funny / how they remain green all year."[62] There is, at times, a complex comfort in the quotidian, in everyday life, and the natural world. But moments like these are temporary at Attica, where, as Dillard concludes, "Pain & suffering mark this day / & all the days of my life."[63]

In "Mending the Existence of Our Times," the penultimate poem in the chapbook, Dillard responds to Robert Frost's beloved poem "Mending Wall." Dillard's poem begins by invoking the New England bard and promising, with a slight tongue-in-cheek tone, "not to steal" Frost's famous lines.[64] Critics have often praised Frost's poem because of its "restrained approach" and "quite subsurface pressure."[65] As Austin Allen writes, "Doubt is what makes 'Mending Wall' a poem and not an editorial ... a subversive classic rather than a scrap of yesterday's news."[66] Dillard's poetry and the poems of many imprisoned poets push against these academic tropes of restraint, subsurface tension, and aesthetic ambiguity. For Dillard, "There are fewer fences to mend / bad dreams [/] plastic meanings / less love [/] more deception."[67] Against the quiet poetics of moderation and self-discipline in Frost's wall poem, the poetics from inside Attica's massive concrete walls turns brassier and more candid: "My poetry is like the silent scream / of convicted voices."[68] In this poem that gives the volume its title and in poems throughout the chapbook, the abolition imagination works not through moderation but through a blunter, more outspoken, and more unambiguous mode of poetic discourse.

The final poem in *Convicted Voices*, "Two Birds," imagines the coming of both a more temperate and symbolic spring, slightly warmer air, rebirth, and perhaps release. In the opening stanza, two birds sing in harmony "tones of freedom."[69] The poem's 'abolition geography,' to borrow a term from Ruth Wilson Gilmore, remains quite local: a sparkling day, Attica's green field, inmates dressed in green also in the yard, a robin flying above the gray prison walls, and crows on the rooftops where New York State troopers fired their rifles a few Septembers ago.[70] Spring, to Dillard, also represents unity and solidarity:

> Black / white some in-between
> a blue net in a peach tree
> black birds of many colors
> hispanic inmate playing
> an african drum
> afro comb in his back pocket.[71]

When prison guards come early one morning to search the cells, Dillard notes that his mouse, presumably a pet, runs from him and hides under his bed. "The fear we shared," he writes, "was equal." But in the final stanza of the poem (and the chapbook), it is the birds that Dillard returns to:

> Free birds / fly high
> by nature you seem happy
> come tomorrow to our windows
> my bread I will share
> unnatural is this atmosphere
> fly my friends fly.[72]

In the unnatural atmosphere of Attica, robins and crows and black birds become the representatives of freedom. Their continual return allows the poet to reimagine or continue to imagine his freedom beyond these horrible, un-mending walls of Attica. And it is imperative to Dillard to maintain those "tones of freedom" in his daily life because, as he asserts in the opening poem of the chapbook, "Incarceration begins / when a mind refuses to think."[73]

A journalist who visited McCarthy's workshop nearly seven years after the uprising described a continuing sense of militancy in the participants' writings: "The poems say and do things beyond the dictionary definitions and grammatical pattern of words. . . . At Attica, the idea of poetry as a liberating force was clearer because the walls were tangible."[74] Imprisoned writers at Attica, from Tisdale's workshops of the early 1970s to McCarthy's of the later 1970s, imagined, like Mariame Kaba would four decades later, that "it's time for a jailbreak of the imagination."[75] In their writings, published in small press anthologies, chapbooks, and other ephemera of Attica print culture, they sought to create and cultivate that imagination with poetry.

The writing and publishing culture at Attica continues to reverberate through the vastly expanded prison writing programs of today. PEN America launched its Prison and Justice Writing Program in 1971 in the wake of the uprising at Attica. Today, the vastly expanded PEN program sponsors a Prison Writing Contest, a Mentor Program (one-on-one writing mentorship via correspondence), a Writing for Justice Fellowship, a monthly newsletter, a podcast series, and an annual prison writing awards anthology. The program also recently released *The Sentences That Create Us: Crafting a Writer's Life in Prison*, a comprehensive anthology of short essays and "how to" guides by prison writing teachers as well as formerly and currently imprisoned writers.[76]

Acclaimed memoirist and poet Randall Horton, who began his writing career in a workshop at Montgomery County Detention Center in Rockville, Maryland, while serving a sentence for seven felony convictions, recently received a Creative Capital grant for a project, "Radical Reversal," that will allow him to set up permanent recording studios inside prisons and detention centers for imprisoned women and men to practice musical and spoken word performance, sound engineering, and digital editing.[77] Randall's project quite literally creates what Angela Davis and her coauthors call "the radicalness of the imaginary as a space for what is yet unthinkable, at the edge of the possible."[78] Horton, the PEN America program, and countless other abolitionary workshop practitioners of the contemporary moment are the inheritors of the work Celes Tisdale, Dudley Randall, and others began in the months and years after prisoners at Attica began using poetry workshops and small press publishing to build the foundation for new abolitionary imaginations.

Notes

1 Mariame Kaba, *We Do This 'Til We Free Us: Abolitionist Organizing and Transforming Justice* (Chicago: Haymarket, 2021), 4.
2 Angela Y. Davis, Gina Dent, Erica R. Meiners, and Beth E. Richie, *Abolition. Feminism. Now.* (Chicago: Haymarket, 2022), 16.
3 Details on Broadside Press come from two sources: Julius E. Thompson, *Dudley Randall, Broadside Press, and the Black Arts Movement in Detroit, 1960–1995* (Jefferson: McFarland & Company, 1999) and Melba Joyce Boyd,

Wrestling with the Muse: Dudley Randall and the Broadside Press (New York: Columbia University Press, 2003).

4   With Gwendolyn Brooks and others, Randall mentored and, through Broadside, eventually published Knight's first two books, *Poems from Prison* (1968) and *Belly Song & Other Poems* (1973). Knight also edited an early anthology of prison writers, *Black Voices from Prison*, that was released by the US socialist publisher Pathfinder Books in 1970.

5   James Sullivan, "Real Cool Pages: The Broadside Press Broadside Series," *Contemporary Literature* 32, no. 4 (1991): 552–72, here 565.

6   Ibid., 566.

7   Davis in ibid., 566–67.

8   In a phone conversation with Tisdale on June 29, 2022, Tisdale made this remark about the publishing industry. He also credited Gwendolyn Brooks with urging Randall to publish the Attica anthology which she had seen on one of her visits to Randall's house in Detroit. On the history of Tisdale's workshops at Attica, see Mark Nowak, "Introduction: Celes Tisdale's Poetry Workshop at Attica," in *When the Smoke Cleared: Attica Poems and Journals*, ed. Celes Tisdale (Durham: Duke University Press, 2022), 1–24.

9   Joy James, "Introduction: Democracy and Captivity," in *The New Abolitionists: (Neo)Slave Narratives and Contemporary Prison Writings* (Albany: State University of New York Press, 2005), xxi–xlii, here xxv.

10 Ibid., xxxii.

11 *Betcha Ain't: Poems from Attica*, ed. Celes Tisdale (Detroit: Broadside Press, 1974), 41.

12 Email interview with Joseph Bruchac, fall 2016.

13 Ibid.

14 *The Last Stop: Writing from Comstock Prison*, ed. Joseph Bruchac (Greenfield Center: Greenfield Review Press, 1974), 16.

15 A-Jabar, "This Is a Recording," in *The Last Stop: Writing from Comstock Prison*, ed. Joseph Bruchac (Greenfield Center: Greenfield Review Press, 1974), 17–21.

16 Ibid., 17.

17 Ibid. Because A-Jabar's poem uses in-line slashes as caesuras, I use a bracketed slash [/] to signal in-line slashes when citing his poem within paragraphs.

18 Ibid.

19 See Orlando Patterson, *Slavery and Social Death: A Comparative Study* (Cambridge, MA: Harvard University Press, 1985).

20 A-Jabar, "This Is a Recording," 18–19.

21 Ibid., 21.

22 Russell N. Baird, *The Penal Press* (Evanston: Northwestern University Press, 1967), 9.

23 Ibid., 19.

24 Brother Thomas Hagen, "Death spoke," *Attica News*, July 31, 1974, A–4.
25 Ibid.
26 Sullivan, "Real Cool Pages," 571.
27 For court appearances, men imprisoned at Attica were regularly transferred to Erie County Jail, a pretrial maximum-security facility in downtown Buffalo.
28 Bro Bernard Shipman, "Free The Young Dragon," in Attica Brother Jomo, *Awakening of a Dragon* (Buffalo: Attica Bond to Free Jomo, 1974), front inner cover.
29 Ibid.
30 Ho Chi Minh, "Free the Dragons," in Attica Brother Jomo, *Awakening of a Dragon* (Buffalo: Attica Bond to Free Jomo, 1974), back cover.
31 For more on dragons and Ho Chi Minh in prison culture, see Joy James, "George Jackson: Dragon Philosopher and Revolutionary Abolitionist," *Black Perspectives*, August 21, 2018, https://www.aaihs.org/george-jackson-dragon-philosopher-and-revolutionary-abolitionist/.
32 See Ho Chi Minh, "People who Come out of Prison can Build up the Country," *PennState University Library*, 1970, https://digital.libraries.psu.edu/digital/collection/blackhistory/id/23/. The four-line lineation is used in most translations of the poem. See, for example, this version: Ho Chi Minh, "Prison Diary," 5th ed. (Hanoi: Foreign Language Publishing House, 1972), 88, https://www.bannedthought.net/Vietnam/HoChiMinh/HoChiMinh-PrisonDiary-1972.pdf.
33 Brother Jomo, "Don't I Know You?" in *Awakening of a Dragon* (Buffalo: Attica Bond to Free Jomo, 1974), unpaginated.
34 Ibid.
35 Ibid.
36 Ibid.
37 In-line slash denoted with bracketed slash [/].
38 Stefano Harney and Fred Moten, *The Undercommons: Fugitive Planning & Black Study* (Wivenhoe and New York: Minor Compositions, 2013), 73, https://www.minorcompositions.info/wp-content/uploads/2013/04/undercommons-web.pdf.
39 Attica Brother's Legal Defense, *Fighting Back: Attica Memorial Book 1974* (Buffalo: Attica Brothers Defense Fund, 1974), 2.
40 Ellis Robinson, "Psalm of Nixon," in *Fighting Back: Attica Memorial Book 1974* (Buffalo: Attica Brothers Defense Fund, 1974), 22.
41 Dalau Asahi, "Hunger," in *Fighting Back: Attica Memorial Book 1974* (Buffalo: Attica Brothers Defense Fund, 1974), 50.
42 Ibid.
43 Ibid.
44 Ibid.
45 Ibid.

46 W. L. Wilson, "Suddenly," in *Fighting Back: Attica Memorial Book 1974* (Buffalo: Attica Brothers Defense Fund, 1974), 83.

47 Ibid.

48 Heather Ann Thompson, *Blood in the Water: The Attica Prison Uprising of 1971 and Its Legacy* (New York: Pantheon, 2016), 213.

49 Wilson, "Suddenly," 83.

50 Ibid.

51 W. L. Wilson, "No More Keys—No More Locks," in *Fighting Back: Attica Memorial Book 1974* (Buffalo: Attica Brothers Defense Fund, 1974), 97.

52 Bernard Shipman, "Death," in *Fighting Back: Attica Memorial Book 1974* (Buffalo: Attica Brothers Defense Fund, 1974), 93.

53 Jaja S/N Michael Phillips, "Surrender in Attica 9/13/71," in *Fighting Back: Attica Memorial Book 1974* (Buffalo: Attica Brothers Defense Fund, 1974), 94–95, here 94.

54 Ibid., 95.

55 Jaja S/N Michael Phillips, "Death of a Comrade," in *Fighting Back: Attica Memorial Book 1974* (Buffalo: Attica Brothers Defense Fund, 1974), 101.

56 Ibid.

57 Ibid.

58 Ronald Reagan, "Remarks at the Annual Meeting of the International Association of Chiefs of Police in New Orleans, Louisiana," Ronald Reagan: Presidential Library & Museum, September 28, 1981, https://www.reaganlibrary.gov/archives/speech/remarks-annual-meeting-international-association-chiefs-police-new-orleans.

59 Information on McCarthy's workshops comes from a series of emails with him in 2021 and 2022 as well as a Zoom interview conducted on June 16, 2022.

60 Antu Satya (Lawrence I. Dillard), "Today I See," in *Convicted Voices* (Lakeville: La Huerta Press, 1979), unpaginated. In-line slash denoted with bracketed slash [/].

61 Ibid.

62 Ibid.

63 Ibid.

64 Antu Satya (Lawrence I. Dillard), "Mending the Existence of Our Times," in *Convicted Voices* (Lakeville: La Huerta Press, 1979), unpaginated.

65 Austin Allen, "Robert Frost: Mending Wall," *Poetry Foundation*, August 20, 2019, https://www.poetryfoundation.org/articles/150774/robert-frost-mending-wall.

66 Ibid.

67 Satya/Dillard, "Mending the Existence of Our Times," unpaginated.

68 Ibid.

69　Antu Satya (Lawrence I. Dillard), "Two Birds," in *Convicted Voices* (Lakeville: La Huerta Press, 1979), unpaginated.

70　See Ruth Wilson Gilmore, *Abolition Geography: Essays Toward Liberation* (London: Verso, 2022).

71　Satya/Dillard, "Two Birds," unpaginated.

72　Ibid.

73　Antu Satya (Lawrence I. Dillard), "Incarceration," in *Convicted Voices* (Lakeville: La Huerta Press, 1979), unpaginated.

74　Bob Bickel, "Writer Helps Inmates Find Poetry in Prison," *Democrat and Chronicle*, May 14, 1978, 4.

75　Kaba, *We Do This 'Til We Free Us*, 25.

76　For more on PEN America's Prison and Justice Writing Program and these publications, see https://pen.org/prison-writing/.

77　For more on Randall Horton's "Radical Reversal," see https://creative-capital.org/projects/radical-reversal/.

78　Davis et al., *Abolition. Feminism. Now.*, 16.

11

An Autofictional Intervention into Working-Class Literature

Karin Struck's *Klassenliebe* and the *Werkkreis Literatur der Arbeitswelt*

Christoph Schaub

Klassenliebe (Class Love), the autofictional debut novel by the then 25-year-old Karin Struck, was published in 1973 at a time when the social and cultural developments that would come to characterize life under neoliberal capitalism first began to appear on the horizon in West Germany. Among these transformations were the weakening of "traditional class affiliations and identities" and the "individualization of lifestyles."[1] At the same time, in the new social movements, the significance of "issues of identity and recognition" increased, while questions of redistribution began to slowly move further into the background.[2] The way *Klassenliebe* intervened in the literary and political public sphere of its time bears the mark of these emerging shifts. The novel examines class society, (proletarian) identity, and subjectivity, but in doing so emphasizes the personal as something that is at least as important for the understanding of (working-)class experiences as social position. *Klassenliebe* explores experience predominantly as the interiority of a socioculturally formed yet singular individual (an individual in crisis at that), and less so with respect to what Raymond Williams terms a (transindividual) 'structure of feeling.'[3]

The emphasis Struck puts on the personal marks a difference to the literature of the labor movement of the interwar years, which in many instances was concerned with shared class experiences and often represented political collectives.[4] At the same time, *Klassenliebe* appears to foreshadow the current transnational trend in autofictional and autosociobiographical writing about class society that was triggered by the success of Didier Eribon, Annie Ernaux, and others. Not too dissimilar from Struck, contemporary German writers mobilize the personal to explore changing class positions and a diverse working class that encompasses both heterogeneous cultural groups and a plurality of singular individuals.[5] For Struck, the personal opened an avenue for positioning herself in her immediate literary environment, in which writers and activists attempted to make a working-class literature. Her novel problematized how this project largely disregarded the individual and relegated many—often gendered—desires, emotions, and issues to the private sphere and thus beyond politics. One may well argue, as Ulka Anjaria's contribution to this volume also indicates, that in the context of the labor movement it is usually women who use literature politically to address the question of what counts as political in the first place. Emphasizing the personal allowed *Klassenliebe* to explore this issue with respect to the counter-public sphere from within which activists challenged hegemonic understandings of literature and promoted engaged writing in early 1970s West Germany.

In what follows, I will use the tension—to be outlined in the next section—between 'being part of' and 'not fitting into' the working-class literature of her immediate environment in order to analyze Struck's literary politics. The political uses of literature can best be understood, I contend, with respect to their actual historical manifestations—a critical operation that also prevents us from misconceiving literature as "an ahistorical medium to which political qualities can be arbitrarily assigned."[6] Struck's intervention, I argue, is most successful when her novel—due to its aesthetic form, the themes it emphasizes, and its narrator's cultural and political positioning—is able to lay bare blind spots and exclusionary politics in the project of making a working-class literature. Struck's point of reference, as I explain below, was in the first place the literary politics of the group *Werkkreis Literatur der Arbeitswelt* (Literature of the Working World Workgroup). Yet in the novel, her usage of the term *Arbeiterliteratur* (working-class literature) also evokes a much broader tradition that she criticizes without clearly defining (but for which she appears to see the *Werkkreis* as symptomatic); it refers to understandings of working-class literature in the academia of the time that she finds reductive, and it names forms of workers' literary articulation marginalized in prevalent understandings of working-class literature. In particular, Struck's intervention, then, concerns the question of individuality, the relation between public and private, and the depiction of the working class. But the novel does not contribute to discussions (and initiatives) among the author's contemporaries concerning the structural transformations necessary for the making of a working-class literature and enabling, more broadly, collective, democratic, and counter-public agency in the literary field, which, in the eyes of many, was determined by the culture industry.[7] In my analysis, I thus pose the question as to the political uses of literature on several interconnected levels: the historically situated politics of literary representation as well as the related formal strategies that affect what becomes visible as political within, and through, a text, and the practices, institutions, and organizations that enable and constrain political uses of literature, such as political organizing around literature.

Struck and the Reception of *Klassenliebe*

The recent rise in German writing about class has changed the scholarly perspective on *Klassenliebe*, a text that had hitherto left its mark in German literary history mainly as a foundational text of the *Neue Subjektivität* (New Subjectivity) and an important work in what has sometimes been called, imprecisely, women's literature.[8] Scholars now emphasize how the link between *Klassenliebe* and (the working) class was crucial in the novel's historical context, as it concerned the author's biography and self-understanding, the debates in the literary field, and the content of the novel. Born in 1947 as the daughter of farm workers who fled the GDR for West Germany when she was six years old, Struck was a social climber through education. In the early 1970s, she worked on a PhD thesis on the "Aesthetics of Working-class Literature, 1970–1972." She never finished the dissertation, but *Klassenliebe* appears to be its continuation in a different form.[9] Her research focused on the *Werkkreis Literatur der Arbeitswelt*, an organization that promoted writing by workers.[10] The *Werkkreis* is also a central topic in the novel, and unsurprisingly so, as Struck herself had been a member of this literary organization and of the DKP, the German Communist Party.[11]

When *Klassenliebe* was published in the spring of 1973, it was discussed rather disapprovingly in left-wing media and literary circles. In May 1973, when Struck participated in a meeting of the *Dortmunder Gruppe 61*—the first major group in West Germany to engage through literature with the industrial working world—the prominent writer Max von der Grün argued that Struck's writing lacked a "class standpoint."[12] The far-left magazine *konkret* called the novel an individualistic "collection of all the illusions that sometimes count as 'left-wing.'"[13] *Unsere Zeit*, the newspaper of the DKP, criticized the text for its lack of a standpoint, its emphasis on individuality, and its unrealistic depiction of the working class.[14] Richard Limpert, a respected working-class writer of the *Werkkreis* who is mentioned in the novel, saw *Klassenliebe* as a thought-provoking text by a promising young author, but also insisted that—because of its challenging form—the novel would resonate with workers "only in individual cases."[15] Whatever their verdicts, Struck's contemporaries situated *Klassenliebe* with respect to debates about the making of a working-class literature.[16]

That *Klassenliebe* did not sit well with contemporary critics on the left is hardly surprising. It did not fit neatly into what, in the West Germany of the early 1970s, was understood predominantly as the working-class literature emerging (or supposed to emerge) from the labor movement, neither historically nor contemporaneously, neither formally nor thematically. Whereas working-class literature, according to the highly politicized perspective of the time, prefers either "operational [operative]"[17] genres such as reportage, workers' correspondence, and agitprop plays, or genres able to represent a social totality such as the novel, *Klassenliebe* employs a mix of genres coded as private: the diary, the dream protocol, the letter. Whereas working-class literature represents collective experiences and events in the spheres of work and politics, Struck's novel is dedicated to the interior and personalized life of its autodiegetic narrator, Karin Strauch, covering the time from May 16 to August 25, 1972. And whereas working-class literature relies on a proletarian standpoint, or at least on one in line with the objectives of the labor movement, the perspective of *Klassenliebe* is messier: the novel is narrated from an experience of in-betweenness and out-of-placeness caused by a not-yet-successful process of upward mobility that is accompanied by anxiety, shame, depression, and rage. Karin is situated between the classes and also stands between two men that represent different social positions: her husband H., whose background is also proletarian, and her lover Z., a bourgeois intellectual.[18] The tension between 'being part of' and 'not fitting into' that marks the novel's position in the literary subfield of working-class literature is embodied by the text's narrator.

Klassenliebe, *Werkkreis Literatur der Arbeitswelt*, and Working-Class Literature

We can examine the uses of literature as a medium of politicization by situating *Klassenliebe* with respect to the *Werkkreis Literatur der Arbeitswelt*. In *Klassenliebe*, Karin mentions the *Werkkreis* throughout: she reflects on reading and duplicating its publications, participating in its meetings, and collaborating with writers organized in it. For the novel's first-person narrator, as for its author,[19] the *Werkkreis* is a significant context for developing her own writing and for thinking about the nature of working-class literature. Founded in 1970, the organization was the outcome of conflicts within the *Dortmunder Gruppe 61*. In the eyes of some of its members, this group had failed to support working-class writers and had become too oriented toward the bourgeois literary market.[20] By May 1972, when Karin began her notations in *Klassenliebe*, the *Werkkreis* had organized about 150 members (most of whom were workers and salaried employees), encompassed twenty literary workshops across West Germany, ran an internal publication (*Informationsdienst*) to facilitate discussions, held meetings of delegates and educational seminars, and had also organized two reportage competitions and published selected contributions in anthologies.[21]

The *Werkkreis* saw itself as a sort of successor to the proletarian-revolutionary literature of the Weimar Republic under changed sociocultural circumstances and worked toward creating the conditions necessary for a collective production and discussion of texts meant to affect change beyond the literary sphere and particularly in the workplace.[22] The organization's program of 1970, drafted by Erasmus Schöfer, promoted the collaboration of workers and salaried employees with intellectuals and professional writers; it sought to establish collective forms of organization; it understood its literature as a force for representing and changing reality (from a proletarian standpoint); it located its writers and target audience within the working class; it favored a realistic aesthetics rich in information and documentation; and it advocated for "the abolishment of the privileges of culture and education."[23] In contrast to many political organizations at the time, the organization was not sectarian but welcomed communist, social-democratic, and nonaffiliated activists and emphasized collaboration with trade unions.[24] The members of the *Werkkreis* were as much interested in the form and content that working-class literature should take as they were concerned with building a counter-public infrastructure for the production, distribution, and reception of working-class literature. From 1972 onward, however, the *Werkkreis* also cooperated with the major publishing house Fischer, which indicates the limits and conditions of the group's counter-public agency within a capitalist market.

As Horst Hensel, a prominent activist of the *Werkkreis*, writes in retrospect, the organization's project was partially based on a "fetishistic" and "idealized" understanding of the working class and the labor movement as a "class-conscious formation."[25] This view of the proletariat lacked any actual foundation in 1970s West Germany. For a variety of reasons, such as the repercussions of National Socialism and the so-called economic miracle, the kind of proletarian milieus that had been foundational to a politicized working-class culture in the Weimar Republic no longer existed and the aspirations and lifestyle of the majority of workers had changed.[26] In addition, the readers of the *Werkkreis* publications, which by the early 1980s had reached a circulation of more than one million, were largely not workers, but students and left-wing intellectuals.[27] *Klassenliebe* traced these tensions within the *Werkkreis*'s project to create a working-class literature.

In the novel, Karin criticizes "young workers in the Werkkreis" for not being able to recognize the complexity of labor relations and for ignoring the intersections of class and gender, as they do not conceive of domestic and care work as work due to it being "unpaid."[28] She also takes aim at what she considers resentment against people perceived as intellectuals, in particular when they are, like her, from a proletarian background but attend(ed) university.[29] In a different notation, Karin reflects upon a female "salaried employee in the Werkkreis who is writing a trashy novel [Kitschroman],"[30] and, elsewhere, claims that (female) workers who read such novels have "an aesthetic desire."[31] In another passage, Karin notes how, during a *Werkkreis* meeting, she was unable to tell the story of "the trainee Burkhard" who "owned every volume of Karl May." For her, his reading biography points to an unwillingness in the *Werkkreis* to "analyze the fantasy of the old [*ollen*] workers."[32] The underlying assumption that the *Werkkreis* was mostly blind to the kind of literature that workers may predominantly have read takes its plausibility from the historical disconnect between the organization's target audience and its actual readers.

Karin's reflections about what counts as the working class in the *Werkkreis* remain fragmentary, but they expose exclusions and weak points within the organization's project. She seeks to advance a comprehension of the proletarian experience that is more expansive and complex than what is captured by the idea of a largely homogeneous and class-conscious proletariat. For Karin, the working class ultimately constitutes a question: "who's that, the working class, who, who, the old [*ollen*] workers, who are they?"[33] In other words, *Klassenliebe* shifts and destabilizes what is intelligible as the working class in the counter-publics of the *Werkkreis*.[34] This realistic impulse characterizes Struck's interest in the political uses of literature, as her novel questions ahistorical premises of contemporary literary politics.

Karin not only articulates criticism of the *Werkkreis* and working-class literature more generally, but also explores the possibilities of a different kind of working-class literature which is never realized in the diegesis. While the novel, symptomatically, identifies no (alternative) agent of social change, Karin situates her own literary project with respect to what can be understood as the writing of the history of minorities and moves away from an understanding of the proletariat as the revolutionary subject: "The history of patients has not been written. . . . The history of workers, the history of women, the history of black people, the history of children, the history of the people."[35] Yet for Karin, such an alternative literature cannot simply focus on heroic and public events, the representation of which too often betrays a romanticizing image of proletarians. Instead, it should concentrate more on the everyday and the life of the mind; it should even, to some extent, take inspiration from the way the bourgeoisie use literature:

> What has been written so far about the working class, about the simple people, about the little people, about the old [*ollen*] workers, about the

farmers with the biggest potatoes, that's nothing but a waste of paper. As if it were enough to describe rallies, the organization of communist factory cells, the development of class struggles. Those old [ollen] workers are not marionettes. Who's screaming "psychologism"? Who? The bourgeoisie have made every detail of their life great through their literature.... To make great. Where to start? And how?[36]

Karin wants to use literature to elevate "every detail" of proletarian life and culture and to 'diversify' it. The poetics of enumeration in these sentences indicates such a desired shift in the representation of the working class.

Rather than building on, say, the *Bildungsroman* of nineteenth-century bourgeois realism, however, Karin is attracted to literary forms more characteristic of modernist writing. Indeed, Karin likens her project to Marcel Proust's *À la recherche du temps perdu*,[37] to an "archaeology,"[38] and to an exploration of the unconscious. For her, literature is about recovering what has been buried. This includes the neglect effected by forms of working-class literature that marginalize private dimensions of the proletarian experience. Seeking an analogy with film late in the novel, Karin speculates about

> a literary technique that would be able to immerse itself in the stream of those subterranean dramas ... the barely perceptible vibrations in the perception, feeling, and thinking of those old [ollen] workers.... I would like to make a movie about my father, who's getting dentures, who's crying because he is getting dentures, who is laughing and saying, now I have much whiter teeth than you, Karin, about the barely perceptible vibrations of that old [ollen] worker who's losing his teeth, only about that, the at once most artistic and most social movie.[39]

Several aspects of this passage are important. First, according to Karin, aesthetics and engaged art are not seen as opposites in working-class cultural production. Second, a central topic of such a different kind of working-class literature would be the most mundane aspects of visible everyday life. Third, this literature would also be about recovering what lies below the surface, what is "barely perceptible." Importantly, the shape Karin sketches for her project adds a different layer to her criticism of the *Werkkreis* and working-class literature more generally. The problem, according to Karin, is not simply that they operate with unrealistic assumptions about proletarians. They also (she alleges) exclude the private sphere, the unconscious, individuality, and everyday life from literary representation. By doing so, they fall back behind what bourgeois literature has accomplished and, moreover, miss the chance to develop a concept of politics that extends beyond the public sphere. It is important to address two aspects here: first, we have to analyze the understanding of the political on which Struck bases her literary intervention into contemporary working-class literature; and second, we have to examine the very literary form that this intervention takes.[40]

Individuality and the Political between the Public and the Private Sphere

Karin's criticism of working-class literature, the labor movement, and left-wing politics revolves around the significance attributed to individuality and the private sphere. Her diagnosis of what she perceives as the Left's historical shortcomings is unequivocal: "'The individual' was only known as a cuss word.' As is still the case in the labor movement today."[41] For Karin, an impoverished language is symptomatic of this contempt for individuality. The "set-phrase language [*Formel-Sprache*]"[42] and "pathetic categori[es]" used in left-wing discourse reflect a "mechanistic image of man [*Menschenbild*]."[43] At the same time, the disregard for the private sphere makes invisible in political discourse the intersections of class and gender that Karin experiences in her life but to which she cannot formulate a feminist answer in her notations.[44] Karin suggests, however, that "the attempt to make oneself alive again" is "the condition for everything, 'for being able to fight the system.'"[45]

Four years after the publication of *Klassenliebe*, an essay by Struck indicates how the author's thinking about the political is close to that of the novel's narrator. In "Das Private ist das Politische" (1977; The Private Is Political), Struck describes how, following her activism in the DKP and the SDS (Socialist German Students' League), her "long march through the jungle of private challenges"[46] influenced her thinking about the relation between public and private. She realized that "each of our so-called private problems is a moment of the epoch in which we live, we only have to translate it [into something political]."[47] And she argues: "Our most personal substance is literally the foundation of our political faculties. . . . Our most personal biography connects us with others, and only our ability to be private enables us to be in a community."[48] This understanding of the political as something emerging from the personal and the private sphere animates Struck's political use of literature.

It is undeniable that political and theoretical insights of second-wave feminism mark Struck's thinking about the political, not least given the adaptation of one of its central slogans for her essay's title.[49] But I would argue, without suggesting any influence, that what Struck articulates in *Klassenliebe* also resonates with how the contemporaneous Frankfurt School theory treated the question of the public and private spheres. I am thinking of Oskar Negt and Alexander Kluge's *Öffentlichkeit und Erfahrung: Zur Organisationsanalyse von bürgerlicher und proletarischer*

Öffentlichkeit (Public Sphere and Experience: Toward an Analysis of the Bourgeois and Proletarian Public Sphere), which was published just one year before *Klassenliebe* in 1972. In their book, the authors argue that "[p]roletarian life does not form a cohesive whole, but is characterized by the blocking of those elements that, in reality, hold it together."[50] One of the reasons for this lies in the fact that the way the public is thought about and practiced in bourgeois society "exclude[s] the two most important areas of life: the whole of the industrial apparatus and socialization in the family."[51] This "traditional public sphere" is thus characterized by "the mechanism of exclusion between public and private spheres."[52] Struck herself notes this dynamic when asking whether the "opposition between private and public, between private and political [is] only constructed."[53] If the *Werkkreis* is concerned with making the sphere of industrial work an issue of political debate, *Klassenliebe* addresses, in an expanded sense, what Negt and Kluge call "socialization in the family." Throughout the novel, the first-person narrator demands that love and sexual relationships, the relationship with her parents, mother- and parenthood, gender relations, and the realm of the household and the everyday need to be significant parts of working-class literature. In this sense, the *Werkkreis* and Struck's political uses of literature can be seen as complementary. Taken together, they address "the whole of the industrial apparatus and socialization in the family."

Moreover, reading *Klassenliebe* with Negt and Kluge allows for a different way of describing what the novel criticizes as the language and the politics of working-class literature. Similarly to Karin, Negt and Kluge diagnose that "the labor movement's linguistic resources" have been "exhausted"; yet they name different causes: "[f]ifty years of counterrevolution and restoration."[54] In addition, *Klassenliebe* and *Öffentlichkeit und Erfahrung* coincide with respect to how the bourgeois organizational logic of the public sphere affects left-wing politics and culture. Negt and Kluge argue that a "split[ting]-up [of] the revolutionary process into essential and inessential, into what is of value to the revolution and what is useless,"[55] has occurred—that is, a "split[ting]-up" into the public and the private that mirrors the commodification of life. Even within the students' movement, in which Struck participated and which is a frequent object of criticism in *Klassenliebe*, Negt and Kluge locate two tendencies: "mobilization via the mechanism of political value abstractions; and the more difficult and slow constitution of emancipatory interests."[56] If "[a]bstract mobilization, which relies above all on ethical and merely political impulses," predominates, it "necessarily creates a mechanism of exclusion that eliminates concrete interests because they cannot stand up to the legitimating political weight of world events."[57] Karin attacks this kind of reduction of the political when she claims that a working-class literature that only emphasizes factory cells and rallies but that does not explore the meaning of her father getting dentures is "a waste of paper."[58] *Klassenliebe* probes an intervention into working-class literature not governed by "political value abstractions."[59] For this reason, the novel criticizes "set-phrase language" and emphasizes the private sphere and individuality.

Despite the fact that Struck's novel and Negt and Kluge's analysis of the public sphere converge in some respects, a fundamental difference exists as well: Negt and Kluge locate "the core of proletarian cultural revolution [in] the organization of collective proletarian experience."[60] For Struck, as for Karin, the participation in such attempts (*Werkkreis*, DKP, SDS) resulted in severe disappointments and "a need to work as an individual and in the private realm [*im Einzelnen und Privaten*]."[61] In fact, in "The Private Is Political," Struck claims: "Writing became action [*Handeln*] for me. I learned that reading and writing were actions, likely more intensive ones than rallies and direct political action. I found out that writing was an engagement with community, with politics."[62] For Struck, the act of writing itself became central to her understanding of literature's political uses. If this was, on the one hand, a response to the dilemmas and disappointments she experienced in the context of left-wing organizing, her move toward the personal, as explored and represented through writing, aimed to transform the experiential basis of politics. What was relegated to the private sphere should thus be articulated in the public sphere to question and broaden what counts as political therein—such was the proposition that *Klassenliebe* put forward. By publishing what she wrote privately and thereby contributing confrontationally to debates about working-class literature, Struck used her writing to intervene politically. Yet in doing so, her own work was increasingly separated from the collaborative development of texts that the *Werkkreis* considered to be essential to the organization of a counter-public sphere (although the narrator describes being involved in such work in *Klassenliebe*). When it came to making the private political, however, the way Struck used literary form came to play a particularly important role.

Politics of Form, Autofiction, and Documentary Writing

The writing and publication of *Klassenliebe* fell into a phase when "new developments in the aesthetic-poetological convictions in the Werkkreis"[63] first began to gain some ground—that is, a new openness to more traditional literary forms like the novel. Up to that point, operative and documentary genres, such as report and reportage, had predominated the organization's literary practices. This had been punctuated by the two reportage competitions that the *Werkkreis* had organized in 1969 and 1971 and that had focused on the workday and the workplace.

If one looks at the reportages published in the anthology of the second competition, several aspects stand out.⁶⁴ Although structurally diverse, all the texts are well organized, use clearly structured sentences, and hew closely to the competition's topic without digressing. The texts deliver information about working conditions, point to how these could be improved, and describe actions taken. Throughout, the many male and fewer female authors, some of whom remain anonymous, are highly critical of labor relations and specific superiors. When relating personal experiences, the authors are primarily concerned with representing their experiences as those of the members of their social class and profession. Some texts highlight—and sometimes dedicate considerable space to—the drastic psychological consequences of harsh and exploitative working conditions. But they do not explore thoroughly interiority or the interrelations between the workplace and other spheres of workers' lives. Instead, they document conditions and experiences that they are able to 'prove': by writing reportages, they make use of a literary genre coded as public, engaged, and factual.⁶⁵

Against this background, *Klassenliebe*'s politics of form becomes visible as an element of Struck's political use of literature.⁶⁶ Along with the novel's propositional discourse and its predominant topics, literary form is essential to the text's intervention. This is so because genres, for example, enable and delimit a particular knowledge and thus influence what can(not) become visible in a text.⁶⁷ The formal choices Struck made already articulated the topic of individuality and the relation between public and private, for which there was little room in working-class literature according to Karin. Struck's choice of genre and mode of writing was, then, itself a political intervention into certain kinds of working-class literature, in particular as it drew attention to the limitations of operative and documentary genres.

Without using the term, Struck describes her own literary practice in the sense commonly used to define autofiction. She writes that she "presents the private material to the public in an utter and inextricable mix of autobiography and fiction."⁶⁸ Such an understanding of her literary practice matches the fundamental definition of autofiction as a mode of writing (rather than as a genre) characterized by "different forms of the more or less paradoxical combination of the referential pact and the fictional pact."⁶⁹ Autofiction implies not simply *any* kind of referential relation, but specifically one that is articulated through an autobiographical dimension that associates author and narrator (or a character in the text). The paratextual designation of *Klassenliebe* as a novel, the text's defamiliarizing adaptation of its author's name as the narrator's (Karin Strauch/Karin Struck), and the countless congruences between the biography of the narrator and that of the author make the text a paradigmatic autofictional novel.

Because it combines autobiography with the blurring of boundaries between fictional and factual texts, *Klassenliebe* clashes formally with the literary discourse and practice of the early *Werkkreis*. In contrast to the *Werkkreis*'s reportages, which tend to focus almost exclusively on generalizable social experiences and thus on position rather than personality, *Klassenliebe* deals more extensively with the specific biography of an individual. This does not mean that Karin ignores the fact that her experiences are socially produced and result partially from her (precarious) social position between classes; it means only that she foregrounds individuality and emphatically approaches the social through the experience of the individual. Additionally, the novel's autofictional mode interrogates the extent to which a documentary literary politics that excludes the fictional can successfully negotiate individual lives in class society. Here, autofiction is presented in partial opposition to reportage insofar as it is better able to promote the personal within the literary public: Struck appears to prefer autofiction because it offers a useful way to make the private public and thus "translate it"[70] into something political.

At the same time, *Klassenliebe* presents itself as a document of Karin's socially formed (interior) life. This is an effect of the genres used to manifest the text's autofictional mode, but it also results from the linguistic style the novel employs. Struck's text combines the genres of the diary, the intimate letter, and, to some extent, the dream protocol. In the text, the boundaries between these genres are blurred: all of them tend to require a first-person narrator and are coded as private—in contrast to the reportage or the novel. If these genres often function as documents of private lives and everyday history, the novel's autofictional mode supports and intensifies such an understanding. That most of the text's entries are dated precisely with the day, month, and year further emphasizes the novel's documentary character. In addition, *Klassenliebe* constructs its documentary dimension stylistically. Karin's notations are associative, digressive, contemplative, and full of contradictions and ellipses. This aura of immediacy that *Klassenliebe* purposefully constructs is also supported by "mistakes in the areas of orthography, interpunctuation, and syntax."[71] An "open structure" characterizes the text: it "wants to come across as direct, spontaneous, and appellative; like a letter, it wants to address its readers directly."[72] Thus, the way the text uses the genres of diary and letter also serves to destabilize the boundaries between public and private. All of this suggests to readers that what they encounter in the book are Karin's immediate, unpolished, unedited utterances, that they hold in their hands a document of her life from May to August 1972. The text's designation as a novel simultaneously alerts readers to the fact that they face a carefully crafted work of art. Still, through its fabricated documentary character, *Klassenliebe* foregrounds its narrator's purportedly immediate and authentic experiences.

Presenting itself as the document of Karin's life, the novel inserts the personal into the public sphere as an area of life that is profoundly political. It thereby differs from—and complements—what the reportages written for the *Werkkreis*'s competitions accomplished through the painstaking documentation of the conditions of wage labor: to make public and politicize "the whole of the industrial apparatus."[73] Instead, *Klassenliebe*'s politics of form challenges the separation of public and private by focusing on individuality and interiority as crucial parts of a social life characterized by class and gender relations.

The shape of an alternative working-class literature remains at best fragmentary in *Klassenliebe*. However, with regard to the literature of the *Werkkreis*, which in *Klassenliebe* is taken as symptomatic of prevalent practices, forms, and understandings of working-class literature more broadly, the strength of Struck's political use of literature was how her text negotiated the politics of literary representation: that is, how literature, on the level of a text, can expand our sense of what counts as political by shifting "the distribution of the sensible"[74] that regulates who can participate and what is (in)intelligible in a particular context. In other words, Struck uses literature to politicize areas of society and culture otherwise not visible as political. She achieves this not only through her novel's discourse but also by developing a politics of form that stands in productive tension with some dominant genres of working-class literature as they were used at the time in the *Werkkreis*. Finally, this politics of form also resonates with what has been called, in the context of 1968, a "revolution in perception" that changes the "patterns of perception, thought, and classification."[75]

Yet Struck's literary politics did not engage the question of what role literature—its production, distribution, and reception—could play in organizing people in specific historical contexts. This question was central to the political use of literature in the *Werkkreis*, which sought to build an infrastructure to enable the collaborative production and publication of texts, literary and political debate, and the promotion of workers and salaried employees as writers. Arguably, Struck's writing was a response to her disappointment with such kinds of left-wing organizing, and her project became "to work as an individual and in the private realm"[76] and to then intervene publicly through the publication of her literary work. Rather than contributing to the collective (or even collectivist) projects of working-class literature, Struck "fashioned herself with [*Klassenliebe*] as the daughter of workers *and* a left-wing intellectual writer"[77] and in so doing she also positioned herself successfully in the literary market.[78] Her political use of literature, then, was limited in terms of its ability to work collaboratively toward broader structural change in the literary field and beyond. Like the literary politics of the *Werkkreis*, which was unsuccessful in building international connections,[79] Struck's intervention also remained constricted to local and national scales (despite the novel's occasional references to international events and texts of world literature). Reading *Klassenliebe* in the context of the *Werkkreis Literatur der Arbeitswelt* shows that the understanding of the political uses of literature can be enriched by site-specific studies. Such analyses should focus on the (dis)connections between textual discourse, the politics of form, and extratextual practices and organizations. The reason for this is as simple as it is important: these (dis)connections crucially remind us that literary texts become 'politicized' through their complex and urgent engagements with their immediate sociocultural and historical contexts.

Notes

1. Oliver Nachtwey, *Die Abstiegsgesellschaft: Über das Aufbegehren in der regressiven Moderne*, 8th ed. (Berlin: Suhrkamp, 2018), 188. Unless otherwise noted, all translations from German are from the author.
2. Ibid., 187.
3. See Daniel Hartley's article in this volume.
4. For some examples, see Christoph Schaub, *Proletarische Welten: Internationalistische Weltliteratur in der Weimarer Republik* (Berlin and Boston: De Gruyter, 2019).
5. See Christoph Schaub, "The Poetics of Personal Authenticity: Diversity, Intersectionality, and the Working Class in Contemporary German Literature," in *Re-imagining Class: Working-Class Identity and Intersectionality in Contemporary Culture*, ed. Michiel Rys and Liesbeth François (forthcoming with Leuven University Press in 2024).
6. See Ivana Perica, "Politische Literatur und Politik der Literatur, Revolution und Evolution: Schnittstellen von politischer Theorie und kritischer Literaturwissenschaft," in *Politische Literatur: Debatten, Begriffe, Aktualität*, ed. Christine Lubkoll, Manuel Illi, and Anna Hampel (Stuttgart: Metzler-Verlag, 2019), 93–107, here 98.
7. From the late 1960s onward, West Germany saw a plethora of debates and initiatives to democratize and organize the literary field in collective and anticapitalist ways. These actions encompassed publishing houses, the book trade, and literary criticism as the institutions of the production, distribution, and reception of literature. The literary agents envisioned and attempted to build counter-publics that worked against the split between producers and consumers. See Carolin Amlinger, *Schreiben: Eine Soziologie literarischer Arbeit*, 2nd ed. (Berlin: Suhrkamp, 2021), 192–228.
8. Until recently, scholars mentioned class only briefly, see Ingeborg Gerlach, *Abschied von der Revolte: Studien zur deutschsprachigen Literatur der siebziger Jahre* (Würzburg: Königshausen & Neumann, 1994), 47–9; Ulrich Breuer, "Nackt wandern: Karin Strucks *Klassenliebe* im Bekenntnisdiskurs (der siebziger Jahre)," *Zeitschrift für Literaturwissenschaft und Linguistik* 126 (2002): 103–27, here 114–15. For one example of the new scholarship on *Klassenliebe*, see Eva Blome, "Rückkehr zur Herkunft: Autosoziobiografien erzählen von der Klassengesellschaft," *Deutsche Vierteljahresschrift für Literaturwissenschaft und Geistesgeschichte* 94, no. 4 (2020): 541–71.

9   See Karin Struck, *Klassenliebe* (Frankfurt am Main: Suhrkamp, 1973), 10.

10 See Ariane Neuhaus-Koch, "Karin Struck und die Arbeiterliteratur," in *Schreibwelten – Erschriebene Welten: Zum 50. Geburtstag der Dortmunder Gruppe 61*, ed. Gertrude Zepl-Kaufmann and Jasmin Grande (Essen: Klartext, 2011), 267–72, here 267.

11 See Gerd Koenen, *Das rote Jahrzehnt: Unsere kleine deutsche Kulturerevolution 1967–1977*, 5th ed. (Köln: Kiepenheuer & Witsch, 2011), 274.

12 See Neuhaus-Koch, "Karin Struck," 269–70.

13 Rolv Heuer, "Bon jour, Proletariat," in *Karin Struck: Materialien*, ed. Hans Adler and Hans Joachim Schrimpf (Frankfurt am Main: Suhrkamp, 1984), 186–8, here 187.

14 See Monika Kummerhoff, "Unbewältigtes Thema," in *Karin Struck Materialien*, ed. Hans Adler and Hans Joachim Schrimpf (Frankfurt am Main: Suhrkamp, 1984), 229–30.

15 Richard Limpert, "Klassenhiebe," in *Karin Struck Materialien*, ed. Hans Adler and Hans Joachim Schrimpf (Frankfurt am Main: Suhrkamp, 1984), 192–3, here 192.

16 Similarly, Sven Glawion understands *Klassenliebe* as "an intervention into the working-class literature of the time." See his "Als Arbeitertochter unter Marx' Erben: Eine Lesart zu *Klassenliebe* von Karin Struck," *Revista de Estudos Alemães* 8 (2019): 45–72, here 66.

17 Gerald Stieg and Bernd Witte, *Abriß einer Geschichte der deutschen Arbeiterliteratur* (Stuttgart: Klett, 1973), 12.

18 On the conflicts in these relationships as class conflicts, see Glawion, "Als Arbeitertochter," 50–2.

19 See Neuhaus-Koch, "Karin Struck," 267–8. I speak of Karin when I mean the text's autodiegetic narrator and of Struck when I refer to the novel's author, although the boundaries between them are fluid due to the novel's autofictional mode.

20 See Alfred Strasser, "Der Übergang von der Dortmunder Gruppe 61 zum Werkkreis Literatur der Arbeitswelt," in *Schreibwelten – Erschriebene Welten: Zum 50. Geburtstag der Dortmunder Gruppe 61*, ed. Gertrude Zepl-Kaufmann and Jasmin Grande (Essen: Klartext, 2011), 230–6.

21 See Michaela Wiegand, "Chronik des Werkkreises 1968–2019," *Literatur in Westfalen: Beiträge zur Forschung* 17 (2020): 427–34.

22 See Werner Jung, "Literatur von unten: Der Werkkreis Literatur der Arbeitswelt," *Literatur in Westfalen: Beiträge zur Forschung* 17 (2020): 157–93, here 160–3.

23 See Horst Hensel, "Das Programm des Werkkreises," *Literatur in Westfalen: Beiträge zur Forschung* 17 (2020): 257–60, here 258.

24 See Wiegand, "Chronik," 429; Koenen, *Das rote Jahrzehnt*, 257–315.

25 Horst Hensel, "Realistisch schreiben und Partei ergreifen: Nachbilder aus dem Werkkreis Literatur der Arbeitswelt," *Literatur in Westfalen: Beiträge zur Forschung* 17 (2020): 239–50, here 249.

26 See Hans-Ulrich Wehler, *Deutsche Gesellschaftsgeschichte: Bundesrepublik und DDR 1949–1990* (Bonn: Bundeszentrale für politische Bildung, 2009), 153–62.

27 See Hensel, "Realistisch schreiben," 249.

28 Struck, *Klassenliebe*, 104.

29 See ibid., 49–50.

30 Ibid., 221.

31 Ibid., 76. The significance of aesthetics and of individuals' desires were issues Struck and the *Werkkreis* disagreed on. See Neuhaus-Koch, "Karin Struck," 267; Gerlach, *Abschied*, 47–9.

32 Struck, *Klassenliebe*, 206, 207.

33 Ibid., 254.

34 One limitation of Struck's own representation of the working class lies in that her novel leaves unaddressed the presence of migrant workers in Germany, the so-called *Gastarbeiter*.

35 Struck, *Klassenliebe*, 139.

36 Ibid., 246–7.

37 See ibid., 247, 243.

38 Ibid., 202–3.

39 Ibid., 270–2.

40 Phrasing the problem in this way implies two assumptions: first, that Karin's project can be likened to some extent to Struck's, which the novel's autofictional character supports, and second, that *Klassenliebe* functioned on some level as such an intervention. The novel's discourse and the contemporary reception of Struck's text buttress the notion that *Klassenliebe* indeed functioned as a literary intervention.

41 Struck, *Klassenliebe*, 180.

42 Ibid., 49.

43 Ibid., 44.

44 See Glawion, "Als Arbeitertochter," 53–5.

45 Struck, *Klassenliebe*, 123.

46 Karin Struck, "Das Private ist das Politische," in *Karin Struck Materialien*, ed. Hans Adler and Hans Joachim Schrimpf (Frankfurt am Main: Suhrkamp, 1984), 53–8, here 54.

47 Ibid., 57.

48 Ibid., 58.

49 On the complicated reception of Struck in feminist literary studies, see Breuer, "Nackt wandern," 115–17.

50 Oskar Negt and Alexander Kluge, *Public Sphere and Experience: Toward an Analysis of the Bourgeois and Proletarian Public Sphere*, trans. Peter Labanyi, Jamie Owen Daniel, and Assenka Oksiloff (Minneapolis and London: University of Minnesota Press, 1993), xlv.
51 Ibid., xlvi.
52 Ibid., 12.
53 Struck, "Das Private ist das Politische," 54.
54 Negt and Kluge, *Public Sphere and Experience*, xliv.
55 Ibid., 44.
56 Ibid., 87.
57 Ibid.
58 Struck, *Klassenliebe*, 246.
59 Negt and Kluge, *Public Sphere and Experience*, 87.
60 Ibid., 186.
61 Struck, "Das Private ist das Politische," 54.
62 Ibid., 57.
63 Jung, "Literatur von unten," 182.
64 See Werkkreis, *Ihr aber tragt das Risiko: Reportagen aus der Arbeitswelt*, ed. Peter Fischer (Reinbek bei Hamburg: Rowohlt, 1971).
65 Werkkreis, *Ihr aber*, n.p.
66 The expression 'politics of form' refers to the site-specific political force that "aesthetic forms" can possess, insofar as they "develop out of what is inherited and thus constitute expressions of the dominant and the residual, yet they may also express aspects of subordinate or emergent cultural formations. Specific narrative and formal structures may function as historically situated bearers of dominant cultural values or as markers of critique that are aimed at uncovering structures that enforce domination and subordination; alternatively, they may express more negotiated and ambivalent standpoints." Greta Olson and Sarah Copland, "Toward a Politics of Form," *European Journal of English Studies* 20, no. 3 (2016): 207–21, here 210.
67 See Michael Bies, Michael Gamper, and Ingrid Kleeberg, "Einleitung," in *Gattungs-Wissen: Wissenspoetologie und literarische Form*, ed. Michael Bies, Michael Gamper, and Ingrid Kleeberg (Göttingen: Wallstein Verlag, 2013), 7–18.
68 Struck, "Das Private ist das Politische," 53.
69 Frank Zipfel, "Autofiktion: Zwischen den Grenzen von Faktualität, Fiktionalität und Literarität?", in *Grenzen der Literatur: Zu Begriff und Phänomen des Literarischen*, ed. Simone Winko, Fotis Jannidis, and Gerhard Lauer (Berlin and New York: De Gruyter, 2009), 285–314, here 311.
70 Struck, "Das Private ist das Politische," 57.
71 Glawion, "Als Arbeitertochter," 47.
72 Breuer, "Nackt wandern," 122, 121.

73 Negt and Kluge, *Public Sphere and Experience*, xlvi.
74 Jacques Rancière, *The Politics of Aesthetics: The Distribution of the Sensible*, trans. Gabriel Rockhill (London and New York: Continuum, 2004).
75 Ingrid Gilcher-Holtey, "Einleitung," in *'1968' – Eine Wahrnehmungsrevolution? Horizont-Verschiebungen des Politischen in den 1960er und 1970er Jahren*, ed. Ingrid Gilcher-Holtey (München: Oldenbourg Verlag, 2013), 7–12, here 9, 8.
76 Struck, "Das Private ist das Politische," 54.
77 Glawion, "Als Arbeitertochter," 65. Emphasis in original.
78 *Klassenliebe* sold about 200,000 copies within ten years. See Breuer, "Nackt wandern," 108.
79 See Hensel, "Realistisch schreiben," 241.

12

Feminism and Progressive Writing in Twentieth-Century India

Ulka Anjaria

Political writing in India has a rich history, which coalesced with the founding of the All-India Progressive Writers' Association (AIPWA) in 1936. The inaugural meeting of the AIPWA called for a literature rooted in contemporary realities rather than the fanciful domain of fairy tales and religious texts, as part of a national, and increasingly international, decolonial politics.[1] While some writers involved in the AIPWA were affiliated with Marxism and/or the Communist Party, which influenced anticolonial thinkers across the world, it should not be characterized simply as a Marxist literary movement.[2] As Snehal Shingavi writes, the question of Marxist aesthetics has to be considered differently in the colonized world, where "artists . . . were at the intersection of various kinds of intellectual, political, and aesthetic commitments," with the effect that "the aesthetic and political notions put forward through various organs of the Communist Party were translated, reinterpreted, reimagined and refigured."[3] Indian writers' "intellectual interests were necessarily varied as they tried to adapt European theories of history to their own colonial contexts. Their models of internationalism were both communist and non-communist, including pan-Islamism and pan-Asianism. . . . They defined themselves at various times as socialist, communist, humanist, secularist, progressive, internationalist, and Gandhian."[4]

The specificity of Indian progressive writing was further deepened by women writers, who had to navigate not only the various ideological positions that characterized Indian politics but also questions of individual rights, sexual politics, and bodily autonomy that were often not considered political. Ania Loomba argues that in India the women's movement had to contend with the strong influences of Hindu asceticism and Gandhism, which led to a rigid and sexually prudish politics within the Communist Party and left many women with no choice but to "unsex"[5] themselves and emulate male ascetic models in order to be part of the movement. While in the 1940s there was an attempt "to explode conventional attitudes to gender and sexuality" and "to question the bracketing of romance from political commitment,"[6] overall progressive intellectuals who were focused on what they saw as more immediate nationalist and internationalist concerns considered love and sexuality individual, romantic, and bourgeois.[7]

This chapter offers a new perspective on the political uses of Indian literature during and beyond the anticolonial movement through a focus on two major female authors, the Urdu writer Ismat Chughtai (1915–91) and the Bengali writer Mahasweta Devi (1926–2016), both of whom reimagined the nature of progressive writing at two different seminal moments in twentieth-century India by writing female characters who challenge structures of power and authority through resistance, refusal, joy, and desire. Both Chughtai, writing amid and following the nationalist movement, and Mahasweta, two decades later, were ideologically committed to progressive politics but their writings give space for the flourishing of individual women whose momentary refusals rarely precipitate revolution, but nevertheless narrate the meeting of the private and the public, where female potential can engender new politics and ways of being. The writerly histories of both authors take us across major events in the global Left, from the Chinese Revolution and Bandung to 1968, the Naxalite movement, the Cold War, and beyond, but their writings are—with the exception of Mahasweta's *Mother of 1084*, discussed below—noticeably aloof from these global events. They are more interested in giving space to the imaginative potential of everyday Indian women than in linking women's stories to world-scale events. Thus, while personally they spoke up against colonialism and capitalism, their fiction offers a politics founded in the body—the desiring body, the wounded body, the enraged body. This productive friction between their political commitments and their literary writings suggests the insufficiency of a definition of progressive writing that is limited to explicitly political texts. Through a reading of a few of Chughtai's and Mahasweta's important texts, this chapter argues that a richer history of political writing in India and across the colonized world is served by attending not only to collective revolutionary potential but also to moments of individual heroism and dissent founded in the female body and imagination.

"Straight Paths Are Frequently Dull"

Ismat Chughtai (1915–91) was born into a large family in North India and quickly became influenced by her older brother, who was a published writer. She began writing early and insisted on continuing her education rather than getting married. She worked as a teacher and headmistress and later wrote for Hindi films. She was prolific, publishing dozens of short stories, novels, plays, and screenplays. She found her way to the progressive writers via her mentor Rashid Jahan,[8] a doctor, writer, and the only female contributor to the controversial book *Angaaray*, which came out in 1932 and angered many orthodox Muslims for its critical and what was seen as blasphemous portrayal of religion.[9] Chughtai read *Angaaray* "on the sly"[10] and took inspiration from Jahan, whom she found "bold" and who "used to speak all sorts of things openly and loudly," so that Chughtai "just wanted to copy her."[11] Along with Jahan, Chughtai participated in the first meeting of the AIPWA in 1936.

Chughtai found the progressive writers both friendly and politically inspiring. She was empowered by the group's internationalism, their commitment to social justice, and their rejection of inherited literary norms. She was excited to be a communist, recording in her autobiography: "I had a new love in my life—Communism!"[12] In another essay, she wrote,

> The progressive group I became affiliated with, the one in Bombay, was such an insolent, interesting, rebellious, and bold group, and I spent so many enjoyable moments with alert, carefree, outspoken, open-hearted, candid and intelligent young people that I didn't even realize we were there to relieve the world's pain and help humanity. Even so, I loved the slogans of the Communist Party so much that they became like a reflection of my own uncontrolled, free and riotous mindset.[13]

But even as she found the politics of the progressive writers freeing, she also bristled against the aesthetic constraints she faced from within the AIPWA. Her novels and stories were seen as too deviant and inward looking, and her focus on middle-class characters made her politics suspect. As she explained:

> The party's policy became more strict, and it was decided that progressive writing can only be writing about farmers and workers (*ki taraqqi pasand adab wahi hai jo kisaan mazdoor ke bare mein likha jaye*). It's clear that I couldn't understand farmers and workers as intimately as I could feel the hardships of people of the middle and lower classes. And I've never written based on hearsay, I've never written being bound by my principles, I've never written according to the dictates or any party or association. Free speech was my nature and is still my nature.[14]

She also found herself unable to turn against friends and family members who did not share her politics: "I do not strongly oppose even the most narrow-minded, conservative people," she wrote. "Every human being is the mirror of his environment (*har insaan apne mahol ka aks hota hai*) and is imprisoned in that environment. One cannot push or drag him out." This elicited criticism from her fellow progressives that she was inconsistent and "self-contradictory (*tazaad*)." But these criticisms did not deter her: "Contradiction is a sign of life. I am not a 'Taj Mahal' that is balanced from all angles (*tavaazun hi tavaazun*). Innumerable questions are always wrestling in my mind. Straightening them, then entangling and re-straightening them (*suljhaana, uljhaana aur phir suljhaana*) is life."[15]

Indeed, Chughtai's fiction demonstrates this interest in contradiction and complexity, especially as they constitute the inner lives of women. The psychological, the sensual, and the "visceral"[16] drive her fiction rather than the political, public, or ideological. Where there are politics, they occupy the background; the primary interest seems to be the fantastical and libidinal energies of the human mind and body. For instance, Chughtai's novel *Tehri Lakeer* (The Crooked Line, 1942) begins with the narrator lamenting the number of children being produced by the women of Shamman's family, complaining that her home feels "more like an animal shed rather than a house."[17] Neglected by her mother, the baby Shamman becomes attached to Unna, her wet nurse, whom she watches "roll[ing] on the hay"[18] with her lover and whose "rounded softness"[19] she loves to cuddle. When Unna is sent away, Shamman is miserable until she finds refuge in the love of her older sister Manjhu, on whom she becomes similarly fixated, walking in on Manjhu bathing and dirtying herself with mud so that Manjhu would have to scold and clean her. In these brief episodes, we see how questions of love and affection are channeled through the twin affects of desire and disgust: the animality of reproduction, the fixation on women's bodies—especially breasts—the obsession with dirt, and the desire for punishment. These continue to mark Shamman's early years: she is repelled by the prospect of courtship or marriage and finds herself drawn to substances like mud and saliva and blood. She has an early proto-sexual experience with the sweeper's daughter that involves going

> behind the cow's stall and stroll[ing] with their arms wrapped around each other. Sometimes they tossed about in the sand like rolling pins. Then they pitched fistfuls of sand as if it was water.... Making spoons out of dried leaves, they scooped up sand and swallowed mouthfuls.... Like pregnant women, they relished the aroma of mud.[20]

The imbrication of dirt, desire, disgust, and homosociality suggests a queer refusal of patriarchy and of the institutions of marriage and childbearing. Indeed, Shamman exhibits a strong desire to get an education rather than get married, breaking away from the role expected of girls in the family. But none of this is presented via the language of modernity that featured in the rhetoric of other progressives of the era who advocated for women's rights and women's education.[21] In *The Crooked Line*, education is not a way out for a young woman but another ambivalent experience filled with desire (for instance, for the various young women at her school boarding house whom she is attracted to) and disgust (at the changes in her pubescent body, which she finds repulsive). Thus, the standard account of *Bildung*, in which the child leaves their oppressive home situation to find intellectual and social freedom in the public world of books and ideas, is continually foreclosed in *The Crooked Line*; the novel refuses the standard temporality of growth and development in which actions educate or culminate, and there is no clear political or even personal awakening. As Priyamvada Gopal writes, Shamman's growth "engages jaggedly with th[e] process of the 'worlding' of the 'new' Indian woman, underscoring—through her own eccentricities, achievements and traumas—its unevenness, triumphs and failures."[22]

Indeed, the very title of the novel, "the crooked line," suggests the idea of being wayward or undisciplined that constitutes an alternative vision to the standard narrative of progress. The theme of crookedness, unevenness, or jaggedness recurs throughout Chughtai's oeuvre; as the narrator says in another short story, "Ziddi" (The Wild One):

> Sometimes we go astray and, without being aware, digress from the crooked path (*tehre raaste se*) to the straight one; often the difference between the straight and crooked paths is barely discernible. . . . Why do people always strive for the straight path? Straight paths are frequently dull, well-lit and flat. Taking this route even a donkey, if it isn't disturbed along the way, will arrive at its destination. But these crooked paths, littered with unseen pits, hidden thorns, sharp stones, pain, heartache, where does one encounter these?[23]

Here, crookedness marks a space of eccentricity, whimsy, hardship, and desire—a space that honors individuality rather than suppressing it in favor of the 'straight path' of ideological certainty. We also see this in Chughtai's recurring interest in obsession—obsession which we might consider unhealthy because it never leads to love or union. *The Crooked Line* sees Shamman variously obsessed with a number of family members, friends, and lovers, which fills her with desire but also fear and dread. In the short story "Til" (Mole), Chaudhury becomes obsessed with Rani; his desire for her is coupled with loathing. Obsession is a long-standing theme of Persian and Urdu poetry; Chughtai modernizes it by stripping away its idealization and aestheticizing it through modernist tropes of stream of consciousness and defamiliarization, such as in "Mole," when the eponymous mole comes to life: "transformed into a black stone by

[Chaudhury's] revulsion, the mole crashed against his forehead."[24] The psyche is a site of danger and potential destruction in Chughtai; many of her characters are on the border of being mentally unwell; sometimes instability comes from social structures like patriarchy or domesticity but it is also the nature of the mind itself, whose dark and perverse longings constitute a rich subject for Chughtai.

Chughtai is most famous for her story "Lihaaf" (The Quilt), which was published in 1942 and for which she was accused of obscenity and had to stand trial two years later. "The Quilt" tells the story of a girl who gets sent to live at an older relative's house by her parents who are worried about her refusal to conform to gender norms, with the assumption that the visit will discipline her and ultimately make her marriageable. But what she finds when she arrives is that the Nawab is uninterested in his wife and finds pleasure in entertaining young men instead. His wife, Begum Jan, is left ignored in the *zenana*, which leads her to initiate a physical relationship with her female maid, Rabbo—a relationship that the protagonist, herself barely sexually mature, cannot understand, but only glimpses through nighttime movement under the eponymous quilt, which she watches and then eventually participates in with a mix of fascination, desire, and unnamable revulsion: "The dusk had plunged her room into a claustrophobic blackness, and I felt gripped by an unknown terror (*ek namaloom dar*). Begum Jan's deep dark eyes focussed on me! I started crying. She was clutching me like a clay doll. I started feeling nauseated against her warm body."[25] Her queer past suggests desire, but her lack of knowledge about sex and especially about female sexuality make her frightened by the sexual excess taking place under the quilt, which she never fully grasps until the end of the story when a "corner [of the quilt] was lifted one foot above the bed." But what she sees, she says, "I will never tell anyone, not even if they give me a lakh of rupees."[26]

Here too the theme of the story is less visibility or identity but secrecy, fear, and desire, which render it politically inscrutable. The protagonist does not become empowered as a queer subject at the end; by contrast, her experience is overwhelmed by visceral feelings she is unable to understand. As in *The Crooked Line*, there is no revelation, so that when she finally sees the sexual action with her own eyes she is unable to articulate it. It is clear that this story, like so many others of Chughtai's, is more influenced by Sigmund Freud than Karl Marx—which is perhaps fitting for this period marked by colonial censorship, and indeed the reason Chughtai was not found guilty of obscenity is quite literally because no vulgar words could be identified in the text. Thus, the narrator's inability/unwillingness to name the lesbian sexual act she witnesses simultaneously works as a way for the author to assert female subjectivity and desire, even as it remains unarticulated in the political domain. At the time, Chughtai defended the story against her critics by asserting that she was simply documenting the kinds of activities she had witnessed as a child:

Nobody ever told me that it was a sin to write on the subject dealt with in "Lihaaf." Nor have I ever read in any book that it is a crime to write about gender choice. Perhaps my brain is not fitted with [a] delicate brush, but with a cheap camera. Whatever it sees, it clicks, and the pen in my hand is left helpless (*jo kuch dekhta hai, khat se button dab jata hai aur mera qalam mere haath mein bebas hota hai*). My brain leads the pen and I am in no way able to interfere in the relationship between my pen and my brain.[27]

Chughtai defends her writing through a dual rhetoric of realism on one hand—"whatever it sees"—and bodily autonomy on the other—"my brain leads the pen"—which define the competing impulses that constitute her fiction. Indeed, this comment mediates between realism's mimetic potential and its ability to imagine and bring to light new realities.[28] For what Chughtai writes about in "The Quilt" are not simply facts that can be physically documented but social realities that require a discerning, feminist eye. Begum Jan's "loneliness (*tanhayi*)"[29] after her husband "deposited her in the house with all his other possessions and promptly forgot about her"[30] was likely the condition of many women living in seclusion, but one not often documented. Nawab's "strange hobby (*ajeeb-o-gharib shauq*)"[31] of courting young men and Begum's sexual relations with her maid offer a queer counterpoint to the conventional representation (in the period, as well as today) of the enforced heterosexuality and sexual repressiveness of middle-class Muslim domesticity. And most clearly, the substance of the story is constituted by the interior contours of a child's mind as she copes with her burgeoning sexuality. None of these topics ever surfaced to nationalist or progressive politics, but, published while the Second World War raged around her and independence grew imminent, they contribute to a broader sense of the political in the era of decolonization.

After Indian independence in 1947, Chughtai continued to work in the Bombay film industry, penning several screenplays and novels about deviant, misunderstood, and frustrated women. These screenplays too do not immediately reflect a Marxist worldview, but considering them in relation to psychoanalysis and gender critique offers a more complex understanding of progressive writing than one generated solely from Marxist aesthetic principles. Through Partition, the India–Pakistan wars, and the global revolutionary moments of the 1960s, Chughtai's literary focus remained on the interior: the domestic space and the space of the inner mind, as part of—rather than despite—her commitment to progressive writing.

"Everyone Is Afraid of Mary"

Mahasweta Devi was a prolific Bengali writer based in West Bengal. Born a decade after Ismat Chughtai, she began her activist career by volunteering for famine relief in 1943 and later married the communist playwright Bijon Bhattacharya and became involved in leftist politics in West Bengal, especially surrounding issues of bonded labor, tribal rights, and environmental exploitation. She began her career in the 1950s, writing mostly historical fiction told from the perspective of subaltern characters,[32] and in the 1970s began to write short stories and novels set in the present as well. Her literary influences include Tarashankar Bandyopadhyay, a Bengali progressive writer interested in questions of rural representation and especially the representation of Adivasis, indigenous communities criminalized by the colonial government and long ignored by mainstream middle-class society and the state. As Mahasweta explained in an interview:

> The tribals and the mainstream have always been parallel. There has never been a meeting point. The mainstream simply doesn't understand the parallel.... Tribal land is being sold illegally every day, and usurped by mainstream society all over India, especially in West Bengal. In North Bengal, extensive lands are being converted into tea gardens, fruit orchards. They can't keep their land; there is no education for them, no health facilities, no roads, no way of generating income. Nothing is done for them although so much money is allotted for them. They do not want money; they want facilities; they want to live the life of an honorable poor Indian.... But they are denied everything.[33]

Like Bandyopadhyay, Mahasweta spent time among Adivasi communities in West Bengal and Bihar, learning about their ways of life, culture, politics, and language.[34] She also participated in political organizing around issues such as bonded labor.[35] She was both a journalist and a fiction writer,[36] raising awareness around issues faced by Adivasis and also featuring Adivasi characters, especially Adivasi women, in her fiction.

Whereas she shared a political commitment to representing the hardships faced by marginalized communities with Bandyopadhyay, many of her stories contain strong female characters who are able to enact remarkable resistance in the face of violence and oppression. This resistance is sometimes collective, but is mostly ad hoc, founded on individual strength of character, a unique personality, or a temporary act of refusal—most of which would not 'count' as resistance in a purely Marxist framework. For Mahasweta, these moments of refusal are realistic because they are founded in the relative freedom given to Adivasi women compared to their counterparts in many Hindu and Muslim communities.[37] But even as she justifies women's resistance as ethnographically accurate, these stories puncture the social realist politics of the writings via fantasy and utopia. Her writings thus offer a sense of political futurity—but one based in the remarkability of her female characters rather than in a complete upturning of the exploitative system.

For instance, Mary, the protagonist of "Shikar" (The Hunt),[38] is introduced as a strong and powerful woman, often seen wielding a machete and threatening those who come in the way of her ambitions. As the daughter of a white man who raped her mother, she is partly outside the Oraon Adivasi community, which gives her a certain freedom, enabling her to harvest and sell the Mahua growing on the landed property without consequences: "Everyone is afraid of Mary (*Mary ke shobai bhoy kore*)."[39] Despite many men wanting to be her lover, she chooses to marry a Muslim man, Jamil, and also to wait until they have saved up enough money before marrying. Eventually, industrialists come to the region to cut down and sell the valuable sal trees growing there. The *tehsildar* in charge of the deforestation becomes obsessed with Mary, bringing her gifts and pursuing her even after she makes it clear she is not interested: "'You think I'm a city whore (*shohorer randi*)? You want to grab me with a sari? If you bother me again I'll cut off your nose.'"[40] The annual hunt comes around, and this year women are to perform it, an occasion that arises once every twelve years. On the eve of the hunt, the *tehsildar* accosts Mary and she gets away only by promising that she will come to him "on the day of the feast."[41] She meets him at the appointed time, drinks with him and seduces him, and then murders him with her machete.

The story activates the relative sexual freedom enjoyed by Adivasi women and puts it in a context of modernization, whose drive for development and national resource extraction has led to the deforestation of Adivasi land through the collusion of local landowners and urban profiteers beginning after independence in 1947 and continuing to this day. Mary's racial hybridity allows her a space apart from the traditions of Oraon custom, but it is her inherent pride that allows her to reject the various men who try to claim her. The *tehsildar*, on the other hand, represents the collusion of national, corporate, and patriarchal violence: "He thought, the business of felling trees in this forest is most profitable. Mary can make his stay profitable (*nafajonok*) in the other sense as well."[42] But Mary is undaunted by his pursuit. She uses the occasion of the hunt, in which rules are permitted to be broken, and in particular this rare year when women run the hunt, as an occasion to perform her own "shikar"— to fell the biggest beast: "Today a small thing cannot please her. She wants to hunt the big beast (*Shikar chai, boro shikar*)!"[43] The women's hunt is an experience full of sensory joy, liquor, food, and revelry, including queer sexual fulfillment: in the midst of the fun, Mary grabs a woman who is too old to take part in the hunt but is still drinking and enjoying herself, "and says, 'I'll marry you after I play the hunt. Then I am the husband, you the wife (*ami bor, tui bou*).'"[44] The murder of the *tehsildar* is also presented as a kind of joyous sexual victory, inverting the sexual dynamics that structure mainstream Indian life; once she has killed him, "Mary comes out. Walks naked to the cut. Bathing naked in the cut her face fills with deep satisfaction. As if she has been infinitely satisfied in a sexual embrace (*jeno purushshongo korey oshesh tripti peyeche oo*)."[45]

In Mahasweta's story "Giribala" too, the protagonist's hardships are countered by a final act of refusal. Giri is married at fourteen to Aulchand, a drug addict and layabout; she works while raising four children and protecting her small dowry from the greedy hands of her husband. Ever looking for a quick buck, Aulchand sells their oldest daughter to a brothel under cover of having her married, to Giri's utter dismay. The context of the story is one of exploitation—Adivasi and low-caste girls are sold into the sex trade because of poverty and the pressure to have daughters married, the police are in league with gangs, and women have little agency over their own lives or the lives of their children. Yet, within this restrictive context, Giri does her best to make her own decisions. First, after the birth of her fourth child, she decides to get sterilized without her husband's knowledge. She refuses to sell her silver jewelry even when he asks her to. She tries to arrange her second daughter's marriage herself, but that fails as well and that daughter too is duped and sold to a brothel. This last tragedy makes Giri realize that the problem lies with her husband and her life will never improve as long as she stays with him. Thus, she leaves with her remaining two children in tow. Although the villagers criticize her for leaving, Giri herself "only regretted that she had not done this before. . . . As this thought grew insistent and hammered inside her brain, hot tears flooded her face and blurred her vision. But she did not stop even to wipe her tears. She just kept walking."[46] The end of the story sees Giri finally determine to take her fate in her own hands.

The end of another of Mahasweta's most well-known stories, "Draupadi" (1978), also contains an act of bodily refusal as Draupadi, after being brutally raped by a group of policemen, exits the jail cell naked, laughing, and covered with blood, to face Senanayak, the "specialist in combat and extreme-Left politics (*somor oo baamponthi ugro raajniti specialist*)"[47] sent to suppress the local Adivasi revolt: "'What's the use of clothes?'" she rhetorically asks him. "'You can strip me, but how can you clothe me again?' . . . Draupadi pushes Senanayak with her two mangled breasts, and for the first time Senanayak is afraid to stand before an unarmed target, terribly afraid."[48]

The ability of individual women to refuse and even escape the oppressions they face might be credited to Adivasi culture, but it is clear that it is Mahasweta's utopic imagination that consistently places these remarkably strong women at the center of her fiction. In all these cases, the social context is marked by structural inequality—capitalism, nationalism, Brahminism, patriarchy—but the resistance that succeeds in defying it is individual, ephemeral, and even idiosyncratic.[49] Thus, Mahasweta's politics seem to be as much about cultivating a space for the flourishing of human freedom as witnessing and recording the dire circumstances in which many rural Indians live.

This experimentation with the nature of political representation continues in Mahasweta's 1974 novel *Hajaar Churashir Maa* (Mother of 1084), whose historical context is much more central to its story. The novel is set immediately following state repression of the Naxalite Movement (1967–71) in West Bengal, a Maoist-influenced armed resistance born out of popular disillusionment with the Indian state and influenced by contemporary global revolutionary movements.[50] Beginning in a Bengali town called Naxalbari, the movement brought together the disempowered rural poor, who sought to rise up against "oppressive landlords,"[51] and middle-class university students in cities like Kolkata (then Calcutta) fired up by revolutionary ideology and frustrated by their own lack of prospects. In the cities, the youth waged a guerrilla war, to which the heavily militarized police responded with torture and repression.[52] The movement caused significant dissent among leftists in the state and led to a split within the Communist Party.[53] It ended with an "organized massacre of the Naxalites in 1970–1971, perpetrated by the police, the party in power, hired goons, and even parties of the Left Establishment acting in unholy collusion."[54]

Mother of 1084 begins after the Naxalite suppression and is focalized not through Brati, the middle-class young man involved in the movement and killed by police (and dumped in the morgue as the eponymous corpse #1084), but through Sujata, his mother, on one single day, two years after Brati's death. Centering Sujata is another imaginative choice on Mahasweta's part; as a middle-class, largely apolitical person, Sujata has no real interest in the structural injustices which spurred the movement, but registers its violent repression through her grief over the loss of her son. As memories of that fateful evening come back to her, she starts to see her own middle-class domestic existence through Brati's eyes. For instance, hearing of Brati's death, her husband's first instinct had been to cover up the story so their family name would not be tarnished. Her memories take her not to a new understanding of injustices faced by the rural poor, but to the rot at the center of bourgeois life. In an attempt to learn more about who Brati really was, Sujata meets with the mother of Somu, one of his friends. Somu's mother is less well-off than Brati's family but despite that, their home had been a truer home for Brati before his death. So when Sujata returns to her own house after these visits, she sees her domestic space as if through a distorting filter: "Sujata crossed the passage and slowly entered the drawing room. Flowers in all the vases. Bright, bright lights. The roses a deep red. Ah, those who had pledged their faith in the red roses and the glowing lights had shifted their allegiance long ago. Yet the roses remained as red as ever, the lights as bright as ever—Betrayal!"[55] Her renewed perception, experiencing light and color as hypocrisy and thus seeing her own home anew, suggests what Freud called the *unheimlich*. Indeed, as in Freud, Sujata is no longer able to distinguish "whether an apparently animate being is really alive; or conversely, whether a lifeless object might not be in fact animate,"[56] and thus her family appears to her as the living dead—walking corpses—flipping the story that begins with the dead corpse of a revolutionary: the one who seeks to live gets shot, and those who remain alive are in fact long dead. By tracing Sujata's story rather than Brati's, the novel unearths a set of deeper social ills that cannot necessarily be solved through revolutionary action.

Thus, in this novel, Mahasweta shifts the focus from the documented history of the Naxalite movement as well as the contemporary male-authored fiction that emphasized middle-class alienation and disillusionment[57] to the kinds of domestic, psychic, and bodily wounds that public action against the state is often inattentive to. Although Sujata is different from Mahasweta's other protagonists in her lack of heroism and is marked by her regularity rather than any exceptionality, her story allows the novel to make a deeper political critique that sidesteps the question of the relevance of the Naxalite movement for a global Marxist politics in favor of a story about an ordinary woman's loss and pain which is unlikely to be written into revolutionary history.

Like Ismat Chughtai, Mahasweta Devi opens up new insight into the political uses of literature by putting pressure on universalist models that assume that the primary focus of progressive politics and progressive writing is, and always should be, class struggle. Both writers center the bodies and minds of women characters to displace the dominant perception that politics lies primarily in the public sphere, in revolutionary action, and in rational dissent. From the 1930s through the 1970s, this contributed to an expanded understanding of the political by allowing for spaces of alienation and distortion as well as joy, desire, and momentary freedom rather than awaiting a grand revolutionary upheaval. These authors, together with others worldwide, recast the literary medium not only as a space to document injustice but also to imagine new futures. They pushed the boundaries of political thinking to chart new trajectories of both witnessing and hope in the literary text and, in doing so, scripted an entry for feminist writing into progressive thought.

Notes

The author would like to thank Sahid Mondal and Auritro Majumder for their assistance with the Bengali originals of Mahasweta's works.

1 Premchand, "Sahitya ka Uddeshya [The Purpose of Literature]," in *People's Art in the Twentieth Century: Theory and Practice*, ed. Jana Natya Manch (Delhi: Jana Natya Manch, 2000), 74–87.

2 See Ania Loomba, *Revolutionary Desires: Women, Communism, and Feminism in India* (Abingdon: Routledge, 2019), 25.

3 Snehal Shingavi, "India-England-Russia: The Comintern Translated," in *Comintern Aesthetics*, ed. Amelia M. Glaser and Steven S. Lee (Toronto: University of Toronto Press, 2020), 109–32, here 109.

4   Ibid., 127.
5   Loomba, *Revolutionary*, 55.
6   Ibid., 107.
7   Ibid., 107–8. This applied to some male writers too: writers like Saadat Hasan Manto, whose stories sensitively portrayed pimps and prostitutes as protagonists, were also criticized by progressive writers.
8   See Tahira Naqvi, "Introduction," in *The Collectors' Chughtai: Her Choicest Stories*, trans. Tahira Naqvi (New Delhi: Women Unlimited, 2021), vii–xix.
9   See Snehal Shingavi, "Introduction," in *Angaaray*, by Sajjad Zaheer, Ahmed Ali, Rashid Jahan, and Mahmud-uz-Zafar (Gurgaon: Penguin Random House India, 2014), vii–xxiii, here viii.
10 Ismat Chughtai, *Kaghazi Hai Pairahan: The Paper Attire*, trans. Noor Zaheer (Karachi: Oxford University Press, 2016), 88.
11 Naqvi, "Introduction," x.
12 Chughtai, *Kaghazi* [English], 251.
13 Ismat Chughtai, "Taraqqi Pasand Adab Aur Main" (Progressive Literature and Me), in *Ismat Chughtai Naqd Ki Kasauti Par*, ed. Jameel Akhtar (Nai Dilli: International Urdu Foundation, 2001), 25–32, here 25.
14 Ibid., 29–30.
15 Chughtai, *Kaghazi* [English], 305. Urdu quotations are from Ismat Chughtai, *Kaghazi Hai Pairahan* (Lahore: Rohtas Books, 1992), 213–14.
16 See Neetu Khanna, *The Visceral Logics of Decolonization* (Durham: Duke University Press, 2020), 85–108.
17 Ismat Chughtai, *The Crooked Line*, trans. Tahira Naqvi (New York: The Feminist Press, 1995), 2.
18 Ibid.
19 Ibid., 3.
20 Ibid., 7.
21 See Preetha Mani, *The India of Indian Literature: Gender, Genre, and Comparative Method* (Evanston: Northwestern University Press, 2022), 161–3.
22 Priyamvada Gopal, *Literary Radicalism in India: Gender, Nation and the Transition to Independence* (London: Routledge, 2012), 70.
23 Ismat Chughtai, "The Wild One," in *The Heart Breaks Free & The Wild One*, trans. Tahira Naqvi (New Delhi: Women Unlimited, 2019), 71–144, here 134. Urdu quotations are from Ismat Chughtai, *Ziddi* (Lahore: Rohtas Books, 1992), 90–1.
24 Ismat Chughtai, "The Mole," in *The Quilt and Other Studies*, trans. Tahira Naqvi and Syeda S. Hameed (New Delhi: Kali for Women, 1990), 110–26, here 121.
25 Ismat Chughtai, "The Quilt," in *The Quilt and Other Studies*, trans. Tahira Naqvi and Syeda S. Hameed (New Delhi: Kali for Women, 1990), 7–19, here

16. Urdu quotations are from Ismat Chughtai, "Lihaaf," *Rekhta*, no date, https://www.rekhta.org/stories/lihaaf-ismat-chughtai-stories?lang=ur.
26. Ibid., 19.
27. Chughtai, *Kaghazi* [English], 77. Urdu quotations are from Chughtai, *Kaghazi* [Urdu], 79.
28. See Jens Elze, "Realism, Political Aesthetics, and (New) Materialism," in *Realism: Aesthetics, Experiments, Politics*, ed. Jens Elze (New York: Bloomsbury, 2022), 1–19, here 5.
29. Chughtai, "Quilt," 8.
30. Ibid.
31. Ibid.
32. See Auritro Majumder, *Insurgent Imaginations: World Literature and the Periphery* (Cambridge: Cambridge University Press, 2020), 124–5.
33. Mahasweta Devi, "The Author in Conversation," in *Imaginary Maps: Three Stories by Mahasweta Devi*, trans. Gayatri Chakravorty Spivak (New York: Routledge, 1995), ix–xxii, here x–xi.
34. See Mahasweta Devi, "Tarashankar's World of Changes and the New Order," *Indian Literature* 12, no. 1 (1969): 71–9, here 71–2.
35. See Devi, "Author," xii–xiv; see also Devi, "Tarashankar," 73.
36. See ibid., xii, xv–xvi.
37. See ibid., xviii.
38. The exact date of publication of "Shikar" and "Giribala" (discussed below) does not seem to be known. Original dates are not referenced in any of Gayatri Spivak's translations and the Bengali editions in which the stories are reprinted often have no dates.
39. Mahasweta Devi, "The Hunt," in *Imaginary Maps: Three Stories by Mahasweta Devi*, trans. Gayatri Chakravorty Spivak (New York: Routledge, 1995), 1–17, here 5. Bengali quotations are from Mahasweta Devi, "Shikar," in *Mahasweta Debir Premer Golpo* (Kolkata: Abanindranath Bera, 2004), 139–53.
40. Ibid., 11.
41. Ibid., 13–14.
42. Ibid., 9.
43. Ibid., 16.
44. Ibid., 14.
45. Ibid., 17.
46. Mahasweta Devi, "Giribala," in *Of Women, Outcastes, Peasants, and Rebels: A Selection of Bengali Short Stories*, ed. Kalpana Bardhan (Berkeley: University of California Press, 1990), 272–89, here 289.
47. Mahasweta Devi, "Draupadi," in Gayatri Chakravorty Spivak, *In Other Worlds: Essays in Cultural Politics: Essays in Cultural Politics* (New York: Routledge, 1988), 179–96, here 188. Bengali quotations are from Mahasweta

Devi, "Draupadi," in *Agnigarbha* (Kolkata: Bamacharan Mukhapadhayam 1980), 163–80.
48 Ibid., 196.
49 Auritro Majumder points out that Mahasweta's stories depict a powerful internationalism even while they are deeply locally situated. He shows how even a character like Draupadi who has limited access to the global media exhibits a "consciousness of the international" and that the story "indirectly, and directly, aligns [Draupadi] with ongoing anticolonial resistances worldwide, whether these are in Asia, Africa, or the Black Americas." Majumder, *Insurgent*, 137.
50 See Rajeshwari Dasgupta, "Towards the 'New Man': Revolutionary Youth and Rural Agency in the Naxalite Movement," *Economic and Political Weekly* 41, no. 19 (2006): 1920–7, here 1920–1; see also Amitabha Chandra, "The Naxalbari Movement," *Indian Journal of Political Science* 51, no. 1 (1990): 22–45, here 27.
51 Chandra, "Naxalbari," 26.
52 See Jawhar Sircar, "In a Calcutta Gripped with Naxal Violence and Police Brutality, People Lost Sons, Brothers and Friends," *The Wire*, March 11, 2021, https://thewire.in/history/calcutta-naxal-violence-police-brutality-1971.
53 See Chandra, "Naxalbari," 29–30.
54 Samik Bandyopadhyay, "Introduction," in *Mother of 1084*, trans. Samik Bandyopadhyay (Calcutta: Seagull Books, 2001), vii–xx, here xiv–xv.
55 Mahasweta Devi, *Mother of 1084*, trans. Samik Bandyopadhyay (Calcutta: Seagull Books, 2001), 92.
56 Sigmund Freud, "The Uncanny," in *The Standard Edition of the Complete Psychological Works of Sigmund Freud, Volume XIVV (1917–1919): An Infantile Neurosis and Other Works*, ed. and trans. James Strachey (London: Hogarth, 1955), 217–56, here 225.
57 See Aruna Krishnamurthy, "The Revolutionary Man in Naxalite Literature," *Journal for the Study of Radicalism* 11, no. 1 (2017): 135–61.

PART III

Political Uses of Literature Today

Legacies and Departures

13

Cultural Politics after the Arab Spring

A New *Lotus* for a New World?

Maryam Fatima

The politics of literature is not the politics of its writers. It does not deal with their personal commitment to the social and political issues and struggles of their times. Nor does it deal with the modes of representation of political events or the social structure and the social struggles in their books. The syntagma "politics of literature" means that literature "does" politics as literature—that there is a specific link between politics as a definite way of doing and literature as a definite practice of writing.[1]

Contemporary Arab literature is political because . . . all literature is. But beyond that it is political because, in recent decades, local and global political machinations have reduced the raw materials of existence in the region to rubble. Arab writers, each in their way, create what they will out of this, and the residue of politics and its consequences will inhere in what they produce. But contemporary Arab literature, like literature generally, can be a humanizing force against the often brutal and alienating conditions of its own production. It can provide a counter to, rather than confirmation of, sweeping generalizations and orientalizing stereotypes.[2]

In the winter of 2016, one of the most prominent cultural magazines of the mid-twentieth-century Third World project, which had been discontinued in the early 1990s, was given a new lease of life.[3] *Lotus* magazine (known previously as the *Journal of Afro-Asian Writings*), based in Cairo (and later, Beirut and Tunis), was published by the Permanent Bureau of the Afro-Asian Writers' Association (AAWA) between 1968 and the early 1990s. Hailed for its anti-Eurocentric and internationalist orientation, the magazine had served as a platform for bringing together literatures from the erstwhile colonized world. Funded and sustained by internationalist Soviet cultural bureaucracies, the magazine was discontinued after the dissolution of the Soviet Union. The second iteration of the magazine was launched by the refashioned AAWA, now known as the Writers' Union of Africa, Asia, and Latin America (WUAALA) to correct the older formation's lack of tricontinentalism. Unfortunately, a lack of funding seems to have marred this second endeavor too and the magazine appears to have been discontinued after only three issues. However, its brief resurgence, recalling both the promise and pitfalls of Third World cultural politics, raises important questions about literature's political usefulness and the nature of political literature.

Relaunched after two and a half decades, the new magazine builds on and deviates from the old *Lotus*'s conceptualization of 'political literature' and 'cultural politics.' In addition to conceptualizing a more capacious Global South geography, the new *Lotus* also broadens its scope of cultural intervention by unhitching itself from the ideological strictures of the previous magazine, as it claims to recenter the 'literary.' Editor-in-chief Mohamed Salmawy's editorials mark it as an antidote to ethnic and religious conflicts, a bridge for cultural convergence, and a platform for understanding.[4] Such statements come over as trite and have understandably been taken to represent the magazine's lack of "ideological orientation or conceptual incoherence."[5] And yet, Salmawy also refers to the task of the Third World writers to be the "conscience of their nations,"[6] reminiscent of mid-century discourses on political literature that had served as the conceptual coordinates of old *Lotus*'s theorizations of committed anticolonial writing, including *adab al-iltizām* (Arabic), *littérature engage* (French), the Progressive Writers' Movement (Hindi-Urdu), and social realism (most expansively construed). Even before Jean-Paul Sartre's concept of *littérature engage* was introduced in the Arabic literary sphere by Taha Hussein in 1947, various notions of literature for social reform had been hugely popular from the late nineteenth century onward. Similarly, the Progressive Writers' Movement in South Asia, which strongly advocated for social realist literature to represent the common man, emerged from (and partly as a response to) earlier reformist literature which had also departed from the abstractions of Urdu lyric poetry and toward simple edificatory prose.[7] In some form or the other, debates about the political and social role of literature and which genres and forms best respond to this need have been raging for nearly two centuries.

I contextualize the new *Lotus*'s refusal to explicitly name these discourses in identifying its intervention through what has been theorized as the postpolitical moment that came to mark populist political mobilizations such as the Arab Spring or the Occupy movement. I also offer that within that context, *Lotus*'s 'ideological incoherence' is less an explicit instantiation of the post-political discourse and more of a rhetorical gesture or populist strategy of disavowing established politics and political norms that were pervasive during the Occupy years. This rhetorical gesture of disavowal or the friction between older and newer reconfigurations of the magazine does raise several important questions that resonate with this volume's timely call to interrogate how mid-twentieth-century discussions of literature's political usefulness are mobilized by contemporary cultural actors (either to align themselves with or to distance themselves from) in order to respond to current crises of migration, globalization, and climate precarities: How might the new *Lotus* be imagined in the absence of a Third World project? What relationship does the magazine elucidate between literature's political nature and the politics of the literary? How does the newly imagined *Lotus* intervene in the long-standing debate concerning just how political postcolonial or Third World literature is? Can we use contemporaneous discussions on 'post-politics' and 'antipolitics' to interrogate the stakes and limitations of depoliticizing aesthetics?

One of the stories carried in the relaunched *Lotus* captures the ethos of this refashioned literary institution and political moment. The Ugandan writer Hilda Twongyeirwe's short story "Baking the National Cake" is set in the fictional Republic of Kabira, whose president is retiring after five successive terms. The nation has been under twenty-five years of 'Islamic rule' and is reeling from authoritarianism and corruption, malaises that are all too familiar for several postcolonial nations in Africa and Asia. An economic crisis is raging in Kabira as the country's coffers are emptied by the political establishment and international agencies are demanding accountability. Kabira's vice president, embodying the corruption of the political establishment, and an honest cabinet minister, who hopes to bring about change, are vying to be appointed successors. At the end of the story, the president decides to not appoint a successor and announces his rerunning for another term to maintain 'continuity' and 'stability' through the economic crisis. The story is narrated from the honest cabinet minister David Okello's point of view, who feels that he deserves the presidency after having put in the hard work over the years and having covered the tracks of the president and the vice president as they squandered public funds on their private lives. The story ends abruptly as things go on as before even though a storm is raging inside David. He continues to perform his duty toward the president and the nation of Kabira. The story is a poignant take on political status quo and the failed promises of anticolonial liberation and, as such, it rehearses the arc of decolonization from colonial administration to corrupt and authoritarian national rule.

This story captures the emotive thrust of the magazine and provides a glimpse into the unfinished work of decolonization that the relaunched magazine could have extended. It shapes the ethos of my investigation into the past and present of this literary institution. In the first section of this chapter, I highlight some of the significant similarities and differences between the two iterations of the magazine. This is important for thinking through the changing vicissitudes of the 'political' and the 'literary' from the Third World project to the Global South. In the second section, I analyze the opinion pieces published in the magazine and the politics of nomenclature in the post-political context. How does the cultural politics of the decolonial moment dovetail into the culturalist politics of the postcolonial? What remains and what gets left behind? At the end of the chapter, I turn to ongoing conversations on postcoloniality and ask: If the earlier *Lotus* allows us to recuperate the pre- of the postcolonial, how does its contemporary instantiation help us think through the future/ities of postcolonial thought?

What's New (or Not) about the New *Lotus*: From Anticolonial Cultural Politics to (Multi)Culturalist Politics

The cultural Cold War had bolstered significant literary production with Soviet cultural bureaucracies and the Congress for Cultural Freedom (CCF) established by the Central Intelligence Agency (CIA) of the United States vying for ideological hegemony in Third World nations. The magazines funded by these agencies, such as *Transitions* and *Lotus*, had lavish and stunning layouts which evinced the institutional support they received. *Lotus*'s eventual discontinuation after the dissolution of the USSR further affirms the crucial significance of nonmarket, state-based patronage in anticolonial cultural production. The relaunched *Lotus* lacks much of the fanfare of the older iteration, the most jarring difference being that the magazine looks different in different languages. The English version does not carry Mohamed Salmawy's editorials and not all literary works are translated across the three languages.

The most crucial difference, of course, is the tricontinental orientation of the magazine, as also evidenced in the change of the association's name from Afro-Asian Writers' Association to the Writers' Union of Africa, Asia, and Latin America. In correcting the bicontinental focus of the Afro-Asian nexus, this move is imagined as realizing the fully internationalist potential of the formation. In his editorial, Salmawy notes,

There is no doubt that the Union of African and Asian Writers, in its old form, is aware of all this and understands the depth of the ties that unite the countries of the South, as they call them. It sought to include the federations of writers in Latin America, to shape the union and bring it in full circle. Our success in doing so represents an important step on the road to building a large, resilient, and strong cultural defense line against any attempts of penetration aimed at erasing the identity of our countries and changing our cultural, political, and social priorities.[8]

While commendable, this is not entirely translated into equitable representation of Latin American literatures in the magazine. The centrality of Palestinian liberation is routinely emphasized. South African apartheid and Palestinian liberation had been core issues on which the Afro-Asian People's Solidarity Organization (AAPSO) had centered its cultural work. In 2019, the Lotus Prize for Literature (which had been awarded to illustrious anticolonial writers such as Mahmoud Darwish, Faiz Ahmad Faiz, and Chinua Achebe by the AAWA between 1969 and 1988) was reinstated by WUAALA. The Palestinian government committed fifty thousand dollars to the award in order to recenter Palestinian cultural production at the forefront of Arab culture. This continued commitment to Palestinian liberation by WUAALA is significant given the increasing number of countries that are now establishing diplomatic ties with Israel, ending decades-long policies of nonrecognition. This positions the magazine at a distance from Gulf states whose 'oil money' is derided and whose muffling of dissent is criticized in no uncertain terms.

Salmawy's editorial pieces articulate the magazine's cultural politics as defined around the cultural and political connections across a tricontinental geography as he posits "cultural communication" as "a first line of defense" against the linguistic and cultural hegemony of economic superpowers.[9] A second editorial includes a scathing critique of the stifling of dissenting voices and opposition, both in the United States (in covert ways) and in other countries such as Saudi Arabia (the killing of the *Wall Street Journal* journalist Jamal Khashoggi). Additionally, the incarceration of intellectuals and writers and the targeting of dissidents by state-owned media houses are highlighted as unjust and major impediments to freedom of expression.[10] Salmawy's editorials offer parallels to Youssef Al-Sebai's editorials from the early years of the old *Lotus* where he outlined Afro-Asian literature as an "effective tool" for communicating the "principles of freedom and human dignity" and in "the condemnation of imperialist crimes."[11]

There is no doubt that the genuineness of Afro-Asian literature lies in its attachment to the value of freedom. There is no doubt either, that within the Afro-Asian societies, economic freedom cannot be separated from political freedom to guarantee the basic rights for development and prosperity. In this respect it is impossible to separate political democracy from economic democracy.[12]

While Al-Sebai's editorial reflects on the task of building national cultures postindependence, Salmawy's piece points to the continued hegemony of the Global South by economic superpowers. But Salmawy's work goes a step further in identifying internal or domestic aggressors, something that the old guard was hesitant to do.[13]

Some other newer political realities and sociocultural changes that the magazine tries to comprehend include terrorism, antigovernment or anticorruption movements in Arab nations, and diasporic themes of exile and alienation. Several articles also present newer ways of understanding the changing terrain of literary production vis-à-vis the internet. The magazine's most exciting contributions are the articles exploring contemporaneous political events and formations such as Safa Elnaili's "An Abused Country," which tackles the political and cultural ramifications of Muammar Gaddafi's 42-year rule of Libya by looking specifically at the manipulation of the public through language. Among other things, the article traces the political discourse that emerged on online platforms such as Facebook, where most of the political debate and significant mobilization took place during the Arab Spring.[14] This includes the emergence of new words or phrases to denote certain political factions (humorously and critically): "new forms of words emerged, such as compound words where two words are joined together, an English word and an Arabic word."[15] One such example includes the 'double-shafra' (meaning the double code) used for Libyan exiles returning to Libya after Gaddafi's assassination to denote their double loyalty and possibly their unfaithfulness (as they are accused of being secret agents working for foreign governments).

I would push against Hala Halim's argument that in its "design, format, and content, the relaunched *Lotus* does not forcefully affiliate itself to its predecessor."[16] While it is undeniable that the editorials present little ideological alignment with the previous *Lotus*, in design and format, the magazine does recall its predecessor, albeit as a shadow of the original. The different sections that make up the magazine are similar—essays, poems, and short stories forming the bulk of the issues, with a few reviews and editorials. The third issue also contains a special section on Mongolian literature, harkening back to the special sections that the older *Lotus* used to carry to spotlight the literatures of particular nations. The literatures represented are wide ranging, as before—Uganda, Vietnam, Pakistan, Ethiopia, and South Africa. The inclusion of Latin American writers is commendable, even if it is quite marginal to the largely African and Asian makeup of the magazine. The literary works—short stories and poems—are a mix of an older generation of writers such as reprints of stories by the Thai writer Sri Burapha as well as newer voices such as the South African Isabella Morris.[17]

The literary pieces published in the magazine, then, move between older and newer sociopolitical realities. This dynamic move may not have been an intentional part of the design, but it does produce one significant effect: it conceptualizes a critical bridge between the two versions of the magazine. Inadvertent as it may be, this bridging allows us to see the enduring links between the two historical moments: decolonization of the 1950s–70s and the post-political or postcolonial moment of the 1990s–2010s (a point we will come back to at the end).

As I have argued elsewhere, despite funding from the Soviet Union which came with stipulations for promoting socialist realism in one form or another, the editors at *Lotus* "prioritized the formation and canonization of Afro-Asian literatures that emphasized ideas of decolonization over socialist or Marxist ideals in the way Moscow may have expected."[18] If even the earlier instantiation of *Lotus*, embedded within the cultural politics of Third World anticolonial movements, did not always publish ideologically cohesive literary works, what might we make of the new *Lotus*'s refusal to identify itself closely with the old one? And how might we read the literature published in the new *Lotus* and its conceptualization of the relationship between literature and politics? In pursuing this line of questioning, it is less useful to track the ideological orientation of individual literary works and more instructive to probe how this literature is framed by the editorials and essays in the magazine. This allows us to trace the shift in the discourse on literature and its usefulness itself within the changing context of the move from a politics of anticolonial liberation to a more identity-based politics of culturalism or multiculturalism. By 'culturalist politics,' I am signaling here academic critiques of liberal multiculturalism that exposed it for its "institutionalized neutralisation of cultures" or "an experience of the Other deprived of its Otherness—the decaffeinated Other."[19] In this chapter, the move from the cultural politics of Third World socialism to the culturalist ethos of the late 1990s and 2000s captures the fault lines between the antagonisms of class conflict and the management of cultural difference in a neoliberal order.

What's in a Name? The Post-Political after the Arab Spring

The interval between the end of the old *Lotus* and the reissuing of the new *Lotus* (1990–2016) is quite telling. This decade and a half in between witnessed shifts, transitions, and remapping of the relationship between literature and politics. For example, Egyptian writers and poets identified as the "nineties generation" articulated their move away from the doctrines of *adab al-iltizām* (committed literature) of the "sixties generation" (authors of decolonization), especially through the medium of the literary journal or the cultural magazine.[20] Whether this was truly a break from earlier literary trends or an extension/modification of them is not settled. However, what is significant for the discourse on political literature or the politics of literature is the rhetorical break this represented. Arabic cultural and literary journals had served as the primary site for the theorization of notions of *iltizām* for the greater part of the twentieth century. In this discourse, the writer's commitment was defined in relation to the colonial condition and the production of national cultures in the wake of independence, with debates on the role of the committed writer reverberating "from translocal circles from across Arab geographies to the transnational AAWB and AAPSO conferences."[21]

Munir Meyzad's essay "Arab Spring or Long Islamic Winter," in the second issue, helps identify the historical and geopolitical context that the relaunched *Lotus* responds to. While Meyzad's essay cannot be taken to represent the magazine's editorial perspective, it does help us map the two landmark political moments that the relaunched magazine seems to be born out of (or emerging into): the attacks on New York's World Trade Center on September 11, 2001, and a decade later, the wave of antigovernment protests that swept across North Africa and the Middle East and came to be identified as the Arab Spring. The Occupy movement, which had played out almost simultaneously in the United States and shared much of the populist energy of the Arab Spring, is conspicuous in its absence.[22] As is evidenced by Salmawy's editorials, the magazine responds to the intensification of Islamophobic rhetoric in the United States post 9/11 and the revival of Orientalist stereotypes of Arab countries. And in identifying the Arab Spring (or rather, registering disappointment at its failures, as Meyzad's "Long Islamic Winter" implies), the essay posits the entrenchment of democracy and antiauthoritarian ethos as a significant task that the relaunched *Lotus* undertakes.[23]

Jodi Dean locates the "politics of no politics" or the "post-political" among active participants in the Occupy movement as the absorption of "the ideological message of democratic hegemony."[24] The post-political condition or post-democratic governing has been theorized as being marked by "the predominance of a managerial logic in all aspects of life, the reduction of the political to administration where decision-making is increasingly considered to be a question of expert knowledge and not of political position."[25] In the absence of organized class politics, inherent political antagonisms and social hierarchies are displaced onto the terrain of 'manageable problems.' For the purposes of my analysis, the post-political typifies tactics of political disavowal, or in the aftermath of the Third World project or the repercussions of the Arab Spring, a generalized reluctance to be associated with earlier forms of political organizing. Further, my chapter is aligned with Nicolas Van Puymbroeck and Stijn Oosterlynck's suggestion that tactics of political disavowal serve "the needs of global capitalism and multicultural humanitarianism" and should be afforded a central role in political and sociocultural analyses.[26] The new *Lotus*'s proposed intervention in charting out a relationship between literature and politics can by no means be considered apolitical or post-political but it does emerge within that context and understandably grapples with its pervasiveness. This is mostly reflected in the politics of naming.

Nothing captures this move from a politics of anticolonial liberation to a more identity-based politics than the following quotation from the Iraqi writer Fadhil Thamir's essay "Cultural and Literary Silk Road: We Must Speak," published in the second issue:

> The colonialist discourse artificially created an imaginary place such as "The Third World," an over inclusive term that usually comprises continents such as Africa, Asia and Latin America to show that they are inferior to the Western World. The term post-colonialism is not restricted to the time after colonialism or the time following the politically determined Independence Day, it is rather an engagement with problematics of the past and present of historical experiences of the colonized peoples.[27]

The most striking thing about this quote is of course the attribution of the term "Third World" to colonialist discourse, which misses the opportunity to connect with the anticolonial politics that the old *Lotus* was born out of and gave shape to. What does the disavowal of Third Worldism and the enthusiastic endorsement of postcolonialism reveal? Clearly, colonialism and its lasting destructive legacies have not fallen out of its purview. The preference given to postcolonialism because it allows for an engagement with the "problematics of the past and present of historical experiences of the colonized peoples" must be commended. This is far from an apolitical stand. The fierce academic debates around pedagogies of multiculturalism, postcolonial literature, and world literature can help us contextualize these moves. The criticism of such pedagogies, which have espoused the inclusion of literatures from around the world in the Euro-American college syllabi, has pointed to them as tokenistic attempts to engage with non-European literatures. Such specializations are called out for being relatively easy, not involving in-depth knowledge of other cultures and languages, and feeding American isolationism.[28] However, these (valid) critiques are particularly about the Europhone attempt to understand the non-Europhone and do not apply to *Lotus* as such, which is produced in and by Third World cultural actors. But, the other critique of identity studies—multicultural or postcolonial (and lately, world) literary studies—as offering what Arjun Appadurai calls an "aesthetics of decontextualization," or being bereft of class and power analysis under the garb of a pluralist or culturalist approach, can be useful in locating the politics of the relaunched *Lotus*.[29]

Historically, the dissolution of the Soviet Union brought into sharp relief the discontent with ideologically heavy or doctrinal literatures that had been brewing for quite a while. The signs of the disavowal of the term Third World, which came to be associated with pejorative senses over time, had already begun to appear at the end of *Lotus*'s run. The Permanent Bureau moved from Beirut to Tunis in the wake of the Lebanese civil war and the siege of Beirut by Israel in 1982. In Tunis, the Palestinian author Ziad Abdel Fattah became the editor-in-chief from 1983 until the end of the magazine in the 1990s and devoted his tenure to rectifying the damage of "Soviet interference" and the editors' ideological commitment to communism with his own more "liberal sensibilities."[30] Fadhil Thamir's essay in the new *Lotus* allows us to see the subtle but significant entrenchment of this liberalism even in postcolonial studies: "It is time to react scientifically and objectively to defend our identity, civilizations and cultures without being narrow-minded or falling into a new fundamentalism that might imprison our insights in the past alone."[31] It is a rendering, albeit unfair, of the earlier politics as being temporally restricted to around the time of independence and not engaged with the protracted damages of colonialism. Again, the instructive thing here is not whether Thamir's characterization is fair or unfair, but the extent to which earlier anticolonial discourse has become unfashionable. The article's wholehearted embrace of the postcolonial scholarship of Gayatri Chakravorty Spivak and Homi Bhabha captures the most significant shift from anticolonialism to postcolonialism or what can be characterized as a move from cultural politics to culturalist politics.

Thamir's essay ultimately favors the framework of the "Silk Road": "it is an umbrella name for our inspirations, sufferings and dreams. We could discover everyday new ties and links that unite us strongly and firmly."[32] As a political and cultural intervention, this seems quite similar to the emphasis on Afro-Asianness of the previous magazine cultivated through the concept of 'co-discovery' or parallelization of African and Asian literatures in order to promote familiarity with each other's works, which they had been lacking "despite their common schooling in the nuances of European literature."[33] The preference for a term like the "Silk Road" connotes a *longue durée* of connectivity sans the political rhetoric of the Afro-Asian.

There are other essays that further contribute to this focus on multiculturalism, such as Nguyen Dang Diep's "The Reform of Modern Vietnamese Poetry." In his essay, Diep introduces the two broad categories of the New Poetry (South Vietnamese, Romanticist/individualistic, influenced by the West) and the revolutionary poetry (North Vietnamese, radical/collective, influenced by the Soviet Union). Diep theorizes a third kind to have emerged since the 1986 Reform which initiated Vietnamese literature's "integration into the global world."[34] This integration, he writes, is "more comprehensive and inclusive"[35] and "multilateral and multichannel,"[36] acknowledges diasporic Vietnamese literature within the fold of Vietnamese literature, and has greater and faster reach because of the internet. Diep hails Vietnamese poetic creation after the reunification of North and South Vietnam as essentially "heteroglossic."[37] While celebrating the opening of "cultural exchanges"[38] that followed as having contributed to more unique literary works, Diep also cautions against the erosion of 'local' ethos. Ironically, his proposal for a "culture filter system"[39] that would ensure "poetic techniques received from the global world are harmonious with traditional cultural values of Vietnam"[40] recalls exactly the kind of cultural planning of the earlier decades he seems to be articulating a move away from.

What emerges from essays such as Thamir's and Diep's is that the distancing from the Third World cultural project or the disavowal of earlier models of political writing is not complete. And it does contrast with Salmawy's editorials, which tend to be more direct in both identifying the political issues that this literary endeavor tackles and how they are legacies of earlier political formations. This gap or elision allows room for thinking through the afterlives of anticolonial thought in the everyday practice of postcolonial literary production.

Conclusion

The new *Lotus*'s rhetorical gesture of the disavowal of the Marxist and socialist realist legacy, despite continuing its cultural politics in one form or another, could be explained by two factors. First, the cultural Cold War had exerted too much pressure on Third World cultural actors for them to align themselves with either cultural bloc. By not associating with the politics of the earlier *Lotus*, the relaunched magazine disassociates itself from the history of that enmeshment or "Soviet interference." Second, this might be a rejection of politically overdetermined readings of Third World or postcolonial literatures. Writers working in non-European languages or from the formerly colonized countries often contend with the a priori reading of their work as necessarily political. This is captured in the famous debate between Fredric Jameson and Aijaz Ahmad on the category of 'Third World' literature. The term that is missing from the essays published in the magazine and Salmawy's editorials but that definitely contextualizes the relaunched magazine's political and cultural intervention is the 'Global South.' Siba Grovogui's reminder is instructive:

> Although the term Global South gained currency at the end of the Cold War, when the term Third World seemed to fall into disfavor, the change does not signify a renunciation of the "Third World." It merely signals an adjustment in ideological and political positioning to reflect the new forms of contentions around the legacies of colonialism. Thus,

the Global South captures the spirit of Third World engagements in that it continues to invite re-examinations of the intellectual, political, and moral foundations of the international system.[41]

For Hala Halim, the relaunched journal is "a historical bridge from the post-Bandung era."[42] And as such, it provides "a case study for reflecting on the vicissitudes of the relationship between the Third World and the Global South."[43] In rethinking the relevance of the postcolonial in the twenty-first century, Robert Young traces a whole host of political issues that do not fall within "the template of the classic paradigm of anticolonial struggles" but actually reveal the extent to which the postcolonial remains.[44] For Young, these include settler colonialism, illegal migrants, and political Islam.[45] The issues identified by Mohamed Salmawy—authoritarianism and the muffling of dissent, the rise of terror, and the dangers of Islamophobic rhetoric—mark the magazine as a critical, even if not the most compelling or self-aware, extension of anticolonial thought in the twenty-first century. If we are to follow Young's lead and think of the postcolonial not as a theory or a discipline whose 'end' can be proclaimed but as a continuing political project, then we are better positioned to understand the two iterations of the magazine as part of the same continuum of responses to politics and literature. In response to this volume's critical interrogation of the allure of the instrumentalist framework for writers, this chapter has offered a historical approach to studying literary institutions instead of assessing the political efficacy of individual literary works or writers. The enterprise of Third World cultural politics forces us to rethink the resistance to instrumentalist writing that postmodernist approaches seem to have normalized. Although the CIA's CCF programmatically promoted liberal individualism in opposition to socialist realism during the Cold War, it is less likely to be read as an instrumentalist use of literature. And even though it is not the immediate focus of this chapter, it is significant to remember that this is because contemporary notions of what constitutes literature and literariness are premised on Eurocentric and neoliberal logic of literary value.[46] The brief but significant resurgence of *Lotus* magazine, and the move away from the politics of its earlier iteration, lays bare how the imagining of literature's political and cultural efficacy is intimately tied to shifts in political culture.

Notes

1 Jacques Rancière, "The Politics of Literature," *SubStance* 33, no. 1 (2004): 10–24, here 10.
2 Mai Al-Nakib, "Arab Literature: Politics and Nothing But?" *World Literature Today* 90, no. 1 (January/February 2016): 30–2, here 32.

3   For a historical overview of the Third World as a geopolitical and cultural product and not as a place to denote 'underdeveloped' countries, see Vijay Prashad, *The Darker Nations: A People's History of the Third World* (New York: The New Press, 2007).

4   See Mohamed Salmawy, "On the Importance of Cultural Convergence," *Lotus*, no. 1 (2016): 4–5.

5   Hala Halim, "Afro-Asian Third-Worldism into Global South: The Case of Lotus Journal," *Global South Studies: A Collective Publication with The Global South*, November 22, 2017, https://globalsouthstudies.as.virginia.edu/key-moments/afro-asian-third-worldism-global-south-case-lotus-journal.

6   Salmawy, "On the Importance of Cultural Convergence."

7   On how Egyptian authors of the "nineties generation" articulated their move away from *adab al-iltizām* (committed literature), specifically through the medium of the literary journal or the cultural magazine, see Nancy Lithicum, "The Cultural Newspaper: 'Akhbar al-Adab' and the Making of Egypt's Nineties Generation," *Alif: Journal of Comparative Poetics*, no. 37 (2017): 229–61.

8   Mohamed Salmawy, "Culture and the Defense of Identity," *Lotus*, no. 2 (2017): 6–7, here 7.

9   Ibid., 6.

10 See Mohamed Salmawy, "In Defense of Freedom of Expression," *Lotus*, no. 3 (2018): 4–5.

11 Youssef Al-Sebai, "Editorial Note," *Afro-Asian Writings*, no. 1 (1968): 6–12, here 7.

12 Ibid., 8.

13 This could be explained as strategic essentialism or the need of the hour, but Salmawy's pointedness presents a welcome change and must be commended.

14 On how social media technologies reshaped the Arab Spring's repertoire of communications, see Paul Gerbado, *Tweets and the Streets: Social Media and Contemporary Activism* (London: Pluto Press, 2012).

15 Safa Elnaili, "An Abused Country: Language as a Weapon to Force and Resist New Political Ideologies in Libya," *Lotus*, no. 2 (2017): 49–56, here 52.

16 Halim, "Afro-Asian Third-Worldism into Global South."

17 The old *Lotus* also routinely carried reprints of already published works despite a concerted effort to seek and even commission new writing. For contextualization within debates on literary valuing, singularity, and cultural authority, whereby works of literature are accorded the status of avant-garde by the economy of prestige (as opposed to being for consumption by the masses), see Günter Leypoldt, "Singularity and the Literary Market," *New Literary History* 45, no. 1 (2014): 71–88.

18 Maryam Fatima, "Institutionalizing Afro-Asianism: Lotus and the (Dis)Contents of Soviet-Third World Cultural Politics," *Comparative Literature Studies* 59, no. 3 (2022): 447–67, here 453.

19 Slavoj Žižek, "Liberal Multiculturalism Masks an Old Barbarism with a Human Face," *The Guardian*, October 3, 2010, https://www.theguardian.com/commentisfree/2010/oct/03/immigration-policy-roma-rightwing-europe.
20 See Lithicum, "The Cultural Newspaper," 232.
21 Chandni Desai and Rafeef Ziadah, "*Lotus* and Its Afterlives: Memory, Pedagogy, and Anticolonial Solidarity," *Curriculum Inquiry* 52, no. 3 (2022): 289–301, here 295.
22 *Time* magazine declared 2011 "the year of the protester" to celebrate the simultaneous and largely spontaneous eruption of popular movements in the United States, Spain, and the Arab world.
23 Meyzad's essay ends rather ominously and proclaims that the new millennium will witness "the rise of the Arabic Civilization and the fall of USA." Munir Meyzad, "Arab Spring or Long Islamic Winter," *Lotus*, no. 2 (2017): 42–5, here 42. This kind of extolling of "Arabic Civilization" recalls the strong undercurrent of Arab/ic hegemony in the earlier *Lotus*, which did a huge disservice to the magazine's mission.
24 Jodi Dean, "After Post-Politics: Occupation and the Return of Communism," in *The Post-Political and its Discontents: Spaces of Depoliticisation, Spectres of Radical Politics*, ed. Japhy Wilson and Erik Swyngedouw (Edinburgh: Edinburgh University Press, 2014), 262–77, here 261.
25 Erik Swyngedouw, "Apocalypse Forever?: Post-Political Populism and the Spectre of Climate Change," *Theory, Culture & Society* 27, no. 2–3 (2010): 213–32, here 225.
26 Nicolas Van Puymbroeck and Stijn Oosterlynck, "Opening up the Post-Political Condition: Multiculturalism and the Matrix of Depoliticisation," in *The Post-Political and Its Discontents: Spaces of Depoliticisation, Spectres of Radical Politics*, ed. Japhy Wilson and Erik Swyngedouw (Edinburgh: Edinburgh University Press, 2014), 86–109, here 89.
27 Fadhil Thamir, "Cultural and Literary Silk Road: We Must Speak," *Lotus*, no. 2 (2017): 46–8, here 47.
28 Dorothy M. Figueira, "Comparative Literature versus World Literature," *The Comparatist* 34 (2010): 29–36, here 30.
29 Arjun Appadurai, *The Social Life of Things: Commodities in Cultural Perspective* (Cambridge: Cambridge University Press, 1986), 28.
30 Sumayya Kassamali, "You had no Address: Faiz in Beirut," in *The East Was Read: Socialist Culture in the Third World*, ed. Vijay Prashad (New Delhi: LeftWord Books, 2020), 50.
31 Thamir, "Cultural and Literary Silk Road," 48.
32 Ibid., 46.
33 Rossen Djagalov, *From Internationalism to Postcolonialism: Literature and Cinema between the Second and the Third Worlds* (Montreal and Kingston: McGill-Queen's University Press, 2020), 71. See also Fatima, "Institutionalizing Afro-Asianism," 454–7.

34 Nguyen Dang Diep, "The Reform of Modern Vietnamese Poetry," *Lotus*, no. 2 (2017): 63–71, here 69.
35 Ibid.
36 Ibid.
37 Ibid., 68.
38 Ibid., 69.
39 Ibid.
40 Ibid.
41 Siba Grovogui, "A Revolution Nonetheless: The Global South in International Relations," *The Global South* 5, no. 1 (2011): 175–90, here 175.
42 Halim, "Afro-Asian Third-Worldism into Global South." The Bandung Conference of 1955 held in Indonesia was a watershed moment in world history, bringing together representatives and state leaders from twenty-nine recently liberated countries from Africa and Asia. Aiming to foster cultural and economic cooperation among participating nations, it solidified the presence of a significant anticolonial bloc and put into motion several cultural and political formations that together formed the formidable Third World project.
43 Halim, "Afro-Asian Third-Worldism into Global South."
44 Robert Young, "Postcolonial Remains," *New Literary History* 43, no. 1 (2012): 19–42, here 22.
45 Ibid.
46 For a historicist discussion, see Aamir Mufti, *Forget English! Orientalisms and World Literature* (Cambridge, MA: Harvard University Press, 2016).

14

Segments of a Larger Narrative

Political Formalism and Working-Class Story Cycles

Dirk Wiemann

How do *political* uses of literature differ from ostensibly nonpolitical ones—such as those, for instance, that Rita Felski so persuasively advocates in her 2009 post-critical manifesto *Uses of Literature*? Writing against the attitude of "analytical detachment, critical vigilance, guarded suspicion"[1] she perceives as dominant in literary criticism, Felski pleads for a more moderate and "respectful"[2] engagement with the text, and for the acknowledgment of "ordinary motives for reading"[3] that focus on jouissance, immersion, self-intensification, enchantment, aesthetic surrender, and generally a relaxed relation to theory and politics. In line with similar calls for "reparative"[4] or "generous"[5] readings that claim to restrict themselves to "register[ing] what the text itself is saying,"[6] Felski's manifesto has effectively helped delegitimize critique as an abuse of literature promulgated by "politically minded critics"[7] hell-bent on maltreating any text until it confesses its clandestine complicity with hegemonic ideology. For a relaxed post-critical practice, by contrast, the ulterior function of criticism is to trace how literature helps to "amplify and replenish our sense of *how things are*."[8] Both literature and its analysis thus become an exercise in befriending the given and making peace with the status quo. But what if Felski is telling only half the story? What if the constellation she designs (that of the affirmative literary text in the hands of the "politically minded" critic) simply rules out the possibility that literature itself may not be happy with "how things are," that texts may be opposed to the status quo even before any critic enters, that the critique of what is, far from being forcefully imposed by some suspicious hermeneutician, may very much be "what the text is saying"? Literature would then "amplify and replenish our sense of how things are" but in its very doing so heighten 'our sense' of why things have to be changed. In what follows I will try to draft a few preliminaries for such a political use of literature (both as an aesthetic event and as a social institution) and conclude with a reading, hopefully generous, of a contemporary working-class text that I consider a paradigmatic example of the kind of situational transcendence that literature may articulate.

Congruence, Transcendence, and Other Questions of Form

The terms *situational congruence* and *situational transcendence* were first deployed by the German sociologist Karl Mannheim, who, in the late Weimar Republic and after 1933 in British exile, put forward an elaborate 'diagnosis of our time': an ideology critique intended to account for the deeply polarized climate of irreconcilable agonism in the 'age of extremes.' In his writings from the 1920s through the 1940s, Mannheim observes a widespread friction between a "situationally congruent" resignation to the given situation and a "situationally transcendent" longing for that which established reality withholds: "all those ideas which do not fit into the current order are 'situationally transcendent' [the German original is 'seinstranszendent,' i.e., 'transcendent of existence/being'] or unreal. Ideas which correspond to the concretely existing and *de facto* order are designated as 'adequate' and situationally congruous."[9] It is within this tension between *Seinstranszendenz* and *Seinskongruenz* that, according to Mannheim, modern subjectivities take their shape.

Mannheim remained persistently puzzled by the sources of situational transcendence. Why do subjects not simply comply with the fait accompli of their situations? What are all those counterfactual ideas or desires that keep resurfacing irrepressibly throughout recorded history made of? In other words, how does that which is not part of the 'situation' come into it all the same? Fredric Jameson devotes his important study of science fiction and/as utopia precisely to this question. At the outset, *Archaeologies of the Future* confronts the "great empiricist maxim, nothing in the mind that was not first in the senses": a maxim whose bleak consequence it would be "that even our wildest imaginings are all collages of experience, constructs made up of bits and pieces of the here and now" so that, as it were, "our imaginations are hostages to our own mode of production."[10] The objective of Jameson's book is the pursuit of the numerous ways in which literature presents an excess and egress from this imprisonment in the given—if only in the negativity of an inverse utopia (which is not a dystopia) whose affordance it is "to body forth . . . the atrophy in our time of what Marcuse has called the *utopian imagination*, the imagination of otherness and radical alterity."[11] Situational transcendence thus comes not (as in Alain Badiou's radical ethics or Derek Attridge's very differently radical aesthetics) as the plenitude of a truth event or an experience of incommensurable singularity but as the marking of an absence, the "demonstration (*manifestation*) of a gap in the sensible itself."[12] It is through the manifestation of these gaps that *dissensus*—which constitutes, for Jacques Rancière, "the essence of politics"[13]—is enabled: an intervention that "places one world in another"[14] on the premise of a prior disarticulation of the apparently unpierceable seamlessness of established reality. A political use of literature would thus consist primarily in the ability to articulate and facilitate a sustained resistance to realism in the name of unrealized potentialities.

For Mannheim, the formation of subjects from the tension between *Seinstranszendenz* and *Seinskongruenz* is to a large extent contingent on "the general historical-social *form* of existence,"[15] that is, on the ways in which the material infrastructure, the social relations, the meaning-making narratives, and the epistemic premises of any given situation are patterned. Mannheim thus grasps the socius at large in terms of a set of "composed relationalities"[16]—a phrase that literary theorist Anna Kornbluh introduces as her basic thumbnail definition of form as such. In ways not foreseen by the post-critical preference for 'surfaces,' the category of form experienced a veritable revival over the first two decades of the twenty-first century, especially among what Felski would call "politically minded critics." This return of formalism as political theory owes mostly to the influence of such thinkers as Jacques Rancière or critics like Caroline Levine, in whose works form figures as the key category linking the aesthetic and the political. Thus, Levine postulates that "forms, defined as patternings, shapes, and arrangements . . . organize both social and literary objects,"[17] and she explicitly refers to Rancière's notion of the "distribution of the sensible" to stake a political claim for her own formulation of formalism.[18] For Rancière, it is the contest over "who can have a share in what is common to the community"[19] that constitutes the political as an essentially formal struggle over composed relationalities, arrangements, and rearrangements of bodies in social space. If "political formalism"[20] posits that society is 'like' a text, then this is a purely structural analogy that puts emphasis on the relations between interlocking composites of all kinds and at all possible scales of the (social) text.

The return of form may plausibly be read as a response to the (perceived) dominance of 'anti-formal' theories and politics that precede, as well as coexist with, the new formalism. Thus, Kornbluh openly polemicizes against a prevalent "enthusiasm for formlessness"[21] steeped in a self-defeating "absolutization of the dissent from formed relationality—institutions, standing formations, the state—into the messianic horizon of destituency that forestalls the constitution of new futures."[22] In this understanding, futurity cannot be delinked from form, with the important proviso that form demands to be grasped not as a fact but a process and a practice through which the "formativeness," the "speculative capacities of form"[23] play out. Constitutive of new futures, form*ing* (rather than form) is then a situationally transcendent generative act that brings forth novel articulations and redistributions of the social. At the same time, it is an incessant process whose outcome will always remain provisional, to be superseded by ever 'new futures.' Given this inherent processuality of form, no social formation is ever a fully "sutured totality,"[24] and hence the "incompletion in the social order"[25] remains ineluctable: not as a lack to be bemoaned but as a categorical openness that enables the political contestability of each and every established form. If the political, then, is crucially formal, the reverse is also true: the formal is eminently political. In this scenario, where "the aesthetic form *is* the political content,"[26] literature has a particular and privileged role to play.

Dissident Participation

Yet literature is not simply a medium that forms; it is also one that has been and keeps being, formed, re-formed, and certainly de-formed by factors that are largely external to it. Thus, in Western modernity, literature has been invested with a set of "organizing practices [that] bring together all the materials of the technical and organizational infrastructure of the institution," while "the imaginative or creative practices bring together all the materials of the aesthetic event that are handed down across the millennia, . . . all those artistic forms that give expression to literary content."[27] Of course, these sets of "practices," be they "organizing" or "imaginative," are historically contingent and subject to contestation and change—change, however, by infrastructural shifts, long-term demographic and educational developments, perhaps also by sustained political intervention, but certainly not through voluntarism. In this light, what does and does not count as literature is to a large extent determined by the rules of literature as an institution, it being understood that institutions, too, "can be seen as forms in the sense that [they] are ways of organizing heterogeneous materials."[28] The degree of compliance with the rules of the institution determines to what extent an utterance will, or will not, be intelligible as 'literature.' Composed relationalities are therefore inscribed into the very makeup of literature, and they simultaneously constrain and enable the production, circulation, and reception of any act of literary forming.

Like all practice in the open air of history, literary forming involves both the agentive dimension of creating the as yet inexistent *and* the necessary compliance with given and inherited circumstances. A 'realist' approach to literature would strive to account for the dialectics of agency and structure, their mutual and reciprocal entanglement. This would enable a politics of dissident participation that neither simply wishes away nor unconditionally succumbs to the established norms that regulate what is and what is not literature, and what is and what is not a proper way to 'use' it. 'Dissident participation' is a strategy delineated by Sabine Hark, who proposes that any interventionist and transformative politics has to operate not only on the terrain prepared and structured by the norm-imposing hegemon but to a certain extent in compliance with these norms:

> To change a field means to first of all change the rules of the game. The transformation of the rules, however, does not only demand a certain degree of virtuosity in understanding and navigating them, but it asks for . . . the acceptance of the rules—and be it out of pragmatic necessity.[29]

The "rules of the game" of literature are surely manifold. Here I can only briefly touch on one of many key entries in the contemporary code of 'the literary': the norm of literature as autopragmatic.[30] No doubt this is a merely functional feature that says nothing about what literature *is* (or even what an individual text seems to *say*) but very much about how literature is to be *used*. According to the autopragmatic paradigm, the 'appropriate' way of using literature is, as it were, to treat it (borrowing from Kant) as 'purposiveness without purpose.' Pragmatics, in short, distinguishes literature as non-pragmatic. This distinction has been firmly entrenched in the course of the historical institutionalization of the literary field that in "a long and slow process of autonomization presents itself as an inverted economic world: those who enter it have an interest in disinterestedness."[31] Like other art forms, literature, then, derives its use value from its uselessness. To intelligibly operate in that field implies a degree of compliance with the autopragmatic paradigm, and this is not a matter of choice. For as soon as one produces or receives a text as primarily instructive, informative, practically applicable, and so on, one is certainly still "in language" but no longer "in literature."[32] Dissident participation begins with the politicization of this normative framing of literature. Theorists of artistic activism have argued for precisely such a testing out and expanding of the rules of the game. Thus, instead of a post-critical or "anti-instrumentalist" scenario, Oliver Marchart argues for an "agitational" art practice that politicizes its users by confronting them with "the experience of antagonism."[33] While

Marchart advocates a head-on departure from the autopragmatic paradigm, Hito Steyerl proposes stretching it from within to its extremes:

> [D]uty free art ought to have no duty—no duty to perform, to represent, to teach, to embody value. It should not be indebted to anyone, nor serve a cause or a master, nor be a means to anything. Duty free art should not be a means to represent a culture, a nation, money, or anything else.[34]

While this assertion reads very much like any declaration of independence from the stock of high-modernist avant-garde manifestos, Steyerl's project is to decisively redefine what "artistic autonomy"[35] means in the age of neoliberal real subsumption and an increasingly refeudalized patronage system, where art takes place no longer in a relatively clearly demarcated semiautonomous "field" (Bourdieu) or "subsystem" (Luhmann) but instead in the messiness of postmodern capital's placeless omnipresence. The autonomy of art is therefore no longer located in, and secured by, the model of the ivory tower of heroic modernism; instead, "duty-free art" is funded by and founded on a wild assemblage of sponsoring/enabling agencies including

> the dictator's contemporary art foundation, the oligarch/weapon manufacturer's tax-evasion scheme, the hedge fund's trophy, the art student's debt bondage, leaked troves of data, aggregate spam, and the product of huge amounts of unpaid "voluntary" labor.[36]

What these disparate and incommensurate 'actors' have in common is their transnationalism, their situatedness in the global. It is on this account that Steyerl proposes to think of duty-free art not simply as overdetermined by, but also as a potential response to, globally deregulated finance capital and the nation-state as a key geographical scale at which neoliberalization operates. Precisely by playing along with the rules of the game, that is, by stubborn fidelity to the autopragmatic paradigm, duty-free art has the capacity to participate in dissidence and to rethink the potentials of autonomy as such. It could, Steyerl suggests, "try to understand political autonomy as an experiment in building alternatives to a nation-state model that continues to proclaim national culture."[37] Steyerl's considerations are interesting first of all because they sketch out a scenario in which art is seemingly exempt from social obligations ('duty free') but in fact harnessed to ulterior interests foreign to itself. Yet subservience—the subjection to an outside force—is only one constraint on autonomy; the other one in Steyerl's account is commitment. Of these constraints, the former is imposed, the latter self-chosen, the former situationally congruent, the latter transcendent. What Steyerl proposes to be the potential of duty-free art—namely to "understand political autonomy as an experiment"—is a scenario for a political use: one that find its contours in a perspective decidedly beyond the nation-state and its cultural forms.

Neither Marchart nor Steyerl addresses *literary* practices in their scenarios of artistic activism. This is not accidental but indicative of the deep entrenchment of the autopragmatic paradigm in the literary field, and also of the arguably even more firmly entrenched notion of reading as a strictly individual, secluded activity. This notion is hardly ever interrogated by present-day political formalists, many of whom take a deep interest in the dissident, status quo-transcendent energies of literature but leave the scene of reception untouched: for Levine as well as Rancière or Kornbluh, the 'dissensus' instantiated by literature is an individual experience that an isolated reader undergoes in private. Whether this privacy of the reader is celebrated as "idiocultural" self-possession and singularity[38] or decried as isolation and alienation[39] is of minor importance as long as it remains unquestioned as an indispensable and unalterable integral moment of literature as a social institution in Western modernity since the early nineteenth century.[40] It is true that there have been attempts to historicize and problematize this individualization as a symptom of, for example, capitalist modernity,[41] of the attendant gendered division of labor,[42] and/or the colonialist universalization of Western cultural paradigms;[43] but these analyses—invaluable though they are in their focus on the political uses of literature—have by and large been superseded by a powerful individualistic turn in literary theory that shifts attention from the political to the ethical impacts of the reading process as an engagement with the worlds of (fictional) others.[44] This is not to deny that a vibrant discussion is ongoing concerning the "transformative power of literature"[45] under the auspices of an obviously pressing demand for a reformulation of literature as activism; yet the discussants mostly take for granted and reproduce the notion of the apparently ineluctable privacy of reading and accordingly address *ethical* rather than *political* dimensions of reception.[46]

What I have called a 'realist' approach to literature has to be cognizant of this entrenched individualism, neither uncritically accepting and thereby reproducing it nor idealistically denying its normative force. A balancing act on the thin line between patience and impatience, such an approach will critically foster the manifold budding experiments to enrich literature with a 'commonist'[47] dimension (as in some varieties of performance poetry or activist readings), but it will be wary of the illusion that the edifice of literary individualism will be brought down by, say, Kae Tempest or the Refugee Tales project. In other words, the work of political formalism remains crucial for any speculation on the political uses of literature.

In this light, the notion of a confrontational and agitational aesthetics as advocated by Marchart strongly resonates with the way literature works as a medium formative of situationally transcendent positions, and it also clearly resonates with Steyerl's call for a transnational political imaginary. This, I would argue, is specifically apparent in such areas of literary production that are premised on an antagonistic relation to the hegemonic form of existence as well as on an internationalist outlook. One prominent exemplary field of literary practice is arguably the body of contemporary working-class writing under the auspices of neoliberal capitalism.

Similar to Steyerl's call for duty-free art to experiment with alternatives to the nation-state model, literary critics tend to find a transnational horizon inextricably inscribed into the body of the working-class text or even into the institution of working-class literature and its uses. Thus, in their discussion of the "global phenomenon of working-class literature(s)," John Lennon and Magnus Nilsson frame working-class writing as a world literature in its own right.[48] The uses of that 'alternative' body of world literature are, however, distinctly different from those of the corpus of works on which the agencies of the established literary institutions (including world literature studies) focus. This is a literature that primarily lends itself to a reading not of cosmopolitanism but rather of *internationalism*. Peter Hitchcock, in his tentative delineation of a project of studying working-class writing in the twenty-first century, emphasizes how "globalization now calls into question the parochial subtext written into national literary formations."[49] In his later full-length study of literary, photographic, and cinematic "labor mimesis,"[50] he expands more rigorously on the thesis of an inherent internationalism of both worker experience and worker representation: "something as pervasive as worker experience has within it the lineaments of a properly global aesthetic."[51] Certainly, this literary internationalism is by no means 'realist' or situationally congruent. Far from it: it is essentially counterfactual—situationally transcendent—given that globalization, the actual internationalization of production and extraction, "leads not to the internationalization—internationalism—of the workforce."[52] It is in this sense that Sonali Perera programmatically invokes "working-class writing as a mode of internationalism in an age of comparative advantage and outsourcing."[53] This corpus, Perera suggests, calls for a rethinking of the institution of (world) literature itself, namely, for "a political concept of world literature that is collaborative in form and internationalist in its tropes, themes, and structural and structuring aspects."[54] In the hope of bringing together the various strands of the argument so far, I will use the remainder of this chapter to discuss the options for alternate uses of literature by proposing a politically formalist reading of one exemplary piece of contemporary working-class literature: Deepak Unnikrishnan's short-story cycle *Temporary People* (2017).

Temporary People: Working-Class Writing as Interrupted Repetition

Temporary People is a collection of linked stories focusing on South Indian labor migrants in the Persian Gulf region. Though announced as

"A Novel" on its title page, the book is technically a story cycle, a form whose potential affordances are not entirely congruent with those of the novel. Commenting on the generic oddity of the book, Shafeeq Karinkurayil proposes that *Temporary People* should not be read as just a novel but more specifically as a migrant novel: a preemergent form which he understands as a representational apparatus not of the larger socius of the nation but of "the live bonds of intimacy"[55] within a spatially dispersed yet intensely connected community. Such a reading appears compatible with the postulates articulated in pioneering studies of the story cycle, which frequently assume isomorphism of the cycle's macrostructure and the social form of community. Most explicitly, Dunn and Morris suggest that we read contemporary story cycles as revisions of the nineteenth-century village sketch that was deemed to "capture a 'sense of place' in many minute particulars, including among these particulars an ethos of community that reflects a complex network of human lives."[56] Before adding my own suggestions and speculations on the specific political uses of this specific literary form, I will try to delineate a more rigorously 'formalist' approach to the story cycle.

Linked collections like Unnikrishnan's create "a structured series in which the component texts are no longer isolated"[57] and yet remain visible as self-sufficient units that could, and frequently do, stand alone. The fact that four of Unnikrishnan's stories have been published in magazines and edited anthologies prior to their inclusion in *Temporary People* testifies to this autonomy. As a consequence, the macrostructure of a story cycle hovers between the continuity of a fully articulated whole and the mere cumulation of bounded elements; in more strictly formalist terms, between sequentiality and segmentivity. As Brian McHale points out in a different context, the foregrounding of the segmentive (which clearly is the effect of the story cycle's architecture) and the recurrent interruption of continuity both emphasize the 'gappiness' of the sequence.[58] What ensues, then, is a structure that may best be described as *interrupted seriality*—a term that, as I will discuss in the last part of this chapter, allows for a reading of *Temporary People* (and the form of the story cycle in general) in the context of class, or, more precisely, working-class writing.

The perforated, 'gappy' structure of Unnikrishnan's collection is highlighted by the conspicuous diversity of the component narratives. The book is composed of twenty-eight "vignettes that feature different text types, such as parables, poems, formal reports, dramas, and monologues"[59] that are held together, at first glance, only by the shared topical focus on South Asian labor migration in the Gulf. Yet there are also overt pointers to the overall coherence of the collection. Thus, the volume is divided into three 'books' of nine or ten numbered 'chapters' each: a structuring device that appears to signal that the stories are to be read as tributaries to a larger narrative arc with a totalizing linearity. The introduction of the novelistic composition by way of chapterization arguably evokes a sequentiality that is, however, hardly manifested in the reading process, where the transition from one 'chapter' to the next yields only so many non-sequiturs. This refusal to gratify the narrative desire that energizes a conventional reading for the plot points to the inaccessibility of precisely such an overarching plot that would ultimately allow for narrative closure and discharge of meaning. In this sense, *Temporary People* is deliberately 'deficient' and so is, upon closer inspection, even the nomination of the individual stories, not as 'chapters' but as 'chabters.' Almost, but not quite: some readers have deciphered this idiosyncrasy as "a nod to native Arabic speakers whose mother tongue doesn't use the 'p'-sound, and replaces such with a 'b'-sound."[60] Malayalam speakers, on the other hand, may remark that the avoidance of *p* recurs to the specifics of Malayali English, whose phonetics privileges voiced over voiceless plosives. Thus, misspelling not only indicates an ironic distance to the generic protocols of the novel but also captures the processes of transnational exchange: languages appear to flow into each other and merge in the contact zone of a text that simulates the specifics of nonstandard Englishes derived from the encounter with widely different languages. But contact zones, as Mary Louise Pratt emphasized long ago, are hardly ever harmonious havens of multicultural cross-pollination but mostly spaces of "copresence, interaction, interlocking understandings and practices often within radically asymmetrical relations of power,"[61] which in *Temporary People* manifest in the confluence of differently empowering languages. While English is the uncontested lingua franca of Anglocentric globalization, Arabic is the hegemonic language of the 'locals' as distinct from the numerous subordinate vernaculars of the "temporary workers"[62] from various regions of South Asia, Eastern Africa, or the Philippines.

Temporary People zooms in mostly on migrant labor from Kerala, and the problem of translation and the "mangling of language"[63] in a deeply asymmetrical contact zone provide one central subject of many of the stories. Translatability and its limits are indeed at the heart of the problem of class identification in the book, whose author himself hails from a *pravasi* background and, as he recounts in an interview, "was raised in a city [Dubai] by parents who barely got by."[64] Originally a Sanskrit word for 'migrant' but also 'bird of passage,' the term *pravasi* has been adopted by Hindi as well as Malayalam, the regional language of Kerala spoken by the majority of *pravasis* in the Gulf region. *Pravasi* thus signals how mobility and transferability of lexical material from one Indian language to another occur prior to all actual transnational displacement. India is in fact a space of constant intranational translation that engenders a principal "migratory poetics"[65] almost by default: a confluence of numerous languages that requires no diasporic or expatriate experience but inheres in the polyglot constitution of a polity the majority of whose members are fluent in at least two or three vernaculars and may in conversation nonchalantly switch languages three or four times within one sentence.

The Western reader is likely to associate this inherent *polyglossia* first of all with the early work of Salman Rushdie and his self-description as a 'translated man.' Yet where Rushdie, writing in the heyday of postcolonial euphoria, celebrates the migrant as the harbinger of 'newness' by way of intermixture, mongrelization, and hybridization, Unnikrishnan's outlook is much bleaker. It is true that in *Temporary People*, the figure of the 'translated man' remains as central as it was in, say, *The Satanic Verses*, but as *pravasi*, it takes on the distinct class character of guest worker with all the constraints and disadvantages this implies. The 'translated man' is therefore no longer a representative of "elite postcolonialism" speaking as a revamped "native informant"[66] to a metropolitan audience but a member of a heavily disenfranchised itinerant global workforce. "Limbs," the epigraphic opening micronarrative that is prefixed to the story cycle, sets the tone right at the outset:

> There exists this city built by labor, mostly men, who disappear after their respective buildings are made. Once the last brick is laid, the glass spotless, the elevators functional, the plumbing operational, the laborers, every single one of them, begin to fade, before disappearing completely.[67]

Invisibilized and spectral, these construction workers and other laborers persist only in the products they made and which apparently exhaust them to the point of complete erasure, turning them into "ghosts haunting the facades they helped build."[68] While readers may for good reason be led to associate this ghostliness with the Marxian specter of the proletariat, these resonances are almost completely blocked by the full disarticulation of this proletariat that has no presence except in the reified form of "their respective buildings," which are, of course, not 'theirs' at all.

Temporary People thus opens with a sketch of class relations for which no class consciousness exists. It is therefore fitting that the workers should name themselves by a translated term—*pravasi*—that the book as a whole then renders untranslatable. Three 'chabters' in the cycle are titled "Pravasis," and all three are distinctly nonnarrative. The third of them, with which the book closes, is in fact entirely nonverbal and consists only of a schematic drawing of a multitude of stylized human figures with suitcases, neatly arranged on the page in an orderly seriality reminiscent of the abstraction of a bar code rather than pictorial representation. (Figure 14.1)

What this 'closure' evokes is the subjection of migrant labor to the quantifying regime of immigration quotas in the abstracting mold of governmental campaigns that Benedict Anderson has discussed under rubric of "bound serialities";[69] in Unnikrishnan, it is the flight from language altogether into the domain of the graphic that underscores the evidence producing and standardizing effects of such enumerative procedures that

FIGURE 14.1 *Drawing, from Deepak Unnikrishnan,* Temporary People *(London: Restless Books, 2017), p. 252. © Restless Books.*

require the "impermissibility of fractions"[70]—in this case, the schematic reduction of individuals to the single feature of their status as *pravasis* signaled by the baggage they carry. In this respect, *Temporary People* closes on a deeply pessimistic note in which much of the effort of the text as a whole—namely the figuration of "authentic worker experience"[71]—appears to have been erased in the bound serialization of the concluding diagram, much like the workers who fade and disappear after the consummation of their tasks.

The point, however, is that these migrant workers have never fully materialized in the first place at any point in the book—at least not in terms of anything approaching a class identity. This becomes apparent in the first two "Pravasi" chapters/'chabters,' which, in sharp contrast to the nonverbal closure, offer an excess of words: long columns or endless chains of terms that might serve as synonyms of that titular term, *pravasi*. Chapter/'Chabter' 4, book 2, titled "Pravasis?", consists of three packed pages of (composite) nouns that all denote menial occupations and, occasionally, professions, opening with "Tailor. Hooker. Horse looker. Maid. Camel rider,"[72] and closing with

> Earth digger. Stone breaker. Foundation putter. Infrastructure planner. Rule follower. House builder. Camp builder. Tube-light installer. Helmet wearer. Jumpsuit sporter. Globetrotter. Daydreamer. City maker. Country maker. Place builder. Laborer. Cog. Cog? Cog.[73]

Obviously, not all terms in the list are from the same paradigm. There is, for instance, a substantial discrepancy in terms of prestige and income range between, say, the "stone breaker" and the "infrastructure planner." Moreover, not all entries are really occupation related, as the inclusion of the "daydreamer" exemplifies; but such terms that exceed the identification through (under)paid labor are so rare that their inclusion in the list underscores how nonrepresentative they are for the definition of the *pravasi*. Guest workers are, it seems, first and foremost identified with their work: an ontological fiat that returns us to the withering-away of the workers after their work is done. But of course, the point of the list lies in its cynical closure, where the indispensable constitutive function of migrant labor—"City maker. Country maker. Place builder"—is highlighted as if to evoke a sense of the dignity of labor, which is then summarily sucked into the full reification of the ultimate denominator, "cog": a wry and laconic ascription that the speaker (or some hitherto silent addressee) immediately questions but that thereby all the more receives the opportunity to be reconfirmed as a nonnegotiable verdict. And yet one might ask whether the cog-ification of the *pravasi* is necessarily disempowering. It prepares, one could argue, for one more attempt to define "what the word pravasi really means: absence":[74] a definition that ties in with the vanishing construction workers whose ghosts haunt the facades of the buildings they have made. Priya Menon persuasively argues that the "absent-present ghosts of Gulf-*pravasis* form the foundation upon which Unnikrishnan constructs the text's spectral architecture,"[75] thereby pointing to (but not elaborating on) the 'gappy' macrostructure of *Temporary People*.

What needs to be added is that the 'architecture' of the book is not only conspicuously perforated but at the same time elaborately patterned. Unlike most story cycles that are marked by relative stylistic coherence, *Temporary People* accommodates a remarkably wide range of styles and genres. This foregrounding of formal heterogeneity emphasizes the gaps between the individual tributary texts and renders the transition from one segment to the next precarious. Analogous to sharp cuts that interrupt filmic continuity, the abrupt stylistic and generic shifts between stories recurrently trip up the reading flow and make it more effortful to integrate the individual segments into whatever constellation. I would like to propose to return at this point to political formalism proper and to read the dominance of segmentivity over synthesis politically: as a figuration of the "interrupted seriality" that Sonali Perera introduces as the defining feature of working-class writing.[76] While Perera's focus is primarily on novels from Mulk Raj Anand to A. Sivanandan and Bessie Head, her theoretical lens with its premium on segments rather than sequences is exceptionally germane to the analysis of more 'gappy' forms like the story cycle.

The notion not only of interrupted seriality but of "repeated interruptions"[77] allows for fascinating speculations on Unnikrishnan's politics of form. This understanding of repetition provides an alternative to the hauntological reading proposed by Menon, who interprets the "cyclicality of spectral repetition"[78] as a correlate of the ghostliness inherent to *pravasi* existence. While not fully following Menon's interpretation, I second her emphasis on the way chapter titles and themes recur and resurface across significant gaps: "For instance, three stories in two different books have the same title, 'Blattella Germanica,' in which stubborn German cockroaches, 'programmed to live,' repeatedly take over the narrator's multiple homes in two different cities."[79] Conspicuous repetitions like these may, adopting Perera's model, point to a trajectory that refers back to the more general problem of what a political use of literature might look like. Perera retrieves from Karl Marx's *Eighteenth Brumaire* a distinction between bourgeois and proletarian revolutions in terms of their plot dynamics, as it were: while the former "storm quickly from success to success," the latter "constantly engage in self-criticism, and in repeated interruptions of their own course. They return to what has apparently already been accomplished in order to begin the task again."[80] Transposing to literature this "figural logic of repeated interruptions,"[81] Perera identifies the recurrent "stops and starts of serialized form"[82] as formative of the novels she discusses, and it is my contention that Unnikrishnan's story cycle, too, is constituted on precisely this autocritical pattern. In this light, repetition and interruption do not articulate only, and perhaps not even primarily, a "sense of disjunction and dissociation"[83] but also, to some extent, a resilient and patient upholding of situational transcendence, if only in the domain of literary form, in a decidedly a-revolutionary setting. In such a perspective, the overtly disjunct component parts may become re-legible as 'cogs,' as segments of a larger narrative for whose future realization there is no guarantee whatsoever. Admittedly, this may seem to be a pretty ethereal 'political use' of literature, one that runs the risk of rendering literature an inefficient angel rather than a rising lion. But whoever said that literature is, or can be, capable of achieving more than that, given its current status as duty-free art?

Notes

The author would like to thank Satish Poduval (EFLU Hyderabad) for helpful information on the phonetics of Malayali English and on the etymology and dissemination of the term *pravasi*.

1. Rita Felski, *Uses of Literature* (Oxford and Malden: Blackwell, 2009), 2.
2. Ibid., 7.
3. Ibid., 14.
4. Eve Kosofsky Sedgwick, *Touching Feeling: Affect, Pedagogy, Performativity* (Durham and London: Duke University Press, 2002), 128.
5. Timothy Bewes, "Reading with the Grain: A New World in Literary Criticism," *Difference* 21, no. 3 (2010): 1–33, here 8.
6. Stephen Best and Sharon Marcus, "Surface Reading: An Introduction," *Representations* 108, no. 1 (2009): 1–28, here 8.
7. Felski, *Uses of Literature*, 55.
8. Ibid., 35. Emphasis added.
9. Karl Mannheim, *Ideology and Utopia: An Introduction to the Sociology of Knowledge*, trans. Louis Wirth and Edward Shills (London: Routledge and Kegan Paul, 1979 [1929]), 175.
10. Fredric Jameson, *Archaeologies of the Future: The Desire Called Utopia and Other Science Fictions* (London: Verso, 2005), xiii.
11. Ibid., 289. Emphasis in original.
12. Jacques Rancière, *Dissensus: On Politics and Aesthetics*, trans. Steven Corcoran (London and New York: Continuum, 2010), 39. Emphasis in original.
13. Ibid.
14. Ibid.
15. Mannheim, *Ideology and Utopia*, 116. Emphasis in original.
16. Anna Kornbluh, *The Order of Forms: Realism, Formalism, and Social Space* (Chicago: University of Chicago Press, 2019), 4.
17. Caroline Levine, *Forms: Whole, Rhythm, Hierarchy, Network* (Princeton: Princeton University Press, 2015), 13.
18. See ibid., 17.
19. Jacques Rancière, *The Politics of Aesthetics*, trans. Gabriel Rockhill (London: Continuum, 2004), 12.
20. Kornbluh, *The Order of Forms*, 17.
21. Ibid., 79.
22. Ibid., 165.
23. Tom Eyers, *Speculative Formalism: Literature, Theory, and the Critical Present* (Evanston: Northwestern University Press, 2017), 186.

24 Ernesto Laclau and Chantal Mouffe, *Hegemony and Socialist Strategy: Towards a Radical Democratic Politics* (London: Verso, 2001), 105.
25 Kornbluh, *The Order of Forms*, 29; see also Eyers, *Speculative Formalism*, 196.
26 Victoria Wohl, *Euripides and the Politics of Form* (Princeton: Princeton University Press, 2015), 18. Emphasis in original.
27 Stephen Tötösy de Zepetnek, "Systems Theories and the Study of Literature and Culture," *Comparative Literature* 67, no. 1 (2015): 1–10, here 5.
28 Levine, *Forms*, 56.
29 Sophia Vögele, "Dissident Participation and Its 'Post_Colonial' Implications: An Exploration of Positionalities of Critique Considered Regarding the Institution of High (Arts) Education," in *Taking Sides: Theories, Practices and Cultures of Participation in Dissent*, ed. Elke Bippus, Anne Ganzert, and Isabell Otto (Bielefeld: transcript, 2021), 225–8, here 228. The given passage is Vögele's own translation from Sabine Hark, *Dissidente Partizipation: Eine Diskursgeschichte des Feminismus* (Frankfurt am Main: Suhrkamp, 2005).
30 See, for example, Terry Eagleton, *Literary Theory: An Introduction* (Oxford: Blackwell, 1983); K. M. Newton, *Twentieth-Century Literary Theory: A Reader* (New York: Macmillan, 1993); Derek Attridge, *The Singularity of Literature* (London: Routledge, 2004); and Derek Attridge, *The Work of Literature* (Oxford: Oxford University Press, 2015).
31 Pierre Bourdieu, *The Rules of Art: Structure and Genesis of the Literary Field*, trans. Susan Emmanuel (Stanford: Stanford University Press, 1996 [1992]), 215–16.
32 See Attridge, *The Singularity of Literature*, 61.
33 Oliver Marchart, *Conflictual Aesthetics: Artistic Activism and the Public Sphere* (Berlin: Sternberg Press, 2019), 40.
34 Hito Steyerl, *Duty Free Art: Art in the Age of Planetary Civil War* (London and New York: Verso, 2016), 97.
35 Ibid.
36 Ibid.
37 Ibid.
38 Attridge, *The Singularity of Literature*, 22.
39 See Lennard J. Davis, *Resisting Novels: Ideology and Fiction* (New York and London: Methuen, 1987), 3.
40 See Abigail Williams, *The Social Life of Books: Reading Together in the Eighteenth-Century Home* (New Haven: Yale University Press, 2017).
41 See, for example, Fredric Jameson, "Third-World Literature in the Era of Multinational Capitalism," *Social Text* 15 (1986): 65–88.
42 See Nancy Armstrong, *Desire and Domestic Fiction: A Political History of the Novel* (New York and Oxford: Oxford University Press, 1987).

43 See Firdous Azim, *The Colonial Rise of the Novel* (London and New York: Routledge, 1993).

44 See, for example, Martha Nussbaum, *Love's Knowledge: Essays on Philosophy and Literature* (Oxford: Oxford University Press, 1990) and *Poetic Justice: The Literary Imagination and Public Life* (Boston: Beacon Press, 1995); Dorothy Hale, "Fiction as Restriction: Self-Binding in New Ethical Theories of the Novel," *Narrative* 15, no. 2 (2007): 187–206; Gayatri Chakravorty Spivak, "Righting Wrongs," in *Other Asias* (Oxford: Blackwell, 2008), 14–57.

45 Betty Wilson, "Literature and Activism, Literature as Activism: Case Studies from Caribbean Women's Writing in French," *Caribbean Quarterly* 66, no. 3 (2020): 405–24, here 420.

46 See Shady Cosgrove, "Reading for Peace? Reading for Peace? Literature as Activism – An Investigation into New Literary Ethics and the Novel" (2008), https://ro.uow.edu.au/creartspapers/82.

47 For the term 'commonism,' see Pascal Gielen, "Common Aesthetics: The Shapes of a New Meta-Ideology," in *Commonism: A New Aesthetics of the Real*, ed. Nico Dockx and Pacal Gielen (Amsterdam: Valiz, 2019), 75–87, here 83. Tellingly, here too the focus is on the visual, cinematic, and performative arts while there is hardly any reference to literary practices.

48 John Lennon and Magnus Nilsson, "Introduction," in *Working-Class Literature(s): Historical and International Perspectives*, ed. John Lennon and Magnus Nilsson (Stockholm: Stockholm University Press, 2017), ix–xviii, here x.

49 Peter Hitchcock, "They Must Be Represented? Problems in Theories of Working-Class Representation," *PMLA* 115, no. 1 (2000): 20–32, here 30.

50 Peter Hitchcock, *Labor in Culture, or, Worker of the World(s)* (Cham: Palgrave Macmillan, 2017), 29.

51 Ibid., 9.

52 Sonali Perera, *No Country: Working-Class Writing in the Age of Globalization* (New York: Columbia University Press, 2014), 3.

53 Ibid., 4.

54 Ibid., 14.

55 Mohammed Shafeeq Karinkurayil, "Novel as a Genre of Migration: Reading *Temporary People*," unpublished manuscript (forthcoming), 13.

56 Maggie Dunn and Ann Morris, *The Composite Novel: The Short Story Cycle in Transition* (Woodbridge: Twayne, 1995), 23.

57 Mara Santi, "Performative Perspectives on Short Story Collections," *Interférences littéraires* 12 (2014): 145–54, here 150.

58 Brian McHale, "Affordances of Form in Stanzaic Narrative Poetry," *Literator* 31, no. 3 (2010): 49–60, here 50.

59 Juliane Strätz, "Subverting Late Capitalist Comfort: Affective Connections in Deepak Unnikrishnan's *Temporary People*," in *Comfort in Contemporary*

Culture: The Challenges of a Concept, ed. Dorothee Birke and Stella Butler (Bielefeld: transcript, 2020), 133–48, here 140.

60 Priya Menon, "*Pravasi* Really Means Absence: Gulf-*Pravasis* as Spectral Figures in Deepak Unnikrishnan's *Temporary People*," *South Asia: Journal of South Asian Studies* 43, no. 2 (2020): 185–98, here 196.

61 Mary Louise Pratt, *Imperial Eyes: Travel Writing and Transculturation* (London: Routledge, 1994), 7.

62 Deepak Unnikrishnan, *Temporary People* (Gurgaon: Penguin, 2017), 112.

63 Ibid., 76.

64 Michael Barron, "How Novelist Deepak Unnikrishnan Post-Modernized the United Arab Emirates," *Culture Trip* (2017), https://theculturetrip.com/middle-east/united-arab-emirates/articles/deepak-unnikrishnan-temporary-people-interview/.

65 Sneharika Roy, *The Postcolonial Epic: From Melville to Walcott and Ghosh* (London and New York: Routledge, 2018), 17.

66 Gayatri Chakravorty Spivak, *A Critique of Postcolonial Reason: Toward a History of the Vanishing Present* (New Haven: Harvard University Press, 1999), 358.

67 Unnikrishnan, *Temporary People*, 3.

68 Ibid.

69 Benedict Anderson, *The Spectre of Comparisons: Nationalism, Southeast Asia and the World* (London: Verso, 2002), 36.

70 Ibid.

71 Hitchcock, *Labor in Culture, or, Worker of the World(s)*, 76.

72 Unnikrishnan, *Temporary People*, 137.

73 Ibid., 139.

74 Ibid., 186.

75 Menon, "*Pravasi* Really Means Absence," 197.

76 Perera, *No Country*, 14.

77 Ibid., 100.

78 Menon, "*Pravasi* Really Means Absence," 12.

79 Ibid., 196.

80 Karl Marx, "The Eighteenth Brumaire of Louis Bonaparte," in *Surveys from Exile: Political Writings. Vol 2*, ed. David Fernbach, trans. Ben Fowkes (Harmondsworth: Penguin/New Left Review, 1973 [1852]), 143–249, here 150.

81 Perera, *No Country*, 124.

82 Ibid.

83 Menon, "*Pravasi* Really Means Absence," 197.

15

Sedimented Reading Habits? The Future Utopia in Contemporary African Science and Speculative Fiction

Peter J. Maurits

A tension exists between contemporary African speculative and science fiction (ASF) and debates about these works, as the following two examples illustrate. First, as the Malawian author Shadreck Chikoti states in an interview for Geoff Ryman's *100 African Writers of SFF*, war and poverty on the continent complicate thinking about a better African future. Science fiction (SF) authors like him, however, can use what he considers the political force of the SF genre: they "envision, create, and so we can think about the future. There is this quote . . . from Abraham Lincoln that says, 'If you want the future then create it yourself.'"[1] Indeed, Chikoti himself wrote the introduction to the short story collection titled *Imagine Africa 500*, which imagines Africa 500 years in the future, and he also wrote a seemingly future utopian novel titled *Azotus: The Kingdom*. Yet his professed concern with the difficulty of imagining or even creating a better future for Africa appears to be in contrast with those works. In the introduction to *Imagine*, Chikoti explains that the volume is about the "exciting prospects about Africa's future" as well as about "our darkest nightmares."[2] But the nightmares dominate: it is true that *Azotus* is set "somewhere in the future"[3] and starts by describing an apparently utopian society; however, in Ryman's words, the novel finally presents us with "one of the worst imaginable futures for Africa."[4] As Chikoti himself agrees, his novel "mirrors"[5] the regime of the

Malawian autocrat Kamuzu Banda, who ruled from 1964 to 1994. *Azotus* is thus neither about the future nor about a better future. My second example is taken from Chiagozie Nwonwu, cofounder of the literary magazine for African science and speculative fiction *Omenana*, who was asked in an interview with the Heinrich Böll Foundation what he thinks inspires "African sci-fi writers the most."[6] The interviewer presupposes that it is either "the fascination with the endless possibilities of the future or simply [a] dissatisfaction with the current realities," but Nwonwu responds that the present and especially the past figure most prominently in *Omenana* submissions.[7] He continues that in *Omenana* they see "far fewer stories about the endless possibilities that the African future holds . . . and we mostly don't see anything that hints at a future with possibilities. When we do get stories about the future in *Omenana*, we are not shocked to see dystopias and future reflections of the discord of the present."[8]

The tension that I mentioned thus derives, on the one hand, from the assumption that contemporary ASF involves 'better future narratives' (what I will be calling 'future utopias') and, on the other hand, from the relative absence of this narrative form from ASF works. I begin by addressing this tension because SF (and its subgenre of the narrative utopia)—due to its narrative strategies of speculation and extrapolation and due to the prominence of the *topos* of the future—has long been considered the preeminent genre for imagining alternative or better futures. This opinion is shared widely by scholars, authors, and fans alike. Consequently, SF has been thought of as a deeply political and even subversive narrative form because it can supposedly think beyond the status quo and imagine or even help facilitate a new social order. When, for various reasons, a significant increase in the production, circulation, and consumption of ASF occurred after the global financial crisis of 2007-8,[9] a similar discourse about the political use of the genre emerged alongside it. The two examples above evidence this and, to give an impression of the magnitude of the phenomenon, it is worth explicating that they are far from exceptional. Consider, for instance, the following selection of further, shorter citations, which all claim a political use of ASF based on a presumed capacity to imagine alternative futures: Ivor Hartmann wrote in his groundbreaking ASF short story collection, "SciFi is the only genre that enables African writers to envision a future from our African perspective."[10] Ayodele Arigbabu noted in his short story collection, "Science fiction . . . allows the writer to imagine ordinarily 'unthinkable' scenarios . . . dare the future, give courage to others."[11] Author and *Brittle Paper* founder Ainehi Edoro maintained, "[s]cience fiction is a transformational art."[12] Prominent ASF figure Nnedi Okorafor said, "[s]cience fiction is one of the greatest and most effective forms of political writing"; ASF is "ready to come forth. And when it does: imagine the new technologies, ideas, and sociopolitical changes it will inspire."[13] It is thus unsurprising that Rodney Likaku and Joanna Woods, who in their study of Malawian ASF perhaps expectedly start from the assumption that ASF is about "creat[ing] a possible . . . future," and conclude with frustration that "the current generation of Malawian [SF] writers fail to adequately postulate possible futures, or practical possible worlds."[14] Nor is it remarkable that Ryman writes, puzzled, that "so many people say African science fiction is about . . . envisaging a future for Africa. And then most of the speculative fiction available seems to be about the past or traditional gods and monsters":[15] "so much of the work isn't futurist."[16]

The question that the above raises, and to which this chapter aims to give more pointed form, is this: If ASF is not about future utopias, why do we keep saying that it is? In the following three sections, I shall suggest that the prominence of future utopia in ASF debates results, first, from the influence of Afrofuturism, and second, from SF's 'inferiority complex,' originating in the pulp era and paradoxically shaped as SF exceptionalism through decades of SF debates. I claim, in other words, that ASF has been viewed in part through the lens of previously established theoretical frameworks. In the third and final section, I will argue that while this is understandable to a degree, it not only misrepresents the political impulse of ASF but also obscures just how ASF is used politically. I shall illustrate this through a discussion of the short fiction of Tlotlo Tsamaase, which very deliberately sidetracks the concern with the future in order to render the everyday legible as dystopian.

Recovering Counter-Futures: The Importance of Afrofuturism 2.0

A possible reason for the prominence of future utopias in ASF debates is the genre's complex proximity to Afrofuturism. Afrofuturism has been a prominent topic of academic and public debates for over a decade. It is now well known that Mark Dery coined the term in his 1994 volume *Flame Wars*; that the term's genealogy goes back at least to W. E. B. Du Bois's early twentieth-century short fiction; and that Afrofuturism may be considered an aesthetic response, to use Jayna Brown's terms, by "racialized and colonized subjects [which] have been excluded from 'the human,' a category made ontological through the naturalization of Western imperial origin narratives."[17]

Rather than revisit this history once more, I wish to draw attention to the way in which Afrofuturism can be understood as having reemerged or reintensified after 2010 (although it had never completely disappeared before then). This process of revitalization, I suggest, involved a reconceptualization of Afrofuturism that placed a more explicit focus on the creation of future utopias as well as on political activism. In her study on the Afrofuturism hashtag, Grace Gipson observed that after a period of intense online activity in the 1990s, Afrofuturism lost its momentum to such a degree that she considers "2002–2011 to be a dormant period."[18] While Gipson comments specifically on internet-based Afrofuturism, Reynaldo Anderson and Charles E. Jones—who spoke of the emergence of "Afrofuturism 2.0" in 2016—suggest that her point possesses broader validity. Like Gipson, Anderson and Jones describe a decline in the use of the term and they note that the "last several years have seen an explosion of interest in . . . Afrofuturism."[19] Also in 2016, Anderson specified that Afrofuturism had "blossomed into a global movement the last five years."[20] He explains that this new "wave" represented a shift away from the Eurocentric question about the deliberate erasure of African history in North America and toward a more explicit critique of Euro-American narratives about the past, the present, and the future.[21] He cites Kodwo Eshun to specify that, now, "Afrofuturism may be characterized as a program for recovering the histories of counter-futures,"[22] in which, in other words, Afrofuturists take the future into their own hands.

For Anderson, then, Afrofuturism 2.0 is not just a literary or artistic phenomenon but also a "critical" project, rooted in the radical politics of Negritude and the Black Arts Movements of the 1960s and 1970s, and aiming to lay the foundations for a future humanity which is "not bound up by the ideas of the enlightenment."[23] A focus on imagining alternative futures with an affinity for activism may indeed be observed in post-2010 Afrofuturist works/studies more generally. Ytasha L. Womack writes, for example, that "black people are minimized in pop culture depictions of the future" and adds: "It's one thing when black people aren't discussed in world history. . . . But when, even in the imaginary future . . . people can't fathom a person of non-Euro descent . . . a cosmic foot has to be put down."[24] For Womack, the people who do this work—imagine a different future for Black people—are Afrofuturists. Tiffany E. Barber writes that Afrofuturism has become an "umbrella term for considering how science fiction, fantasy, and technology can be used to imagine and reimagine lost pasts and new futures for alienated, black 'others.'"[25] Gipson suggests that Afrofuturist works are "prescriptions for a promising future,"[26] and Ingrid LaFleur defines "Afrofuturism as a way of imagining possible futures through a black cultural lens."[27] Faithful to the activist thrust of her arguments, she ran for mayor of Detroit in 2017 with an Afrofuturist agenda.

Afrofuturism, in this sense, differs from scholarship on race in SF or on so-called Black SF—although there is a significant overlap. For example, Sharon DeGraw's study traces how eugenics found its way into SF works of writers such as Edgar Rice Burroughs and how it influenced the type of futures/story worlds they imagined.[28] Isiah Lavender III highlights how George Schuyler's *Black No More* (1931) imagined a cure "to turn darkies white,"[29] thus confronting such "unspoken white desire for blacks to vanish, leaving behind a seemingly white world" in the future.[30] Like

DeGraw, Lavender is ultimately concerned with "trac[ing] the development of scientific racism through literary, cultural, and scientific discourses and how this shapes [SF]."[31] Even Samuel R. Delay, who, due to his inclusion in Dery's *Flame Wars*, is understandably considered an Afrofuturist, ultimately has different concerns. He observed in 1976 that he was one of the few Black SF writers in North America and addressed why it was important that there be more: if SF "has any use at all, it is that . . . it gives us images for our futures."[32] SF creates "images of tomorrow; and our people need them more than most."[33] Nevertheless, as he would later add with great insistence, and in contrast to 2.0 Afrofuturists, "Science fiction is not about the future; it uses the future as a narrative convention"[34] and is thus similar to the "parallel world" convention, which presupposes that "history had turned out differently. [SF can be] set in an alternative past . . . present [or] future."[35]

In the ongoing debate about the definition of ASF, there now appears to be an emerging consensus that, at the very least, it is not the same as Afrofuturism. In their 2009 article on ASF, Delphi Carstens and Mer Roberts already labeled Afrofuturism an "African-American discursive practice."[36] In a related vein, Dilman Dila wrote in 2015 that "[s]ome liken [ASF] to Afrofuturism, but I don't like that idea, for African Americans . . . operate in a slightly different world [with] a richer pool of resources and opportunities compared to us who work and live on the continent."[37] And Nwonwu wrote in 2018 that the two aesthetic currents are different because "our experience is vastly different" and because ASF "isn't part of a movement, [there is no] collective wish to influence politics or culture."[38] Mohale Mashigo also says ASF is an aesthetic response to issues "unique to us" Africans (2018), while Afrofuturism is based on experiences of exclusion and racism specific to a North American "minority [which is] divorced or violently removed from their African roots, so they imagine a 'black future' where they aren't a minority and are able to marry their culture with technology."[39] She continues that in Africa, however, representational issues are different: "my television screen showed stories populated by black people speaking indigenous languages, so I have never suffered from a lack of representation as such."[40]

To understand ASF we need to take into account the relations and conditions of literary production. While this should entail distinguishing ASF from Afrofuturism, there is reason to assume that ASF and Afrofuturism influenced each other reciprocally. What Lisa Yaszek says of Afrofuturism is also true of ASF: it "appropriate[s] . . . the narrative techniques of science fiction"[41] and relies on SF traditions at large. But there are three other lines of reciprocal influence that I want to highlight. First, Carstens and Roberts already indicated that despite their differences, Afrofuturism can be useful to ASF in showing how to be in "dialogue with the past" and yet also craft "viable futures out of distinctive cultural motifs."[42] Second, the new "wave" of Afrofuturism described above intersects with the ASF boom. Earlier I argued that ASF "can be said to have occurred in part in the discursive space created by the GFC [global financial crisis]."[43] And while there is no space here to develop this argument, it seems more than likely—considering their near simultaneous reemergence or boom—that ASF and Afrofuturism share a social concern and a social referent, even if they focus on the African and North American continent, respectively. When Anderson writes in the wake of the success of the film *Black Panther* (2018) that "it is up to Africans to take it to the next level. And that could become afrofuturism 3.0,"[44] it appears to me that he taps into a not unproblematic discursive template according to which Africans must somehow catch up, while overlooking this simultaneous post-2010 traction of both Afrofuturism and ASF. Third, the separation of ASF and Afrofuturism was not always as clear as it is currently. Writer and artist Masiyaleti Mbewe recalls that she and other African futurists initially "call[ed] ourselves Afrofuturists. We're only now trying to detangle that identity. . . . [W]e noticed that the prefix 'Afro-' is the label used all the time to describe anything done by black people. Why can't we define things ourselves?"[45] Currently, Okorafor is among the most vocal figures advocating the distinction between the two aesthetic currents, but just as Mbewe, in 2017 she would discuss her work in the context of Afrofuturism,[46] as did esteemed ASF author Lauren Beukes.[47] Alena Rettová, in her landmark article on ASF in African languages, laments the "label of Afrofuturism or futurism" has not been applied to African literature, and adds with moderate optimism that recently, people have started "rectifying the situation."[48] She cites part of the Afrofuturist canon (Yaszek, Eshun) to make her point and in part focuses on how such works suggest "ways to construct this future."[49]

My claim, then, is that the aesthetic currents of Afrofuturism and contemporary African SF were co-constitutive to a degree, which promoted reciprocal flows of ideas. This was facilitated by the conjuncture of generic proximity, coterminosity, and partly shared literary/aesthetic ancestors, and by the initially porous borders between the two categories. This influence crucially included the flow of ideas about the future utopia from Afrofuturism to ASF.

Overcoming the Pulp (Science) Fiction Label

A second possible reason for the friction central to this chapter is ASF's connection to SF debates at large. SF writers, scholars, fans, and critics have long complained, displaying what may be described as a deeply rooted inferiority complex, that the genre was treated with "disdain,"[50] that it was not considered literature but rather genre or even pulp fiction. Responses to this position have been manifold and include a self-identification as marginal, for which Damon Knight's *The Futurians*, a nonfictional historical account of SF fans who became (famous) SF writers, is exemplary. Each of the real-life protagonists in Knight's book is described as deficient or impaired in some way: Hugo Gernsback was "unimpressive,"[51] Frederik Pohl was "emaciated" and "pale,"[52] Robert A. W. Lowndes had a "clubfoot,"[53] and so on. Dery escalated this type of response in a not unproblematic way, stating that "the sublegitimate status of science fiction as a pulp genre in Western literature mirrors the subaltern position to which Blacks have been relegated throughout American history."[54]

A more common way of responding to SF's perceived status problem was the attempt to break down the "ghetto walls of the popular [so] SF can (re)join the 'mainstream' of fiction" through different forms of justification.[55] The justification mechanism was associated with SF since its birth as a genre in the opening pages of Gernsback's first issue of *Amazing Stories*, in which the term SF was eventually coined. Opening with a justification, Gernsback wrote that the "reader may well wonder, 'Aren't there enough [fiction magazines] already, with the several hundreds now being published?'"[56] He continued that this was the case but that SF (which was then still called 'scientifiction') offered

> charming romance intermingled with scientific fact and prophetic vision. [These stories] make tremendously interesting reading—they are also always instructive. They supply knowledge ... in a very palatable form. [They] have the knack of imparting knowledge, and even inspiration, without once making us aware that we are being taught.... Prophecies [are] made in many [works and they blaze] a new trail ... in literature and fiction, but in progress as well.[57]

Gernsback thus distinguished SF from other pulp magazines on the basis of an SF exceptionalism consisting of SF's literary novelty, political efficacy, and the quasi-supernatural power of the prophet, with Jules Verne's predicting the submarine almost "to the last bolt" in his *Vingt Mille Lieues sous les mers* (1869–70) as his most famous example.[58] In line with this, *Amazing Stories*'s slogan was "Extravagant fiction today. Cold fact tomorrow."[59] Despite Gernsback's accomplishments, SF critics blamed him for associating SF with pulp and for its consequent bad reputation. Brian Aldiss wrote that Gernsback was "one of the worst disasters ever to hit the science fiction field" for "segregat[ing]" SF into pulp magazines and being "utterly without any literary understanding."[60] James Blish complained that SF exists beyond Gernsback's "ghetto" but is judged "exclusively by its bad examples."[61] Reflecting on these anti-Gernsbackian sentiments, Roger Luckhurst observes that despite the "suppression" of Gernsback's legacy, his "initial elaboration of the conditions on which the genre has come to be defined" remains determinative until today, even if these foundational generic conditions are now sometimes framed differently.[62] Thus, Luckhurst explicates, Gernsback's claim that SF stories are based on "scientific laws" is now treated as a token of the stories' "scientific rigor" and an imaginative "extrapolation" of available science; his claim that SF imparts knowledge is now framed as SF's "educative role"; his comments on blazing a trail for literature and progress are now framed in various ways as claims for SF's "cultural significance."[63]

In extension of Luckhurst's argument, I suggest that Gernsback's concept of 'prophecy' was also discredited and repackaged rather than abandoned. This most famously, but not exclusively, occurred in Darko Suvin's widely influential early work, which is characterized by a dislike for Gernsback that appears inseparable from his desire to lift SF out of the realm of pulp fiction. He did so by associating SF with classical literature, a project Delany called "pedagogic snobbery (or insecurity),"[64] and by establishing a more scientific-sounding SF exceptionalism in which SF is the only literary genre capable of cognitive estrangement and the "only meta-empirical genre which is not at the same time metaphysical."[65] He unpacked that while SF, like much "dominant literature," had "a mature approach analogous to that of . . . science and philosophy," only SF "shares the omnitemporal horizons" thereof.[66] This allowed for a focus on "possible futures"[67] and, because SF from the nineteenth century onward had employed "temporal extrapolation and centered on sociological . . . modelling,"[68] it also allowed for the genre to "be used as a hand-maiden of futurological foresight in technology, ecology, sociology, etc."[69] Explicitly aware of the resonance with Gernsback's prophecy, against which he was writing, Suvin added that "SF should not be treated as a prophet."[70] In Suvin, then, what Gernsback had dubbed "prophecy"[71] is rearticulated using terms such as "extrapolation," "omnitemporal horizons," and "possible futures"—all of which were designed to lend SF a more 'scientific' veneer.[72] The supposed potential to foresee possible futures remained central to SF's perceived political and subversive nature—to its "cultural significance"—even if, in resonance with Nwonwu's remarks, commenters like Basil Davenport pointed out that "science fiction has been at its least imaginative in inventing alternative societies, especially alternative good societies."[73]

Gernsback's legacy, including Suvin's influential opposition to Gernsback, is seldom an explicit topic of debate in the ASF context but its repercussions are still widely noticeable. For example, I pointed out earlier how Okorafor echoes Gernsback's comments on Verne's submarine,[74] and Gernsback's slogan 'fiction today, fact tomorrow' can be heard without much difficulty in the passage from Okorafor I cited above. In a related spirit, Anwuli Okeke wrote that ASF is about "learning" and "development" and that "entrepreneurs . . . are building the Africa of tomorrow, and they will need . . . the input of African science fiction . . . to build a future that is beneficial for all."[75] Ivor Hartmann even appears to be paraphrasing Gernsback when he says that "only" SF can "envision a future" for Africa and that it does so in a "not purely academic [but] readily understandable" fashion through fiction.[76] My claim, then, is that ASF's future utopian concern is inherited in part through the ways in which SF's legitimacy crisis manifested as SF exceptionalism in much SF scholarship.

The Case of Tlotlo Tsamaase: Future Utopia or Everyday Dystopia?

Based on the above, then, I argue that the prominence of future utopia in ASF debates to an important degree results from the tendency to understand ASF through the theoretical frameworks of Afrofuturism and SF studies. It is important to add that using these frameworks is at times justified and necessary: on the one hand, ASF, like Afrofuturism, is a form of SF, and ASF authors often self-consciously use canonical SF intertexts and conventions; on the other hand, even though ASF claims the status of SF, it is not always recognized as such. As Rettová has commented, in the context of African literature "there seems to be a nearly systematic avoidance of the label 'sci-fi' [and instead] sci-fi elements are reinterpreted as a mere 'replacement' of more traditional themes and motifs," or are understood as folkloric to suit the magical realist label.[77] In Michelle Louise Clarke's words, "SF from Africa" must at once "fight . . . to be read as SF [to] transform the traditional conventions of the genre [and to] contest . . . reductive notions of Africa nurtured within the Western imagination."[78] Thus, not only could disavowing the theoretical lens of Afrofuturism and SF studies in the ASF context hinder understanding, but it may also constitute exotification. Nevertheless, even keeping this in mind, applying the lens of SF studies and of Afrofuturism can also distort our understanding of ASF as the friction this chapter opened with demonstrates, and as the case of Tsamaase's short fiction will further show.

At my point of writing, Tsamaase has published fifteen short stories since 2014, written predominantly in the registers of horror, fantasy, myth, and SF. These stories are chiefly set in urban areas of Botswana and its main themes are, overwhelmingly, exploitation and dispossession, mostly of women. A coherent project is recognizable throughout Tsamaase's work, although just eight stories are recognizably SF ("Eco-Humans," "Eclipse our Sins," "Dreamports," "Virtual Snapshots," "Season of Safety," "Behind our Irises," "District to Cervix," "Material*Skin*"). Tsamaase is explicitly aware of SF conventions, remarking that her forthcoming novel "extrapolate[s] our current reality's issues,"[79] and that it relies on the SF body-swapping/controlling trope, which appears in most of her SF stories. In line with this, 'the (predominantly female) body' can be seen as her work's central figure.

Importantly, although her SF stories are set in an unspecified future, there are no future utopias and, often, there is no future in the future at all, or the future is suspended. In "Season," for example, the protagonist is subject to violent abuse and her boyfriend is "slowly killing future possibilities";[80] in "Thoughtbox," the protagonist realizes that the future is based on lies and adultery; analogously, the protagonist of "They Don't Believe God Grows in Our Hearts" professes that "The future . . . scares me. . . . Our dreams are swords wrapped around our throats";[81] and in "Snapshots" there is only death in the future. At best, the future in Tsamaase's work provides the possibility of revenge ("Dreamports," "The Palapye White Birch") or rebirth ("Eclipse"). One formal expression of the absent future is the metaphorical prison, which appears in almost all of Tsamaase's stories in the shape of a single location to which the protagonist is confined for most of the story-time. This can be one mind, bed, cell, hut, room, job, telephone booth, and even the womb. Narratively, Tsamaase renders the symbolic value of these spaces by reducing the cast of her characters to a single deeply alienated female protagonist. This results in a profound sense of claustrophobia, which is enhanced frequently by the stories' first-person (collective or singular) focalizers: the respective protagonists of "Season," "Dreamports," and "God" say that "Ours is only one room . . . We're five . . . The house is . . . essentially 18m² of torture";[82] "I'm trapped in a glass room";[83] "I'm bargaining with my window to let me out."[84]

The precarious future, alienation, and claustrophobia are linked—their underlying cause is generally poverty, especially feminized poverty, and most of Tsamaase's protagonists are poor. Poverty, like most events in Tsamaase's short fiction and in contrast to grand SF allegories, is not spectacular but mundane and quotidian: in the story "Eclipse our Sins," it is the inability to pay for "tampons, period-pain medication, anti-depressant medication, food, water . . . necessary things that I can't do without";[85] in "Behind our Irises," it is a "salary that could barely cover my rent. How was I going to pay for transportation, utilities, groceries?";[86] and in "The River of Night," poverty means having to work "weekdays and weekends raw into the night" but not knowing how to "eat this month . . . How [to] pay the rent."[87] In the SF stories, poverty implies the inability to pay for the rationed oxygen ("Eco-Humans," "Eclipse," "Snapshots"). Poverty also forces most characters into low-paying jobs that they deeply dislike—throughout Tsamaase's work runs a refrain of phrases like "I hate my job. I hate my job. I hate my job,"[88] "My horrible job,"[89] the "apocalyptic eight hours of this job I hate,"[90] "my life shackled in a low-paying-demoralising-abusive job"[91]—if there are jobs at all. This precarity is fertile ground for further exploitation, not seldom across former/neocolonial or patriarchal axes in the form of UK-to-Africa tourism or multinational tech corporations. It culminates in the dispossession of the body, since there are only a few ways of escaping or alleviating poverty, such as volunteering to have data-mining devices implanted under one's skin, renting out one's body, giving up bodily autonomy, or allowing corporations to access one's thoughts or mind. As one protagonist says, "my body became theirs."[92]

Tsamaase's fiction thus registers the lived experience of austerity, and the web of connections, which her fiction spins, forms a cognitive map that registers what Diane Pearce has called the "feminization of poverty," that makes such austere, patriarchal everyday life legible as dystopian.[93] And while the settings carry all the local particularity of Botswana, the lived experience described, to borrow from the Warwick Research Collective, "find[s] precise counterparts in the lived experiences of the inhabitants not only of cities elsewhere in the 'global south' but also in certain spaces within cities across the 'global north,'"[94] particularly following the 2007–8 global financial crisis. I want to suggest calling this SF subtype 'micro-dystopic austerity fiction,' to highlight the identity with globally dominant literary trends (the narrative dystopia) as well as the difference from them (claustrophobic one-character settings, no prominent role for the future), and the precarious subject positions it registers. As Fredric Jameson once argued, "texts come before us as the always-already-read," through "sedimented reading habits and categories."[95] As this consideration of Tsamaase's work illustrates, such readerly 'habits' can take the form of a future-directed utopianism that runs the risk of obscuring what is specific about the political work of her stories, and by extension, of ASF. Critics of ASF need to be able to identify such reading habits to specify how ASF pushes beyond them and how it aims to be(come) political.

Notes

The author would like to thank the German Research Foundation (DFG) for their funding while writing this chapter.

1 See Geoff Ryman, "Shadreck Chikoti," *Strange Horizons* 100 African Writers of SSF, Part Four, March 4, 2017, http://strangehorizons.com/non-fiction/100african/shadreck-chikoti/.
2 Shadreck Chikoti, "Managing Editor's Note," in *Imagine Africa 500: Speculative Fiction from Africa*, ed. Billy Kahora (Lilongwe: Pan African Publishers, 2015), 5–7, here 7.
3 Shadreck Chikoti, *Azotus: The Kingdom* (Blantyre: Malawi Writers Union, 2016), 19.
4 Ryman, "Shadreck Chikoti."
5 Ibid.
6 Chiagozie Nwonwu, "But Africans Don't Do Speculative Fiction!?" *Perspectives*, no. 3 (December 2018): 14–17, here 16.

7   Ibid.
8   Ibid.
9   See Peter J. Maurits, "On the Emergence of African Science Fiction," in *The Evolution of African Fantasy and Science Fiction*, ed. Francesca T. Barbini (Edinburgh: Luna Publishing, 2018), 1–18, here 17.
10 Ivor W. Hartmann, *AfroSF: Science Fiction by African Writers* (Zimbabwe: Story Time, 2012), 8.
11 Ayodele Arigbabu, *Lagos_2060: Exciting Sci-Fi Stories from Nigeria* (Lagos: Dada Books, 2013), 9.
12 Ainehi Edoro, "The New Image of Africa in Black Panther," *Perspectives*, no. 3 (December 2018): 6–9, here 7–8.
13 Nnedi Okorafor, "Sci-Fi Stories that Imagine a Future Africa," *TED*, filmed November 2017, https://www.youtube.com/watch?v=Mt0PiXLvYlU, 8:33–8:56.
14 Rodney Likaku and Joanna Woods, "Writing the Possible and the Future: Style in Malawian Speculative Fiction," *Journal of Humanities* 25, no. 2 (2017): 1–25, here 2.
15 Geoff Ryman, "Living in an African Future," *The Manchester Review* 18 (July 2017), http://www.themanchesterreview.co.uk/?p=8046.
16 Geoff Ryman, "Endnote: Afro-? African-? Astro-?" *Strange Horizons* 100 African Writers of SSF, Part 12, October 26, 2018, http://strangehorizons.com/non-fiction/endnote-afro-african-astro/.
17 Jayna Brown, *Black Utopias: Speculative Life and the Music of Other Worlds* (Durham and London: Duke University Press, 2021), 8.
18 Grace Gipson, "Creating and Imagining Black Futures through Afrofuturism," in *#identity: Hashtagging Race, Gender, Sexuality, and Nation*, ed. Abigail De Kosnik and Keith P. Feldman (Ann Arbor: University of Michigan Press, 2019), 84–103, here 94.
19 Reynaldo Anderson and Charles E. Jones, "Introduction: The Rise of Astro-Blackness," in *Afrofuturism 2.0: The Rise of Astro-Blackness*, ed. Reynaldo Anderson and Charles E. Jones (Lanham: Lexington Books, 2016), vii–xviii, here xi.
20 Reynaldo Anderson, "Afrofuturism 2.0 & the Black Speculative Arts Movement: Notes on a Manifesto," *Obsidian* 42, no. 1/2 (2016): 228–36, here 228.
21 Ibid.
22 Ibid.
23 Ibid., 229.
24 Ytasha L. Womack, *Afrofuturism: The World of Black Sci-Fi and Fantasy Culture* (Chicago: Chicago Review Press: 2013), 6–7.
25 Tiffany E. Barber, "Cyborg Grammar?: Reading Wangechi Mutu's *Non je ne regrette rien* through *Kindred*," in *Afrofuturism 2.0: The Rise of Astro-*

Blackness, ed. Reynaldo Anderson and Charles E. Jones (Lanham: Lexington Books, 2016), 3–26, here 11.
26 Gipson, "Creating," 101.
27 See Womack, *Afrofuturism*, 9.
28 See Sharon DeGraw, *The Subject of Race in American Science Fiction* (New York: Routledge, 2007).
29 Isiah Lavender III, *Race in American Science Fiction* (Bloomington: Indiana University Press, 2011), 4.
30 Ibid., 6.
31 Ibid., 6–7.
32 Samuel R. Delany, *Starboard Wine: More Notes on the Language of Science Fiction* (Middletown: Wesleyan University Press, 2012), 10.
33 Ibid., 14.
34 Ibid., 26.
35 Ibid., 165.
36 Delphi Carstens and Mer Roberts, "Protocols for Experiments in African Science Fiction," *Scrutiny2* 14, no. 1 (2009): 79–94, here 83.
37 Dilman Dila, "Is Science Fiction Really Alien to Africa?" *Dilman Dila: Storyteller, Writer, Filmmaker*, July 22, 2015, https://www.dilmandila.com/2015/07/science-fiction-literature-africa-sff.html.
38 Nwonwu, "But Africans," 17.
39 Mohale Mashigo, *Intruders: Short Stories* (Johannesburg: Picador Africa, 2018), 56.
40 Ibid. Yet SF *was* arguably a predominantly 'White' genre also in South Africa, hence the representational issues discussed here may in fact be similar after all.
41 Lisa Yaszek, "An Afrofuturist Reading of Ralph Ellison's *Invisible Man*," *Rethinking History* 9, no. 2–3 (2005): 297–313, here 297.
42 Carstens and Roberts, "Protocols," 83.
43 Maurits, "On the Emergence," 17.
44 See Jehan Latief, "Looking to Afrofuturism 3.0," *Design Indaba*, June 29, 2018, https://www.designindaba.com/articles/creative-work/looking-afrofuturism-30.
45 Rafeeat Aliyu and Masiyaleti Mbewe, "Moving Past Afrofuturism," *Perspectives*, no. 3 (December 2018): 10–13, here 10.
46 See Okorafor, "Sci-Fi Stories," 3:10–3:14.
47 See Lauren Beukes, "The Power of Afrofuturism," in Lauren Beukes, Kim Stanley Robinson, Ken Liu, Hannu Rajaniemi, Alastair Reynolds, and Aliette De Bodard, "Science Fiction When the Future is Now," *Nature* 552, no. 7685 (December 2017): 329–33, here 329.
48 Alena Rettová, "Sci-Fi and Afrofuturism in the Afrophone Novel: Writing the Future and the Possible in Swahili and in Shona," *Research in African Literatures* 48, no. 1 (2017): 158–82, here 161.

49 Ibid.
50 Geoffrey Winthrop-Young, "The War of the Worlds (H. G. Wells, 1898)," in *The Novel. Volume 2: Forms and Themes*, ed. Franco Moretti (Princeton: Princeton University Press, 2006), 189–95, here 194.
51 Damon Knight, *The Futurians* (New York: John Day, 1977), 2.
52 Ibid., 7.
53 Ibid., 8.
54 Mark Dery, *Flame Wars: The Discourse of Cyberculture* (Durham and London: Duke University Press, 1994), 180.
55 Roger Luckhurst, "The Many Deaths of Science Fiction: A Polemic," *Science Fiction Studies* 21, no. 1 (1994): 35–50, here 37.
56 Hugo Gernsback, "A New Sort of Magazine," *Amazing Stories* 1, no. 1 (April 1926): 3.
57 Ibid.
58 Ibid.
59 Ibid.
60 Brian Aldiss, *Billion Year Spree: The True History of Science Fiction* (Garden City: Doubleday, 1973), 209.
61 James Blish, *More Issues at Hand: Critical Studies in Contemporary Science Fiction* (Chicago: Advent Publishers, 1970), 119–20.
62 Luckhurst, "The Many Deaths," 40.
63 Ibid.
64 Samuel R. Delany, *Silent Interviews: On Language, Race, Sex, Science Fiction, and some Comics: A Collection of Written Interviews* (Hanover: Wesleyan University Press, 1994), 25.
65 Darko Suvin, "On the Poetics of the Science Fiction Genre," *College English* 34, no. 3 (1972): 372–82, here 378.
66 Ibid.
67 Ibid.
68 Ibid.
69 Ibid., 379.
70 Ibid.
71 Gernsback, "A New Sort," 3.
72 Suvin, "Poetics," 378.
73 Basil Davenport, *The Science Fiction Novel: Imagination and Social Criticism* (Chicago: Advent Publishers, 2021 [1959]), 11–12. Notably, he wrote before the 1960s–70s feminist utopian SF.
74 See Peter J. Maurits, "Legacies of Marxism? Contemporary African Science Fiction and the Concern with Literary Realism," *African Identities* 18, no. 1–2 (2020): 64–79.

75 Anwuli Okeke, "Looking Forward Through the Imagination of Africa," *Vector* 289 (Summer 2019): 15–19, here 19.
76 Hartmann, *AfroSF*, 8.
77 Rettová, "Sci-Fi and Afrofuturism," 161–2.
78 Michelle Louise Clarke, "Torque Control," *Vector* 289 (Summer 2019): 2–14, here 3.
79 See Linda Codega, "Author Tlotlo Tsamaase on the Feminist Sci-Fi Horror of *Womb City*," *Gizmodo*, August 16, 2022, https://gizmodo.com/erewhon-books-tlotlo-tsamaase-sarah-guan-womb-city-1849333086.
80 Tlotlo Tsamaase, "Season of Safety," *Interstellar Flight Magazine*, December 31, 2020, https://magazine.interstellarflightpress.com/season-of-safety-2e5ceaeeee92.
81 Tlotlo Tsamaase, "They Don't Believe God Grows in our Hearts," *Wasafiri* 32, no. 4 (2017): 17–22, here 19.
82 Tsamaase, "Season."
83 Tlotlo Tsamaase, "Dreamports," *Apex Magazine*, December 20, 2021, https://apex-magazine.com/short-fiction/dreamports/.
84 Tsamaase, "They Don't Believe God," 19.
85 Tlotlo Tsamaase, "Eclipse our Sins," *Clarkesworld*, December 2019, https://clarkesworldmagazine.com/tsamaase_12_19/.
86 Tlotlo Tsamaase, "Behind our Irises," *Brittle Paper*, October 16, 2020, https://brittlepaper.com/2020/10/behind-our-irises-by-tlotlo-tsamaase-africanfuturism-anthology/.
87 Tlotlo Tsamaase, "The River of Night," *The Dark Magazine*, November 2020, https://www.thedarkmagazine.com/the-river-of-night/.
88 Tsamaase, "Behind our Irises."
89 Tlotlo Tsamaase, "MaterialSkin," in *Community of Magic Pens*, ed. E. D. E. Bell (Detroit: Atthis Arts, 2020), 134–44, here 138.
90 Tsamaase, "River."
91 Tsamaase, "They Don't Believe God," 20.
92 Tsamaase, "Behind our Irises."
93 Diana Pearce, "The Feminization of Poverty: Women, Work and Welfare," *Urban and Social Change Review* 11, no. 1–2 (February 1978): 28–36, here 28.
94 Warwick Research Collective, *Combined and Uneven Development: Towards a New Theory of World-Literature* (Liverpool: Liverpool University Press, 2015), 151.
95 Fredric Jameson, *The Political Unconscious: Narrative as a Socially Symbolic Act* (London and New York: Routledge, 1983), ix.

16

Literary Activism in Contemporary Africa

Praxis, Publics, and the Shifting Landscapes of the 'Literary'

Madhu Krishnan

In this chapter I outline recent work on literary activism in Africa today. The concept of literary activism is as inchoate as it is (increasingly) ever-present. Whither the 'literary' in literary activism? Whither the 'activism'? For some, literary activism stands apart from so-called market activism, detached from questions of representation and politics, whereas for others, literary activism is intrinsically political, the very act of constituting spaces for literary engagement and activity a radical act of politics. In this chapter, then, I trace the contested genealogies of the term, as well as the tensions which have undergirded it and which are linked to larger concerns about the nature of the 'literary' and its 'uses.' Contra to the argument that literature can and must be disinterested, singular in its forms, I argue that the work of literary activists in Cameroon and elsewhere on the African continent demonstrates how even the most carefully attuned work of aesthetics retains a political use and usage which cannot be separated from the question of activism. To do so, I look at the case of Bakwa (Cameroon), setting its work within a longer continental history of literature and activism which has spanned at least seventy years. Focusing particularly on the ways in which the colonial invasion fractured the creative ecology and linguistic imaginary,

I explore how contemporary efforts to revitalize Africa-centered literary networks around translation can be seen as a crucial node in the larger nexus of social production and political activism.

Literary Activism and African Literature: A Short History

Scholarship on African literatures has always shown a deep preoccupation with the notion of the writer as an engaged intellectual with a significant role to play in the raising of national consciousness, helping to constitute the ostensibly postcolonial nation through the anticolonial struggle. Indeed, since the early twentieth century the African continent in particular has been a key site in which literary engagement has intertwined with the political and social activist movements which have marked its emergence as a zone of ostensibly independent nation-states in the postcolonial era. Work in African studies, for instance, has noted the ways in which the creation of literary collectives such as the Mbari Club, *Transition* magazine, *Black Orpheus*, and university publications like *Darlite*, *Penpoints*, and *Busara* in the 1950s and 1960s enabled the constitution of spaces within which writers and producers were able to engage in complex negotiations around the meaning of modernity, development, and citizenship in an African continent emerging into independence.[1] A few brief examples suffice to illustrate the historical puissance of literary activism for the region: the significant work of Léopold Sédar Senghor, first as a poet and literary activist central to the development of the Négritude movement and pan-African student mobilization in mid-century Paris and later Senegal's first president; the participation, on various sides, of prominent writers, thinkers, and members of the Ibadan-based Mbari literary club, including Wole Soyinka, Chinua Achebe, Elechi Amadi, and Christopher Okigbo, in the protracted Nigerian–Biafran War of 1967–70; the harassment of Rajat Neogy, founder of *Transition* magazine, by the Ugandan government for perceived acts of sedition through the activities of the same publication; the imprisonment (and sometimes murder) of writers across the continent, including Ngũgĩ wa Thiong'o, Kenule Saro-Wiwa, and Chris Abani. As these examples demonstrate, the literary has long served as a key—and sometimes feared—site of sociopolitical mobilization, debate, and engagement on the African continent, with important material effects and implications both for governance and for activist movements operating in the region. Critically, this is a vision of the literary which is neither autonomous nor disinterested, vis-à-vis the production of society and subjectivity more broadly. If, in a Euro-American context, debates around literature and aesthetics have repeatedly returned to post-Enlightenment notions of art as disinterested, what is commonly thought of as 'art for art's sake,' in the African context (and Global South context more broadly) have taken on a rather different quality. Here, the work of writers and cultural producers and their concerted interest in engagement with society through aesthetic and creative forms demonstrate the ways in which art and culture more generally have always served as significant elements of social production and reproduction, a reflection of Raymond Williams's mid-century observation that *all* parts of the social unit interact, engage, and impact upon each other.[2]

While African literary writing—at least in the form of the global novel— is less explicitly or overtly 'activist,' in the commonplace sense, literary activism, particularly on the continent, continues to gain significance.[3] Yet there is little consensus regarding what, precisely, the term means or how to define 'activism' or literary activism. Both 'the literary' and 'activism' remain contested terms. For some, literary activism is a question of aesthetics and form, a championing of the platonic notion of the literary as such. Amit Chaudhuri, for instance, develops an oppositional relation between 'market activism' and literary activism. Where the former is described as "a species of activity that added a fresh—and what soon became an indispensable— dimension to the publishing of novels and, indeed, how the novel would be thought of," intimately connected to "the discovery of new literatures,"[4] the latter is "more desultory."[5] In this view, market activism might be seen as concerned with questions of diversity, literature development, representation, and the cultivation of new publics for these 'new literatures.' Literary activism, by contrast, concerns itself more with the inchoate—and highly contested—question of literary 'value.' For other critics, working definitions conceptualize literary activism as a mode of social production through the opening of spaces and platforms and constitution of networks and publics, particularly those based and centered on the African continent. As I write, with Ruth Bush and Kate Wallis, in a 2021 special issue of *Eastern African Literary and Cultural Studies*, in this view literary activism might be seen as a mode of knowledge production, "an expression of agency that unfurls through a desire for a 'something else' which is not essentialist in its aims and which leverages its own forms of momentum."[6] Still more recent work explicitly delineates literary activism as a concerted and deliberate mode of political intervention both through the production of literary writing under conditions of duress and through its content, address, and publicness. As these various, if not always contradictory, definitions imply, literary activism functions not as a single concept or roadmap for literary engagement, but as a constellation of (sometimes contradictory and incompatible) approaches to understanding cultural production today. In this chapter, I focus explicitly on literary activism stemming from the African continent, exploring one specific case study from Cameroon, with wider ramifications across the continent. Among my preoccupations are questions concerning the relationship between the 'literary' and the 'activism' in the term; the role of individuals, the public, and networks in the constitution of literary activist work; the relationship between praxis and theory in the myriad manifestations of literary activism on the African continent; and the role of institutions and structures in literary activism and its potential legacies. Literary activism is of course a term which has been applied far beyond the African continent. Here, I draw on my own experiences as a researcher, collaborator, coproducer, and friend who has been working with literary activists, writers, editors, translators, and other creatives on the continent for nearly a decade. It should go without saying that my reflections in this chapter are not and could not be comprehensive; Africa is not a country. At the same time, the case studies that I outline at the end of the chapter strike me as representative of the larger patterns and tendencies which have marked literary activist work more broadly.

Well before the term appeared in common usage, the centrality of literary activism to the work of cultural production was made evident on the African continent. Be it through the work of cultural centers and collections such as the Nigeria-based Mbari Club or Nairobi-based Chemchemi (both of which, notably, were funded by Northern institutions, a point I will return to at the end of this chapter); conferences such as the 1962 Conference of African Writers of English Expression held at Kampala's Makerere University, the 1963 Fourah Bay Conference of teachers of Anglophone literature held in Sierra Leone, or the 1973 conference on African publishing held in Ife; the great pan-African festivals held in the 1960s and 1970s in Dakar, Lagos and Kaduna, Algiers, and Kinshasa; school literary societies and their periodicals, newspapers, and other modes of print culture, literary and cultural activity was always tied to larger questions around society, politics, and self-determination.

Both historically and in its present shape, literary activism thus enables a vision of social production which moves away from a polarity between the vertical (leadership) and horizontal (movements) through its broader entanglements and institutional practices, necessitating a critical vision which fetishizes neither and foregrounds the relationality therein. In the 1950s, for instance, the Mbari Club, for which the influential Nigerian literary magazine *Black Orpheus* was published, functioned both as a physical site for meeting and collaboration by anticolonial and radical writers from Nigeria and beyond and as a symbolic location through which a series of aesthetic principles were developed and transmitted to wider publics. Though funded in part by the Congress for Cultural Freedom, an institution of the United States Central Intelligence Agency, the Mbari Club nonetheless operated through a transformation of these modes of financial support into new institutions with specific and singular aims that were not always of a piece with the goals and objectives of the former. Both implicated within the vertical topographies of power during the Cold War era and radical in its fabrication of a space of commoning in which writers and producers could contest and negotiate the terms of literary and social engagement undergirding their work, the Mbari Club cannot be easily categorized as merely one or the other, relegated in a neat binary to either the realm of the air-conditioner or the realm of the veranda.[7] This is but one example of the complex historical interaction of institutions, their creation, transformation, and mutation, through the work of literary activists on the African continent. With the end of the Cold War, the institutional landscape against which literary activism operates again shifted, this time sedimenting around the work of NGOs and donor agencies, including the Ford Foundation (who, until 2016, supported Kenya's Kwani Trust) and the Miles Morland Foundation. As these examples demonstrate, however, literary activism has also always been riven by questions of soft power, funding streams, and the larger role of Northern patrons. At the same time, the work of these foundations, institutions, and meetings was critical to the constitution of modern African literature in English, in particular, but also other languages and ecologies.[8]

Critically, what this early history shows us is the role played by the *literary* as a site through which to constitute, negotiate, and contest the social. Anticolonial thinkers and activists such as Frantz Fanon and Amilcar Cabral notably observed the importance of culture to the constitution of the postindependence nation. Far from acting as supplementary to 'real' social production, in its broadest sense, literature functioned as a key avenue through which ideas about politics, society, morality, and liberation could be elaborated upon and debated. At the same time, this was a specifically *aesthetic* task. That is, rather than operate purely as functional or educative, early debates on African literature and its implications for the (re)production of society centered on questions of form, audience, and language.[9] Crucial to these debates was the understanding that the literary is both a register through which to create publics[10] while also creating these public spaces and networks through which to debate the contours of their own societies and modes of self-fashioning. Moreover, as the history of literary activism has shown, these discussions foreground the ways in which the literary functions as a constellation of activities, aesthetic modalities, and forms, forming bridges across different facets of the book chain and with strong links to university cultures and critical discursive communities. At the same time, literary activist work cannot be seen as strictly provincial or self-referential; rather, what emerges is the existence of broader global networks which enabled—and continue to enable—literary activism, including networks of funding, distribution, critical-academic discursive exchange, and the wider book chain. Thus, it is important to avoid the temptation to fetishize the grassroots or the concept of the independent cultural actor; instead, something rather more complex must be recognized, not least in the present day when questions remain concerning donor involvement, state support (or the lack thereof), infrastructure, and physical resources, the tension between markets and audience, and more. There remain, moreover, broader questions around extractivism, seen for instance in the ways in which work originally enabled by Africa-based literary activism becomes consumed and appropriated by the Global North.[11]

Platforms, Networks, and Gate Opening as Practice

If, as many literary activists claim, central to this work is the concept of gate opening, there nonetheless remains a wider question about what the role of art and cultural production can be in the broader context of the sociality. Indeed, in my many conversations with literary activists, writers, and translators, one frequent refrain is the idea that the individual in question might not actually view themselves as an activist, in the traditional sense, or as engaged in politics directly, but that the mere act of producing cultural work and opening cultural spaces in a context in which there is a deep lack of structural and institutional support is inherently activist in the broader sense. For instance, Ray Ndebi, the Cameroonian translator and cultural producer who currently runs Ônoan Literature, notes how, in the African context, it is important to recall the specific structural circumstances which preclude—and sometimes enable—literary work to emerge. As he notes: "on se rend compte que le niveau est vraiment bas. Mais il n'est pas bas compare aux Français, aux Anglais, aux Américaines. Il est bas compare à ce qu'on peut produire nous-mêmes déjà, à notre propre contexte."[12] Critically, from this comment, what emerges is a sense that literary ecologies and their implication in their wider social and political landscapes should be seen not as a disinterested universal, but rather as embedded within the specific contexts and histories from which they emerge. In particular, when considering the ways in which artistic production displays its articulations with the social unit more broadly, questions of audience, publics, and engagement become paramount. As another Cameroonian translator and the publisher of Éditions Nuances, Mariette Tchamda Mbunpi, observes of her own work: "le fait est que ça [the work of translation and publishing] reste quand même un peu un combat."[13] In this sense, the literary, as such, takes on a different aspect in the context of literary activism in Africa than is often felt as common sense. Rather than view 'art for art's sake' and 'politically engaged art' in opposition, that is, the two are intimately intertwined, with questions of aesthetics, language, and expression emerging as inherently political within their own contexts, involving complex questions of culture, identity, and autonomy against the backdrop of a continued lack of institutional support and neocolonialist expropriation of cultural expression.

Literary Activism in Cameroon: Bakwa, Language, and Social Production

My own work with literary activists began with a series of serendipitous meetings in 2016, when I was invited to the Kampala-based Writivism festival (now defunct), in order to co-convene the first Arts Managers and Literary Entrepreneurs (later changed to Literary Activists—or AMLA) workshop. Over the course of four intense days, I, along with my colleagues Kate Wallis and Ruth Bush (and aided by Grace Musila, who was instrumental in the development of the workshop but unable to attend due to visa issues), worked with thirty-odd aspiring literary activists from sixteen African countries. During this time, our sessions focused on a range of questions around how to develop infrastructures such as magazines, networks, translation platforms, and book distribution outfits, as well as more theoretical issues concerning what it means to be a literary activist. On the back of this particular workshop, I entered into a number of long-standing collaborations with literary producers based on the African continent. In what follows, I outline one of these, Bakwa, to examine some of the ways in which literary activism functions despite, through, and against existing structures (or the lack thereof) on the African continent.

Following my initial meeting at the 2016 Writivism Festival with Dzekashu Macviban, founding editor of Bakwa, I entered into what has now been a collaboration with the collective lasting many years. Our most notable work to date has been the Bakwa-Bristol Literary Translation Project, which was initiated in 2018 with funding from the United Kingdom's Arts and Humanities Research Council (AHRC). Cameroon has a unique history, in terms of its colonial and postcolonial past, and this continues to inform the ways in which Bakwa shapes its aesthetic, literary, cultural, and social missions, all of which are deeply interconnected. Its initial offering, *Bakwa* magazine, was founded in 2011 to, as its founder, Dzekashu Macviban, has noted, "fill a lacuna" and respond to the absence of spaces in Cameroon where writers and critics could publish both creative and critical work.[14] Originally conceived of as a website, Bakwa has since grown into a multimedia collective involved with podcasts, a publishing house, a pop-up library, live literary events, and more. At the time of its founding, Macviban, himself a writer, had little experience with editorial work, nor digital publishing. Moreover, while initially borne of frustration, over time Bakwa has evolved to envision itself as transformative, enabling "writers to re-experience what it means to be published" through a process of "doing everything differently."[15]

With the establishment of Bakwa Books in 2020, Bakwa's work has increasingly turned to the question of language and its ramifications in the Cameroonian context. Language use—and indeed the language of literary production—has particular valences in the country for reasons linked directly to its complex history of colonial rule. From the time of independence to the present day, Cameroon has been beset by violent conflict between its Francophone government and Anglophone separatist movements calling for the creation of an independent nation-state (Ambazonia or Amba Land). Particularly concentrated in the Anglophone North- and Southwest of the country, the 'Anglophone problem,' as it is often referred to, is a legacy of Cameroon's complex colonial history. Once the German colony of Kamerun, following the end of the First World War, Cameroon became a UN Trust Territory administered under British and French mandates. The majority of the territory (roughly four-fifths) was under French control, governed and administered along lines roughly similar to those in Afrique-Occidentale française and Afrique-Équatoriale française, while the remainder (called the Northern Cameroons and Southern Cameroons) was placed under British control. In the decades since their partition, the Anglophone and Francophone regions have developed along differential lines, marked by an asymmetry in resource and wealth distribution (Anglophone areas relatively neglected), and exacerbated by the continued rule of Francophone governments since the independence of La République du Cameroun in 1960. In 1961, a plebiscite determining the fate of the British Cameroons was held, resulting in the unification of the Northern Cameroons with neighboring Nigeria and the Southern Cameroons with the French Republic of Cameroon, and sparking conflict between federalists, separatists, and unionist which has continued ever since.

Cameroon now has two official languages: English and French. Alongside over 250 African languages (including Ewondo, Fang, and Bamoun), French is the main language in eight of Cameroon's ten regions. A 2005 census notes that 57.6 percent of the total population speaks French versus only 25.2 percent that speaks English. Moreover, despite the institution of the National Commission for the Promotion of Bilingualism and Multiculturalism in 2017, few Cameroonians define themselves as bilingual in the sense of being fluent in both English and French, and therefore Anglophone and Francophone remain more acutely *political* than they are *linguistic* identities. There is a popular saying that 'Cameroon is bilingual, but not Cameroonians,' a consequence of the country's policy of 'official bilingualism,' articulated by former president Ahmadou Ahidjo as "[b]y bilingualism we mean the practical usage of our two official languages, English and French, throughout the national territory."[16]

This context is important for understanding Bakwa's current work and, particularly, the growing importance of translation and language to their mission. In recent years, as a deliberately Cameroonian project, Bakwa has sought to engage in the production of wider networks and infrastructures around not only writing, but also literary translation and editing as a means of effecting change at the level of the social. This brings us back to my own collaborative work with them. Following our award of AHRC funding in 2018, I worked with Dzekashu Macviban, Georgina Collins, and Ruth Bush to design a series of workshops around creative writing and translation under the highly imaginative title (to which I will return), "Creative Writing and Translation for Peace." In 2019, we ran two creative writing workshops, one in French, the other in English, facilitated by Billy Kahora and Edwige Dro. Following a period of postworkshop mentorship, we ran a follow-up workshop for emerging literary translators, facilitated by Dr. Georgina Collins, Ros Schwartz, and Edwige Dro. These emerging translators then worked to translate the stories from the creative writing workshops from English to French and vice versa, resulting in the production of a bilingual anthology published by Bakwa Books, *Your Feet Will Lead You Where Your Heart Is/Le crépuscule des âmes sœurs*. At the heart of the project was a distinctly political aim: to attempt, in the context of the 'Anglophone crisis,' to develop lines of communication, empathy, and bridge building between Anglophone and Francophone Cameroonian experiences. As one participant in the workshops explained to us, this sort of work is fundamental due to the fact that, without knowing each other's stories, how can communities come to know each other? At the same time, it would be difficult to characterize the project as explicit in its political aims: participants, including writers and translators, were trained in *craft*, and not limited in the topics, aims, and purviews of their stories. Like all of Bakwa's projects, our primary aim was aesthetic: to nurture and support radical aesthetics and creative thinking. Yet, as the project progressed, it became clear that this is in itself a fundamentally political project.

Since the running of these workshops, from 2019 to 2022 I, along with Georgina Collins, have conducted a number of group and individual interviews with the wider project network. Comments from the participants in these conversations demonstrate the ways in which the aesthetic and the social collide through literary activism, as well as the complexity of thinking of the political use of art in a complex context such as Cameroon. Many of the participants in our writing workshops, for instance, highlight how they themselves only felt the confidence to begin writing careers (or aspire to do so) through participation in government-sponsored activity, such as 'les concours d'écriture,' which are run on an annual basis. One participant, reflecting on his development as a writer, notes how

> Quand j'y pense, j'ai participé à mon premier concours d'écriture, c'était en classe de cinquième. Je pense que j'avais onze ans ou douze ans. Mais moi je ne considérais pas ça comme la littérature. Mais c'est après quelques années que je me suis rendu compte qu'en fait, c'était la littérature que je faisais . . . , la décision d'écrire a commencé en 2015, et c'était toujours par rapport à un concours national d'écriture.[17]

Given widespread complaints by our interlocutors concerning the lack of government support for the arts, particularly literature, and the clear tension which Cameroon's political history has exhibited, it might be surprising that so many emerging writers felt their work began through participation in government-sanctioned and funded activity. At the same time, this is less of a contradiction than it might first appear. In the absence of robust literary networks and infrastructure, for many of our interviewees school, education, and, by extension, participation in these state-sanctioned events were the only entryway into cultural activity. Yet, our workshop participants showed a healthy level of skepticism about how far this could go, one remarking that

> On souffre du manque de projets de cette envergure-là, qui peuvent rassembler, qui peuvent déjà à la base, former des écrivains. À la base. Parce que c'est l'essentiel. Les écrivains sont les moteurs de cette activité. S'il n'y a pas d'écrivains, il n'y a pas d'éditeurs, il n'y a pas de traducteurs, etc. Donc, commencer à la base, former les écrivains, ensuite former les traducteurs, ensuite former quelques éditeurs. Donc, on manque vraiment de ce genre de projets.[18]

Another participant, in this same group conversation, forcefully noted the cause of this situation, observing that "l'Etat ne s'implique pas assez dans la production littéraire des jeunes, pourtant il y a plein de talents là dehors. Il y a beaucoup de personnes qui ont des choses à dire, qui peuvent s'exprimer, mais se découragent. C'est faire pour rien. Il n'y a même pas de motivation, il n'y a pas d'encouragement."[19] Yet another expressed her desire for expanded literary networks and infrastructure, explaining, in response to another participant's plea for an identity as an 'engaged writer,' that

> je ne me vois pas trop comme un auteur engagé parce que ma culture littéraire n'est pas vraiment vaste. Et depuis toujours, j'ai toujours fait tout par passion, par amour. Je n'ai jamais vraiment poussé ma recherche ou ma réflexion. J'écris sur ce que je connais, sur ce que je vis. Et j'ai découvert les livres comme étant un moyen pour éveiller les consciences, mais aussi pour évader.[20]

Since the publication of the anthology, a number of our participant writers and translators have gone on to be commissioned for high profile projects. One translator, Nchanji Njamnsi, for instance, was selected to produce the English translation of Cameroonian writer Hemley Boum's acclaimed novel, *Les jours viennent et passent* (Days Come and Go). Published simultaneously on the African continent by Bakwa and in the United States of America by Two Lines Press, this marks the first occasion in which an internationally published novel by a Cameroonian writer has been translated by a Cameroonian translator. Another translator, Mariette Tchamda Mbunpi, has since founded her own publishing company, Éditions Nuances, dedicated to women's writing from Cameroon and elsewhere which reflects the linguistic realities of African life. As she notes, this project grew from an increasing frustration with the chasm between so-called 'proper' French and the Frenches of daily life in Cameroon and elsewhere in West Africa. For Tchamda, the essential need for Nuances was twofold: to show writers that it is possible to write in one's own vernacular French, and to curate and develop wider reading publics through this same work. More broadly, Bakwa has gone on to conduct a number of public events. This has included editing slams and translation slams intended to enable new capacity for literary production in West Africa itself. Many of the translators from the anthology project have now launched their own Association of Literary Translators in Cameroon.

This, however, returns us to the problem of funding. One irrefutable fact is that the "Creative Writing and Translation for Peace" project would not have been possible without the financial support of the AHRC, and our follow-up activities and research without the income from a European Research Council Starting Grant (and indeed, even the titles of our projects indicate a certain need to 'speak' to Northern funders). Moreover, while I would characterize my work with Bakwa as founded predominantly on friendship and shared ideals, it remains the case that this work depends on my participation as a UK-based academic with access to the aforementioned funding schemes. It is further true that structures and institutions that are Africa-based and Africa-centered remain a struggle, particularly access to high-quality printing and distribution facilities. While this is happily in the process of changing, with publishers such as the Ivoirian Nimba Press dedicated to local editing and printing, there remains a significant gap. At the same time, it would be shortsighted to dismiss literary activist work such as I have described as forever oppressed by the process of NGOization or derealization.[21] One refrain which repeats itself across my many interviews, not just in Cameroon but also in Côte d'Ivoire, Nigeria, Kenya, and elsewhere, is the need to take and use the resources at hand, but to use them for one's own aims and goals. That is, there is a strong sense from the literary activists with whom I have worked that their own ideals are not necessarily compromised by funding bodies. Instead, the efforts to develop larger and more expansive cross-continental networks have supported the emergence of new creative solutions and of an autonomous sense of the larger aesthetic aims and social project of these collectives. These, in turn, have the ability to open new pathways to, as Dzekashu Macviban remarked in October 2019 at the Translation Matters conference in Yaoundé, "seize the means of production." To give one example, while a recipient of external funding for some of her work, the Ivoirian literary activist Edwige Dro has developed a range of methods to ensure sustainable financial backing for her organization, 1949, a library in the popular quarter of Yopougon in Abidjan. These methods have included work through different mentoring projects and workshops, and the 1949 restaurant (tagline: "le restaurant où on lit, la bibliothèque où on mange"),[22] whose affordable prices offer one means of reaching new audiences and publics for the library.

Contra to the argument that literature can and must be disinterested, singular in its forms, I argue that the work of literary activists in Cameroon, as is the case elsewhere on the African continent, shows how even the most carefully attuned work of aesthetics retains a political use and usage which cannot be separated from the question of activism. This is no small thing, in my view, and what I am trying to begin to suggest is that literary activism is one way in which the act of enacting power differently, of producing differently—producing literary work and platforms, yes, but also producing ways of being through an inherently political implication with the social—is critical for understanding its various roles in Africa today. Moreover, to return to Chaudhuri's opposition between 'market' and 'literary' activism, the work of literary activists in Africa demonstrates the ways in which these preoccupations are intimately intertwined. In a context in which structures and infrastructures remain to be built, the economic, the literary, the social, and the political can only function as part of a fundamental whole, albeit one whose constituent parts are sometimes in opposition. Furthermore, if literary activism as described in this chapter is sometimes ambiguous, it is also a space in which individuals and collectives retain a sense of agency, creating their own networks and platforms which, while not always visible to publics in the Global North, remain essential to the development of literary cultures and the constitution of the sociality more broadly. This, in turn, opens spaces through which the very boundaries of the literary and political can be opened to new horizons, based on radical collaborations and a rejection of simple binaries or received knowledge about *how* literary activism should work and oriented more toward a constructive politics that explores *to what end* it works. That is, rather than simply dismantling, literary activism in contemporary Africa provides one model for collective, sometimes fraught, but always creative construction.

Notes

The author would like to thank the European Research Council, from which she received a Starting Grant for her project "Literary Activism in Sub-Saharan Africa: Commons, Publics and Networks of Practice" (LITCOM, grant number 851955).

1   See Nathan Suhr-Sytsma, *Poetry, Print and the Making of African Literature* (Cambridge: Cambridge University Press, 2017); Peter Benson, *Black Orpheus, Transition and Modern Cultural Awakening in Africa* (Berkeley: University of California Press, 1986); Mwangi Macharia, "Nexus/Busara and the Rise of Modern Kenyan Literature," *Social Dynamics* 47, no. 2 (2021): 228–42.

2 See, for instance, Raymond Williams, *The Sociology of Culture* (Chicago: University of Chicago Press, 1981) and Raymond Williams, *The Long Revolution* (Cardigan: Parthian, 2013 [1961]), esp. 67–8.

3 There are of course clear exceptions here, such as the work of Patrice Nganang, a Cameroonian writer who has suffered state persecution for his interventions in the so-called Anglophone crisis.

4 Amit Chaudhuri, "On Literary Activism," in *Literary Activism: Perspectives*, 1st ed., ed. Amit Chaudhuri (New Delhi: Oxford University Press, 2017), 5.

5 Ibid.

6 Ruth Bush, Madhu Krishnan, and Kate Wallis, "Introduction: Literary Activism in 21st Century Africa," *Eastern African Literary and Cultural Studies* 7, no. 1 (2021): 1–9, here 3.

7 See Emmanuel Terray, "Le climatiseur et la véranda," in *Afrique plurielle, Afrique actuelle: Hommage à Georges Balandier*, ed. Georges Balandier (Paris: Éditions Karthala, 1986), 37–46.

8 See, for instance, Rebecca Jones, *At the Crossroads: Nigerian Travel Writing and Literary Culture in Yoruba and English* (Martlesham: Boydell & Brewer, 2019); Khwezi Mkhize, "'Shoot with Your Pen': Isaac William(s) Wauchope's *Ingcamango Ebunzimeni* and the Power of Speaking Obscurely in Public," *Social Dynamics* 36, no. 1 (2010): 222–34.

9 We might consider here debates around the language(s) of African literature animated by individuals such as Obi Wali, Chinua Achebe, and Ngũgĩ wa Thiong'o; questions of form, such as Ngũgĩ's decision to move from prose to theater writing as a means of wider engagement with his intended publics; debates around the validity of African modernisms; the role of the newspaper as a critical platform for constituting what Stephanie Newell calls 'paracolonial' publics; and more.

10 See Moradewun Adejunmobi, "Abiola Irele and the Publicness of African Letters," *Journal of the African Literature Association* 14, no. 1 (2020): 72–89.

11 Examples here include Ayọ̀bámi Adébáyọ̀'s *Stay with Me*, which, though originally a shortlisted winner of the Kwani? Manuscript Prize, only garnered critical attention with its acquisition and publication by Canongate, Jennifer Nansubuga Makumbi's *Kintu*, originally published by Nairobi-based Kwani? in 2014 but only receiving international attention with its American edition published in 2017 by Transit Books, or Teju Cole's *Every Day Is for the Thief*, first published in 2007 by the Nigerian press Cassava Republic and later, to global acclaim, by Faber & Faber in 2014. Of course the production of multiple editions across geographies is a common practice in contemporary publishing. My point here is rather that these serve as instances where *visibility* was denied certain texts—or minimized—until their publication in the Global North, with the profits of course going to these multinational publishing houses rather than the original Africa-based smaller outfits that provided the original editorial labor.

12 Personal interview with Ray Ndebi. In English: "I realize that the level [of work and opportunity] is low. But it is not worth comparing ourselves to

the French, to the English, to the Americans. It is worth comparing what we produce to ourselves, to set it in its own context," trans. M. K.

13 Personal interview with Mariette Tchamda Mbunpi. In English: "The fact is that the work of translation and publishing remains a kind of combat," trans. M. K.

14 Personal interview with Dzekashu Macviban.

15 Ibid. For a publicly available interview on Bakwa's origins, see BakwaCast. "Episode 0: BakwaCast Origins," *SoundCloud*, https://soundcloud.com/bakwacast/episode-0-bakwacastorigins.

16 Cited in Nguh Fon, "Official Bilingualism in Cameroon: An Endangered Policy?" *African Studies Quarterly* 18, no. 2 (2019): 55–66, here 58.

17 In English: "When I think about it, I took part in my first writing competition my second year of middle school. I think I was eleven or twelve. But I did not consider this literature. It was only after many years that I realized that, in fact, I was writing literature. . . . My decision to write began in 2015 and it was always through participation in national writing competitions."

18 In English: "We suffer from a lack of projects of this magnitude, projects which can bring together and, at their heart, nurture writers. At their foundation. Because this is essential. Writers are the motors of this activity. Without writers, there are no editors, no translators, etc. This, to start at the foundation is to nurture writers, then translators, then editors, and publishers. We really lack these sorts of projects."

19 In English: "I don't see myself as an engaged writer because my sense of literary culture is not so vast. I have always done this from passion and love. I have never really researched or reflected. I write what I know, what I live. And I have discovered that books can be both a way to raise consciousness but also a way to avoid it."

20 In English: "I don't see myself as an engaged writer because my literary world is not so vast. I never really pushed my reflection or research, And I've always done it for passion, for love. I write about what I know, what I live. And I have discovered that books can be a way to raise consciousness but also to suppress them."

21 See Sarah Brouillette, "On the African Literary Hustle," *Blind Field Journal*, August 14, 2017, www.blindfieldjournal.com/2017/08/14/on-the-african-literary-hustle/; Ashleigh Harris, *Afropolitanism and the Novel: De-realising Africa* (Abingdon: Routledge, 2019).

22 In English: "the restaurant where we read, the library where we eat," trans. M. K.

CONTRIBUTORS

Ulka Anjaria is Professor of English and director of the Mandel Center for the Humanities at Brandeis University, United States. She researches South Asian literature and film and is the author of *Realism in the Twentieth-Century Indian Novel: Colonial Difference and Literary Form* (2012), *Reading India Now: Contemporary Formations in Literature and Popular Culture* (2019), and *Understanding Bollywood: The Grammar of Hindi Cinema* (2021).

Ben Conisbee Baer is Associate Professor of Comparative Literature at Princeton University, United States. His most recent book is *Indigenous Vanguards: Education, National Liberation, and the Limits of Modernism* (2019). He is also a translator of modern fiction from Bengali.

Hunter Bivens is Associate Professor of Literature at the University of California, Santa Cruz, United States. He received his PhD in German Studies from the University of Chicago and is the author of *Epic and Exile: Novels of the German Popular Front* (2015) and numerous pieces on GDR literature and film and proletarian-revolutionary literature. His current project is *The East German Construction Novel of the 1950s: Work, Affect, and Obstinacy*.

Juan E. De Castro is Professor of Literary Studies at Eugene Lang College of Liberal Arts, The New School, New York, United States. His publications include *Writing Revolution in Latin America: From Martí to García Márquez to Bolaño* (2019) and *Bread and Beauty: The Cultural Politics of José Carlos Mariátegui* (2020).

J. Daniel Elam is Assistant Professor of comparative literature at the University of Hong Kong. He is the author of *World Literature for the Wretched of the Earth* (2020). He has edited Bloomsbury's anthology *Aesthetics and Politics in the Global South* (2022). Currently he is writing a book about anticolonial sociology and a book about M. K. Gandhi's popularity in the United States.

Maryam Fatima is a doctoral candidate in Comparative Literature at the University of Massachusetts Amherst, United States. She researches the connected histories of Urdu and Arabic literary modernities and Afro-Asian literatures of decolonization. Her dissertation, *Partitions and Palimpsests: Transgressions of Form and Territory in Postcolonial Urdu and Arabic Writing*, has been supported by a Mellon-Sawyer fellowship. Her work has appeared in *Comparative Literature Studies*. She is currently coediting a special issue on Late Persianate Literatures for *Philological Encounters*.

Sandra Fluhrer is Assistant Professor of Comparative and German Literature at the University of Erlangen-Nuremberg, Germany. Her research interests include theories and practices of aesthetic experience, forms of theatricality, and the relationship between literature, mythology, and the political. Her second book, on the aesthetics and politics of metamorphosis in European literature and political philosophy, will be published in 2024.

Daniel Hartley is Associate Professor in World Literatures in English at Durham University, UK. He is the author of *The Politics of Style: Towards a Marxist Poetics* (2017) and has published widely on contemporary literature and Marxist theory.

Benjamin Kohlmann is Professor of English at Regensburg University, Germany. He is the author of *Committed Styles: Modernism Politics and Left-Wing Literature* (2014) and *British Literature and the Life of Institutions: Speculative States* (2021). His articles have been published in *ELH*, *PMLA*, *Novel*, and elsewhere. He is working on a global history of the radical bildungsroman, 1820–2020.

Madhu Krishnan is Professor of African, World and Comparative Literatures in the Department of English at the University of Bristol, UK, and Director of the Centre for Black Humanities. She is author of *Contemporary African Literature in English: Global Locations, Postcolonial Identifications* (2014), *Writing Spatiality in West Africa: Colonial Legacies in the Anglophone/Francophone Novel* (2018), and *Contingent Canons: African Literature and the Politics of Location* (2018). She is at present working on a large-scale project on literary activism in contemporary Africa, which explores the ways in which engagement with the literary functions as a mode of social production.

Steven S. Lee is Associate Professor of English at the University of California, Berkeley, United States, where he is also affiliated with the Center for Korean Studies, the Center for Race and Gender, and the Institute of Slavic, East European, and Eurasian Studies. He is the author of *The Ethnic Avant-*

Garde: Minority Cultures and World Revolution (2015) and coeditor (with Amelia M. Glaser) of *Comintern Aesthetics* (2020).

Peter J. Maurits is Postdoctoral Fellow at the Chair of American Studies, University of Erlangen-Nurenberg, Germany. His research focuses on Mozambique, African literature and film, genre, and the adaptation of form. He has published on migration, futurism, and the modern ghost story. His most recent book is *The Mozambican Modern Ghost Story* (2021) and he is currently writing a book on African science fiction.

Mark Nowak's books include *Shut Up Shut Down*, *Coal Mountain Elementary*, and *Social Poetics*. He recently edited *Coronavirus Haiku* (2021) and wrote a critical introduction to Celes Tisdale's *When the Smoke Cleared: Attica Prison Poems and Journal* (2022). A native of Buffalo, Nowak is the founding director of the Worker Writers School (https://www.workerwriters.org).

Ivana Perica works at the Leibniz Center for Literary and Cultural Research (ZfL) in Berlin, Germany. She is a postdoctoral researcher in the Horizon Europe project *The Cartography of the Political Novel in Europe*. She is the author of *Die privat-öffentliche Achse des Politischen: Das Unvernehmen zwischen Hannah Arendt und Jacques Rancière* (2016). Her current book project is about political literature around the conjunctures of 1928 and 1968.

Aurore Peyroles is a research assistant at the Institute for Romance Languages and Literatures at the University of Regensburg, Germany. She holds a doctorate in comparative literature and has published, in addition to numerous articles on literary commitment, *Roman et engagement: le laboratoire des années 1930* (2015) and *Villes en guerre au 19e siècle* (2021). She has recently completed her habilitation project on novelistic representations of the Parisian suburbs.

Christoph Schaub is a research associate in German Literature and Cultural Studies at the University of Vechta, Germany, and has previously held postdoctoral positions at Columbia and Duke Universities. He is the author of *Proletarische Welten: Internationalistische Weltliteratur in der Weimarer Republik* (2019) and a coeditor of the volume *Anthropozäne Literatur* (2022) and the special issue "Figuring the Planet: Post-Global Perspectives on German Literature" (2022, *The Germanic Review*).

Galin Tihanov is the George Steiner Professor of Comparative Literature at Queen Mary University of London, UK. He is the author of six books, including *The Birth and Death of Literary Theory: Regimes of Relevance in*

Russia and Beyond (2019) which won the 2020 AATSEEL prize for "best book in literary studies." Tihanov has been elected to the British Academy and to Academia Europaea. Currently he is completing *Cosmopolitanism: A Very Short Introduction*.

Dirk Wiemann is Chair in English Literature at University of Potsdam, Germany. His most recent monograph, *Anglophone Verse Novels as Gutter Texts: Postcolonial Literature and the Politics of Gaps* (2023), addresses the political potentials and limitations of literary forms. He is also the author of *Genres of Modernity: Contemporary Indian Novels in English* (2008) and *Postcolonial Literatures in English: An Introduction* (2019, with Anke Bartels, Lars Eckstein, and Nicole Waller). He was a founding member of the Research Training Group "Minor Cosmopolitanisms" and director of the bilateral research network "Genre Transactions in World-Literary Space" with the University of Delhi, India.

INDEX

1930s 17 n.7. *See also* committed novel of the 1930s
1949 restaurant 276
1960s. *See* global 1960s; long 1960s

AAPSO. *See* Afro-Asian People's Solidarity Organization
AAWA. *See* Afro-Asian Writers' Association
Abani, Chris 266
abolition 14, 161, 162, 170, 175
absolute 53 n.19
Achebe, Chinua 221, 266, 277 n.9
acting theory 62
activism 6, 16–17, 19 n.23, 265–70, 276. *See also* literary activism in contemporary Africa
activist art 3, 6–9
Adébáyọ̀, Ayọ̀bámi, *Stay with Me* 277 n.11
Adivasi community 206–8
Adorno, Theodor W. 9, 38 n.7, 153
Aesthetics and Politics (ed. Jameson) 9, 82 n.22, 132 n.3
affordances 19 n.28
Africa
  and Hansberry 144
  literary activism in 16–17, 265–78
  world literature 19 n.23
African speculative and science fiction (ASF) 250–64
  importance of Afrofuturism 252–5
  overcoming pulp (science) fiction label 255–8
  overview 16, 250–2
  Tsamaase and future utopia 258–60

African studies 140, 266
Afro-Asian literature 221–3, 226
Afro-Asian People's Solidarity Organization (AAPSO) 15, 221
Afro-Asian Writers' Association (AAWA) 218, 220, 221
Afrofuturism 252–5, 258
agency 5, 8, 10, 276
Agüero, José de la Riva 45
Ahidjo, Ahmadou 272
Ahmad, Aijaz 227
Ahmad, Muzaffar 30, 31
AHRC. *See* Arts and Humanities Research Council
AIPWA. *See* All-India Progressive Writers' Association
A-Jabar, "This iS A recording" 164–7, 177 n.17
Aldiss, Brian 256
Alegría, Ciro 51, 52, 55 n.38
Alipore Bomb Trial 41 n.53
Allen, Austin 174
All-India Progressive Writers' Association (AIPWA) 33, 37, 199, 201
All-India Workers' and Peasants' Party Conference 24
Althusser, Louis 112, 118 n.64, 154
Amauta (journal) 43, 45, 51, 52 n.7
Amazing Stories (magazine) 256
Ambedkar, B. R. 138, 139
Anderson, Benedict 242
Anderson, Perry 102, 113, 118 n.70
Anderson, Reynaldo 253, 255
Angaaray (Zaheer et al.) 201
Angelou, Maya 141

INDEX

anthropology 138, 139
anticolonialism 6, 18 n.19, 225–8
antipolitics 15, 219
antiracism 141–2, 144, 146, 147
Appadurai, Arjun 225
Arab literature 217–31
  overview 217–20, 227–8
  new *Lotus* magazine 220–3
  post-political after Arab Spring 223–7
Arab Spring 219, 222, 224, 229 n.14
Aragon, Louis 60, 87–9
  Les Beaux Quartiers 95
  Le Monde réel 12, 87–99
Arendt, Hannah 98
Arguedas, José María 51, 52, 55 n.38
Arigbabu, Ayodele 251
art
  activist art 3, 6–9
  Artaud on 61
  art for art's sake 9, 266–7, 270
  artistic autonomy 237
  commitments of 1
  duty-free art 237, 245
  literary studies and uses of literature 4
  and politics 1–3
  Popular Front culture 72–3
  socialist art 50–1
  and surrealism 49–50
Artaud, Antonin 56–68
  overview 4, 11–12, 56–9
  and Mexico 53 n.9, 56–8, 62–3, 65 n.8, 68 n.57
  political critique in *Messages révolutionnaires* 59–61
  political theory 61–3
  presence of voice in texts 66 n.18
  reusing to theatricalize life 63–4
    "An Affective Athleticism" 62
    "Ce que je suis venu faire au Mexique" (What I Came to Mexico to Do) 58
    La conquête du Mexique (The Conquest of Mexico) 56, 66 n.15
    "The False Superiority of Elites" 63
    Les Tarahumaras (*The Peyote Dance*) 57, 67 n.51
    "Lettre ouverte aux Gouverneurs des États du Mexique" (Open Letter to the Governors of the States of Mexico) 58
    Messages révolutionnaires (*Revolutionary Messages*) 11, 57, 59–62, 64
    México 57
    "Le Mexique et la civilisation" 68 n.57
    "No More Masterpieces" 64, 68 n.63
    Pour en finir avec le jugement de dieu (To Have Done with the Judgment of God) 61
    "Surréalisme et révolution" (Surrealism and Revolution) lecture 60
    The Theater and Its Double 62, 64
    "Le Théâtre et les dieux" (Theater and the Gods) lecture 61, 62
    "Une Race-Principe" (A Race-Principle) 63
Arts and Humanities Research Council (AHRC) 271, 273, 275
Arts Managers and Literary Activists (AMLA) 271
Asahi, Dalau 171
ASF. *See* African speculative and science fiction
Association of Proletarian-Revolutionary Writers (Bund proletarisch-revolutionärer Schriftsteller) (BPRS) 74, 83 n.40
Attica News (newspaper) 167, 168
Attica prison print culture 161–80
  foundation of small press poetry and print culture 162–7
  overview 14, 161
  poetry and print culture expansion 167–73
  small press poetry and print culture after Attica 173–6

uprising 14, 161–4, 166, 168–73
Attridge, Derek 234
Auden, W. H. 8, 19 n.29
Austin, John 104, 114 n.14
autobiography 124, 191
autofiction 15, 122, 181, 182, 191–2
avant-garde
   and decadence 46–7
   Peruvian literature 11, 43–4, 46–52
   Popular Front culture 12, 72–3
   and realism 9
   Soviet Union 159 n.16
   and Vallejo 43, 48–52
Averintsev, Sergey 156, 157
Awakening of a Dragon (Attica Brother Jomo) 165, 168–71
Azikiwe, Nnamdi 140

Bach, Johann Sebastian 50, 51
Badiou, Alain 234
Baird, Russell N., *The Penal Press* 167
Bakhtin, Mikhail 156, 159 n.9
Bakwa 265, 271–5, 278 n.15
Bakwa magazine 16, 271
Banda, Kamazu 251
Bandung Conference (1955) 231 n.42
Bandyopadhyay, Manik 11, 33–7
   "Chhoto Bakulpurer Jatri" (Travelers to Chhoto Bakulpur) 33–7
Bandyopadhyay, Tarashankar 206
Banerjee, Sibnath 40 n.43
Barber, Tiffany E. 253
Barthes, Roland 95, 159 n.6
   Mythologies 153–4
Basak, Gopal 31
Bataille, Georges 23
Baxter, Carolyn, *Prison Solitary and Other Free Government Services* 167
Becher, Johannes R. 72, 83 n.40
Beethoven, Ludwig van 50
Beigel, Fernanda 45
Beijing Forum on Literature and Art 110, 113
Bengal 33, 41 n.53, 206, 209

Benjamin, Walter 19 n.25, 72, 74, 75, 77, 79, 84 n.47, 153
   "On the Concept of History" 75
   "The Storyteller" 115 n.30
Berdiaev, Nikolai 156
Bergson, Henri 53 n.19, 138, 140–1
Berlant, Lauren, *Cruel Optimism* 80
Bernstein, J. M., *The Philosophy of the Novel* 79–80
Betcha Ain't: Poems from Attica (Tisdale, ed.) 163, 165
Beukes, Lauren 255
Bhabha, Homi 226
Bhattacharya, Bijon 206
Black Arts Movement 162, 163, 253
Blackness 138, 140, 144, 146, 147, 149 n.7
Black Orpheus (magazine) 266, 268
Black Panther (film) 255
Black people
   Genet's *Les Nègres* (*The Blacks*) 140–2
   Hansberry's *Les Blancs* 140, 142–6
   Hurston account 139
   imprisonment 163, 166, 167, 170
   pop culture and SF 253
   workers 130
   writers 163, 166, 170
The Black Poets (anthology) 163
Black SF (science fiction) 253–4
Black Voices from Prison (anthology) 177 n.4
Blish, James 256
Bloch, Ernst 9, 12, 70, 72–3
   "Die Kunst zu erben" (To Inherit the Arts) (Bloch and Eisler) 73
Bloomsbury group 133 n.20
Boas, Franz 139
body 61, 200, 202, 203, 258–60
Boggs, Grace Lee. *See* Stone, Ria (Grace Lee Boggs), *The American Worker* (Romano and Stone)
Bolshevism 25, 28, 51, 52
Botswana 258, 260

Boum, Hemley, *Les jours viennent et passent* (Days Come and Go) 274
bound serialities 242
Bourdieu, Pierre 114 n.14, 152, 237
Boyer, Hersey, "Attica Reflections" 163
BPRS (Bund proletarisch-revolutionärer Schriftsteller) 74, 83 n.40
Brecht, Bertolt 3, 7, 17 n.1, 72, 74, 76, 144
  Lehrstücke 1, 3
  "On Form and Subject-Matter" 1
  "Popularity and Realism" 75, 82 n.24
Brecht–Lukács debate. *See* Expressionism Debate
Bredel, Willi 71, 83 n.40
Breton, André 60, 68 n.53
  Nadja 47
Broadside Press 162, 163, 176 n.3, 177 n.4
Brooks, Cleanth 2
Brooks, Gwendolyn 162, 177 n.4, 177 n.8
  "We Real Cool" 170
Brother Ali, "A View from Erie County Jail" 168
Brown, Jayna 252
Bruchac, Joseph 164, 167
Brühmann, Horst 153
Burroughs, Edgar Rice 253
Bush, Ruth 267, 271, 273

Cabral, Amilcar 269
Calderón, Ventura García 45, 46
Cameroon 265, 267, 271–6
capitalist realism 10, 19 n.33, 80
Cardoza y Aragón, Luis 57
Carstens, Delphi 254
Casanova, Pascale 5, 6
Castoriadis, Cornelius 125
Castro, Fidel 114 n.5
Caudwell, Christopher 122, 125
Cawnpore (Kanpur) 38 n.12
CCF. *See* Congress for Cultural Freedom

CCP (Chinese Communist Party) 104, 109, 110, 113
Central Intelligence Agency (CIA) 220, 228, 268
Chakrabarty, Dipesh 26–7, 40 n.43
Chaudhuri, Amit 267, 276
Chavez, Cesar 168
Chemchemi 268
Chen, Xiaomei 109, 118 n.65, 118 n.70
Chikoti, Shadreck
  Azotus: The Kingdom 250–1
  Imagine Africa 500 (ed.) 250
China
  Cultural Revolution 102, 118 n.64
  and imperialism 117 n.47
  manifesto genre 103, 104, 109–13
  and modernism 13
  overview 12–13
  and Soviet Union 107, 110, 111
chronicles 74–5, 79, 84 n.47
Chughtai, Ismat 15, 200–5, 210
  "Lihaaf" (The Quilt) 204–5
  Tehri Lakeer (The Crooked Line) 202–3
  "Til" (Mole) 203–4
  "Ziddi" (The Wild One) 203
Citton, Yves 92
Clark, Katerina 71, 72, 106, 115 n.30
Clarke, Michelle Louise 258
class 76, 194 n.8. *See also* working class
Claudius, Eduard, *Grüne Oliven und nackte Berge* (Green Olives and Bare Mountains) 76–7
Clayton, Michelle 50
Cleary, Joe 9
Clifton, Lucille 162
close reading 2
Cole, Andrew 151
Cole, Teju, *Every Day Is for the Thief* 277 n.11
Collins, Georgina 273
colonialism 6, 8, 25–6, 45, 225, 227–8
Comintern. *See* Communist International

commitment 87, 88, 93, 99
committed novel of
    the 1930s 87–101
    democratic novels 96–9
    hegemonic 'thrillers' 89–92
    inventing new stories 92–4
    novels of the 'real world' 94–6
    overview 87–9
commonism 238, 248 n.47
communism
    ABC of Communism 29
    conspiracy cases 38 n.12
    German Popular Front novel 69–71, 76
    India and Meerut Conspiracy Case 25–33, 36, 199–201
Communist International (Comintern) 6, 18 n.19, 26, 54 n.25, 69, 70
Communist Manifesto (Marx and Engels) 13, 24, 26, 29, 36, 103–6, 109–12
Communist Party
    and conspiracy 28, 38 n.12
    Germany 12, 69, 70, 183, 188, 190
    global literary history 8
    and Hansberry 140
    India 199, 201, 209
Comstock Prison 164
Conference of African Writers of English Expression 268
Congress for Cultural Freedom (CCF) 220, 228, 268
congruence, situational 233, 234
conspiracy 11, 26–8, 36, 39 n.20
Convicted Voices (Antu Satya) 165, 174
Correspondence (organization and publication) 129
cosmopolitanism 5, 71
Cottrell, Susan, "To My Man in Jail" 162
counter-public sphere 7, 74, 182, 190, 194 n.7
creative writing workshops. *See* writing workshops
critical theory 153

cultural hegemony 92
cultural heritage 73, 75
culturalist politics 220, 223, 226
cultural politics 15, 218, 220, 221, 223, 226–8
Cultural Revolution 102, 118 n.64
culture 59, 70, 74
culture orientée 4, 61–3
Cusset, François 151

Da Costa Dias, Luciana 65 n.8, 66 n.15
Damrosch, David 5
Darwish, Mahmoud 221
Davenport, Basil 257
Davis, Angela 161, 176
Davis, Cleveland. *See* Jomo, Attica Brother
Dean, Jodi 224
decadence 46–9, 53 n.20
decolonization 205, 220, 223
DeGraw, Sharon 253
Deineka, Aleksandr 103
Delany, Samuel R. 254, 257
Deleuze, Gilles 57
de Man, Paul 158
de Mèredieu, Florence 65 n.8
Denis, Benoît 88, 93
Derrida, Jacques 114 n.14, 152, 154
Dery, Mark, *Flame Wars* 252, 254, 256
dialectics 151, 153
diary genre 129, 184, 192
Diep, Nguyen Dang, "The Reform of Modern Vietnamese Poetry" 226–7
Dila, Dilman 254
Dillard, Lawrence I. (Antu Satya), *Convicted Voices* 174–5
Dimitroff, Georgi 70–1
direct agency 5
dissensus 234, 238
dissident participation 236
DKP (German Communist Party) 12, 69, 70, 183, 188, 190
Döblin, Alfred 79, 85 n.78
Dobrenko, Evgeny 115 n.19
documentary genre 190, 192

Dog Day Afternoon (film) 173
dominant storytelling 89, 91, 92, 98–9
Dortmunder Gruppe 61 183, 184
Dos Passos, John, *USA* 12, 88–90, 92–9
Dostoevsky, Fyodor Mikhailovich, *Notes from the Underground* 14, 150
dragon figure 169, 178 n.31
drama 122, 123, 132 n.4, 147
dream protocol 184, 192
Dro, Edwige 273, 275
Du Bois, W. E. B. 138, 140, 144, 252
Dunayevskaya, Raya (code name Freddie Forest) 128
Dunn, Maggie 240
dystopia 252, 260

editing slams 275
Éditions Nuances 274–5
Edoro, Ainehi 251
Egyptian writers 223–4, 229 n.7
Eikhenbaum, Boris 154
Einstein, Albert 27, 73
Eisenstein, Sergei 50, 51, 68 n.55
Eisler, Hanns 12, 70, 72–3
    "Die Kunst zu erben" (To Inherit the Arts) (Bloch and Eisler) 73
Elam, J. Daniel 6
Eliot, T. S. 123
Elnaili, Safa, "An Abused Country" 222
empiricism 138, 139
Endnotes Collective 10, 19 n.34
Engels, Friedrich 29, 105, 106, 132 n.1. *See also Communist Manifesto*
epic genre 23, 75–6, 79, 80
Erie County Jail 178 n.27
Erlich, Victor 154
Eshleman, Clayton 52 n.5
Eshun, Kodwo 253, 255
Esslin, Martin 66 n.9
eugenics 253
European Research Council 275
experience 123, 132 n.5, 133 n.14

Expressionism Debate (Brecht–Lukács debate) 12, 69, 70, 72, 75, 82 n.22

Facebook 222
Faiz, Faiz Ahmad 221
Fanon, Frantz 144, 269
fascism 3, 70, 72, 79
Fattah, Ziad Abdel 226
Fehervary, Helen 84 n.47
Felski, Rita 4, 17 n.6, 234
    Uses of Literature 232
female characters 94, 146, 202, 206, 207, 210, 259
feminism 15, 188, 196 n.49, 205, 210, 263 n.73
Fighting Back: Attica Memorial Book, 1974 165, 170–1, 173
films 50, 173, 187, 205
First All-Union Writers' Congress 71, 81 n.12
Fisher, Mark 10, 19 n.33, 80
Fitzpatrick, Sheila 71
Foley, Barbara 17 n.2
folk cultures 111
folklore 106–7, 139, 258
Ford 129
Ford Foundation 269
Forlorn Hope (prison newspaper) 167–8
form 8–9, 234–5. *See also* politics of form
formalism
    congruence, transcendence, and form 233–5
    cultural 'formalism' 105
    and Marxism 9
    political formalism 16, 234, 238, 245
    Russian Formalism 152, 154–5, 157–8, 159 n.14
Foucault, Michel 152, 154
Fourah Bay Conference 268
Frankfurt School 188
Frank-Kamenetskii, Izrail 160 n.21
freedom of expression 221
Freidenberg, Olga 156–7, 160 n.21, 160 n.23

French Revolution 58, 63, 78
French Theory 151, 154
Freud, Sigmund 204, 209
Frost, Robert, "Mending Wall" 174
future utopias 251, 252, 255, 258
futurism
    Italian futurism 46, 103
    Peruvian "futurists" 45–6, 48
    Russian futurism 103, 104
    theatricality of manifestos 112

Gadamer, Hans-Georg, *Truth and Method* 153
Gaddafi, Muammar 222
Gálvez, José 45
Gandhi, Mahatma 31
Gastarbeiter (migrant workers) 196 n.34
Gavrilov, A. K. 160 n.23
General Motors 129
Genet, Jean 140–4, 147
    Les Nègres (*The Blacks*) 140–4
German Popular Front novel 69–86
    cultural popular front 70–3
    overview 12, 69–70
    popular novel 73–80
Germany
    Communist Party 12, 69, 70, 183, 188, 190
    critical theory 153
    literary field 194 n.7
    literary theory 153, 154
    Struck's *Klassenliebe* and the *Werkkreis* 181, 182, 184, 185
Gernsback, Hugo 256–7
Ghosh, Kishorilal 31
Gibson, William, *Pattern Recognition* 80
Gilmore, Ruth Wilson 175
Gipson, Grace 253
Gladkov, Fyodor 43
    Cement 42
Glaser, Amelia, *Comintern Aesthetics* (Glaser and Lee, eds) 6
Glawion, Sven 194 n.16
global 1960s
    Attica print culture and small press poetry 161–80
    feminism and progressive writing in India 199–213
    Hansberry and solidarity 137–49
    non-Marxist theory 150–60
    Struck's *Klassenliebe* and the *Werkkreis* 181–98
    Williams, Lefort, and workers' inquiry 121–36
globalization 5, 6, 239
"Global South" as term 227–8
Godard, Jean-Luc 102
Goethe, Johann Wolfgang von 5
Gopal, Priyamvada 203
Goricheva, Tatiana 155
Gorky, Maxim 43, 106–8, 115 n.30, 155
Goswami, Manu 40 n.33
Gramsci, Antonio 37, 47, 54 n.21, 92, 118 n.64
Greek novel 160 n.21
Greenfield Review Press 164, 167
Grovogui, Siba 227
Groys, Boris (aka Igor Suitsidov) 114 n.4, 155–8, 159 n.15, 159 n.16, 160 n.20
    "Istoki i smysl russkogo strukturalizma" (The Origins and Meaning of Russian Structuralism) 155–6
Grün, Max von der 183
Guattari, Félix 57
Gussen, James 80

Hagen, Brother Thomas 168
Halim, Hala 222, 228
Hansberry, Lorraine 137–49
    overview 13–14, 137–8
    from Genet's *The Blacks* to *Les Blancs* 140–2
    society as a way of life 146–8
    sociological imagination 140
    sociology's hesitations 138–9
    solidarity in black and white 142–6
    Les Blancs 13, 14, 137, 140, 142–7

The Sign in Sidney Brustein's Window 146
Village Voice essay 141–3
Hansberry, William Leo 140
Hansen, Miriam 74
Hark, Sabine 236
Harney, Stefano 170
Hartmann, Ivor 251, 257–8
Hastings-King, Stephen 133 n.21, 134 n.29
Hawkins, Isiaah, "13th of Genocide" 163
Hayden, Robert 162
Heartfield, John 73
Hegel, G. W. F. 151, 153, 158 n.2
hegemonic 'thrillers' 89–92
hegemony 47, 54 n.21, 92
Heidegger, Martin 116 n.41, 156, 158
Heller, Agnes 79
Hensel, Horst 185
hermeneutics 153
hermeneutics of suspicion 17 n.6
Herzfelde, Wieland 71
Herzog, Werner 65 n.5
Higgins, John 132 n.4, 133 n.10
high culture 74
Hinduism 138, 139, 200
historical novel 74, 75, 78–80, 86 n.89
history 75–6
Hitchcock, Peter 239
Hobbes, Thomas 61
Ho Chi Minh 114 n.5, 178 n.31, 178 n.32
  "Free the Dragons" 169–71
Holm, David 112, 117 n.48
Horton, Randall, "Radical Reversal" project 176, 180 n.76
La Huerta (poetry magazine) 174
Hughes, Langston 162
Hurston, Zora Neale 138, 139
Hu Shi 104
Hussein, Taha 218
Hutchinson, Lester 31, 40 n.41

IBRL. *See* International Bureau of Revolutionary Literature

India 23–41, 199–213
  Chugtai's fiction 201–5
  conspiracy, intention, program 27–32
  feminism and progressive writing 199–213
  intranational translation 241
  literature and the useless in interwar India 23–41
  Mahasweta Devi 205–10
  overview 11, 15, 23–5, 199–200
  paranoid reading to headless organization 25–7
  waste as proof 33–7
indigenismo 11, 43, 46, 51
indigenista writing 42, 43, 51
individualism 51, 170, 228, 238
individuality and private sphere 187–90, 192
Inside: Writings by Attica Inmates, 1977–78 174
instrumental agency 5
International Bureau of Revolutionary Literature (IBRL) 69, 83 n.40
International Congress of Writers for the Defense of Culture 72
"Internationale" (anthem) 23–4
internationalism 6, 18 n.19, 27, 71, 72, 199, 213 n.49, 238–9
interventionist art 2–3, 6, 16
interventionist thought (eingreifendes Denken) 7, 8
interwar paradigms
  Artaud and *Messages révolutionnaires* 56–68
  committed novel of the 1930s (Aragon and Dos Passos) 87–101
  German Popular Front novel 69–86
  literature and the useless in interwar India 23–41
  manifesto as lived experience (Soviet Union and China) 102–18
  overview 10–13

Peruvian literature, Vallejo, and Mariátegui 42–55
Iron Mike. *See* Shipman, Bro. Bernard
Islamophobia 224, 228
Israel 221
Ivanov, Viacheslav 156

Jackson, George 14
Jahan, Rashid 201
Jaja S. *See* Phillips, N. Michael
Jakobson, Roman 154
James, C. L. R. (code name J. R. Johnson) 128, 129
James, Joy 163
James, William 138
Jameson, Fredric
   Aesthetics and Politics (ed.) 9, 70, 82 n.22, 132 n.3
   Ahmad debate 227
   The Antinomies of Realism 86 n.89
   Archaeologies of the Future 233–4
   "A Monument to Radical Instants" 79
   "Periodizing the 60s" 17 n.8
   The Political Unconscious 2, 47, 260
   "Reflections in Conclusion" 70, 80
   Sartre: The Origins of a Style 131
Japan 117 n.47
Johnson–Forest Tendency 121, 128, 135 n.53, 135 n.60
Jomo, Attica Brother (aka Eric Thompson/Cleveland Davis) 168–72
   Awakening of a Dragon 168–71
   "Don't I Know You?" 170, 171
Jones, Charles E. 253
Jones, James Earl 141
Jordan, June 162
Josh, Sohan Singh 32, 40 n.34
Journal of Afro-Asian Writings 218. *See also Lotus* (magazine)
Joyce, James 48, 114 n.16
   Ulysses 54 n.25
juxtaposition 49–50

Kaba, Mariame 14, 161, 176
Kahora, Billy 273
Karinkurayil, Shafeeq 240
Kelly, David 173–4
Kenyatta, Jomo 138
   Facing Mount Kenya 139
Kerényi, Karl 160 n.21
Khashoggi, Jamal 221
Khrushchev, Nikita 109
Khrzhanovsky, Ilya, *Dau* project 109
Kiaer, Christina 103
Kipling, Rudyard, *Kim* 26
Kluge, Alexander, *Öffentlichkeit und Erfahrung* (Public Sphere and Experience; Negt and Kluge) 188–90
Knight, Damon, *The Futurians* 256
Knight, Etheridge 162, 177 n.4
Kornbluh, Anna 16, 234–5, 238
Kracauer, Siegfried 74
Kristal, Efraín 53
Krivulin, Viktor 155–7, 159 n.11, 159 n.15
Kwani Trust 269, 277 n.11

labor mimesis 239
labor movement 182, 184, 185, 188, 189
LaFleur, Ingrid 253
language
   and literary theory 152, 155
   Marr's new theory of language 156
   translation in Cameroon 271–2
   Unnikrishnan's *Temporary People* 241–2
Lassere, Davide Gallo 122, 132 n.1
The Last Stop: Writings from Comstock Prison (Bruchac, ed.) 164, 165, 167
Latin America 11, 19 n.23, 42–4, 221, 222
laughter 140–1, 144
Lavender, Isiah, III 253–4
Leavis, F. R. 123
Lee, Steven 6, 63, 68 n.54
Lefort, Claude 122, 125–8, 133 n.25

"L'expérience prolétarienne" ('Proletarian Experience') 13, 122, 126–8, 134 n.29
left-wing melancholy 7, 19 n.25
left-wing storytelling 92
Lehrstücke ("pedagogical plays") 1, 3
Lenin, Vladimir 29, 60, 121
  State and Revolution 29
Lennon, John 239
Leskov, Nikolai 115 n.30
letter genre 184, 192
Levine, Caroline 16, 19 n.28, 234, 238
Levinton, Georgii 160 n.23
Lévi-Strauss, Claude, *Tristes Tropiques* 154
Lewisohn, James, *Golgotha: Letters from Prison* 167
Libya 222
Light from Another Country: Poetry from American Prisons (ed. Bruchac) 167
Likaku, Rodney 251
Limpert, Richard 183
Linkskurve (journal) 83 n.40
literary activism in contemporary Africa 265–78
  Cameroon and Bakwa 271–6
  history of 266–70
  overview 16–17, 265–6
  platforms, networks, and gate opening 270
literary commitment 87, 88, 93, 97, 99
literary radicals 17 n.2
literary realism 9–10. *See also* realism
literary studies 1–2, 4–7, 117 n.47, 196 n.49, 225
literary theory 8, 14, 19 n.26, 152–5, 238
literature
  autopragmatic paradigm 236–8
  dissident participation 235
  literary studies and uses of literature 4–7
  literature as a map of reality 47–8
  and politics 1–3, 7–10, 24–5
  regime of relevance 151–3
  revolutionary political visions 147–8
  task of 94
  and theory 157
  uses of 4–9, 23–5, 232–3
  Williams on 124
littérature engagé 4, 218
Liu, Kang 111, 117 n.58, 118 n.64
long 1930s 17 n.7
long 1960s 3, 6, 7, 13–15, 17 n.8
Loomba, Ania 200
Losev, Lev 157
Lotman, Juri 156, 157, 160 n.22, 160 n.23
Lotus (magazine)
  new *Lotus* magazine 220–3
  overview 15–16, 217–20
  post-political after Arab Spring 223–7
Lotus Prize for Literature 221
Lowndes, Robert A. W. 256
Löwy, Michael 75
Luckhurst, Roger 256–7
Lukács, Georg
  Brecht–Lukács debate (Expressionism Debate) 12, 69, 70, 72, 75, 82 n.22
  in *Linkskurve* journal 83 n.40
  and modernism 122
  on the novel 73, 75, 78–80
  and realism 9, 115 n.30
  The Historical Novel 75, 78–9
  "Realism in the Balance" 75
Lumet, Sidney 173
Lu Xun Art Academy 112

McCarthy, Gerald 174, 176, 179 n.59
McGrath, John 18 n.17
McHale, Brian 240
Machiavelli, Niccolò, *The Prince* 118 n.64
Macviban, Dzekashu 271, 273, 275, 278 n.15
Madhubuti, Haki 162
magical realism 258

Mahasweta Devi 200, 205–10,
     213 n.49
  "Draupadi" 208
  "Giribala" 208, 212 n.38
  Hajaar Churashir Maa (Mother
     of 1084) 200, 209–10
  "Shikar" (The Hunt) 207,
     212 n.38
Mailer, Norman 141–2, 147
Majumder, Auritro 213 n.49
making use 9, 19 n.30
Makumbi, Jennifer Nansubuga,
     Kintu 277 n.11
Malawian ASF 250, 252
manifesto as lived experience 102–
     18. See also Communist
     Manifesto
  China 109–13
  overview 13, 102–5
  Soviet Union 105–9
Mannheim, Karl 233, 234
Manto, Saadat Hasan 211 n.7
Mao Zedong 13, 102–3, 109–13,
     114 n.5, 117 n.48, 117 n.58,
     118 n.64, 118 n.65, 121
  "On Contradiction" 112
Marchart, Oliver 236–8
Marchwitza, Hans 83 n.40
Marcuse, Herbert 154, 234
Mariátegui, José Carlos 11, 43–9, 51,
     52, 52 n.7, 53 n.20
  *7 ensayos de interpretación de
     la realidad peruana* (Seven
     Interpretive Essays on
     Peruvian Reality) 11, 43–5
  "Arte, revolución y decadencia"
     (Art, Revolution, and
     Decadence) 44, 46, 47,
     53 n.20
  *La novela y la vida: Siegfried y
     el profesor Canella* (The
     Novel and Life: Siegfried and
     Professor Canella) 11, 44,
     47, 54 n.22
  "Populismo literario y estabilización
     capitalista" (Literary
     Populism and Capitalist
     Stabilization) 44, 48

"Principios de política agraria
     nacional" 53 n.8
Marker, Chris, *Le Fond de l'air est
     rouge* 6, 19 n.24
market activism 267, 276
Marr, Nikolai 156, 157, 160 n.21
Marx, Karl
  Artaud on 60
  and conspiracy 28
  and India 29, 204
  Soviet resistance to theory 154
  and Spivak 116 n.41
  workers' inquiry 13, 121
  Capital 135 n.57
  Communist Manifesto (see
     Communist Manifesto)
  *Eighteenth Brumaire of Louis
     Bonaparte* 32, 109, 245
Marxism
  and Artaud 11, 60
  BPRS 83 n.40
  and formalism 9
  and India 199
  Lefort and workers' inquiry 126
  literary criticism 122, 125
  Peruvian literature 11, 44
  Soviet resistance to theory 154–7
  and surrealism 60
  Williams and structure of
     feeling 124
Mashigo, Mohale 254
materialism 50, 60
Mayakovski, Vladimir 63, 68 n.54
Mayer, Hans 76
May Fourth Movement 110, 112
Mbari Club 266, 268–9
Mbewe, Masiyaleti 255
Mbunpi, Mariette
     Tchamda 278 n.13
Meerut Communist Conspiracy
     Case 11, 24, 26–33, 37
Menon, Priya 244
Merleau-Ponty, Maurice 127,
     133 n.25, 134 n.26, 134 n.28
  *Phenomenology of
     Perception* 125–6, 134 n.40
metapolitics 4
Metrodor (journal) 157, 160 n.23

Mexico 53 n.9, 56–63, 65 n.8, 68 n.54, 68 n.57
Meyzad, Munir 230 n.23
 "Arab Spring or Long Islamic Winter" 224
Middle East 19 n.23
Middleton, Stuart 132 n.5
migrant workers 196 n.34
migratory poetics 241
Miles Morland Foundation 269
militant structures of feeling. *See* structure of feeling
Miller, Tyrus 79
Mingus, Charles
 Changes One 173
 "Remember Rockefeller at Attica" 173
modernism
 Peru, Vallejo and Mariátegui 46, 47, 51
 Popular Front culture 73, 74, 80
 proletarian modernism 69, 80, 81 n.3
 and realism 9–10, 13, 103, 122, 132 n.3
 social modernism 73
 Soviet Union and China 13, 113
 vernacular modernism 74
Monferrand, Frédéric 122, 132 n.1, 134 n.28, 135 n.48
Mongolian literature 222
montage 6, 98
Morris, Ann 240
Morris, Isabella 222
Moten, Fred 170
Mothé, Daniel (Jacques Gautrat) 135 n.49
Mshaka (Wille Monroe), "Formula for Attica Repeats" 163
Müller, Heiner 58, 64
multiculturalism 223, 225, 226
Mundial (journal) 44, 54 n.22
Murphy, James F. 84 n.40
music 131, 173, 176
Musila, Grace 271
Mwandishe, Kuweka Amiri, "The Nigger Cycle: For Angela Davis Kidnapped by the F.B.I. on Oct. 13, 1970" 162
myth 106, 108

national anthems 23
National Socialism (Nazism) 71, 78, 79, 81 n.2, 185
Naxalite movement 209, 210
Nazrul Islam, Kazim 23–4, 29, 37 n.2
 Bisher Banshi (The Poison Flute) 24
Ndebi, Ray 270, 277 n.12
negative dialectics 153
Négritude movement 253, 266
Negt, Oskar, *Öffentlichkeit und Erfahrung* (Public Sphere and Experience; Negt and Kluge) 188–90
Nemiroff, Robert 144, 149 n.14
Neogy, Rajat 266
Neruda, Pablo 51
 Heights of Macchu Picchu 53 n.8
Neue Subjektivität (New Subjectivity) 183
New Criticism 2, 17 n.2
Newell, Stephanie 277 n.9
New Left Review 124
new paternalism 141, 142
newspapers 91, 167–8, 277 n.9
Nganang, Patrice 277 n.3
Ngũgĩ wa Thiong'o 266, 277 n.9
Nietzsche, Friedrich 14, 150, 155
Nigeria 266, 268, 275
Nilsson, Magnus 239
Nimba Press 275
Nimbkar, R. S. 30
Nixon, Richard 171
Njamnsi, Nchanji 274
Nkrumah, Kwame 138, 140
non-Marxist theory 150–60
nonsynchronism 12, 81 n.4
Noorani, A. G. 39 n.20
Norris, John Lee, "Just Another Page" 163
novels
 and autofiction 191–2
 committed novel of the 1930s 87–101

democratic novels 96–9
fictional status 92
German Popular Front
    novel 12, 69–86
Greek novel 160 n.21
historical novel 74, 75, 78–80,
    86 n.89
popular novel 73–80
proletarian novel 74
revolutionary political visions 147
social novel 79
working-class literature 124,
    184, 190
Nwonwu, Chiagozie 251, 254, 257

objective correlative 123
obsession 203
Occupy movement 219, 224
Okeke, Anwuli 257
Okigbo, Christopher 266
Okorafor, Nnedi 251, 255, 257
Omenana (SF magazine) 251
Ônoan Literature 270
Oosterlynck, Stijn 224
organology 61

Palestinian liberation 221
pamphlets 8, 35, 37
pandemic 57, 64
paranoia 26
Paris 1968 riots 66 n.9
Pasternak, Boris 108, 156
Patterson, Orlando 166
Pearce, Diane 260
PEN America 176, 180 n.76
Pennybacker, Susan 27
Perera, Sonali 6, 239, 245
Perry, Imani 146
personal, emphasis on 181, 182,
    190, 192
Peruvian literature 42–55
    avant-garde and decadence 46–7
    literature as a map of reality 47–8
    overview 11, 42–4
    Peruvian context 44–6
    Vallejo and avant-garde 48–52
Petrov, Petre 108–9, 116 n.41
peyote 57

Phillips, N. Michael (Jaja S) 172–3
    "Death of a Comrade" 172–3
    "Surrender in Attica" 172
Plato 152
Plessner, Helmuth 61
poetry
    Attica print culture and small press
        poetry 161–80
    foundation of small press poetry
        and print culture at
        Attica 162–7
    overview 2, 14, 161
    poetry and print culture expansion
        at Attica 167–73
    small press poetry and print culture
        after Attica 173–6
    Urdu poetry 203, 218
Pohl, Frederik 256
Poliakova, Sofia 157, 160 n.21
political agency 5
political autonomy 237
political formalism and working-class
        story cycles 232–49
    congruence, transcendence, and
        form 233–5
    dissident participation 235–9
    overview 16, 232–3
    political formalism 16, 234,
        238, 245
    Unnikrishnan's *Temporary
        People* 239–45
political literature 15, 112, 218,
    224
political unconscious 2, 47, 131
political uses of literature
    abolition, Attica print culture, and
        small press poetry 161–80
    Artaud and *Messages
        révolutionnaires* 56–68
    chapter organization 10–17
    committed novel of the 1930s
        (Aragon and Dos
        Passos) 87–101
    contemporary African science and
        speculative fiction 250–64
    cultural politics after Arab
        Spring 217–31
    definitions 23–5

feminism and progressive writing in India 199–213
German Popular Front novel 69–86
Hansberry and solidarity 137–49
literary activism in contemporary Africa 265–78
literary studies and uses of literature 4–7
literature and politics beyond 'left-wing melancholy' 7–10
literature and the useless in interwar India 23–41
manifesto as lived experience (Soviet Union and China) 102–18
non-Marxist theory 150–60
overview 1–19
Peruvian literature, Vallejo, and Mariátegui 42–55
political formalism and working-class story cycles 232–49
Struck's *Klassenliebe* and the *Werkkreis* 181–98
Williams, Lefort, and workers' inquiry 121–36
politics
 definitions 98
 literary studies and uses of literature 4–7
 and literature 1–3
 literature and politics beyond 'left-wing melancholy' 7–10
 metapolitics 4
politics of form 191, 193, 194, 197 n.66, 245
politics of literature 217, 224
popular (definition) 75
Popular Front 12, 33, 69–73. *See also* German Popular Front novel
popular novel 73–80
Pospelov, Gennady 154
postcolonialism 220, 223, 225–8
postcritique 18 n.15
post-politics 15, 219, 224–5
post-Structuralism 151
Pound, Ezra 131
pragmatics 236

Pratt, Mary Louise 241
print cultures. *See* Attica prison print culture
Prison and Justice Writing Program 176, 180 n.76
prisons. *See also* Attica prison print culture
 metaphorical 259
 music programs 176
 newspapers 167–8
 poetry workshops 14, 163, 164, 173–6, 177 n.8
private sphere 187–90
Progressive Writers' Movement 218
progressive writing 15, 200, 201, 205, 210, 218. *See also* All-India Progressive Writers' Association
proletarian modernism 69, 80, 81 n.3
proletarian novel 74
proletarian realism 110
proletariat 105, 126–7, 184–7, 189, 190, 242, 245
Proust, Marcel 114 n.16
 À la recherche du temps perdu 187
public sphere 189, 190
Puchner, Martin 103–6, 109, 110, 112, 114 n.5, 114 n.14, 118 n.64
 Poetry of the Revolution 13, 103
pulp fiction 252, 255–7
Pyatigorsky, Alexander 160 n.20

racism 130–1, 138, 140–7, 162, 166, 172, 253–4
Radek, Karl 54 n.25, 114 n.16
Rancière, Jacques 16, 87, 234, 238
Randall, Dudley 162, 163, 167, 176, 177 n.4, 177 n.8
reading practices 2, 24–5, 33–4, 36–7, 96–8, 238
Reagan, Ronald 173
realism. *See also* socialist realism
 capitalist realism 10, 19 n.33, 80
 German Popular Front novel 12, 69, 70, 80
 magical realism 258

and modernism   9–10, 13, 103, 122, 132 n.3
Popular Front culture   73
proletarian realism   110
social realism   42–3, 46, 49, 52, 206, 218
and workers' inquiry   122
The Red Poppy (ballet)   116 n.33
Refugee Tales project   238
regime of relevance   151–3
reportage   73, 184, 185, 190–2
Rettová, Alena   255, 258
revolution
　and aesthetics   102–3
　Artaud on   61–3
　China   102, 109, 112, 118 n.64
　Cultural Revolution   102, 118 n.64
　and decadence   53 n.20
　French Revolution   58, 63, 78
　and modernism   13
　Peruvian literature   45, 46
　and revolutionaries   10
　Russian Revolution   26, 58, 102
　Williams on   75
revolutionary romanticism   106
Ricoeur, Paul, *Temps et récit*   94
Rivera, Diego   68 n.54
Roberts, Mer   254
Robinson, Ellis, "Psalm of Nixon"   171
Rockefeller, Nelson   162, 171
Rockhill, Gabriel   5
Rogozinski, Jacob   64
Rohde, Erwin   160 n.21
Rolland, Romain   27
romance   94
Romano, Paul (Phil Singer), *The American Worker* (Romano and Stone)   13, 122, 128–32, 135 n.54
romanticism   106, 152
Rushdie, Salman, *The Satanic Verses*   242
Russian Formalism   152, 154–5, 157–8, 159 n.14
Russian Revolution   26, 58, 102
Ryman, Geoff   250, 252

Salmawy, Mohamed   218, 220–2, 224, 227, 228, 229 n.13
Salmon, Christian   89–91, 98
samizdat magazines   14, 150, 155, 157, 159 n.11
Sanchez, Sonia   162
Saro-Wiwa, Kenule   266
Sartre, Jean-Paul   94, 95, 125, 131, 133 n.25, 134 n.26, 218
　What is Literature?   88
Saudi Arabia   221
scénarisation   92, 93
Scharer, Peter   41 n.53
Scherpe, Klaus   80
Schild, Kathryn   107, 116 n.31
Schmitt, Carl   25, 61
Schöfer, Erasmus   185
Schuyler, George, *Black No More*   253
Schwartz, Ros   273
science fiction (SF)
　Black SF   253–4
　contemporary African science and speculative fiction   16, 250–64
　importance of Afrofuturism   252–5
　Jameson on   233
　origin of term   256
　overcoming pulp (science) fiction label   255–8
　overview   16, 250–2
　SF studies   258
　Tsamaase and future utopia   258–60
Scrutiny (journal)   123
SDS (Socialist German Students' League)   188, 190
Seale, Bobby   169
Al-Sebai, Youssef   221–2
sedition   24, 26
Seghers, Anna   70, 72, 74–5, 77, 83 n.40, 84 n.47, 86 n.85
　Die Entscheidung (The Decision)   80
　Die Rettung (The Rescue)   74
　The Seventh Cross   77–8, 85 n.64
semantic paleontology   156, 157
semiotics   153, 155, 157

Senghor, Léopold Sédar 266
The Sentences That Create Us: Crafting a Writer's Life in Prison (anthology) 176
September 11, 2001 attacks 224
SF. *See* science fiction
Shaikh, Juned, *Outcaste Bombay* 40 n.45
Shih, Shu-mei 111, 117 n.47
Shingavi, Snehal 7, 199
Shipman, Bro. Bernard (aka Iron Mike) 169, 170, 172
   "Death" 172
Shklovsky, Viktor 154, 155
Sholette, Gregory 3, 8
Siao, Emi (Xiao San) 107, 108, 116 n.33
"Silk Road" as term 226
Singer, Phil. *See* Romano, Paul (Phil Singer), *The American Worker* (Romano and Stone)
situational congruence 233, 234
situational transcendence 233, 234, 245
Slezkine, Yuri 116 n.31
small press poetry 161–80
   foundation of small press poetry and print culture at Attica 14, 161–7
   poetry and print culture expansion at Attica 167–73
   small press poetry and print culture after Attica 173–6
Smith, Patti, *The Peyote Dance* 57
socialism 24, 25, 131
Socialisme ou Barbarie 13, 121, 125, 133 n.21
   Socialisme ou Barbarie journal 126, 128
socialist art 42, 50–1
Socialistic Fallacies (Guyot) 24, 25, 38 n.5
socialist realism
   German Popular Front novel 71, 82 n.14
   and manifestos 103, 105–10
   and modernism 13, 103
   Peruvian literature 42, 48–51
   Petrov on 116 n.41
   proletarian realism 110
   revolution and aesthetics 103
   Soviet Union 69, 105–9, 115 n.19
social media 222, 229 n.14
social modernism 73
social novel 79
social realism 42–3, 46, 49, 52, 206, 218
social theory 137–8, 148
society 138, 139, 143, 146–8
sociological imagination 139, 140, 148
sociology 13–14, 137–9
Soledad Prison 162, 164
solidarity 14, 146–8
Sontag, Susan 11, 49–50, 57–8
Soundwalk Collective 57
South Africa 221, 262 n.40
Soviet Union
   and China 107, 110, 111
   Cultural Revolution 105
   literary theory 157
   and *Lotus* magazine 218, 220, 223, 226
   manifesto genre 103–11
   and modernism 13
   Popular Front culture 71
   and realism 9
   resistance to theory 14, 150, 154, 157–8
   socialist realism 69, 105–9, 115 n.19
   Structuralism 155–8, 159 n.16
Soviet Writers' Congress 13, 105–11, 113, 116 n.31
Soyinka, Wole 266
Spanish Civil War 69, 76
speculative fiction. *See* African speculative and science fiction
speech act theory 104, 114 n.14
Spies, Bernard 78
Spinoza, Benedict de 135 n.60
   Ethics 130
Spivak, Gayatri Chakravorty 5, 109, 116 n.41, 212 n.38, 226
Spratt, Philip 30
Sri Burapha 222

Stalin, Joseph   28, 29, 105, 111, 113, 116 n.31
Stal'skii, Suleiman   107–8
Stanislavsky, Konstantin   112
Stendhal (Marie-Henri Beyle)   150
Steyerl, Hito   237–9
Stone, Ria (Grace Lee Boggs), *The American Worker* (Romano and Stone)   13, 122, 128–32, 135 n.54
story cycles   240, 242, 244, 245
storytellers   115 n.30
Struck, Karin   181–98
  overview   181–3
  individuality and private sphere   188–90
  politics of form, autofiction, and documentary   190–4
  reception of   183–4
    Klassenliebe (Class Love)   15, 122, 181–93
    "Das Private ist das Politische" (The Private Is Political)   188, 190
    Werkkreis and working-class literature   184–8
Structuralism   153–8, 159 n.16
structure of feeling   121–36
  conceptual innovation of Williams   122–5
  Lefort's 'proletarian experience'   125–8
  location   134 n.37
  and Mariátegui   47
  overview   13, 121–2
  Romano and Stone's *The American Worker*   128–32
  and Struck   181
  and style   132 n.4
student movements   189, 209, 266
Suitsidov, Igor. *See* Groys, Boris
Sullivan, James   162, 168
surrealism   44, 47–51, 60, 144
"suspicious readers"   2
Sutherland, Christopher, "At Last"   163
Suvin, Darko   257

Tagore, Saumyendranath   24, 25, 36
Takhtadzhian, S. A.   160 n.23
Tarahumara community   57, 58, 61, 63, 67 n.51
Tate, Allen   2
Tchamda Mbunpi, Mariette   270, 274–5
Tebhaga revolt   33
Tellkamp, Uwe, *Der Turm* (The Tower)   80, 86 n.85
Tempest, Kae   238
Thamir, Fadhil   226
  "Cultural and Literary Silk Road: We Must Speak"   225, 226
theater   56, 60, 62–4, 104, 147, 277 n.9
Thengdi, D. R.   31
theory
  critical theory   153
  definitions   151
  French Theory   151, 154
  and ideology   157
  interventionist thought   7
  literary theory   8, 14, 19 n.26, 152–5, 238
  non-Marxist theory   150–60
  regime of relevance   151–3
  Soviet resistance to   14, 150, 154, 157–8
  and theory   151, 153, 154, 157
"Third World" as term   225–7, 229 n.3
Thompson, Eric. *See* Jomo, Attica Brother
Thompson, Heather Ann, *Blood in the Water*   171–2
thought crime   27
thriller genre   89–91
thug figure   28
Timofeev, Leonid   159 n.9
  "Verse and Prose"   154
Tisdale, Celes   167, 173, 176, 177 n.8
  Betcha Ain't: Poems from Attica   163
Todorov, Tzvetan   154
Tomashevskii, Boris, *Teoriia literatury: Poetika*   154
Toporov, Vladimir   156, 157

totalitarianism 98, 159 n.16
transcendence, situational 233, 234, 245
Transition (magazine) 220, 266
translation 17, 241–2, 266, 270, 272–5
Tretyakov, Sergei 72
Tribune Ouvrière (newspaper) 128
Tsamaase, Tlotlo 16, 252, 258–60
 "Behind our Irises" 258, 259
 "Dreamports" 258, 259
 "Eclipse our Sins" 258, 259
 "Eco-Humans" 258, 259
 "The River of Night" 259
 "Season of Safety" 258, 259
 "They Don't Believe God Grows in Our Hearts" 259
 "Thoughtbox" 259
 "Virtual Snapshots" 258, 259
Tshombe, Moïse Kapenda 146
Twongyeirwe, Hilda, "Baking the National Cake" 219–20
Tynianov, Iurii 154–7

unconscious 2, 47, 131, 187
underground 14, 150
Unnikrishnan, Deepak, *Temporary People* 16, 239–45, 243
Urdu poetry 203, 218
uses of literature 4–9, 23–5, 232–3. *See also* political uses of literature
utopia 16, 206, 233, 234, 251, 252, 255, 258

Vallejo, César
 and avant-garde 43, 48–52
 Mariátegui personal contact 52 n.7
 overview 11, 42–4
 Peruvian context 42–5
  Amauta works 43
  Arte y revolución (Art and Revolution) 50, 52 n.6
  "Autopsia del superrealismo" (Autopsy of Surrealism) 11, 48, 49

 Contra el secreto professional (Against the Professional Secret) 52 n.6
 "Ejecutoria del arte bolchevique" (Judgement on Bolshevik Art) 51
 Escalas melografiadas 52 n.1
 España, aparta de mí este cáliz (Spain, Take This Chalice from Me) 43, 49
 Fabla salvaje 52 n.1
 Los heraldos negros (The Black Heralds) 43, 45
 "Un hombre pasa con un pan al hombro" (A Man Walks by with a Baguette on His Shoulder) 44, 49–51
 "Me estoy riendo" (I am Laughing) 43
 Poemas humanos (Human Poems) 11, 43, 49
 "Poesía nueva" (New Poetry) 43
 "Prohibido hablar al piloto" (It Is Forbidden to Talk to the Driver) 43
 "Sabiduría" 43
 "Telluric and Magnetic" 53 n.8
 Trilce 42, 43, 45, 49
 El tungsteno (Tungsten) 42–4, 46, 48, 49, 51
Van Puymbroeck, Nicolas 224
Vasudevan, Hari 25
Verne, Jules 257
 Vingt Mille Lieues sous les mers 256
verse theory 155
Vietnamese literature 226–7
The Village Voice 141–3
violence 76, 78, 92, 143–4
Voloshinov, V. N. 25

Wali, Obi 277 n.9
Walker, Alice 162
Wallis, Kate 267, 271
Warburg, Aby 63, 68 n.55
Washington, Sam, "Was It Necessary" 163

Weber, Samuel 64
Weimar Republic 3, 70, 74, 81 n.3, 185, 233
Weiskopf, F. C. 74
Weiss, Peter, *Aesthetics of Resistance* 80, 86 n.88
Wells, H. G. 27
Werkkreis Literatur der Arbeitswelt (Literature of the Working World Workgroup) 15, 182–7, 189–93
White, Edmund 149 n.9
white antiracism 141–2
Whitehead, Colson, *The Intuitionist* 80
whiteness 142, 146
Williams, Raymond
  on drama 132 n.4, 133 n.8
  on revolution 75
  on social unit 267
  structure of feeling 13, 47, 122–8, 131, 132 n.4, 134 n.37, 181
  on working-class culture 135 n.47
  The Long Revolution 130
  Marxism and Literature 124, 133 n.14, 133 n.19
  Politics and Letters 124–5
  "When Was Modernism?" 3
Wilson, W. L. (aka Xmielex), "Suddenly" 171–2
Wimsatt, William K., *The Verbal Icon* 2
Witherspoon, Jim, "County Jail" 162
Witherup, William 164
Wolf, Christa 80
Womack, Ytasha L. 253
women
  female body 200, 202, 203, 258
  female characters 94, 146, 202, 206, 207, 210, 259
  labor movement 182
  women's literature 183
  women writers 15, 182, 200, 274
Woods, Joanna 251

workers' inquiry 13, 121–2, 126–32, 132 n.1, 135 n.53
working class 71, 77, 121, 124, 135 n.47
working-class literature 232–49
  congruence, transcendence, and form 233–5
  dissident participation 235–9
  overview 16, 232–3
  Struck's *Klassenliebe* 15, 182–7, 189–91, 193
  Unnikrishnan's *Temporary People* 239–45
  as a world literature 239
world literature 5, 106, 107, 225, 239
Das Wort (journal) 69, 75
Wright, Stephen 9, 19 n.30
writers, function of 94
Writers' Union of Africa, Asia, and Latin America (WUAALA) 218, 220, 221
Writing for Justice Fellowship 176
writing workshops
  creative writing 14, 273, 275
  prison poetry 14, 163, 164, 173–6, 177 n.8
Writivism Festival 271

Xi Jinping 110, 113

Yan'an Conference on Literature and Art 13, 110–13, 117 n.56, 118 n.64, 118 n.65
Yaszek, Lisa 254, 255
Young, Robert 228
Your Feet Will Lead You Where Your Heart Is/Le crépuscule des âmes soeurs (anthology) 273
Yurchak, Alexei 104–5, 114 n.14

Zhdanov, Andrei 105, 106
Zhmud, Leonid 157, 160 n.23